OMAR BRADLEY

⋆⋆ GENERAL AT WAR ⋆⋆

Jim DeFelice

D0953630

REGNERY
HISTORY

Library of Congress Cataloging-in-Publication Data

    DeFelice, Jim, 1956-
      Omar Bradley : general at war / by Jim DeFelice.
        p. cm.
      Includes bibliographical references and index.
      ISBN 978-1-59698-139-3 (alk. paper)
      1. Bradley, Omar Nelson, 1893-1981. 2. Generals--United States--Biography. 3. United States. Army--Biography. 4. World War, 1939-1945--Campaigns. I. Title.
      E745.B7D45 2011
      355.0092--dc22
      [B]

2010046874

Published in the United States by
Regnery Publishing, Inc.
One Massachusetts Avenue, NW
Washington, DC 20001
www.regnery.com

Manufactured in the United States of America

10 9 8 7 6 5 4 3 2 1

Books are available in quantity for promotional or premium use. Write to Director of Special Sales, Regnery Publishing, Inc., One Massachusetts Avenue NW, Washington, DC 20001, for information on discounts and terms or call (202) 216-0600.

Distributed to the trade by:
Perseus Distribution
387 Park Avenue South
New York, NY 10016

To all the quiet heroes following in Bradley's footsteps.

CONTENTS

First Impressions

Northern Africa, February 23, 1943

The C-54 Skymaster ducked down from the clouds, its Pratt & Whitney radials pulling it toward the long, tan dagger jutting into the azure ocean ahead.

Africa.

As the plane dropped lower, green blotches appeared: trees spared the fury of the working bulldozers that razed the nearby land, turning it burnt yellow even as the aircraft dropped. A short, precariously narrow gray line appeared in the sand ahead. Ants were running near it.

Not ants, but men. Not a line but a runway, unfinished. The men were laying steel planks to widen and extend it.

General Omar Bradley, stiff and tired from a flight that had begun the night before in Brazil, roused himself and gazed out the window.

"We're landing, sir," said Chet Hansen, one of the general's two aides.

Bradley nodded. Taciturn, he continued to gaze out the window as the military transport bumped onto the steel grid, its wheels whining. A gust pushed the aircraft hard to the side as it landed; the Air Corps pilot mastered it, keeping the drab green airliner on the runway as he feathered the engines and went hard on the brakes. The short strip gave him little room for error.

The same might be said for the tens of thousands of Americans stretched out between the airport and the far-flung foothills of Tunisia well to the east. Three months before, the troops had landed in North Africa, full of hope and vigor, sure that they would bring the war against the Axis to a quick and victorious conclusion. Now they weren't so sure. Their offensive had stalled badly. The reality of war had proven considerably more frightening than most had thought possible. Facing experienced German veterans, they had stumbled badly. Indeed, things were worse than most realized, as they had benefited from a good portion of luck at the start of the campaign, unnoticed as it may have been.

Luck had run out in a pass far to the east in Tunisia. There the young American force had been severely whipped in a mountainous area known as Kasserine Pass. At roughly the same time the C-54 was setting down, the architect of their defeat was repositioning his Panzers, threatening a strike that would break the young force entirely.

Bradley rose from his seat and made his way to the door with a mixture of anticipation, energy, and undoubtedly some apprehension. Though he was a general, he'd never been this close to war before. Though he was regarded as a master tactician—and had instructed thousands in the art—his plans had never been put to the test of real combat. And though he was held in the highest esteem by men who had already proven themselves under fire, he himself had never heard an angry bullet crease the air nearby. At fifty, he was a virgin to combat.

This would not have mattered much if he was coming to take a staff job, or even if he intended only to fulfill the role of an observer, in theory the job he had been assigned. But Omar Nelson Bradley, while modest in speech and demeanor, had ambitions that extended beyond the job of advisor or assistant. He wanted desperately to lead men into battle. He wanted to win, and he wanted to kill.

Nor had the man who sent him across the Atlantic intended that he merely observe. U.S. Army Chief of Staff George C. Marshall, who'd known Bradley for years, believed he could help turn the faltering U.S. Army around. Originally opposed to the African campaign, Marshall had come to see it as a crucial test for the still inexperienced Army. It was a test that it had to pass, or it would suffer the most dire consequences.

Most Americans, if they've heard of Omar Bradley at all, know him from the 1970 movie *Patton*. Played by Karl Malden, Bradley there is a middle-aged, bespectacled milquetoast who couldn't organize a pickup softball game on his own. Disappearing into the woodwork whenever any *real* fighting needs to be done, Malden is the anti-Patton, a slouch-shouldered mouse incapable of roaring.

Ironically, Bradley—well into his seventies at that point—is credited as a consultant on the movie. Parts of his memoir, *A Soldier's Story*, formed the basis for the screenplay, which does track the historical events relatively accurately. Indeed, the screenplay itself casts Bradley in a fairly favorable, if clearly supporting, role. But anyone watching the movie can't be blamed if they end up wondering exactly how Omar Bradley came to lead the largest American military force ever assembled.

No one expects a movie to accurately portray history, but Bradley has fared just as poorly in many allegedly accurate histories as well. Called everything from a conservative infantryman to an unimaginative plodder, his designs for the war have been lost in a raft of misconceptions. His personality has been distorted until he appears the exact mirror image of who he really was. His achievements have been handed to others, his failures magnified out of all proportion.

But perhaps the worst thing is that he has been forgotten or miscast even by serious historians. Bradley, even more than Eisenhower, the architect of the American victory in Europe, rarely appears in more than a cameo in many accounts focused on the campaign.

There are a number of reasons for this, but the most important is Bradley himself. He was, in a word, undramatic. And that has always been out of fashion in America.

By all accounts, Bradley was a man of moderate behavior, a mature leader who thought before he spoke, who risked his life but didn't call attention to it. He allowed his subordinates to take credit and glory. When he disagreed with his superiors, he did so discreetly. He dressed for the field, and looked it. He lived, for much of the war, in a truck.

Based on the testimony of his peers, Bradley was one of the great tacticians of the war, praised by everyone from paratroop commander James Gavin to Supreme Commander Dwight Eisenhower. But his real asset was his ability to get results from his commanders—he was as much an enabler as a creator of success. The keys to this were his intelligence, his humanity, and most of all his ability to keep his ego largely in check: a rare quality in a general of any rank, let alone one who ended his career with five stars.

That quality sprang directly from Bradley's character, forged in turn-of-the century Midwestern America. Bradley was, first and last, a believer in values that, even during the War, would have been cynically termed "small-town"—self-reliance, respect for others, humility. He was the product of an America that had only recently conquered the frontier, an America where brain and brawn fit together naturally. It was a time when being an athlete brought more responsibilities, not less, a place where a man hunted for food and worked out math problems for fun, an America where calling attention to one's achievements cheapened them irrevocably.

When so much of our perception of history depends on drama and flash, is there room for a man who personified quiet competence?

Yes. For beyond the flash and drama of the moment, the real achievements of the war depended on men like Bradley. And still do.

The irony is that Bradley's war years were full of drama and flash; they've just never been written about. He barely escaped death several times and was at every battle dramatized in the movie Patton—closer, often, to the bullets than the movie's hero. If Bradley hadn't been a general, he would have been a virtual Zelig (or, to use a character from military literature, a *Private Yankee Doodle*), on hand for every major land conflict in the European Theater of the war. Few men experienced as much of the war as Bradley.

Bradley is more typical of his generation than either Patton or Eisenhower, generals who receive many times as much ink in the history books. Though the nickname "the GI General" was a bit of a misnomer—most GIs were not professional soldiers, officers, or infantrymen—he was at least spiritually closer to them than most of the so-called "brass" of the war. The vast majority of GIs who fought in World War II never considered themselves heroes. For them, heroism, sacrifice, and perseverance under fire was just doing their job. They liberated the world and created the American Century. Omar Bradley, unsung and humble, was one of them.

To understand America in World War II, one has to know Omar Bradley. There should be many biographies of him. He should appear more prominently in general histories. His decisions should be more carefully analyzed in the context in which they were made, not used as a straw man for feel-good pronouncements that ultimately avoid the harsh realities of war.

I was amazed some years ago to find that Bradley had never been the subject of an in-depth biography. Gradually I came to believe that the lack of that kind of study was not only an indication of how far he had slipped from public memory, but also a cause of it. His memoirs, especially *A Soldier's Story*, tell his story well. But an impartial, easily accessible summary and evaluation of his life has been missing, until now.

My aim here his to tell Bradley's story, focused on World War II, setting right some of the misperceptions, and showing how it is impossible to understand America's victory in Europe without understanding Omar Bradley. And so, we start at the beginning...

CHAPTER 1

Preparing a General

Omar squinted through the trees, watching for movement. The young boy could hear the squirrel's chatter and the click of its nails against the hard bark of the surrounding trees, but he couldn't see the critter.

He moved forward slowly, trying not to step on the dried leaves. The squirrels in the Missouri woods near his house were wary creatures, used to dealing with hunters far more formidable than a boy barely old enough to read. Most local farmers hunted regularly to supplement their crops, and squirrels were an important source of meat.

Something moved in the branches ahead. The boy froze, squinted.

Just the wind, rustling the leaves.

He stepped again. Something near the top of the tree ducked to the right. The squirrel! It disappeared around the trunk of the tree.

Omar looked over to his father, a few yards away. His dad nodded, then began moving to his right, gingerly slipping through the nearby trees. The boy raised his rifle.

A pair of hunters had a much easier time against the small prey if they worked together. In this case, the tactics were simple but effective. One would wait facing the tree, while the other circled around, in effect flanking the enemy. Drawing closer, the hunter at the rear would make just enough noise for the squirrel to spot him. The animal would seek cover, moving around the tree—and square into the sights of the first hunter.

It was an old tactic, but one that required a fair amount of skills. One had to be stealthy and patient, calm at the moment of attack, capable of analyzing the tactical situation—flanking your prey too close to another tree or too high in the canopy was a waste of time.

And there was marksmanship. Even at the comparatively close distance of ten or twenty yards, hitting a target as small as a squirrel with an iron-sighted rifle was not an easy task.

Omar steadied the single-shot Stevens and fired. The .22 caliber bullet whistled past the animal, a clean miss.

The squirrel, either petrified or oblivious, didn't move. Omar reloaded calmly, cocked, fired.

Another miss.

His hands flew across the rifle. He aimed, sure of a dead-on shot this time. His finger squeezed at the trigger. The bullet jumped from the gun. His body contained the shock of the rifle. It was a true shot, following the mark precisely.

But once more, the bullet sailed off into oblivion. The squirrel sniffed the air. Danger might be nearby, but this spot seemed safe enough. Dejected, Omar looked to his father.

His father motioned for the rifle. Quietly, he adjusted both sights, putting them into line with the barrel. Then he took the weapon and lifted it to his shoulder.

"If I don't knock his eye out," Omar's father said, "something is very wrong with the sights."

The sharp ping of a rifle shot creased the air. The squirrel—shot through the eye—fell dead to the ground.

Embarrassed by his misses, Omar would long remember that day: sight your weapon properly before you set out. Success depends on attending to all details, small and large, before battle.[1]

Omar Nelson Bradley often went hunting with his dad on the family's sodbuster farm in Randolph County, Missouri, not far from the three-room log house where he was born, February 12, 1893. His mother, Sarah Elizabeth (Bessie) Hubbard, had been born in the same small house seventeen years earlier. His father, John Bradley, had met Bessie while working as a teacher at the local school. When they married, he was twenty-five; she was sixteen.

Their son's unusual first name was a tribute to Omar D. Gray, a newspaper editor. His second name was that of a local doctor. Unfortunately, Omar seems not to have known why his parents chose those names. One was a man of letters, the other a man of science. Both were prominent in the community, and would have seemed good models for the boy to emulate. Speculating further, the newspaper editor's politics— a prominent part of his trade at the time—seem to have celebrated the common man against the big Eastern interests. John's decision to give the editor's name to his son was as much a statement of values as a way to make him unique.

Described in Bradley's autobiography *A General's Life* as "a crude three-room log house,"[2] the Hubbard family home was probably a little older than many of the houses in the area, but its size was fairly typical. Much of Missouri was still sparsely settled, with forty-square-acre family farms dominating the irregular landscape. Clark County's roots extended to the early decades of the nineteenth century. Many early settlers were from the South. Regional and family ties as well as politics played a strong role there during the Civil War, when many local citizens, including Bradley's paternal grandfather, enlisted in the Confederate army. But local loyalties were divided—Bradley's maternal grandfather had served in the Union.

Still, no matter their individual histories, the families had much in common. As the opening lines of *A General's Life* put it, they were "plain Missouri farmers, proud, honest, hardworking and poor. Desperately poor."[3]

The U.S. Census counted 24,803 people in Randolph in 1890, and 24,442 in 1900. They were spread out. The population in Clark, the closest town to the Hubbard homestead, was counted at 194. Moberly, an important railroad depot and the largest city in the area, had some 8,209 residents. The area was growing—Moberly had increased by about a third from its 1880 population. Still, there were fewer than five thousand homes and only some six thousand families living in the entire county just prior to Omar Bradley's birth.[4]

Raised in a family of farmers and mostly self-taught, Omar's father had a yen for learning, but it wasn't until he was nineteen years old that he began attending school for the first time. Two years later, he became a teacher himself. Like his son, he seems to have possessed a gift for math. He also loved reading and valued books. When he started teaching at a new school, John Bradley would often ask local leaders and businessmen to help him raise funds to buy books and start a library. Years later, Omar remembered fund-raisers like ice cream socials where the money was raised a few cents at a time.[5]

Love of learning aside, almost certainly one of John Bradley's main qualifications as a young teacher would have been his ability to keep order. Athletic, he was more than a match for the rambunctious teenagers who would run roughshod over other instructors.

While the local school district was centered around Higbee, it spread out over a considerable distance. There were nearly a dozen schools. These were the famous one-room schoolhouses, where teachers grouped their students by age and ability, conducting lessons on everything from the alphabet to great literature. While the upper bounds were obviously set by the teacher's own educational background, most students would find their limits more quickly, their attendance constrained by the family's need to make a living on the prairie.

The teachers were not well paid. John never made more than forty dollars a month from his teaching, though the district did supply housing for his family. He supplemented his income by laboring on local farms during the summer. The family occasionally took in borders as well.

At least in her son's eyes, Omar's mother Bessie was the archetypal frontier woman, the sort of resourceful person the mid-West was built by. Her household garden supplied much of the family food; her baking was essential to the family meals. She sewed all her own clothes with a Singer sewing machine. Eventually, she used those sewing skills to support the family as well. She's described in *A General's Life* as "blue-eyed, strong-minded and entirely gray-haired before she was twenty . . . an unfailing cheerful and resourceful woman. She was a strict, attentive, though far from doting mother."[6]

Bessie came from a tight knit family that remained close through difficult times. When her older sister, Emma Jane Bogie, died in 1897, Bessie's mother helped her son-in-law care for their two young daughters, Nettie and Opal. When she died a few months later, the Bradleys took in the girls, ages seven and six, making the three and a half-year-old Omar an instant baby brother. Omar himself had a baby brother, Raymond Calvert, born in February 1900. But the child died short of his second birthday in January 1902, the victim of scarlet fever.

A photo taken of the family when Omar was six years old reveals John as a solid, well-built man of barely average height with a moustache and buttoned suit, posing with one hand on his son in front of him. Omar's mother, in a black dress, stands off to their right, a visible gap between the others.[7] It's a very formal family photo, and Bessie is the only one near smiling.

Father and son formed a tight bond during Omar's early years. They would walk to school together at what must have seemed like a quick pace for the young child, though almost a dawdling one for his father, seventeen minutes a mile. The walks gave them time to discuss many things: hunting, books, and baseball, the sport a particular passion of John's. At night, the cold house meant that father and son often shared a bed for warmth. John would quiz Omar on math problems, honing an innate ability with numbers and reinforcing Omar's inclination to logic.

The Bradleys attended the Church of Christ, a born-again Christian church that John had been raised in. (Bessie, originally a Baptist, joined after marriage.) Outside of services, the family had few formal observances of religion; they neither said Grace at the table nor read much from the Bible. Nonetheless, Omar remembered them as having deeply held Christian convictions, living a "Christian life in every sense of the phrase."[8]

Baseball had a strong influence on Omar. John Bradley enjoyed the sport, which was gaining enormous popularity at the time. Omar spent many summer afternoons in the pastures playing ball. His cousin, interviewed years later by Clay Blair for *A General's Life*, remembered that as Omar got older, he could throw a ball three hundred feet, or roughly the distance from home plate to the right field wall in a modern stadium—an impressive toss, even for today's professionals.

Indoors, Bradley played toy soldiers, creating forts and mock battles using the .22 caliber shells for men and dominos for walls and barriers. Cannons were fashioned from a pea shooter to support the troops. The childhood battles were fantasized replays of the Revolutionary War, with the British generally taking it on the chin.

But play was generally a small part of Omar's day, even when school was out of session. His first chores included gathering kindling each morning for the stove, and fetching water from the well out back. Later, he helped with farm chores and some of the odd jobs John Bradley did to earn money.[9] Omar helped his father gather honey (some seventy years later he still remembered the stings). Father and son would also dig yellow root or goldenseal, a common ingredient of medicine at the time. While he considered hunting recreation, he would regularly take his rabbit pelts and sell them, earning more money for ammo. He was a good shot; among the stories Bradley later told was one about nailing eggs tossed in the air[10] while shooting from the hip.

John's shifting school assignments meant that Omar attended a variety of grammar schools, at least four by the time he reached sixth grade according to the family records. Educationally, this probably wasn't very disrupting—he had the same teacher, after all. But it did mean a different set of friends during these early days, and may have tightened his relationship with his father.

When he was twelve, the family moved to Higbee, buying a house there. This allowed Bradley to attend the school there, probably with the idea that it would prepare him for college. The house they bought, purchased at a sheriff's auction, cost $515. The $450 mortgage strained family finances to the point that Mrs. Bradley took a job as a telephone operator to earn extra money. A switchboard was installed in one of the bedrooms, and Omar and his two cousins took turns at it each night, handling the odd overnight call. Omar's father, meanwhile, continued to teach at the rural schools, walking about seven miles every day.

Higbee was not a one-room schoolhouse town. Students attended class by grade level. By age, Omar was a seventh grader, but tests showed he was more advanced, and he was placed with the eighth graders for the 1905–06 school year. By the end of the year, Omar was ranked first among the twenty-two boys and girls in his grade. The next year—considered the "sophomore year" at the school—there were only twelve students. Omar thrived, finishing with a grade point average of 98.66.

One evening toward the end of January 1908, John Bradley came home late from work, exhausted by his six-mile trek. That was unusual; even in the winter, exercise seemed to agree with him. Worn down and coughing from what seemed to be a very bad cold, he went to bed.

It turned out he had a fever. There was a good deal of illness going around town, and John's condition didn't seem particularly bad; he was a healthy man in good physical shape. But the doctor found that his lungs had begun filling with fluid. Within days, pneumonia killed him. He was forty.[11]

Omar was too sick to go to the funeral. His father's sudden death shook the small community. There was standing room only at the funeral.

"No matter how hard they had tried to suppress their emotions," wrote the *Higbee Weekly News*, "the strongest among the large crowd turned from the casket with tears in their eyes. To die universally regretted is a privilege accorded but few."[12]

Omar, just entering his teen years, had lost not just a father and role model, but a teacher, hunting companion, and probably his closest friend. He remembered that winter—one of the warmest on record in that part of the state—as the coldest ever.

The family could no longer afford the mortgage on the house, so his mother rented it out (it was later sold at a sheriff's auction), and they moved to Moberly. Moberly, Missouri, was a railroad town, relatively new and "big"—if a population just under nine thousand can be considered big. It was certainly larger than Higbee, and it provided more opportunities for work. Bessie worked as a seamstress and rented out rooms in their leased house.

Omar added some money by taking a paper route, but school was his primary concern. At Moberly High School, he was assigned to the tenth grade, repeating the grade he had last completed at Higbee. The next year, in the fall of 1909, the school officials decided he had been left back unfairly and jumped him ahead to the senior class.[13]

Whatever the effect on his studies, the arbitrary promotion helped Omar in one sense: it put him in the same class with his neighbor, Mary Quayle. He slowly developed a crush, though they never actually dated. Bradley said later that he was too busy with his paper route and sports, but his innate shyness around girls and women was certainly a much bigger factor. Still, he got to know the Quayle family quite well. They attended the same church, and he took Sunday school lessons from Mary's mother Eudora. The friendship would eventually blossom into a romance.

By now, Bradley was a self-described "baseball nut." His skills made it easy for him to make friends on the baseball diamond. The school did not have an organized team, but the students made their own arrangements, and Bradley with his tall, sinewy frame was a popular player. Away from the field, he seems to have felt he was something of an outsider, not really fitting in with young people who had known each other from early youth. The pressure of his family finances might have been another factor. He spent the summer of 1909 working in the supply department of Wabash Railroad.

In the late winter of 1910, Omar and another boy collided while skating one night on the local lake. They came together so fast and hard that Bradley's teeth were damaged. The hard-pressed family couldn't afford medical attention. Already shy, he became self-conscious about how he looked, pressing his lips together whenever he was photographed. It was a habit that stayed with him for the rest of his life, as he remained painfully self-conscious when his photo was being taken—even when, paradoxically, he demonstrated little care for how he looked otherwise.

That summer, Omar went back to his old job at the railroad. He got a quick promotion, becoming a helper in the mechanical division working on the steam engines. Paid seventeen cents an hour, he worked six days a week. That was about half the average pay for all railroad workers in America, but not a bad wage considering his experience.[14] The position was exactly the sort that a young man with ambitions might start in.

But Omar wasn't planning a career with the railroad. He was saving money for college. He had decided to become a lawyer, and planned to attend the University of Missouri in Columbia. Any worries he had about not being able to support his mother once he left for college were somewhat alleviated when Bessie married a local widower, John Robert Maddox on Christmas Day 1910, though Maddox himself was poor and raising two young sons.

At some point that spring or early summer, Bradley chanced to strike up a conversation with John Cruson, who ran the Sunday school at his church. Cruson liked the seventeen-year-old. There was much to like: athletic and intelligent, Omar was hard-working and conscientious.

Cruson asked Omar about his future plans. Omar told him he was saving money to attend the University of Missouri in the fall.

"Why don't you try for West Point?"

"I couldn't afford West Point."[15]

Cruson smiled and told him that West Point didn't charge tuition. Rather, it paid its students—in exchange, of course, for their committing to serve in the U.S. Army as commissioned officers.

Bradley told this story throughout his life, making it sound as if his interest in West Point was primarily financial: it was a free way to get a college education. But that seems far too simplistic. For one thing, while he may have been so uninformed about West Point that he believed he had to pay tuition, he would certainly have found out a great deal about the school by the time he decided to apply. The Army was an institution unto itself, not joined lightly. Whether he saw it as a pathway to becoming an engineer—a guess, but a likely one given the school's reputation—it still represented a major switch in direction, one that a contemplative person like Bradley would have considered with some seriousness.

The admission process to the Point was formidable, and Bradley faced another obstacle—his mother didn't think it was a good idea. But talking about it with her apparently convinced him to go ahead and apply. He wrote a letter to his congressman, William M. Rucker, seeking an appointment to the school. Rucker had already made his allotted appointment that year, however, and told Omar he would have to wait another year before applying.

Too long, thought Omar. He was about to drop the idea when the law on appointments was changed, giving the congressman another nomination. There was another young man ahead of Bradley, but Rucker offered him a chance to take the exams anyway; this would allow him to become an alternate in case the other boy failed the tests. Omar had eight days to decide—which meant, if he said yes, he had eight days to study.

The decision almost came down to money: Omar didn't want to spend the money on a train ticket "with the odds stacked so heavily against"[16] him. He sought out J. C. Lilly, the local superintendent of schools, to ask for his advice. Lilly told him to take his shot. Even if he failed, it would be good experience.

And yet Bradley still couldn't bring himself to spend the money. He decided he would take the test if—and only if—the railroad would "give me time off and a free pass to St. Louis."[17] The railroad did both.

The qualifying exams stretched over four days. The stumper for Bradley was not English, a subject he'd always had trouble with in school, but rather algebra, the subject he'd always done best in.

His mind seemed to go blank reading the problems. It had been two years since he last studied the subject in school. He had trouble with calculations, couldn't remember formulas. It was a disaster.

Despairing two hours into the four-hour test, he gave up. Omar rose from his desk and walked toward the proctor. But the officer was reading a book, and was so engrossed in it that he failed to notice Bradley— or perhaps he just decided to ignore him, silently urging the would-be recruit to take another shot.

Bradley decided he wouldn't disturb him and went back to his desk. Somehow, equations materialized from the fog of his memory, and Bradley was able to do enough of the exam to pass, though by his recollection just barely.

The congressman's first choice, who had been studying for a year, did not. Bradley was offered the appointment.

"I felt a twinge of guilt about Dempsey Anderson [the other candidate, whom he had met while taking the tests], as though I had taken away something that was his," Bradley says in *A General's Life*. "I offered to decline the appointment, thinking he might somehow regain it, but he said, 'Indeed not. You have won.'"[18]

Here was a decision that was literally the most important he had ever made in his life to that point, and Bradley was ready to give up a place he had earned through a difficult competition. The moment illustrates a deep facet of his character, something more than just sensitivity to other's feelings, or altruism. Even as a teenager he seemed to have a well-developed sense of universal justice: it wasn't fair that a usurper took someone else's "position," even if *he* was the usurper.

An undertone of bemusement and even wonder comes through when the story is told in *A General's Life*. One might be tempted to credit his co-writer, but it's present in his interviews and other source material as well. Bradley comes off as unassuming because he *was* unassuming. Given that the bulk of the interviews and stories came after he was a five-star general, it's an even more remarkable character trait.

West Point is located on the western bank of the Hudson River in New York, about sixty miles north of New York City. Overlooking a strategic spot where the waterway forms an elbow bending to the west, a garrison above the river there was one of several important camps George Washington used to house troops during the latter stages of the Revolutionary War. Most infamously, the fort was commanded by General Benedict Arnold when he decided to desert to the British.

West Point remained a garrison and training area after the war, and in 1802 became the site of the U.S. Military Academy, the Army's premier training school for young officers. Throughout much of the Academy's history, it was known for turning out engineering students, and is often cited as the role model for engineering colleges throughout the U.S. Among its many famous graduates was George Washington Goethals, the engineer responsible for the Panama Canal.

When Bradley arrived in 1911, the Point and the Army were in the middle of a boom. Following the Spanish-American War and action in the Philippines, the U.S. Army had a shortage of trained officers, and congress authorized the expansion of the classes. Bradley was one of the beneficiaries of this expansion.

The Army itself was relatively small, with roughly 133,000 soldiers. The recent wars notwithstanding, it was still very much a frontier force.

Economically, the country was growing rapidly, but America was not a world power in a military sense. Its standing army and navy paled compared to those of Europe, and would continue to do so even after World War I. This was a reflection of many deeply held American attitudes, beginning with George Washington's famous admonition not to get involved in "foreign entanglements." Thanks partly to geography, there were no great threats facing the country that demanded a large military. Nor could the country have supported one easily. Federal budgets were financed primarily by excise taxes and tariffs through the nineteenth century. The unpredictable nature of these taxes and the difficulty of collecting large amounts through them necessarily kept government spending low. And that in turn meant a very small standing army and navy.

Bradley was joining a fairly small club, and he was joining as one of its elite. Despite his background, there would be no obstacles to his advancement through the ranks if he worked hard and proved himself. And if he chose to leave the Army, he would have a reasonably good education for civilian life.

Bradley's graduating class of 1915 would prove to be an exceptional one, producing a large number of generals, including two (Bradley and Dwight D. Eisenhower) who became five-star generals. Of the 164 graduates, 59 became generals, a rate that is said to be the highest of any class to graduate the Academy. Its success set the class apart, and it became known and celebrated as "The Class the Stars Fell On."[19]

It can be argued that to some extent, the class's achievements were a result of a peculiar set of circumstances—the men who graduated as young lieutenants had the benefit of serving during an expansionary era for the Army, and found themselves in the middle of a war at exactly the age and experience level when colonels are promoted to generals. In that sense, they were in the right place at the right time, however ironic it may be to use that phrase to describe a war. On the other hand, their achievements would prove to be outsized, the individual records attesting to their unusual abilities.

Bradley's grades on the entrance exam were good enough to get him into the school, but they were far from the best in his class. The 265 men

20 ★ OMAR BRADLEY: GENERAL AT WAR

were divided into 28 divisions according to those scores. Bradley started at 24 in math, his best subject; he was in division 27 in English and history. But that was largely a product of his preparation for the exam. Bradley finished his first year ranked 49th in his class, eventually graduating at 44th.

Bradley's late appointment meant he missed the actual start of the term, which began in June with a seven-week "summer camp." During that time, new cadets—called "plebes" their first year—lived in tents on the grounds and received a kind of basic introduction to military life and skills. Hiking and shooting were at the core of these skills, and the boy who'd learned to hunt at four excelled at them. Bradley thus missed out on an early opportunity to set himself apart as a class leader.

He also missed the West Point tradition of "beast barracks"—the difficult ritual that involved merciless hazing of the newcomers by upperclassmen. The hazing at the time was quite cruel, even inhumane, and in fact continued well after beast barracks. But if Bradley was singled out for particular attention during his first year he never complained. He thought hazing (called "crawling" at the time) was a great "leveler," removing preconceived notions of merit and replacing them with military discipline and a recognition of the command structure and privileges of rank.

His status as a late-comer earned him and the others the title of an "Augustine," a play on words referring to the month they started. Bradley felt that the Augustines were discriminated against, with none promoted to cadet officer until their senior year.[20]

Bradley won respect among his classmates for his athletic ability. Not long after he arrived, the Army baseball coach, Sam Strang Nicklin, watched the long, lean plebe play in an intramural game. Bradley hit a long home run and made several good throws to the plate from the outfield. The coach made a point to look him up after the game, complimenting him on his throwing arm. The following spring, Omar went out for baseball. He didn't make the first team—that would have been unusual for a freshman—but he was added to the squad nonetheless. Being on the baseball team removed some of the restrictions normally placed on plebes. Omar was allowed to sit at a team table, mix with upper classmen on the team, and avoid a good deal of hazing while on the fields. He was popular enough to be inducted into an illegal Greek fraternity.

The following year, Omar became the team's starting left fielder. He was a good player on a good team. Not only did Army have a winning season—16–6—but they beat Navy 2–1 in a contest surely celebrated long and hard at the time.

Bradley lettered as the starting left fielder on a pair of excellent teams in his final two years. Characteristically, he calls the 1914 squad's record "middling," when it was actually 10–5, a winning percentage professional teams would kill for. In his final year, the record was an even better 18–3.

Bradley also played football, starting with the jayvee squad in his second year. He made varsity as a backup center the next, and played in a handful of games over the rest of his school career. The teams were outstanding, but most important for an Army man, they all beat Navy. Bradley hurt his knee playing, however; the injury would plague him on and off for the rest of his life.

Bradley came to West Point a hair shy of six feet tall but skinny: he weighed 145 pounds. He says he gained more than thirty pounds by his second year. Even then, he was more rangy than heavy. As his sinewy frame filled out, his strength, endurance, and energy became obvious. Someone nicknamed him "Darwin," allegedly because he looked like an ape.[21] The nickname didn't quite stick; "Brad" did.

One other physical characteristic deserves note: Bradley's hair was already going gray, a trait he inherited from his mother.

In his military courses, Bradley discovered that he had a knack for small-team tactics, or what might be called the science of the battlefield— examining and analyzing positions and forces. Bradley joined a small group of cadets in an informal seminar on tactics led by a lieutenant, Forrest Harding. Conducted at night after regular classes, the sessions provided some of the most important professional preparation Bradley received at the Point.

★ ★ ★ ★

It was at West Point that Bradley first met Dwight Eisenhower. Not only were they both members of the same class, but as athletes they were both members of Company F, Bradley joining in his second year. Eisenhower would probably have been a star running back had he not injured his knee during his plebe year; he consoled himself with cheerleading. At the same time he earned something of a reputation as a rebel.

Though the two young men were friends, they were not extraordinarily close. Their personalities were very different: Eisenhower liked to talk; Bradley was hardly loquacious. More to the point, Bradley tended to follow the Point's rules where "Ike" often flouted all but one: honesty.

In a class of 164 graduates, everyone knew each other fairly well, and by 1915, Eisenhower had taken Bradley's measure. Editing the yearbook in their final year, Eisenhower chose a quote for Bradley's entry:

"True merit is like a river; the deeper it is, the less noise it makes." And he suggested, "If [Bradley] keeps up the clip he's started, some of us will some day be bragging to our grandchildren that, 'Sure, General Bradley was a classmate of mine.'"[22]

Bradley went back to Missouri during the summer of 1913, his first visit since starting at West Point. Mary Quayle was home as well. She'd finished St. Cloud Normal School. Qualifying as a teacher, she had accepted a job at Albert Lea in Minnesota. The pair started seeing more of each other. Their relationship blossomed, continuing with letters after both went back to their respective schools. By the time Bradley graduated West Point, they had become engaged.

The young Bradley seems to have been particularly shy around girls. He says he never dated during high school, and in the four years he was at West Point attended only one hop (or dance); in his own words he "dragged" a girl to the dance.

In *A General's Life*, Mary is described with a single sentence: "Pretty, bright, ambitious and domineering, like my mother." The description is sandwiched between accounts of Bradley's playing baseball in Moberly and his first assignment as an officer in the Army.[23]

Reading a section about his wife a little later on, one can almost hear his co-author trying to coax a full description onto the page. She had strong likes and dislikes, says the book, "and did not hesitate to order Second Lieutenant Bradley around." And he emphasizes her education and experience as a teacher and college student, remarking on her maturity and interests. "She wanted to expand her horizons still more." What attracted Bradley—or at least what he admitted to—were Mary's sense of justice and humanity, and her intellect. Fine qualities, certainly, though not usually those one lists when describing a passionate romance.[24]

But there seems to have been a quiet passion between them, one that endured despite the rigors of military life. During World War II, Bradley wrote to his wife often if not every night, and he had a photo of her on his desk. Overly demonstrative shows of emotion were not in his character, even on the written page: his wife habitually complained that his letters were far too short.

Bradley presented Mary with an engagement ring soon after graduating from West Point in 1915. The wedding was set for a year later, a not unusual arrangement, especially considering Bradley's military commitments and the war in Europe. There were other ominous signs of pending dangers. Americans were casting a wary eye to Mexico, where the revolution of 1910 had unsettled the border area. U.S. intrigue culminated in the U.S. assault on and takeover of Vera Cruz in 1914, a move against Mexican General Victoriano Huerta and a strike against German influence at the same time. The city's capture cut off Huerta's access to German money and supplies through the port. Continued unrest along the border would lead to the so-called Punitive Expedition conducted by General John J. "Blackjack" Pershing in 1916.

Fighting rebels and *banditos* was hardly glamorous, and the border area was the last place most young second lieutenants wanted to go. It wasn't so much the danger, though of course there was plenty of that. The living conditions, even by the standards of the time, were rough. The troops were isolated from their families, spending much of their time in the field either patrolling or pursuing Mexican "outlaws" along the badlands and open desert of the border. This was in direct contrast to life at other posts, where an officer could easily afford decent quarters and perhaps share a servant with others. Duty was so light that even a lowly lieutenant might find himself free at noon.

West Point shavetails were allowed to request their first postings, though requesting and getting were not necessarily the same thing. Bradley's standing in his class, though good, was not quite high enough to win an appointment to either the corps of engineers or the artillery; like the bulk of his classmates, he went into the infantry. (Artillery service promised faster promotions, and thus was highly sought after. The Corps of Engineers was perhaps the Army's most celebrated branch, with successes like the Panama Canal to its credit, and experience in the Corps translated very well once separated from the service. There was also the Signal Corps, with its nascent aviation section—ironically regarded as one of the least desirable posts at the time.)

Bradley asked to be assigned to the 14th Infantry Regiment stationed in Alaska and Washington, and won that assignment. After a three-month furlough, during which he got engaged, he reported to Spokane, joining the regiment's Third Battalion.

Many a young lieutenant's true education only begins after he wins his commission, and if that was an exaggeration in Bradley's case, it wasn't by much. He found himself surrounded by officers and non-commissioned officers with considerably more experience; the battalion first sergeant, for example, was a major in the reserves.

The flipside of this experience was the uneven strength of the enlisted corps. Privates earned $13 a month; they generally had to serve for years before being considered for promotion (and a raise) to corporal. The poor pay discouraged many men from making a career of the Army, or even staying on for their full hitch. Desertion was common.

Officers had it considerably better, even when starting out. Bradley was making $141.67 a month, and had his room in a three-bedroom duplex paid for. He, his two roommates, and two other officers kicked in and hired a black cook to prepare their meals.

Bradley's early specialty was drilling the men on the parade ground, but he soon found a second calling as counsel for the defense in the many court martials; after winning a case for a robbery suspect, he became sought after by every prisoner in the stockade. Perhaps recognizing his skills, the commander appointed him a member of the court, making him change sides.

As an officer, Bradley's physical size and bearing were as critical as his intellect. He was big enough to wrestle the battalion's wrestling champ to a draw, though he would wryly admit years later that he could only avoid being pinned for five minutes. On New Year's Eve in 1915, Bradley stepped into an alcohol-fueled brawl between a group of local soldiers and civilians in town, managing to get all the men home without bloodshed or serious injury. He didn't use threats or even, apparently, blows. His method of dealing with his men was more like the sort of persuasion one would expect from a coach or captain of an athletic team: C'mon boys, let's get home, he barked. And they did.

Bradley's easy life in Portland came to an abrupt end in the spring of 1916, when General Pershing's pursuit of Pancho Villa over the border raised Mexican feelings to the point where war was threatened. Pershing's campaign began after a number of raids by Villa that claimed U.S. lives, including the razing of Columbus, New Mexico. Shut off from the Mexican railroads, Pershing used trucks and cars to move his men. His force also included six airplanes, used as scouts. (Though their use was historically important, neither the motorized vehicles nor aircraft were central to the fight.)

While the expedition would burnish Pershing's reputation as a leader, it was not particularly successful; Villa was able to continue making raids and escaped capture. A lieutenant in Pershing's army, George S. Patton, had his first brush with wider fame when he personally killed Julio Cardenas in a gunfight. Cardenas was Villa's second in command and a hardened fighter. Patton is said to have notched his pistol afterwards;

strapping Cardenas's body to the hood of his car to bring back to Pershing. True or not, the story was the first of many to burnish the Patton legend.

Bradley was one of the thousands of soldiers rushed south as tensions peaked, but like most of them, he saw no direct action. There were immediate personal consequences, however. His marriage to Mary Quayle had to be postponed. Unfortunately for Mary, she learned of the postponement not from Bradley, but from a headline in the local newspaper:

War orders delay marriage
Lt. Omar Bradley called to border war
Soon to wed Miss Mary Quayle[25]

According to Bradley, a reporter from the *Moberly Democrat* had learned of the mobilization plans and phoned him to find out what was going on. After talking to the journalist, Bradley decided that rather than sending a telegram or calling his bride-to-be—phones were not yet ubiquitous—he'd write a letter. The letter arrived after the newspaper, and did nothing to assuage Mary's feelings on being scooped.

As tensions with Mexico eased, Bradley and his company were sent to Arizona, where they drilled and went on maneuvers. He described his posts at Douglas and Yuma as "disagreeable," brushing over them in his autobiography.

The details were more telling. The men lived in tents and patrolled desert wilderness; they froze at night and sweltered during the day. The roads were primitive at best and nonexistent at worst. Using trucks to move men was new, and the vehicles made it such a chore that it would have been hard to predict how it would revolutionize warfare. Yet the hands-on experience with the vehicles was useful to the young officer, who saw both the potential and the problems, as well as some ways around them. Bradley supervised a truck hike where the vehicles had to be pulled over a shallow river crossing after the bridge went out; it took two or three hundred men with ropes pulling the vehicles one at a time to get them across. It was another early experience that he would never forget.

Even in camp, sand got into everything. Bradley would sit in his tent, working at his desk, and find his feet completely covered. His unit was undermanned, and Lieutenant Bradley found himself heading supply, personally counting horses and mules before breakfast, then heading construction efforts in the afternoon, supervising the soldiers as they built more permanent quarters. From designing a sewer system to helping his men unload fourteen train cars of uncut lumber, Bradley was busier than he had ever been in the Army. But while it was exhausting, the jobs also required his full-range of skills, from brains to brawn. Realizing his ability, Bradley's commander kept adding jobs. The lieutenant handled them all without complaint—or at least none that he voiced.

There was one responsibility that he made time for gladly: coaching the regimental baseball team. And in whatever spare time he had left, Bradley worked with a young setter, hoping to use the dog to hunt. (It turned out he didn't have much of a chance to test the dog's skills.) Hunting remained a passion, which he indulged whenever possible. Later on, Bradley would train another setter to hunt with him, keeping him for fourteen years until just before World War II.[26]

In October, Bradley and his classmates were promoted to First Lieutenants. On December 28, 1916, he and Mary wed in Columbia, Missouri, where her family had moved to be near her and her sister while they went to college.

Moberly is some thirty miles as the crow flies north of Columbia; the two cities were connected by railroad. Bradley's mother and stepfather missed the wedding. According to Bradley, this was because it would have cost too much for them to come.

The excuse seems to be a blatantly face-saving one, though who it's sparing isn't clear.

Train fares were in the area of two to three cents per mile at the time; it could have cost Bradley's mother as much as four dollars to watch her son get married, with perhaps another two or three to stay overnight. Bradley notes that his mother was still "poor as a church mouse." But he had also just been given a promotion that raised his salary to $206 a month, a good wage for the time. If Bradley truly wanted his mother at the wedding, surely he could have found the funds to get her there.[27]

Bradley had no best man at the wedding: no friends (or relatives) close enough to stand up for him in Missouri, and no Army friends whom Bradley felt he could (or should) ask to take time off to do the same. Part of the reason may have been Bradley's characteristic feeling that he shouldn't impose on others, but the wedding was also a sign of the separation between his two worlds—his former civilian life and the Army. The former would continue to fade in importance.

After a brief honeymoon in Kansas City, the newlyweds visited an Army friend of Bradley's in Texas, then went to Arizona and California. They were back in Yuma by January 11, 1917, where they rented a two-room house.

Not yet twenty-four, Bradley was tall and prematurely gray. He hated Yuma, describing duty there as boring and routine. Worse, the only entertainment he and Mary could find were visits to superior officers, or as he put it years later, a "tedious round of formal calls on superiors for tea or coffee."[28] He applied for a transfer back to the First Battalion in the Alaskan wilderness.

Though approved, the transfer was never implemented. The United States declared war against Germany on April 6, 1917. Bradley's unit was tasked with training recruits. He tried to transfer out of the 14th Infantry—rightly, he saw combat as a sure ticket to advancement after the war—but nothing worked. In January 1918, he took over command of the Regiment's Company F. Just under a hundred men strong, the company was assigned to guard the copper mines near Butte, Montana.

There was little danger of a German invasion that deep into the heartland, but the strategic importance of copper made labor unrest in the area a matter of national security. Bradley was assigned to keep the mines open.

Bradley arrived in town that January in the middle of a cold spell, with temperatures hitting 40° below zero—close to, though not quite a record. But the temperature was the only thing in town that was cold. To Bradley, Butte seemed barely removed from the frontier days, and he thought nearly everyone in town was packing a gun. The town had been the scene of considerable labor and political unrest, and the local IWW[29] leadership was described to him as a bunch of anarchists determined to shut down the mines.

When the IWW planned a general strike for St. Patrick's Day, March 17—the date would have been chosen to resonate with Irish-American miners—Bradley turned out his company of troops. With the crowd threatening to riot, Bradley ordered live rounds and fixed bayonets. He made a show of force on Main Street. There was some violence, though how much is not clear. The local news accounts said the soldiers arrested fifty men, but the strike itself fizzled. Bradley was praised by the local press.

That September, Bradley led a raid on the Metal Mine Workers Hall, arresting about fifty members of the IWW who had fliers calling for a general strike. The most prominent among them was William F. Dunn, a newspaper editor who would be subsequently charged with sedition for statements opposing the war.[30]

Anti-labor feelings mixed with patriotism and anti-German sentiment, not only in Montana but throughout the country. Montana passed a strict anti-sedition act that made it a crime to "utter, print, write or publish any disloyal, profane . . . contemptuous, slurring or abusive language" about the country, its soldiers, or its flag. According to historian Clemens P. Work, seventy-nine people were convicted under the law; nearly all were poor laborers. As it happened, Dunn was one of the few exceptions. Well-known as a critic of the state government and mine operators, one of whom he accused of hiring German spies, his alleged slurs were in print where they could be easily seen—and presumably influence others. He was convicted of sedition, but then won a reversal on appeal. He would eventually become an important figure in the American Communist Party.

Workers at the time were protesting poor pay, unsafe conditions at the mine, and a "rustling card system" used to single out labor agitators and others, preventing them from working. The company actively bullied the state government and openly strove to break the unions. The conflict would continue for years, with occasional outbreaks of violence. In 1919, after Bradley had been reassigned, soldiers ordered to break up a strike bayoneted nine workers, and a clash with company officials the following year saw two men die, with over a dozen others shot.

Bradley took no role in the politics; he looked back at the matter simply as an officer following orders. He told a local newspaper after St. Patrick's Day, "We got orders to assist the police in quelling a riot and had no alternative but to quell it. I am glad nobody was seriously hurt, but I would rather have seen a lot of people hurt than to feel that my boys fell down on the job. I am proud of every boy in my command."[31]

His experience at Butte was tinged by personal loss. Mary arrived in the city some seven and a half months pregnant. In February, she went into labor. The baby boy was stillborn. The death, Bradley admitted, touched him greatly, reminding him not only of the loss of his brother Raymond, but also of his father more than a decade earlier.

Mary's mother Dora took the body back to the cemetery in their hometown, burying the infant boy next to Mary's father. Bradley remained at his post.

Except for the labor agitation and baseball, Bradley found Army life in Butte dull. It didn't help that the war in Europe was reaching a high point that summer, with fresh American troops supplying a needed boost to the Allies. Bradley got a routine promotion to major, but otherwise life seemed an unrelieved routine.

That changed in September 1918. The 14th Infantry Regiment received orders to report to Camp Dodge in Des Moines, where it would form the core of the 19th Infantry Division—and then ship out to France.

The young major was beyond excited. Given command of the Second Battalion, 14th Regiment, he fell eagerly into a training program under the direction of officers just back from the front. But almost as soon as the unit started drilling, soldiers began turning up at sick call in droves. Within days, the camp hospital overflowed with victims of the Influenza Epidemic of 1918.

The disease seemed arbitrary, even petulant. Five men in Bradley's ninety-six-man company got sick, but none so seriously as to die. A company that had just come from Alaska saw eighty-five of its eighty-six men fall ill, with twenty-six dying. Bradley escaped the epidemic himself, but chafed at the disruptions it caused. The unit's training schedule was upended, and he began to think he was never going to get into the war.

His desire to go to France was an indication not of blood lust, but of ambition. He'd made the Army his family and his future. Like most other officers of his day, he realized that combat experience—however slight—represented a game changer, an indelible recommendation in the resume. Pershing was a clear example: his early career in the Indian wars and then the Spanish and Philippine conflicts had helped him advance. Bradley no doubt wanted to test himself and the theories about tactics and combat he'd learned, but long-term considerations were never far from his mind.

One Saturday evening in early November, Bradley took his wife into town. Suddenly they heard whistles and church bells sounding. The Armistice had come. The war was over.

Bradley had heard rumors that the war would end, but hadn't believed them. Now the proof was all around him.

His career, he thought, had just died. He'd never make general now.

The Army had grown tremendously in just two years; now it shrank nearly as fast. Bradley was ordered to Camp Grant in Illinois, where he helped close what had been one of the country's largest military facilities. (The camp would later be used by the National Guard and the Civilian Conservation Corps. It played an important role in World War II when, besides being used as an induction and training center, it housed enemy POWs.)

Bradley was bored by the assignment. Unsure what to do about his career, he decided with his wife that he should try and get a post in the state of Washington, an area they loved. He requested a job teaching ROTC.

Teaching—whether it was drilling, tactics, or mathematics—always appealed to Bradley. It was a job Bradley never described as dull or boring. His father had been a teacher, and Bradley seems to have inherited or learned a knack for the profession from him.

The transfer came through, but to Bradley's surprise, he was assigned not to the Pacific Northwest, but to the area the Army designated "Northwest"—North and South Dakota. He headed to Brookings, South Dakota, to teach at a small agricultural school there.

It could have been worse. Just prior to receiving that assignment, Bradley was ordered to take command of a unit headed for Vladivostok, Siberia, during the Allied intervention in 1919. But his presence on a court martial of sixteen black soldiers accused of raping a white woman prevented him from taking the assignment. Bradley found the court martial case so distasteful that he didn't talk about it later, but he was happy not to go to Siberia.[32]

Bradley liked teaching the ROTC classes, though he found that he had nowhere near as much time with the students as he wanted—only three hours a week. He helped coach the football team and gave boxing and gymnastics instruction, which made him popular with the students as well as the school officials. The drill unit was highly regarded, a change over previous years. He took to wearing a moustache in a bid to make himself look a little older.[33]

A bureaucratic snafu or some other mix-up kept Bradley from being evaluated while at the post, a problem in an army where assignments and promotions rested on the results of annual efficiency reports. When the adjunct general's office investigated, a solution was imposed: Bradley received an average evaluation. It was the lowest he would get in his career.

Bradley saw it as an injustice and a slight, and not without good reason—it could easily prevent him from choice assignments in the future. He admitted to being still somewhat bitter fifty years later.

The obscure posting to Brookings turned out to be a prelude to a job with a considerably higher profile: math professor at West Point.

It's not precisely clear how or why Bradley was chosen to join the faculty as a math instructor in September 1920. He doesn't seem to have requested the post, and in the interviews and remembrances throughout his life expressed surprise at getting it. According to *A General's Life*, the head of the math department, Colonel Charles P. Echols, remembered him and chose him for the assignment. Bradley would also have been recommended because of his general qualifications, the fact that he was a Point graduate, and his posting as an ROTC instructor. But perhaps the biggest factor was simply the need for teachers—the staff had to be increased to meet the larger enrollment.

The Academy was in the midst of a reorganization and expansion following World War I. General Douglas MacArthur, a hero of the First World War, had been chosen its superintendent. MacArthur brought a number of changes to the Academy, hoping to update its curriculum and training.

Some of the changes were welcomed, like the expansion of intramural programs that increased the cadets' physical activities. Others were roundly criticized, including MacArthur's attempts to expand the curriculum, adding courses in social sciences and the arts while decreasing time in such studies as math. MacArthur also generally loosened the rules governing cadets. They were allowed to smoke and given passes long enough for them to get to nearby New York City by train for the afternoon or evening.

But perhaps nothing was so controversial as the new superintendent's official ban on hazing. The ban was essentially forced by Congress and followed the highly publicized suicide of a plebe, but even so it made

MacArthur less than popular. Even Bradley disliked it, and it is not surprising that the practice returned once MacArthur moved on.

For Bradley, hazing and the strict rules governing the cadets' behavior were part of the introduction to Army discipline. Together, they showed a plebe exactly where he was in the chain of command—pretty low—but they also taught him respect for the institution. Army discipline could be a life saver under fire—one learned to take orders without questioning them. It also provided a road map for advancement through your career, as demonstrated by a cadet's experience at West Point: take your lumps, play by the rules, work hard, gain seniority, and soon you would be the one giving orders.

Or teaching the classes. Bradley was one of thirty-seven math instructors. He and other newcomers had to attend afternoon courses to stay ahead of the plebes they were instructing. The coursework cut into his free time, taxing what was otherwise an extremely pleasant assignment. But that wasn't so bad, he figured—he'd have an easier time the next year.

But the next year he was moved up to what was called yearling math, a more advanced course for the sophomores. Once again he found himself spending his afternoons studying to stay ahead of his students. And then the third year was descriptive geometry. The fourth year he was appointed instructor for the teachers' introductory course. He couldn't catch a break.

Bradley's duties didn't cut *too* deeply. He had enough time to join the Free Masons,[34] and learned to golf with his friend Matt Ridgway. Bradley also once again became an intramural coach. This was not wholly a matter of choice, as he and other young instructors were doled out assignments soon after arriving. His was soccer: a problem, since he didn't even know the rules to the sport. He managed to trade jobs with a colleague who'd been appointed a football coach but had no experience in the sport. The switch worked out well—their companies won the respective championships.

Though this was the Roaring Twenties, Bradley and his wife missed most of the excitement. They were teetotalers at this point and also didn't smoke, which must have left them in a distinct minority at the time.

Cigarette smoke bothered Mary, and this helped cut down their social life even further; they tended to avoid gatherings where there would be a lot of smoking. New York City was not that far away, and they would sometimes drive down for dinner and a show.

Bradley regularly played cards with a group of friends, enjoying a pastime he would continue throughout his Army career. He did quite well at it, at least if the claims in *A General's Life* are to be believed. According to the book, Bradley played according to a system that had him mentally calculate the winning odds on every hand, folding if they were under 70 percent.

The system there is described as conservative, but in actual play it would encourage very large pots and gambling for high stakes at regular intervals. To succeed—Bradley claims he did well enough to supplement their Army income—a player would not only have to take a long view, but would have to be able to sustain high losses without losing his nerve, trusting that the math would eventually work in his favor.

The parallel to a war strategy can easily be seen. Such a general would avoid battles where he did not already enjoy a relatively good chance of winning. He would put a high number of chips on the table for the big battles where he thought he could win. And he would be prepared to persevere in the face of losses.

In his spare time, Bradley studied military history, often visiting the Academy library. He was especially attracted to the Civil War campaigns of William T. Sherman. From Bradley's perspective, Sherman was a master of maneuver, especially adept at bringing a large army into battle and supplying it. The ability to move an army deep into enemy territory, rather than using it to engage in a head-on, set piece battle, was a quality Bradley greatly admired.

This was not necessarily the lesson generally drawn from Civil War battles at the time, nor were such tactics necessarily in vogue in military thinking. The main lessons drawn from World War I, still being digested, had to do with static defenses and trench warfare. Not having seen action in France, Bradley was perhaps freer to draw his own conclusions about the proper conduct of war.

Bradley and his wife were still trying to have a child. They suffered another disappointment in 1920, when she miscarried—"another depressing personal setback"[35] as *A General's Life* puts it. Finally, in December 1923, Mary gave birth to a girl. They named her Elizabeth, giving her Omar's mother's name.

As the end of his fourth year at West Point approached, Bradley began looking for a new assignment. He was overdue for a foreign posting, but none of the choices seemed particularly enticing. Finally, he decided to pick Puerto Rico. After applying, he discovered that he could qualify for duty as a student in the Infantry School at Fort Benning, a relatively new institution at the time. The assignment was far more interesting, as well as career enhancing. Bradley applied and was accepted for the advanced class—he was to go from teacher to learner that fall.

He had ten weeks furlough before reporting. Bradley had been investing some of his extra money in the stock market, only to lose it as the market turned against him. Partly because of that, he decided to spend his ten weeks off working on a massive construction project just to the south—the Bear Mountain Bridge.

At ten dollars for a twelve-hour workday, the pay would be a welcome supplement.

Bradley hadn't been working for too many days when one of the suspension cables snapped. One of the strands hit his wristwatch, snapping it off. The incident made him reassess his decision. He quit and spent the rest of his vacation fly fishing. Characteristically, Bradley was to say later that he only decided to forgo the extra job after learning that very same evening that he had made ninety dollars from the stock market. Even the most primal emotions like survival were always balanced by logic and calculation.

Then as now, the courses at Benning were viewed as both practical and helpful to an officer's career. The school introduced Bradley to the infantry weapons World War I had made critical, machine guns and automatic rifles especially. He learned how to use them all.

Fortuitously, the main thrust of the tactics section at Benning fit well with what Bradley had learned from studying Sherman's campaigns and during his earlier training in small-group tactics. Maneuver, aided by dependable vehicles that could cover long distances quickly, was in vogue at the school, much to the dismay of the veterans of the war in France. And translating theory to practice was an area that Bradley excelled in—he became a coach on the battlefield, leading his team to take whatever tactical position was set out as the object of the exercise.

The combination of intellect and athleticism once more stood Major Bradley well. He finished second in his class.

Duty in Hawaii with the 27th Infantry Regiment followed. It was, as Bradley remembered later, pleasant, and not just because of the weather. He worked half-days most of the time, and generally didn't stand duty on the weekends. His golf game flourished, with his handicap shrinking to a four. He also discovered whiskey, or more properly bourbon, and in *A General's Life* is said to have begun a lifelong habit of relaxing before dinner with a drink or two.[36]

The Hawaiian beaches may have encouraged a more military habit—the use of sand tables to explore and teach tactics. The sand could be easily molded to mimic the terrain, and the three-dimensional effect was a major advance from the squigs and topo lines of a map. The sand made the interplay between combat and terrain that much more obvious and immediate. Terrain could be everything in a small unit battle; using it wisely could easily be the difference between victory and defeat.

It was in Hawaii that Bradley met an officer who would play an important role in his future: George S. Patton. Their meeting was less than auspicious. Patton, who had reverted to his prewar rank as major after serving as a colonel in the war, was G-2, the staff intelligence officer of the Hawaiian Division. In the last year of his assignment, and famous because of his service as a tank commander, Patton was regarded as a caustic and at times eccentric officer—not without reason.

Though the Bradleys and the Pattons lived across from each other, they could hardly have inhabited different social worlds. Outgoing and flamboyant, Major Patton and his wife entertained often; the Bradleys were quiet homebodies.

Bradley may not have liked partying, but he did like shooting, and when Patton invited him to join a trap shooting team he was organizing, Bradley went for a tryout. He missed the first two shots—then hit the next twenty-three, as sturdy a run as anyone could ask.

"You'll do," said Patton.[37]

Bradley stayed in Hawaii for three years, serving his last year as a liaison officer to the Hawaiian National Guard, a post where he nearly died of boredom. He returned to the States and another assignment as a student, this time at Fort Leavenworth, where he was enrolled on the one-year course at the Command and General Staff School.

It was a disappointing course of study, far less innovative than Benning, predictable and behind the times. Bradley had more fun off-campus, playing golf and caring for a friend's horse, which he rode an hour a day, something he seemed to enjoy despite comments by others and in his autobiography that he disliked the animals in general.

About the most memorable thing that came out of that year was the recommendation by a doctor who told Bradley to get all his teeth pulled or risk having a heart attack. Continued infections and abscesses had been bothering him ever since his childhood accident, but Bradley was nonetheless reluctant. Still, at thirty-five, Bradley became toothless. If he'd been self-conscious about his smile before, he was doubly so now.

As classes wound down, two job offers came in—one as treasurer of West Point, the other as an instructor at Fort Benning.

It was no contest as far as Bradley was concerned. In 1929, the Bradley family packed up their things and shipped out to Georgia. It would prove to be the making of his career.

★ ★ ★ ★

The assistant commandant at Fort Benning was Colonel George C. Marshall. Marshall headed the academic department and was therefore Bradley's boss. He would become the single most important influence on his career.

Marshall had served in World War I as a staff officer, winning notice from Pershing and marking himself as a comer in the Army. At Benning, he was updating the curriculum and the infantry at the same time. Marshall wanted to simplify battlefield tactics, apply the hard lessons of the recent war, and prepare officers to make quick and creative decisions based on inevitably limited information. As Marshall biographer Forrest C. Pogue writes, Marshall sought "to teach the art of improvisation, to extricate tactical principles from the procedural formulas in which they had become fixed by the schoolmen."[38] It was a philosophy that meshed perfectly with Bradley's own.

Like all his subordinates, Bradley's relationship with Marshall began as a thoroughly professional one, and never completely lost that character. Marshall always addressed him by his last name, and Bradley would not even think of addressing him as George. The two men did have much in common, and Bradley admired Marshall's probity, a serious streak that extended even to his disapproval of off-color stories, a staple of army life from time immemorial. Neither smoked—Marshall gave up both drinking and smoking for health reasons. Both men liked to hunt, and shared time together in the fields. But Marshall liked the younger man for his ability, not his friendship. Bradley, said Marshall, "was conspicuous for his ability to handle people and his ability to do things simply and clearly."[39]

Bradley began his stint at Benning in the tactical section, working under Joe Stilwell, another officer who would gain fame during World War II. On a personal level, Bradley found Stilwell tough, fully fitting the later label of "Vinegar Joe." But he also considered Stilwell a brilliant officer and tactician.

Bradley saw a connection between mathematics and tactical situations. Math for him was largely a matter of logic, a rigorous way of approaching the world. Tactics were much the same thing: the situation was a math problem, to be attacked with a logical set of rules.

Rules, however, were only part of the answer. Choosing the right one depended on the circumstances. And for Bradley, this often came down not just to the men and firepower at your command, but the geography as well—the terrain and its many facets. Here his youthful experience as a hunter gave him both tools and an insight into the situation. He would go over the terrain of a particular tactical problem, exploring it in great detail. As he told interviewer George Pappas many years later, "Shoot quail over it and you become familiar with every little draw and every little hill."[40]

Marshall demanded that instructors deliver their lectures extemporaneously. Bradley at first "cheated" by writing notes on cards and leaving them on the floor, where he could refer to them just in case. He gradually developed more confidence, and evidently did well enough to impress Stilwell, a notoriously hard grader, who rated him excellent on his efficiency report.[41]

After a year, Bradley was named to head the weapons section, making him one of Marshall's four chief assistants—and the only one still a major. Bradley excelled at this as he excelled at everything at Benning. Marshall rated Bradley "superior" on his last fitness report. His comments:

> Quiet, unassuming, capable, sound common sense. Absolute dependability. Give him a job and forget it. Recommended command: regiment in peace, division in war.[42]

The time a soldier spends in the classroom, both as a student and as a teacher, is often skipped over in the history books. The subject matter is often arcane to general readers, and there's simply no way to dramatize sitting and listening to lectures all day. In Bradley's case, his years in various schools are sometimes mentioned as a vivid (and inherently damning) comparison to the combat others saw in their formative years.

But the interwar years were an extremely important time for the American military, which was reinventing itself in big and small ways. The transition of divisions from "four-square" to "triangular" (to simplify greatly, going from four to three regiments in each) had far-reaching implications. The streamlined organization added to the Army's mobility, a critical American advantage during the war. At the other end of the spectrum, small group tactics—how and when to use supporting fire, say—had a profound effect not just on how units should be organized but how they should be deployed, how they should be equipped, and how they should be handled.

While there were many facets to the changes the U.S. Army underwent during the entire inter-war period, one of the most notable is the emphasis on movement and maneuverability in its battle doctrine.[43] This was despite the fact that the Army had very few vehicles and was shockingly behind other countries in the development of tanks. In ways big and small, the changes were a leap of faith in a conservative and underfunded institution. The doctrines of combined arms, with deep coordination between artillery, armor, infantry, and air power—hallmarks of Bradley's strategy in Europe—would advance light years during the World War, but its seeds were planted here.

Bradley played an integral role in this reinvention, and was intimately involved in the small matters as well as their larger implications. Exactly how far-reaching his influence was may be judged from one example: the use of machine guns in the war.

Bradley's advice prevented the machine gun from being treated in the same manner artillery was organizationally, which would have greatly complicated infantry company operations.[44] And any soldier who either used a machine gun or was able to advance because of a machine gun's indirect fire during the war was following doctrine and procedure written down during Bradley's stint as head of the tactics section at Benning.[45]

Of course, there were downsides to the tactics and methods the Army adopted. An emphasis on movement and maneuverability was all very well, but what was the solution when there was little room to maneuver and speed wasn't possible? Could an army designed to cover vast amounts of terrain in a lightning strike also feature the requisite firepower to blast an enemy ensconced in heavily fortified bunkers? Encouraging improvisation on the part of the local commander was a great idea, as long as the commander was creative. Then again, even a creative commander might choose the wrong solution to a problem: that was part and parcel of being creative.

One thing Bradley learned directly from Marshall: allow your underlings to do their job.

"Once having assigned an officer to his job, General Marshall seldom intervened,"[46] noted Bradley. It was a critical part not just of Marshall or Bradley's style, but would become a hallmark of American military command.

For better or worse, these were the ideas and prejudices that Bradley embraced at Benning, and would take into the war.

Bradley spent four years at the infantry school, time that saw the dawn of the Great Depression, which affected both his personal finances and the state of the Army. Bradley and his wife lost about $5,000 in the Crash and had to take out a loan to pay off their losses—an indication that, like many other people at the time, they had been buying stock on margin, or borrowing to pay for some of the purchase. Bradley had a reputation throughout his life as a man ruled by logic, and that was certainly justified. But there was another side of him that liked risk, at least when carefully considered. He played poker and played the stock market as a young man. Later in life he bet on horses, even developing a mathematical system worked out to guide his betting. [47]

The Army, too, was deeply affected by the Depression. The neglect that had begun right after World War I worsened as the Depression continued.[48] The Army benefited from some New Deal programs, including the Public Works Administration, which not only built a number of barracks and military facilities, but also funded the purchase of $20 million worth of trucks in 1934 and 1935, allowing the Army to phase out its older vehicles and retire many of its horses. But the Depression and the country's recovery were of far higher priority than military preparedness. The 1930s saw the Army's budget continually cut. Bradley, like every other soldier in the Army, found himself on what was called a "payless furlough" for a month—in other words, he received a pay cut equal to a full month's salary. While this was vastly preferable to being out of a job, it still strained personal finances. The Bradleys had a hard time staying current on the loan he had taken to cover his stock market loss.

Douglas MacArthur, by now chief of staff, is said to have engaged in at least one shouting match with the president over proposed cuts. MacArthur was a controversial figure both in the country at large and in the Army itself. During the Hoover administration, he personally led the assault on the Bonus Army veterans at the foot of Capitol Hill and razed their camp on the other side of the Potomac. Two babies died in the incident, still remembered as one of the darkest of the Depression. Though acting *against* President Hoover's explicit orders, MacArthur managed to deflect much of the political blame to the president with a brilliant press conference. Still, the episode hurt his reputation with many Americans, including Franklin Roosevelt, who reportedly considered him the country's most dangerous man, along with Huey Long.

MacArthur had plenty of enemies in the Army itself. He had been a member of the court martial of Billy Mitchell, and though it wasn't clear how he voted (the vote was split and secret), he was distrusted by pilots and other members of the air corps because of it. While fighting strenuously against budget cuts, as chief of staff he was the one who had to find ways to live with them. He cut the tank corps in 1931, a necessary move from a budgetary standpoint, but a devastating one militarily.

Many officers thought MacArthur a vain glory hound, and not without reason. He and General Pershing had a complicated relationship, but while the older general was at times helpful to MacArthur's career, a group of younger officers despised MacArthur for a host of slights and offenses during World War I. MacArthur returned the sentiment. Bradley wasn't a man who hated anyone, but he was a Marshall man, not a MacArthur supporter. Bradley later believed that MacArthur shunted Marshall into a meaningless and dead-end job as a senior instructor of the Illinois National Guard immediately after his Benning assignment.

If Bradley wasn't in a position to engage too heavily in Army politics, he steered even further from civilian. Then as now, most Army officers endeavored to stay out of partisan politics for reasons both practical and patriotic. But a good number of officers were close to the Republican establishment. This wasn't very surprising, given the party's domination of post-Civil War politics. They failed to stem the party's turn toward isolationism. Shared by a large part of the country, it ultimately harmed the Army, keeping it from acquiring the weapons it needed, and leaving it dangerously unprepared for the changes that the end of the Depression brought.

Bradley never advertised his politics, though it's reasonable to assume he was raised a populist Democrat, given his father's strong support for William Jennings Bryan and his being named after an editor associated with the Democrats. Late in his career, Bradley bitterly denounced conservative critics when they attacked him, as chairman of the Joint Chiefs of Staff, for the MacArthur sacking. In *A General's Life*, they're labeled "right-wing primitives."[49] At the time, of course, he was serving Democrat Harry Truman.

On the other hand, Bradley clearly did not identify with the more radical elements of the farmers' progressive movement or the labor movement, and called union agitators "anarchists" when he stopped the riot in Butte. Leaving aside reactions to riots and political attacks, Bradley seems to have been politically moderate and a true believer in a separation between civilian politics and the military. While ambitious for his own career, he was not much of a player in politics, either in the Army or the world at large. One gets the impression that his siding with Marshall in the conflict with MacArthur has everything to do with his positive assessment of Marshall as a man and as an officer, and nothing to do with the politics of the service, let alone an allegiance to either the Democratic or Republican Party.

In May 1931, Bradley got a telegram from his stepfather telling him that his mother had had a stroke. Though she was only fifty-six, it was clear that she was dying. He took an exceptional circumstances leave and went back to Moberly, staying for ten days, the length of his leave. She died three weeks later, June 23, following another stroke.

Never particularly close to his stepfather, Bradley never saw him again.

Bradley spent the next few years punching tickets for his career, attending the Army War College in Washington, D.C., where the outdated ideas bored him practically to death. From there he returned once more to West Point, this time as a tactics officer. In 1936 he made lieutenant colonel and became a cadet training officer. (Technically, this was considered a troop post, and had considerable prestige.) Bradley was on a solid but unspectacular path, a fact brought home to him by his assignment in 1938 to the general staff, the heart of the Army bureaucracy.

As close as it was to the top ranks, a staff job was not necessarily a ticket to them. For every combat general seasoned there, there must have been literally scores if not hundreds of officers who had seen their ambitions shrivel. As Joe Stilwell had told Bradley a few years earlier, trying to talk him out of going to the War College, "Why would you go up there...and prepare yourself for a job you don't want?"[50]

His assignment was less than promising: G-1, or personnel. The only saving grace was the fact that Bradley happened to arrive just as the Army began rapidly increasing in size. As an assistant to Brigadier General Lorenzo D. Gasser in the summer of 1938, he immediately began working on mobilization plans and everything that went with them. Over the next few months, he learned more than he ever wanted to know about the highly technical legislative language needed for Congress.

This might have earned the dutiful Bradley a one-way ticket to oblivion, had it not been for the selection of George Marshall as Army Chief of Staff in 1939.

Originally something of a dark horse candidate, Marshall was supported by Pershing and a number of Roosevelt advisors, including Deputy Secretary of War (later secretary) Louis Johnson, and the president's close personal aide, Harry Hopkins. Marshall chose the general staff, making Gasser his deputy chief of staff and selecting Colonel Orlando Ward his secretary.

Ward, a 1914 West Point grad, had served under Pershing as a cavalry officer; he had also been an artillery officer and was now considered a tank expert. A veteran of both the Mexican and European campaigns, he was somewhat reserved, with a studious appearance. Ward was given two assistants, hand-picked by Marshall. One was Lieutenant Colonel Stanley R. Mickelsen; the other was Bradley, "stolen" from Gasser.

Ward and his assistants were gate-keepers and filters for Marshall, reviewing reports and presenting recommendations, as well as handling more routine matters such as correspondence. The three men functioned as a team, with Ward allowing his assistants an unusual amount of responsibility. Marshall expected them to act as a check on his judgment; after their first week on the job, Bradley recalled, the chief chewed them out for not disagreeing with him once.

Hitler's invasion of France in 1940 made American mobilization even more critical. But as Marshall had warned even before taking his post, the plans only recently adopted were grossly inadequate. The Army was seriously under-equipped. Called up for duty, National Guardsmen found themselves training with broomsticks instead of guns. Tanks were non-existent. There were shortages in every category of weapon.

But the most critical area where the Army lagged was in understanding the enormous task in front of it. *A General's Life* points out that the general staff's mobilization plan aimed at organizing four million men to take part in a world war. It called for a single general—Marshall—to lead that army in Europe. That was essentially the same plan used in World War I, where Pershing led an initial force of four divisions into battle. The 1940 plans underestimated both problem and solution by a wide margin; the draft alone would bring ten million men to the military during the war.

As much as Bradely liked Marshall, he did not want to spend the war as his assistant.

Early in 1941—Bradley didn't record the date—Brigadier General Robert L. Eichelberger, the new superintendent of West Point, stopped by to see Marshall. He also stopped to chat with Bradley. Eichelberger knew Bradley, at least somewhat, from a stint there in 1934–35, when he had been adjutant to the superintendent and the secretary of the academic board. Eichelberger's visit wasn't an accident: he offered Bradley the post of commandant of the cadets.

Bradley had missed out on the job a few years before at West Point, in his opinion because he wasn't friends with the incoming superintendent at the time, Brigadier General Jay L. Benedict. The job would have been considered a promotion in 1938, but now it was a step back. On the other hand, Bradley saw it as a way to get out of boring staff work. It would probably open the way to a command position—combat, in other words. Bradley, always the teacher, also saw it as a way to instruct and influence the men who would be leading troops in combat in what he thought was an inevitable war.

Bradley said he'd take the job.

Eichelberger met with Marshall, and the chief of staff agreed to release Bradley back to West Point. But a few days later, Marshall called Bradley into his office.

"Are you sure you want to go back to West Point?" he asked.

"Yes, sir."

Bradley began enumerating the reasons. Marshall's eyes drifted toward the window. Perhaps he was envisioning the future. Out of reasons, Bradley stopped and waited for his commander to speak.

"How'd you like to have Hodges's job?" he said finally.[51]

Hodges was Brigadier Courtney H. Hodges, the commandant of the Infantry School at Fort Benning. The post was considerably more important and prestigious than the one at West Point. Marshall wanted to move Hodges to chief of infantry but needed a suitable replacement.

The normally deliberative Bradley practically jumped out of his boots taking the job. Marshall agreed and made the arrangements. Then Bradley got sick—severely. Hospitalized at Walter Reed with a case of mastoiditis, he was treated with sulfa drugs, only to find out he was allergic. What had been a relatively harmless infection led to a serious condition. His face ballooned; he broke out in hives. In the meantime, the infection continued to plague him.

For nearly two weeks, Bradley was confined to the hospital bed, gradually losing his patience and growing more and more certain that he was going to lose the Benning post. He celebrated his forty-eighth birthday in bed. Finally he managed to convince the doctors he should be released.

A week later, he left for Benning.

Courtney Hodges would play an important role in Bradley's future, eventually joining him in Europe as his deputy and then becoming commanding general of First Army. Ironically, Hodges had flunked out of West Point because of poor math grades in 1905. He reenlisted as a private the following year. Quickly promoted, he advanced to the officer ranks and was commissioned a second lieutenant in 1909. In France during World War I, he earned a Distinguished Service Cross during action on the Marne.

Bradley and Hodges had been classmates at the Army War College. Bradley knew him as an excellent shot—in fact, Hodges was the Army's national rifle champion. But what really impressed Bradley was Hodges' bearing and personality. Bradley called him the "quintessential Georgia gentleman." Bradley admired Hodges's modesty and what he called his "low profile"—two qualities of his own.

Bradley's assignment implied a promotion, but Marshall didn't mention one, and Bradley thought it impolite to ask. When he got to Benning, he found a telegram waiting for him, saying that the U.S. Senate had approved his appointment as a brigadier general, skipping him past colonel.[52] He was the first member of his West Point class to reach the rank.

One of Bradley's proudest accomplishments at Benning was the expansion of the small Officer Candidate School (OCS) there. The school was supposed to take qualified enlisted men and graduate them as second lieutenants. The concept was highly controversial inside the Army. Marshall had proposed and pushed it; many of his subordinates, including the head of G-1 and Hodges, opposed it. There was more to the opposition than tradition or class conflict. Second lieutenants were generally commissioned after four years at West Point, or a similarly long period in ROTC training. The OCS program was supposed to turn them out quickly—so fast, in fact, that they were called "ninety-day wonders" by critics.

Hodges had established the school because he had been ordered to do so, but he kept it small and gave it low priority. Bradley saw it as a possible solution to the Army's shortage of trained officers. When Hodges and the Army's G-1 department continued to oppose expansion, Bradley went directly to Marshall and got the expansion orders approved. It was one of the few instances where he clearly skirted the chain of command.

The draft netted a number of men who had completed college, giving them the academic background an officer traditionally required, but it's clear from Bradley's comments that these were not the people he was aiming at. Almost fifty, Bradley had served in the Army for years; he was in most ways a member of the elite—a West Point grad and former athlete, not to mention a general. Yet he continued to identify with and value the sort of people he had grown up with: farmers, blue collar workers, and others from the vast cross section of the American middle class. He believed not only that they possessed leadership qualities, but that those qualities could be identified and nurtured, assuming one took the time to do so.

Ticking off leadership qualities in a speech not long after he had retired, Bradley listed a number of factors that he believed a leader should possess: perseverance, moral character, mental and physical energy. But he went into most detail about what he called human understanding:

> Lincoln, to my mind, had this in greater measure than any other man in history—the ability to understand the problems of those who served under him, and to appreciate their feelings in every situation. This includes, in my opinion, regular words of praise, as well as the occasional obligation for words of constructive criticism. It includes a great appreciation for an individual's privacy: Criticism of a man should be given personally, not through impersonal communication, and in privacy, not in public.... Most of all, human understanding is exemplified when a superior listens—and listens attentively— when his subordinates are asked to give their opinions, or when they voluntarily come forward with an idea.[53]

As commandant of Benning, Bradley was responsible for making the camp run smoothly and supporting the units based there. Of particular interest to him, as well as the rest of the Army, was the Second Armored Division, headed by another freshly minted general, George C. Patton.

Patton had given up command of the Third Cavalry the previous summer to join the division, one of two in the Army's newly created

Armored Force. The German advances into Poland and then France had shown not only how important tanks were, but how utterly out of date America's tank units and much of its military thinking were. The Armored Force—led by General Adna Chaffee—consisted of two divisions, the First headquartered at Fort Knox, and the Second at Benning. Patton joined the Second as the commander of the Second Armored Brigade and acted as the division training officer; he was soon promoted to general, then named to head the division when Charles Scott moved up to replace Chafee, who'd fallen ill.

Working essentially from scratch, fashioning doctrine as well as teaching tactics and even inventing procedures such as refueling tanks under combat, Patton built the Second Armored Division from the treads up. The general was a famously mercurial man, as emotional as Bradley was unemotional. His leadership style tended to be explosive and abrasive—he could humiliate an officer for failing to salute—and yet he was also capable of showing great tenderness and concern. Patton was an extremely hands-on leader, constantly injecting himself into the training situations, overseeing everything directly and racing around the practice fields in anything that moved, from scout cars to airplanes. He made an impression wherever he went, turning heads with a siren attached to his light tank.

Contrary to his later legend, Patton's eccentric leadership style did not always work, and some of his biographers say that he had a difficult time organizing the tankers at first. But by the time Bradley arrived at Benning, the Second Armored Division was rounding into shape. It had completed a series of small-scale maneuvers as well as a large drive to Florida, at the time regarded as America's largest armored march, with over a thousand vehicles participating. Perhaps tellingly, less than a tenth were tanks—101 medium and 24 light tanks. The German Panzers that had sped over France had already rendered them obsolete.

While they had met before, this was Bradley's first chance to observe Patton for an extended period as a fellow commander. It's not hard to imagine his reaction to any number of Patton's flourishes—his cursing, his belief in reincarnation, and most especially his treatment of his men. But the two seem to have gotten along well enough for Patton to commend Bradley for his cooperation in a letter after leaving Benning, something he was unlikely to have done if Bradley had been a thorn in his side. (By contrast, Patton feuded at the base with Lloyd R. Fredendall, whom both he and Bradley would later meet in Africa.)

Tanks and mobile infantry were one aspect of the changing face of warfare. Aircraft were another. At Benning, Bradley renewed his acquaintanceship with Major William M. Bud Miley, a fellow West Point graduate and former tactical instructor. Miley had been building and training Army paratroopers at Benning. By the time Bradley arrived, there were three battalions, the 501st, 502nd, and 503rd. A gymnast, Miley placed a great deal of emphasis on the soldier's strength and individual fighting skills, a legacy that lives on today in the Army's elite units. Bradley became a believer in the airborne concept while at Benning, supporting Miley with supplies and other arrangements.

Elizabeth, often called "Lee" by her father,[54] was admitted to Vassar College in 1940. Bradley found time to help her study for her college board exams, delighting in reviewing math and presenting her with algebra problems for practice.[55] He was somewhat amused by the special prep classes that had sprung up to help students prepare for the exams; after all, he hadn't had any time to do that himself when he entered West Point.

Bradley and his wife still enjoyed their time together, Sundays especially. One afternoon in December they went out to the front yard and began weeding the garden.

A car passed by, stopped, and rolled back in reverse. The driver was Harold "Pink" Bull, a friend and instructor at Benning. Bull shouted to the Bradleys:

"Did you hear about Pearl Harbor?"

It was December 7, 1941. The United States was about to enter the war, and Bradley's long apprenticeship was over.

CHAPTER 2

Africa

O mar Bradley tried stretching his legs as he stepped from the
C-54 onto the metal surface of the temporary runway at Dakar
in French Senegal. It was an unusually cool February morning
in 1943. The wind whipped the nearby sand across the open peninsula.
The Senegalese workers wrapped their clothes tighter for protection,
gawking briefly at the plane that had just brought Bradley before going
back to their work.

"Breakfast?" asked Bradley's aide, Chet Hansen.

Bradley nodded. They had just enough time to grab some powdered
eggs and canned bacon in the tar-paper shack that served as the temporary VIP mess before heading back to the refueled plane. The C-54
bumped her way back into the wind, rising northeastward toward Marrakesh, 1,400 miles away.

The flight took several hours, but in a sense it had taken a lifetime for
Bradley to reach this stage. He was headed, finally, to combat—some

forty years after reaching West Point, and some fourteen months after war had been declared.

Bradley had spent those months deeply involved in the business of war, yet far from battle. He was given a second star—the second in his class to make major general—and placed in command of the newly formed 82nd Infantry Division. Working with a stellar staff—Matthew Ridgway was his second in command—and a cadre of officers from the 9th Division, Bradley set up shop at Camp Claiborne, a new base in Louisiana. He took rare steps to make the new inductees feel at home, touches like arranging their gear on their beds and having a hot meal already waiting. In the often impersonal bureaucracy of the Army, these were almost revolutionary innovations, all designed to help build an instant *esprit de corps*. Training also included firing exercises designed to simulate combat, a Bradley innovation.

Throughout the Army, new draftees' poor physical condition—Bradley used the word "marshmallows" to describe them—was notorious. An important part of the program was toughening them up. Among other things, the training included an obstacle course that all soldiers had to complete.

Including Bradley. One day while participating, his hands slipped on one of the swing ropes, and he fell straight into the ditch below…a ditch habitually filled with sewage.

The soldiers roared. Bradley, by now forty-nine and not quite the athlete he once was, took it in stride.

After working with the division for roughly four months, Bradley and the 82nd were expecting to go overseas. But both received unusual orders: in June, Bradley was told to join the 28th National Guard Division at Camp Livingston. A short time afterwards the 82nd, with Ridgway at its head, was designated to become the Army's first airborne division. The designation was a tribute to the unit's superior training; it would go on to an impressive record in the war as one of the country's elite fighting units.

★ ★ ★ ★

If the 82nd was rated high, the 28th was rated low. Very, very low.

The Pennsylvania unit was under-manned, haphazardly trained, and poorly led. This was not unusual for divisions that had come from the National Guard, though the 28th was a particularly brilliant example of ineptitude. Its original commander had left the division to run for governor, a job he seems to have been much better suited for. When an interim general also came up short, Marshall pushed him out and had Bradley take his place.

Bradley did not want the job, but had no choice. He began by shaking up the command ranks from top to bottom, bringing in a large number of OCS officers to fill out the junior ranks. Training regimes were tightened to include more physical exercise. Bradley claims to have joined a twenty-five-mile, full-gear hike incognito, passing among the soldiers as just another grunt. While it's unlikely he went unnoticed, it's not at all unbelievable that he completed the hike carrying the equipment of a few of his men.[1] By late fall 1942, the division was approved for the advanced training before being deployed for combat.

Once more, Bradley began getting ready to go overseas. He moved his wife Mary to Thayer Hotel, a comfortable residence on the edge of the West Point campus in New York. This made it easy for her to see their daughter, attending Vassar College in Poughkeepsie at the time.[2]

Between Christmas and the New Year, the 28th Division moved on to Florida's Camp Gordon Johnson for amphibious training. Rather than making New Year's resolutions, Bradley immersed himself in a whole set of problems, both tactical and logistical, that would need to be solved for combat. He was still working on those problems on February 12, 1943, when he got a TWX[3] or telex from General Marshall congratulating him on his birthday—and telling him that he would soon be appointed to command X Corps.

It was the assignment he had waited his lifetime for. X Corps, headquartered in Sherman, Texas, was destined for the Pacific as part of the Sixth Army. In the days ahead, its most famous battle would come at Leyte, where MacArthur waded ashore to declare, "I have returned."

But it would fight without Bradley. Literally moments after he received his orders, Bradley's telephone rang. He found himself talking to Alexander Bolling, the G-1 or head of personnel for McNair.

He wasn't going to Texas. Marshall had something else planned.

Bolling wouldn't tell him what.

Bradley fished for details, but Bolling refused. Finally Bolling told him that he would be joining a classmate.

That could only be one person, Bradley realized—Eisenhower.

He was going to Africa.

But *not* as a combat commander. Bolling told him he could have two and only two aides accompany him. That made it clear he wasn't getting a division, let alone a corps. Dreading the prospect of yet another job he didn't want, Bradley rounded up his two personal assistants, Chester Hansen and Lewis Bridges, and headed to Washington for instructions.

A week and a half later, Bradley was in Africa, still not entirely sure of his assignment. After a night in Marrakesh, he and his aides squeezed themselves between the cargo in the hold of a C-47 and flew on to Algiers, where Walter Bedell Smith was waiting in Eisenhower's armor-plated Cadillac in a sea of mud. An unusually heavy rain had turned the desert airport into a swamp so wet the steel runway planks were floating.

The rain was one surprise; the cold another. For most Americans, northern Africa was the desert, and the desert meant dry heat—lots of it. But Africa in winter, especially farther east in Tunisia, can actually be quite cold and, occasionally, quite wet. The winter of 1942–43 would prove to be both.

Bradley greeted Bedell Smith warmly. Smith, another of Marshall's "boys," was an old friend from the trapshooting range, a former student and instructor under Bradley at Benning. Now Eisenhower's chief of staff, many found his personality prickly and intimidating. But "Beetle" and Brad got along reasonably well; Bradley found Smith quiet and witty, two characteristics he always admired.

The car took Bradley to Eisenhower's headquarters at the St. George Hotel. Bradley wasn't quite prepared for what he found—upwards of a thousand officers, French and British as well as American, were crowded into the place, trying to exert control over a battle hundreds of miles away.

Tired and recovering from a serious cold or a mild case of pneumonia, Eisenhower took Bradley into his office. Save for a few brief social occasions, mostly at West Point reunions, it was the first time the former classmates had seen each other since graduating. Clearly exhausted, Eisenhower didn't even try to put a happy gloss on the situation.

"I want suggestive corrections," he told Bradley, pointing to a map showing the American retreat in Tunisia. He needed them quickly. While Bradley had been traveling, the American Army had suffered its most serious defeat yet, this one at Kasserine Pass.

The British had been fighting in northern Africa for more than two years when the Americans launched Torch in the fall of 1942. While the British generally outnumbered the Germans and their Italian allies, Field Marshal Erwin Rommel and his Afrika Korps had kept the British at bay in Egypt, Libya, and Tunisia. But the tide slowly turned in favor of the British, and in August 1942 they began a series of victories that drove Rommel back into Tunisia. Ultra, the top-secret project that intercepted and decrypted German communications, played an important role in the campaign.

Though not formally a part of a coordinated attack plan, the Torch landings can be seen as the western pincer of a larger movement against the Axis forces in Africa. As Rommel retreated from British Eighth Army commander General Bernard Montgomery in the east, a second Allied army came at him from the west, cutting off his supply line and attacking him from the flank. Tunisia, the German stronghold in the middle of the two Allied pincers, was the clear target.

The American troops that landed in Torch were divided into two different Army corps. I Corps, under Patton's command, remained to the west, consolidating the Allied gains. II Corps, led by Fredendall, joined with British units pushing eastward into Tunisia. II Corps included the 1st Armored Division under Orlando Ward, the 1st Infantry Division, headed by Terry Allen, the 34th Infantry Division under Major General Charles Wolcott "Doc" Ryder, and the 9th Infantry Division (not yet in the line when Bradley arrived) commanded by Manton Eddy. Additional units included the 1st Ranger Battalion and several artillery regiments.

Heading this eastward thrust was British Lieutenant General Kenneth Anderson, the commander of First Army. Besides the American and British troops, French units, generally poorly equipped, were also under First Army's command, chaffing greatly under British direction.

There were problems from the start. II Corps' divisions were deployed in small units and spread out along the southern flank of the Allied advance. Experience had already shown that this was a poor use of troops in Africa, where they could be easily isolated and overwhelmed. The effect was especially crippling for the 1st Armored Division, as it kept Ward from being able to muster his tanks effectively and made it hard to communicate across the difficult terrain. The 1st Armored Division's tanks were outgunned by German equipment, and were still trying to adapt their tactics to the fast-paced African war.

Almost as critically, Fredendall did not get along with Anderson or his own division commanders, especially Ward.

Historians have lambasted Fredendall for being disorganized and unrealistic. His subcommanders had pretty much the same opinion. The general delivered orders in colorful but clearly unmilitary language, at times talking in ellipses and slang rather than using standard military language. Some of this was a precaution in case his commands were intercepted, but it just added to the overall confusion.

So did the command structure above Fredendall. Anderson, the head of the First Army, had difficulty overseeing the large organization under him, at least partly because he had a 200-mile front. The distance and terrain made it difficult to communicate with his sub-commanders. Orders were given, then countermanded in confusion. The American units were at times unsure whether to follow Anderson's orders or the contrary directions of Fredendall.

"The Allied command structure was so confused that troops in the field had trouble finding out who they were supposed to take orders from and sometimes received conflicting orders from two or more sources," writes Orr Kelly in *Meeting the Fox*, a study of the Allied campaign. "They wondered, with considerable justification and not just in that normal soldier way, if *anyone* was in charge up there."[4]

Eisenhower, in overall charge of the Allied operations, had another layer of command between him and Anderson. British General Harold Alexander—also Montgomery's direct boss—had been made deputy commander for the campaign in January. British officers directed the air and sea forces as well. The practical effects of this were many. The Americans were looked down on as inferior soldiers by the British, and war plans developed by the British gave the Americans a second and even tertiary role. This wasn't simply a matter of pride and bruised egos, though there was plenty of that. Relegating the Americans to a secondary role dictated a strategy where American numbers, to say nothing of their abilities, could not be used to their best potential. This made the Allied attack one dimensional, or at least not as rounded as it could have been. As the Americans increased in ability and numbers, it would exacerbate frictions between the Allies and weaken the potency of their attack.

Based on their performance to that point, it was hard to argue. The American troops had never been in combat before and responded as neophytes often do against an experienced enemy. Their commanders, especially Fredendall, were lacking. But the British were not above criticism themselves. Anderson split up his units and failed to coordinate his front, leaving French as well as American units to be picked off and knocked away by Rommel. Anderson's performance was probably as bad as Fredendall's, and not as defensible on grounds of experience.

The trouble in II Corps came to a head at Sidi-Bou Zid on February 14, when German Panzers surprised the 1st Armored Division in the eastern Dorsals of central Tunisia, routing the division. The attack narrowly missed General Eisenhower himself—the Panzers roared through the Faid and Maizila passes only a few hours after Eisenhower had personally inspected the units guarding them.

Badly battered, II Corps retreated on February 17. The Americans suffered an even worse loss two days later when Rommel's forces overran the defenses at Kasserine Pass. Complete disaster was barely avoided when the 9th Infantry Division managed to hold off the German 10th Panzer with its artillery, thanks largely to the arrival of General Ernest N. Harmon, whom Eisenhower had sent over from Patton's command. Constrained by their lack of supplies, the Germans broke off the attack, but not before leaving the Americans in tatters.

Marshall sent Bradley to Africa as part of a strategy to improve American performance just as the February reverses were starting. He had decided Eisenhower needed a personal representative close to the battlefront. Eisenhower's papers indicate that he listed thirteen possibilities soon after the Casablanca conference. He then narrowed the choices to three, then finally to one—Bradley.[5]

It's not clear how having a "personal representative" was supposed to solve the problem. Eisenhower had already tried this approach, both with Lucian Truscott, who was still in the theater, and Harmon, who assumed an even more nebulous role as temporary deputy II Corps commander.[6] Having another general he knew at his disposal suited Eisenhower, who used personal representatives throughout the war to gather information. But it's not clear why Marshall considered sending Bradley important enough to reverse Bradley's earlier orders and upset other plans.

Obviously, Marshall felt the situation in Africa was critical for the United States, and he wanted a high level officer to help diagnosis a solution. But there must have been more involved. One suspects that in sending Bradley, who was already qualified as a corps commander, he was giving himself and Eisenhower the flexibility to replace Fredendall—if not with Bradley, then with Patton, who was in eastern Africa as head of I Corps.[7] Bradley could then have moved into Patton's slot.

It seems almost sacrilegious to make such a suggestion, but Marshall could even conceivably have substituted Bradley for Eisenhower. This would have given him another subordinate whom he completely trusted, and whom he knew could get along with anyone, a critical quality for dealing with allies. Though Marshall had recently succeeded in getting a promotion for Eisenhower, Ike was still very much an unproven commodity. And given that Marshall planned to lead the invasion of France himself, having Bradley in place below him would not have been a poor option. [8]

The war that was fought here was fierce and foreign. Little in the American training process would have prepared Americans to physically deal with the distances involved, let alone the other realities northern Africa presented. Advances were lightning fast, with tanks covering scores of miles in a day. Then suddenly everything would go into slow motion near a hilltop or a town where defensive positions had been established. Positions could be overrun so quickly frontline troops didn't realize they were behind enemy lines until they received orders to retreat. Minefields were an important element in the battle; fuel supplies and the ability of mechanics to keep vehicles going in a harsh environment were nearly as critical as ammunition.

Tanks and vehicles were crucial to success, but the bulk of the fighting was done by infantrymen. Aircraft could appear without warning far behind the lines, leaving no sector safe; deployed against tanks and vehicles, they could pin down an advance or a retreat before it started.

American journalist Ernie Pyle, whose front-line dispatches remain among the best eyewitness accounts of the war, described one part of the battle in February near Faid Pass like this:

> That Sunday morning hordes of German tanks and troops came swarming out from behind the mountains around Fair

Pass. We didn't know so many tanks were back there, and didn't know so many Germans were either, for our patrols had been bringing in mostly Italian prisoners from their raids.

The attack was so sudden nobody could believe it was in full force. Our forward troops were overrun before they knew what was happening. The command post itself didn't start moving back till after lunch. By then it was too late—or almost too late.

Command cars, half-tracks and jeeps started west across the fields of semi-cultivated desert, for by then the good road to the north was already cut off. The column had moved about eight miles when German tanks came charging in upon the helpless vehicles from both sides.

A headquarters command post is not heavily armed. It has little to fight back with. All that these men and cars could do was duck and dodge and run like hell. There was no such thing as a fighting line. Everything was mixed up over an area of ten miles or more.

It was a complete melee. Every jeep was on its own. The accompanying tanks fought till knocked out, and their crews then got out and moved along on foot....[9]

Before the war, Tunisia's civilian population was estimated at 2.6 million. Besides native Tunisian berbers and Arabs, a small number of French colonists and some other Europeans were scattered through the country, mostly in the urban areas. Though sparse, there was a network of hard-top macadam roads, and cities, towns, and villages had existed for thousands of years. Needless to say, countless civilian farms and buildings were destroyed during battle. When they could, people in the small settlements fled the war as the armies approached. The impact on the civilians in the battle areas, as in all wars, was devastating. If they didn't pay with their lives, they often paid with their possessions, many of which were flattened as collateral damage as the battles raged.

From Algiers, Bradley traveled to II Corps headquarters with Smith and his aides. They swapped a Ford sedan for jeeps with mounted machine-guns near the Tunisia border. The Allies had not yet wrested control of the air from the Luftwaffe, and Smith told Bradley that he had been attacked on the road just the week before.

They traveled with the windshields on the jeeps folded down. The cold African wind whipped at Bradley as they rode down a paved highway studded with truck traffic heading toward the supply depots at Tebessa. Every so often Bradley would spy a peddler by the side of the road, selling his wares. He noted wryly in *A Soldier's Story* that the price of eggs increased with the Allied troop concentrations.[10]

The noise of troops milling about echoed through the canyon walls as Bradley approached Fredendall's headquarters. The Corps command post was located in a mining town called Djebel Kouif, about thirteen and a half miles northeast of Tebessa.[11] The surrounding ground was filled with phosphate, and the sheered landscape dotted with abandoned mines and small settlements. Troops were camped in the woods all around the deep ravine that formed the area. Sleeping in tents on crushed stone floors, they froze at night—and didn't fare much better during the day, when the wind whipped across the high hills and through the ravines.

Nicknamed Speedy Valley by the Americans, the area was also jokingly called Lloyd's Very Last Resort. With great effort and handheld jackhammers, Fredendall's engineers had knocked two enormous tunnels into the ravine wall, and were working to complete a pair of 160-foot, U-shaped bunkers as protection against air strikes when Bradley arrived. The location of the headquarters some ninety miles from the front, to say nothing of the resources expended to build the bunkers, caused many to snicker.

Bradley thought it was an embarrassment.

He was shown to the command post, an unheated old school building that had been plundered before Fredendall arrived. II Corps' staff was shoehorned inside. Bradley and his two aides were given a single windowless room in what he called a "dingy hotel"[12] nearby. Bradley was never one to complain about his accommodations, but placing a two-star general in a single room with his two aides was a clear and very obvious slight by Fredendall, who didn't want him around.

Bradley immediately set out with Smith to get a feel for what was going on. There was one positive surprise: Bradley discovered that II Corps had considerable supplies in its depots, and was able to make good its losses from Kasserine. But that was practically the only positive note. Bradley immediately saw that the British and American officers were bickering, pointing fingers at each other for failures—a marked contrast to the almost surreal air of cooperation at Eisenhower's headquarters.

At the 1st Armored Division, Bradley tactfully told General Orlando Ward and his staff that he was looking for information that would help combat training back home. He got an earful. They may or may not have believed Bradley's stated reason for coming, but they were full of information and, to a large degree, criticism. They were heavily critical of their equipment, especially their tanks—the Shermans were called fire-traps and their half-tracks death traps. (These shortcomings were magnified by how the equipment was used in the battle. Interestingly, Bradley pointed this out for the half-tracks but not the tanks in *A Soldier's Story*.) [13]

The men were also hard on themselves, admitting that their inexperience and tactics had hurt them. But they were even harder on their commanders, most especially Fredendall. Wandering around the division and speaking to noncoms as well as junior and senior officers, Bradley quickly learned that morale was low, things were disorganized, and discipline was lacking.

Fredendall seems to be Exhibit One in the study of how different the demands of peacetime and war leadership truly are. He was extremely well-regarded in the years between World War I and World War II. Marshall, who had made a crusade of clearing out older generals and leaders upon becoming chief of staff, kept him on despite his relative age; he was fifty-nine at the time Bradley met him, one of the oldest corps commanders in the war. Eisenhower chose him as corps commander at Marshall's recommendation, and even praised him in November 1942. [14]

But then came combat, and the man who was supposedly renowned for his leadership abilities turned paranoid, caustic, and indecisive. Uncommunicative with both his own men and his superiors, he stayed away from the front and seems to have made tactical decisions based on whim rather than observation.

Some historians have quibbled over exactly how much fault Fredendall deserves for the American debacle in Tunisia. There is certainly enough blame to be spread to Anderson and to Fredendall's own division commanders. But some measure of his competence may be discerned from the fact that Bradley found his men deployed in defensive positions on the wrong side of the slopes.[15]

Of the many differences between Bradley and Fredendall, the most striking is how differently they dealt with their subordinates. Fredendall treated his division commanders like second class citizens, even though II Corps depended on them for any sort of success. He rarely solicited their advice and disregarded it when it was offered, routinely sent cryptic orders, and often micro-managed them. He rarely approached the front lines or even the division command posts to form his own sense of how things were going. Bradley would prove the opposite in all these things.

Bradley spent three days at the 1st Armored Division. He moved on to the 34th Infantry Division, which had suffered horrendous losses in the Kasserine battle, and heard much the same story. The 34th's positions had been poorly thought out, and were to blame for much of their losses.

Bradley continued his fact-finding mission, visiting the 9th Division in early March. He never remarks on his relations with Fredendall in either *A Soldier's Story* or *A General's Life,* but clearly they weren't good. Even if Bradley hadn't been insulted by the poor quarters he was given, it was obvious that Fredendall was trying to keep him out of things. The Corps commander neglected to tell him that Eisenhower was visiting headquarters on March 5. It wasn't a surprise visit, nor an unimportant one: Ike wanted to discuss reorganizing the command structure so that the American corps would be on the same level as Anderson, removing one layer of confusion and, not coincidentally, a commander whose performance was considered sub par.[16]

Eisenhower reached Bradley by phone, summoning him to the small house he was using for consultations. During a break in the meeting, the two men retired to the porch.

Well? Eisenhower asked.

Bradley, unknowingly, echoed what Harmon had told Eisenhower a few days before—Fredendall's division commanders had lost confidence in him.[17]

Eisenhower, who had twice commended Fredendall during the campaign, nodded grimly. Then he told Bradley that he had already decided to replace Fredendall with George Patton.[18]

And, Eisenhower added, he was thinking of making Bradley deputy Corps commander; once he had combat experience, he could expect a promotion to II Corps commander.

As the story is told in *A Soldier's Story* and elsewhere, Patton asked Eisenhower to make Bradley his deputy commander, telling one of his subordinates, "I don't want any goddam spies running around my headquarters." The story is colorful and funny, but even if true doesn't tell the entire story. Nor does it do Bradley or Patton much justice, as Bradley's appointment was more than a matter of eliminating a conflict in the chain of command. For one thing, Patton could have shunted Bradley aside or even asked for him to be removed if he truly didn't want him "spying." For another, the position hardly lessened the possibility of his "spying" or backstabbing, as many a commander can readily attest.

Even if he was simply being Machiavellian, Patton's treatment of Bradley in the days that followed show that he held him in high regard. Bradley didn't handle paperwork or visit the latrines; he was an active deputy, with an important role in the battle. Patton used him as a sounding board and as his personal representative to Eisenhower, which showed a significant level of trust.

From Eisenhower's point of view, the only complication with appointing Bradley was a suggestion from Marshall that Bradley take Patton's place planning for the Sicily campaign temporarily. Eisenhower discussed it with Bradley, who declined, pointing out that the staff for the invasion had already been working with Patton, and replacing him for a few weeks or months would be pointless. Eisenhower then asked if Bradley was prepared to take over II Corps, perhaps sooner rather than later. Bradley agreed.

Bradley's appointment as deputy corps commander is of some interest to historians because it is often used as that starting point for a supposed conflict between Bradley and Patton. *A General's Life* even complains that his original version of what happened had been misunderstood by one of Patton's early biographers and cited as evidence of professional jealousy. A close examination of the situation shows that it shouldn't be.

The relationship between Bradley and Patton has been an endless source of fascination for experts and casual readers alike. It's easy to see why. On a personal level, the men could not have been more different. Patton was voluble and emotional, flamboyant, given to writing poetry. An avid horseman and a respected theoretician of tank warfare, he was at once a throwback to an earlier age and a revolutionary in the newest.

Bradley was undemonstrative, quiet and logical to a fault. He was a mathematician, not a poet; even when he bet on horses or played poker, he justified his moves with elaborate calculations. He, too, had a subtle and versatile military mind, rooted as much in the practical experience of hunting as in theories of movement and maneuver.

The differences between the two men were not so great in battle. Though Bradley's background and tactical training was in the infantry, as the battles in Tunisia and later showed, his theory of warfare was not radically different than Patton's. Too much is made of what seems on the surface a natural contrast between Bradley as an infantryman and Patton as a tanker (or cavalryman, which in many ways is more accurate). In reality, both men integrated their forces and wielded them in broadly similar ways, or they would have had an impossible time working together.

The one aspect of Patton's command style that mystified Bradley was his general disinterest in logistics and supplies, something he noticed right away in Africa. In II Corps, this would not prove to be a problem for several reasons, most notably the efforts of Wilson, the Corps G-4 or supply officer. Bradley himself would rely on him later not just in Sicily but in Normandy, and declare him "the outstanding G-4 in the entire European war."[19]

Their greatest difference lay in the way they treated subordinates, especially at this stage of their careers. Patton was legendary for being difficult, even harsh; the so-called slapping incidents are arguably better known to the general public than his real accomplishments on the battlefield. Bradley, on the other hand, often acted almost like a benign father figure to the enlisted men under him, and certainly had a much gentler approach than Patton.

These thumbnail images, of course, don't tell the entire story. Patton could be incredibly humane and loving, and his emotional outbursts resulted in support as well as tongue lashings. Bradley expected results on the battlefield, and was considerably more apt to dismiss one of his sub-commanders than Patton. But their differences in approach were very real.

Bradley was turned off by Patton's style, most especially his use of profanity. "I could not accustom myself . . . to the vulgarity with which Patton skinned offenders for relatively minor infractions in discipline," wrote Bradley in *A Soldier's Story*. "While some chuckled delightedly over the famed expletives he employed with startling originality, the majority, it seemed to me, were more often shocked and offended. At times I felt that Patton, however successful he was as a corps commander, had not yet learned to command himself."[20]

Some historians and Patton biographers look at that passage and interpret it to mean only that Bradley was shocked at Patton's language. Bradley, who didn't make much of a show over religion himself, would clearly have been perplexed by the incongruity of reverence and foul-mouthed cussing, as it was called. But Bradley surely knew of other officers who cursed, and when he remarks on it later—at one point he calls Ernie Harmon a "profane tornado"[21]—it is not with any particular approbation. Nor is it likely that the man who had brought peace to a mining town had gentle ears. Bradley's point is much larger. What he is saying is that a general, and specifically a *corps commander*, must act a certain way.

Among the writers who seem to have a particular bugaboo with Bradley is Carlo D'Este, who spends several pages in *Patton: A Genius for War* criticizing Bradley for supposedly hating Patton, going so far as to claim that "Bradley's dislike of Patton stemmed in no small part from his rigid upbringing, in which alcohol and profanity were forbidden." [22] But this seems more than unlikely. Bradley liked bourbon, he had a former bartender as his personal valet, and his aides' diaries are filled with accounts of Bradley giving bottles of liquor to subordinates. His staff held plenty of cocktail parties during the war, and Bradley was present at more than a few. Bradley was not shy about mentioning Patton's faults, and if he truly disliked Patton's drinking, he would have said so. What bothered him about Patton was what bothered everyone about Patton— his apparent lack of judgment.[23]

There is, for example, the famous story of Patton walking over to 1st Infantry Division commander Terry Allen's trench and peeing in it to show how displeased he was that the general might use a trench during an air raid.[24] Or the suggestion, apparently given in earnest, to Orlando Ward that he should let a few officers die because it would be good for enlisted morale.[25]

These are incidents that work well in movies, setting a dramatic scene. They speak of macho bravado, accomplishing in a few seconds what ten or twenty minutes of dialogue might. But in real life, they become something different. Imagine a CEO relieving himself in an underling's desk in full view of the underling's workers, or a police chief being told to make sure some of his lieutenants are killed so the patrolmen will feel good.

Some may object that the military is different, and that there swagger and machismo are an important part of leadership. As true as that is, there are still limits to behavior. In Bradley's opinion—and it should be said, in many others'—Patton was often on the other side of the line.

There is another element to Bradley's complaint about Patton, one that goes deeper to Bradley's character. What Bradley objects to above all is injustice, and in Africa especially he was put off by Patton's severe penalties for relatively minor infractions. Bradley was no slouch on discipline; he objected to loosening of the rules at West Point. Still, his sense of justice was different than Patton's, considerably more practical and steady.

It was not necessarily "by the book" either. Constantine Fitzgibbon, an intelligence officer with the 12th Army Group, found himself in a difficult situation during the September 1944 drive toward Germany. Possessing intelligence that Patton's Third Army flank was threatened by an imminent panzer attack, the young officer had no way to warn them except over an open radio line, forbidden by regulation and rules unless approved by a senior officer. (His colonel could conceivably have "OK'd" the message.) Fitzgibbon, deciding the situation was dire, sent the message; Patton was able to beat off the attack.

Three weeks later, Patton sent a message to headquarters demanding that Fitzgibbon be court-martialled.

Bradley, after hearing Fitzgibbon's side, frowned.

"Look, someone's got to answer this thing," he told Fitzgibbon. "I'm a very busy man. Draft a reply for my signature, will you?"[26]

There appear to have been no flare-ups between the volatile Patton and the stoically laconic Bradley. Bradley disliked Patton's faults, most especially those he interpreted as emotional and impulsive. He believed that Patton's staff work was often inadequate, handicapping the use of his forces in battle. But he also believed Patton to be an effective commander. And he recognized purpose behind Patton's methods, and believed that in the main they worked—for Patton, at least.

Patton, his familiar siren wailing, shrieked into Djebel Kouif March 7 to take command of II Corps. Bradley watched as the procession arrived:

armored cars and half-tracks, then an open staff car with Patton standing, in Bradley's words, like a charioteer.[27] He was a scowling Ben Hur, or more aptly Caesar, casting an angry eye on the forlorn troops he had come to command.

He started by kicking butt, declaring that he was going to rid Africa of Germans and needed officers who were tough enough to get the job done. He wanted them angry as well as quick-witted.

Patton quickly got them angry, at him as much as the Germans, thanks to strict rules about helmets and dress. Soldiers had to wear their helmets at all times, without exception. Officers were expected to wear ties. Leggings, still part of the uniform, were mandatory under Patton. The rules were reinforced with fines and caused a great deal of grousing. But they also immediately showed everyone that things were going to be run differently than in the past.

Patton took over Fredendall's house and gave Bradley a room in it. They set out together soon after Patton's arrival to inspect the 1st Armored Division and the 9th Infantry Division. Both divisions showed the strain of the recent battle. The men of the 34th Division were in somewhat better shape. Still, there were signs of destruction everywhere—broken equipment and a landscape battered by bombs and artillery shells.

Patton did not institute wholesale changes in the staff. On the contrary, he kept two of the most important staff officers—the G-2 or intelligence head, Colonel Benjamin "Monk" Dickson, and the G-4, Colonel Robert Wilson.

While Dickson had correctly warned Fredendall of the likely German attacks before the recent fiascos, at first glance, he wouldn't seem a good pick for a staff officer. He was intelligent and could speak German, but he tended to be somewhat disorganized. Some of his irreverence towards others (not Bradley) and his teasing of other members of the staff must have struck Bradley as a bit much. But eccentric or not, Bradley valued and came to praise his abilities.

Wilson was far more conventional. One glance at the loaded supply and weapons depots made his abilities clear. He and Dickson would play important roles, not only in II Corps but with Bradley in the future.

★ ★ ★ ★

Because of the defeat at Kasserine, the Allied line looked like a backwards C, with the British at the north and the Americans pushed back into the mountains at the south. The American forces in II Corps consisted of some 90,000 men in four divisions arrayed in the Western Dorsal mountains. This force was on the southern portion of the Allied front, facing eastwards. To their west—or on their left—were 50,000 French troops. Next over on the left was a British force, which numbered 120,000.

On the other side of the line, the Germans and Italians held a large swath of territory from Bizerte southwards to Tunis, anchored by a force in defensive positions originally built by the French known as the Mareth line. Below them to the coast was Montgomery's Eighth Army.

Rommel wanted to strike Montgomery in a pincer attack aimed at Medenine, which was an Eighth Army stronghold. The attack would come along the coastline—to the Axis' left. Rommel hoped to stall if not break the Eighth Army's momentum northwards from southern Tunisia. But the plan was overruled by Italian Field Marshal Giovanni Messe, the overall commander of the Axis armies in northern Africa. Instead, the Germans were directed to undertake an attack from their right side, sweeping down and then hooking back north against the stronger part of the British line.

Launched March 6, the German attack failed. Once more, Montgomery was able to use Ultra intelligence to his great advantage. With the Germans falling back, the Allies went back on the offensive.

Alexander's plan called for the British Eighth Army under Montgomery to go north up the peninsula toward Tunis and Bizerte. Meanwhile, II Corps would work against the German flank. The Americans' role was primarily a diversion; by pushing eastward through the hills, they would put pressure on the Germans, forcing them to either protect their flank or retreat.

Patton and Bradley would have preferred a bolder strike aimed at cutting off the Axis troops and trapping them between II Corps and

Montgomery. But both generals realized II Corps was in no condition to pull this off, and did not protest the plan. Bradley, surveying the area, saw that the terrain would work against a lightning tank attack, limiting offensive possibilities even if II Corps had been in top shape. The hills provided plenty of cover for ambushes, whether by antitank units or even properly armed infantry.

From the way the battle unfolded, it seems possible that Patton believed if the Americans captured the high ground beyond Maknassy, Alexander would then allow them to push farther. In that case, II Corps might join in the final pursuit of the Germans.[28] For the moment, though, they stuck to the plan as drawn up by Alexander.

II Corps' operations were divided into three sectors. At the north, a small portion of the Corps would protect the flank against an attack by the Germans. No such attack was ever launched, and the units were not a major factor in the battles that followed. In the area of Maknassy, the 34th Division was tasked to work with British units to attack Fondouk el Aouareb. The pass there, known as Fondouk Pass, had a rail line and was a vital passage through the Eastern Dorsal. The Germans held the high ground on both sides.

Most of II Corps—1st Armored Division and 1st and 9th Infantry Divisions—was concentrated to the south in the area east of Gafsa. After taking Gafsa, the Americans were to take El Guettar and start down the coastal road toward Gabes. This would directly threaten the Mareth Line and the Axis forces in front of Montgomery.

As deputy corps commander, Bradley acted as a kind of jack of all trades before and during the battle. He was a sounding board for Patton, who relied on him for advice, and probably to blow off steam. But most of Bradley's time was spent visiting the division and subcommands. The visits took him quite close to the front. At several points he came under fire.

On March 16, Bradley reported to Patton's staff room to participate in a last-minute briefing before the Gafsa battle. If there was any lingering doubt among the division commanders that Patton had a very different attitude toward his job than Fredendall, it vanished as the briefing drew to a close. Bradley looked on in something close to astonishment as Patton declared, "Gentlemen, tomorrow we attack. If we are not victorious, let no one come back alive.[29]

He then left to pray.

For Bradley—and in his eyes the rest of the II Corps staff—the performance, especially the prayer, bordered on theater. But Bradley would come to realize that Patton was not only sincere about fighting, he was reverent as well, if not in a way that Bradley completely understood.

The American drive against Gafsa was called "Operation Wop," a not-so-subtle reference to the fact that the bulk of the troops guarding the town were Italian. Artillery opened with a barrage late on the night of March 16. But when troops reached Gafsa the following morning, they found it empty; the defenders had withdrawn.

The reporters traveling with Patton reported that the enemy had run in fright.

A few nights later, on March 19, Bradley sat up pondering the continuing drive through the African hills. The roads were mud pits, the weather frigid. Despite Patton's constant hectoring, many of the commanders still thought defensively, worried about the attack that might come, rather than the attack they should make. The soldiers under them were continuing to have trouble; many seemed especially reluctant to close in battle. Still, II Corps was moving ahead, and the American Army was showing progress. The disaster at Kasserine Pass was at last behind them.

A message came in over the Corps radio while Bradley was in the headquarters. He looked at it, then went to find Patton.

Bradley woke him up. It was midnight.

It's John, Bradley told Patton. He tried to keep his voice level. *Your son-in-law.*

John Waters, who served in the 1ˢᵗ Armored Division, had been captured in action that day.

Patton took the news stoically, but he was deeply affected by his son-in-law's capture. He would do everything he could to get information on his whereabouts over the next two years. Eventually, he would find a way to do more.

Taking Gafsa presented the Americans with a pair of roads that ran to the Mediterranean. One went northeast through Sened Station and Maknassy, reaching the sea at Sfax. The Americans called this Gumtree Road; it is said the name came from the Eucalyptus trees lining it.[30] The second, in much steeper terrain, went through El Guettar southeast to Gabes.

Either way, II Corps had done well and was now in position to threaten the German Army by continuing eastward. But on March 19, with Montgomery about to launch what looked to be the final offensive against the Germans, Alexander told Patton to send the 9ᵗʰ Division north, where it would join Anderson's attack on Bizerte. The plan called for it to operate on the far left of the British force, removing it from the American line of command and making it completely dependent on the British. The rest of II Corps was to attack Fondouk, and in military terms "demonstrate"—in other words, make a heck of a lot of noise and scare the enemy, but not actually do anything. The Germans would be driven from Africa without them.

The Americans were being split up and left out of the battle. In effect, Alexander was writing off the three divisions that had just taken Gafsa. At the same time, splitting a division from the main corps and giving it to another commander—one clearly held in low regard, to boot—revealed an attitude just short of contempt toward the American commanders.

This was not entirely unexpected, given Alexander's earlier orders and his opinion of the American force. The worst part, though, was that Eisenhower had agreed to it. Patton, though unhappy, stifled his anger and agreed without protest.[31]

Bradley seethed, interpreting the orders as a direct slap against the Americans and their capabilities. Siphoning off the division violated the general principle that American troops should be commanded by Americans. He immediately began working on an alternative plan for II Corps. Then he convinced Patton that he should present it personally to Eisenhower in an effort to override Alexander's orders.

While Patton was certainly busy with the troops, his willingness to let Bradley go by himself was a sign of trust, not only in the plan but in Bradley himself. As a general rule through the war, Patton presented plans for his forces to his commander himself, and while this was a special case—they were circumventing Alexander and the chain of command—Bradley arguably had less pull with Eisenhower than Patton, who had been Eisenhower's close friend for years. Bradley's plan made better and more ambitious use of American forces than Alexander proposed. It called for the entire II Corps to sweep to the north, using the route behind the mountains that Alexander had proposed for 9th Infantry. Situating itself to the left of Anderson, the Corps would then launch an attack on Bizerte at the tip of the peninsula.

It was a daring plan, and not only in light of the Americans' earlier experiences in Africa. It called for moving an entire corps through the British First Army sector, a logistics puzzle under the best conditions. But if successfully launched, it would place a large force at the rear of the enemy, cutting them off from the sea and threatening a quick envelopment at Tunis. It's easy to imagine what Patton could have done with four divisions rolling up the German rear.

At his meeting with Eisenhower March 23, Bradley argued the military merits. Further, he made his appeal emotional as well as tactical: the Americans, he said, *deserved* a part in the victory. He cited the defeat at Kasserine, suggesting this would be a way to rebound and redeem the Army in the eyes of the people back home. He appealed directly to Eisenhower's goal of keeping the alliance running smoothly—if the Americans were left totally out of the victory, they would feel cheated and relations would sour.

This was not the last time that Bradley appealed to Eisenhower's nationalism. Nor was it the only time in the war that Bradley identified a particular battle plan he favored as being good for American morale.

Eisenhower did not agree to the plan itself—the attack blueprint would be left to Alexander—but he assured Bradley that the Corps would be given its own sector and real objectives in the fight. Ike then sent a letter suggesting this—but not quite ordering it—to Alexander. Alexander eventually modified his orders, allowing II Corps to remain intact and giving it more meaty objectives, though it still played a secondary role in the campaign.[32]

Bradley's plan was never implemented, but it's interesting for several reasons. First and foremost, it demonstrated that he had faith in the American Army, even though he fully appreciated how poorly it had done and how woefully unprepared it had been in the earlier battles. The plan also made use of the Americans' one real advantage at that point in the war: the ability to move large amounts of men and machines over a good distance. It avoided fighting in a difficult area where the Americans had not done well, putting them into an area where the speed and maneuverability of their armor would, if not actually give them an advantage, at least level the playing field.

Not least important, it demonstrates that Bradley was anything but a straight-ahead, smash-mouth strategist, even from his earliest days as a battlefield commander.

Could they have pulled it off?

Simply moving so many men and that much equipment quickly would have been a challenge, but that was the Corps' strongest asset. They would actually have had a decent time to pull the shift off, and with a strong supply line and overall control of the air, it seems likely the divisions could have gotten into place for the jump off.

A more difficult question to answer is whether the divisions would have been up to the battle if they met strong opposition. They were striking at the German underbelly, but that was no guarantee of victory. Bradley's plan called for 1st Armored Division to take a leading role in the advance—surely a leap of faith given its past performance.

With Montgomery's forces still bogged down below the Axis line, II Corps pushed toward El Guettar. The 1st Ranger Battalion made a daring night assault up and across Djebel Orbata, a towering and seemingly impenetrable ridge. The assault overwhelmed the Italian post guarding El Guettar. Patton then sent the 1st Infantry Division down Gumtree road, assigning it to hold the high ground along the road and north of the Gafsa-Gabes road. The 9th Infantry Division followed to the south of Gafsa-Gabes road.

Directed to take Sened Station, the 1st Armored Division captured the town March 21. Its next objective was Maknassy to the east. It set out the next night, arriving after the enemy had already withdrawn. Ward moved on the next night, aiming toward enemy airfields Patton wanted targeted farther east. But the division bogged down. Its vanguard of three infantry battalions, two companies of tanks, and four battalions of artillery ground to a halt before 350 furious defenders in the hills.[33] Patton kept urging Ward on. The positions were strategic; holding them would allow II Corps to push eastward, though at the moment no such attack was authorized or planned.

Bradley went up to the 1st Armored Division command post to help Ward. Patton thought the division's problems were due to Ward's conservative approach to warfare. To Patton, Ward moved too cautiously, allowing the enemy time either to escape or to reinforce its positions. Bradley's own thoughts didn't contradict that, exactly, but he felt that Ward wasn't getting enough tactical help from Patton and was now in a difficult tactical position, having to attack over terrain not suited to his units. A stronger initial strike might have carried the day, but now that the forces were bogged down, a head-on slog up the hills was, if not futile, at least a very difficult task.

Bradley was discussing the situation with Ward after dinner March 24[34] when the phone rang in Ward's command post. It was Patton. His voice was so loud it was easy to overhear as he told Ward he must take that hill.

Lead it yourself, demanded Patton. And don't come back if you don't take it.[35]

Bradley watched Ward put the phone down in shock. He couldn't quite believe what he had heard. Had Patton just told Pinky not to come back if he didn't take the hill? The position was hardly worth a general's life.

Bradley waited silently for the conversation to end, then they went back to discussing the plans for the operation. Ward grabbed a carbine and later that night personally led a small squad up a hill in front of the main objective. They made it up a second as well, but the machine gun fire from the third and last was too much, and once more the objective went untaken. Ward returned to the division command post, exhausted and wounded. Bradley watched a doctor patch the general's eye.

A day or two later, Patton came by and pinned a silver star on Ward for his bravery—though he still chided him for not being aggressive enough. Ward would also eventually get a Distinguished Service Medal for his gallantry. But he didn't win the most important prize, and ultimately the only one that counted: the third hill, which would open up the path to an offensive they weren't allowed to make.

Bradley's visits to the II Corps forces included a small amount of comic relief in the form of gallows humor, especially when speaking with troops that had recently been under fire. Bradley had heard that the half-tracks were too lightly armored to stop German machine-gun fire, so he asked a soldier about it one day.

"No, sir," came the reply. "They only come in one side and rattle around a bit."[36]

Like Ward, Bradley always traveled with a rifle, though he preferred an old 30-06 Springfield to newer weapons. The standard Army rifle prior to the adoption of the M1, the bolt action weapon remained a fine gun in an expert's hands, accurate and true. Bradley would occasionally use it during the war to snag game, though the opportunities in Africa were slim.

But its main purpose was to shoot the enemy. Even though Bradley did not go on patrol or do anything else so foolish, he used it several times against enemy planes.

One afternoon in late March while visiting the 1st Division, Bradley got out of his jeep to speak to some soldiers holding positions along Gumtree Road. A pair of Messerschmitts appeared overhead, coming down for a strafing run at one hundred feet.

My rifle! shouted Bradley to his aides.

But the gun was back in the Jeep, some five hundred feet away. The aircraft disappeared before anyone could retrieve it.

Even if he'd been able to hit the plane, the odds of taking it down were infinitesimal. But Bradley believed shooting at the enemy was a hell of a lot better than just being shot at. It was certainly good for morale, and few soldiers seeing a major general stand up and fire at an airplane would hesitate to fire their own.

If my rifle isn't with you the next time we're buzzed by the Germans, Bradley told Chet Hansen, *you're fired.*[37]

While the Allies had air superiority over the Germans, the Luftwaffe remained a serious threat to individual soldiers. One afternoon Bradley got in his jeep and headed up to the 1st Armored Division, taking along British General Charles Dunphie, an observer. It was one of the first fine spring days Bradley had seen in Africa, and if it weren't for the war, the balmy air and swinging palm trees might have made the drive pleasant. But the war was inescapable, whether in the form of damaged Arab huts near the road or the endless stream of ambulances and trucks they passed through on the way to the front.

Still trying to push east, Patton had directed that an armored task force be created to break through a German bottleneck. Headed by Colonel Clarence C. Benson, the task force of tanks and armored half-tracks had been severely battered when Bradley arrived to check on their progress. Bradley consulted with Benson in a makeshift command post near the road. The only cover were his vehicles and some shallow slit trenches; the war had already shorn the threadbare earth of its trees.

As Bradley began going over Benson's plans, someone sounded an air raid siren nearby. He looked up and spotted a dozen Ju-88 bombers[38] flying in their direction.

Hoping that the bombers would somehow miss them, the anti-aircraft gunners remained silent. The planes passed by.

Then the whistle blew again. The Junkers had spotted them and were returning.

The Americans' anti-aircraft cannons began sending flak skyward as the men ran for cover. A bomb struck so close to Bradley as he ran that his helmet flew off. Hot sand burned his face. Finally he reached the shallow trench and stayed low as the Germans dropped butterfly bombs—anti-personnel shrapnel bombs that used submunitions to kill "soft" targets, i.e., human flesh. Somewhat similar to today's cluster bombs, the weapons were a well-known and feared hazard.

Finally, the bombing ended. Bradley climbed out of the trench. His British observer lay on the ground a short distance away. Bradley's aide, Lewis Bridge, was working over him, using his shirt as a bandage on the man's gaping wounds. Bradley's other aide, Chet Hansen, was tending to Captain Richard Jensen, an aide to Patton. Finally, Hansen looked up. Jensen was dead.

Bradley had Jensen's body brought back to Patton. Tears streamed from the general's face as Jensen was buried that night.

The attack brought home the dangers of the Luftwaffe, and touched off a dispute with British General Arthur "Mary" Conningham, who was commanding the tactical air force in Africa. It was his job to protect II Corps, and in Patton's opinion, that wasn't being done.

Conningham had limited resources and a large number of missions to accomplish. Just before Patton's arrival, the air force had shifted its tactics in an effort to cut down on the Luftwaffe's effectiveness, striking at enemy bases to lessen the air attacks. The strategy gradually paid off, but there is no denying that the American forces were being harassed from the air. The loss of his aide undoubtedly put Patton in a rage, but there were ample examples of Luftwaffe attacks to make his case, even if some find that case subjective.[39]

Patton not only complained to Conningham's air support command, he had his G-3 sent a sitrep noting that the Corps' front lines and division command posts had been bombed. The sitrep was a bit of an exaggeration—it claimed that the Americans had received *no* air cover at all—but the basic facts regarding the consistency of the German attacks were unarguable.

Conningham responded with a radio message contesting the veracity of the sitrep and calling the reports greatly exaggerated. Patton was outraged—even more so when a copy of the radio message was sent to every senior commander in the Mediterranean theater. The British air commander was calling Patton—and by extension Bradley, who'd barely escaped death and provided the details of the attack—a liar and a coward.

Patton grabbed a phone and called Eisenhower to complain. This resulted in a stingy, 27-word clarification and semi-apology from Conningham. The capstone of the incident came when Chief Air Marshall Sir Arthur W. Tedder and American Lieutenant General Carl Spaatz came to see Patton and Bradley about the telegram April 3, hoping perhaps to clear the air and explain the strategy that had removed Allied fighters from overhead. Just as the air commanders began talking about how the Allies had achieved air supremacy, four German fighters flew over the headquarters at low altitude, bombing and strafing the area.

Plaster fell all around. The concussion from the bombs knocked the door frame out of whack, nearly trapping them in the room. Even Tedder had to admit, the raid was the most perfect demonstration of Patton's point possible.[40]

Bradley looked back on the dispute with more philosophy than bitterness, calling it an example of the "sensitivity" between air and ground commands. But it was much more emblematic of American and British relations. The British commanders barely concealed their contempt for the American forces, even as they themselves were doing a poor job.

There was more to worry about than air cover.

With Montgomery starting to make progress, Alexander modified his plans and gave II Corps a greater role in the final offensive. Noting the 1ˢᵗ Armored Division's continued sluggishness, Alexander also suggested to Patton that its commander be relieved. Whether this was the weight Patton needed to go ahead or whether he had reached the same conclusion himself, he decided that Ward would have to go.

He also decided that Bradley should break the news. It was one thing to berate the man and suggest that he die in battle, and another to strip him of his post. For Patton, the latter was the worst that could be done to a commander. And he didn't want to do it in person.

Bradley, who liked Ward and had served under him in Washington, was in a difficult position. He didn't believe that the 1ˢᵗ Armored Division's problems were all due to Ward, but its failure to meet its objectives was glaring. Finally, on April 4,[41] Patton looked across at Bradley at breakfast and told him to tell Ward the news that he was being reassigned.

Bradley went about it with a heavy heart. Ward took one look at him as he arrived in his tent at division headquarters and knew what was up. Bradley said only a few words, shook hands, then left. Ward wrote in his diary that night that Bradley took the news much worse than he had.[42]

Bradley thought that Ward should not have been replaced, and laid out some of the reasons after the war in *A Soldier's Story*.[43] He considered the weather the division's worst enemy, noting that the rain and mud had wreaked havoc on the tanks and other vehicles. Nor had the division been used particularly well, having to operate in hill country where it was easy for them to be picked off by defenders.

Alexander's orders regarding the division have been criticized by others for failing to take the topography and area into account. But Ward could also be faulted for not using enough force in his initial assaults, a fatal error that allowed his enemy to be reinforced. In any event, once he lost the confidence of his commanders, there was no way he could remain in command.

The real bottom line wasn't the weather, the enemy, or excuses. The bottom line was results. No results, no command.

It was an important lesson for Bradley. Unlike Patton, who would never fire another division commander in the war, Bradley would change underlings ruthlessly. If he could fire Orlando Ward, a man for whom he had a great deal of respect, he could fire anyone.

Alexander next formulated a plan to cut off the main German force before it could escape toward Tunis. As part of the plan, II Corps' 34th Infantry Division was placed under the command of British Lieutenant General John T. Crocker, who commanded the British IX Corps. Besides his British divisions and the 34th, Crocker had some French units at his command. His ultimate objective was Sousse, a city on the Mediterranean that the German forces would have to pass through en route to Tunis. The Allied line of attack would go through Fondouk and Kairouan, cutting a jagged dagger through the hills and across Tunisia's throat.

The Americans were assigned to take Djebel Haouareb, the key defense in the Fondouk pass. General Ryder, the division commander, suggested a feint and encirclement. Crocker overruled him, directing the division to make a frontal assault in the pass. Worse, he ordered the unit to do so without having the defenses suppressed or even shelled, fearing that American artillery would kill nearby British troops.

The results were predictable. Facing well-guarded positions amply protected from higher ground, the 34th Infantry Division battered itself against the rocks and enemy. The division came away with little more than heavy casualties. It was a fiasco—and one that should have properly been blamed on Crocker, who had ignored not only the American advice but that of a French general who had battled in the pass earlier in the war.

A British attack from the rear flank also came up short. Djebel Rhorab fell late in the afternoon of April 9, but it still took a suicide attack by British tankers through a minefield—ordered by Alexander—to break through the pass the next day. Even then, the defenders were in good enough shape to slip away and avoid capture.

So, too, did the Axis forces to the south in front of Montgomery. The plan to cut off their escape died at Fondock.

The battles were horrific enough, but Crocker immediately blamed the Americans for his difficulties. The American commanders were too far from the front, the junior officers were weak, and the men incompetent. Crocker shared his criticism with several war correspondents. A raft of stories about how poorly the Americans had done at Fondouk followed. Meanwhile, British troops were praised for their brave showings in the press.

Alexander proposed that the 34th be taken from the line for additional training under British direction. Once again, Patton and Bradley were outraged. Patton, in his diary, blamed Eisenhower nearly as much as the British for the debacle, both on the battlefield and in the media. Both he and Bradley felt that Eisenhower was seeing things from the British perspective far too often, and was failing to defend them—or at least to point out the fact that British deficiencies, with supposedly well-seasoned troops and commanders, were nearly as great as the Americans'. From Bradley's perspective, American problems were being blown out of proportion by the British, who were themselves making serious errors in their deployment.

As the dispute simmered, Bradley offered to take personal command of the 34th and lead it into battle. Alexander, who undoubtedly had been hearing the howls of American protest over Crocker's remarks, agreed to leave the unit on the line with II Corps, and it was incorporated into the plans for what would prove the final battle in North Africa. To both Bradley's and the division's credit, the unit would go on to redeem itself in the following weeks.

In the end, the negative publicity probably helped the American cause, as the news stories about the 34th Division back home prompted Marshall to tell Eisenhower that the Americans *must* have an important role in the victory at Tunisia. It was a matter of national morale.[44] Eisenhower, as always bowing to Marshall's pressure, finally put his foot down and told Alexander the same thing.

National morale in wartime is an important if somewhat amorphous ingredient in victory. Bradley, like some other American generals, tended to assume that what was good for *his* pride was good for the nation's as well, as when he made the argument to Eisenhower that II Corps should be given a larger part in the battle. But his concerns over the 34th Division and the II Corps in general were more than a matter of ego or even national prestige. They went directly to the way American troops were being used to that point in the war—and how they were to be used in the future.

Splitting a division away from its corps command as Alexander originally proposed cut it off from its normal supply and support. British and American supplies were not necessarily compatible. Both armies had radically different ways of doing things. While the new plan put the division under Crocker, it at least kept the 34th Division close to its corps geographically, keeping it closer to its lifeline.

Further, Bradley and the other American commanders feared that, if American units were not commanded by Americans, they would be used poorly—as the 34th Division was by Crocker. Being treated as a junior partner by the British wasn't just humiliating, it was extremely dangerous to the men involved. The Canadian debacle at Dieppe—a poorly thought out, terribly supported "raid" foisted on the Canadians by the British, who then couldn't stand far enough away from the disaster—is but one example of what the Americans feared would happen to them. And it was all the more dangerous given the fact that it was obvious the United States would supply the bulk of men and materials needed for victory.

The other side of this, of course, was the fact that the Americans did not do a particularly good job in Africa, certainly not before Bradley's arrival, and in many cases afterwards. One doesn't have to take the British commanders' word for it, or even the Germans', who looked down on the Americans as the Western version of their own Italian allies. Bradley himself was critical of the Americans' performance—though only to other American commanders.

"[The] campaign showed American soldiers unwilling to close with [the] enemy," Bradley told Lucian Truscott after the Tunisia campaign was over. It was his biggest worry. Americans had to be taught to kill and would need better discipline than they had shown in Africa.[45]

On the other hand, the British were not without their own flaws and failures. The Eighth Army had only recently (and with great pains) improved to the point where it could match Rommel in fighting prowess; even so, its progress whenever the Germans put up heavy resistance was generally slow, even when it had vastly superior numbers and firepower in its favor.

The Americans had every reason to respect the British, and they did. Bradley personally admired Alexander—in *A Soldier's Story*, Alexander is cited as the model of a "great soldier" possessing "reasonableness, patience, and modesty"—Bradley's highest compliments.[46] (Montgomery was another matter.) But there is a difference between respect and awe, and Bradley would never be accused of showing his British commanders or coequals the latter.

With the campaign in Tunisia winding down, Eisenhower decided that it was time for Patton to return to planning for the Sicily campaign. Bradley had demonstrated enough ability to be trusted with II Corps, and Eisenhower set the turnover date for April 15.

Before he left, Patton sat down with Bradley in their command post one last time. The talk soon turned to Patton's plans for Sicily.

How would you like to go with me and take II Corps into Sicily? asked Patton. He wanted II Corps to play a major role in the assault, replacing VI Corps, which was just arriving in Africa.

Bradley was surprised.

In place of Dawley? he asked, referring to Major General Ernest J. Dawley, who was the commander of VI Corps.

I've worked with you and I've got confidence in you, said Patton. *I don't know what in hell Dawley can do. If you've got no objection, I'm going to ask Ike to fix it up.*

Bradley had no objection at all.[47] He and II Corps replaced VI Corps in the invasion master plan.

Even though he was now in charge of the corps, Bradley did not alter his personal command style. Dealing with his division commanders, he tended to work by persuasion rather than coercion. At times his method bordered on the Socratic, as he asked questions and prompted answers. As commander, Bradley had the advantage of the last word, but he clearly preferred to lead by reason rather than fiat.

Today a corps commander can count on instantaneous communication with any of his units, and have reams of intelligence at the press of a computer button. Bradley relied on landline telephones, radio phones (though these could be intercepted), and personal visits. He generally preferred to talk to his division commanders in person, and usually did so once a day. Before getting out of bed each day he telephoned each of his division chiefs for a report.

He made his visits in the afternoon. He traveled by jeep or, when necessary, airplane, flying most often in a two-seat Piper Cub. Working from a command post consisting of tents, he would move often during a campaign in an attempt to keep close to the action. A photograph taken in Tunisia shows him briefing division commanders in the field with the help of a large folded board holding a terrain map. He wears his thin-rimmed glasses, a tie, and leggings; if not for the setting, he could be back in the States giving a course at command school.[48]

In his memoir *Command Missions,* Lucian Truscott describes Bradley calling him from a division command post as soon as he arrived with the 3rd Infantry Division. Bradley needed a unit to relieve a position held by the battered 1st Infantry Division. The sense one gets is of a guided negotiation taking place in double-time:

- There was a problem that could be solved if Truscott could move a combat team up. Was that possible?
- Yes, it was.
- Excellent. Bradley would relay the message.
- Further problems developed. Bradley called Truscott with news that the Germans were defending a position, and he could expect resistance. There would be no armored support.
- Did Truscott have enough staff to operate?
- Yes, it was not a problem.
- In that case, attack with 15th Infantry toward Ferryville. Bradley would attach other units together for a second attack nearby.[49]

Dealing with his staff, Bradley tended to act very much like a college professor running an advanced seminar. According to Colonel Dickson, who spent about a year and a half as his intelligence officer, Bradley invited his subordinates to lay out their positions on an issue, listening to what they said with little comment. When they were finished, he would generally consider the matter—in the case of a tactical situation, restudying his maps—then return with more questions before making a final decision.

He could often be quite subtle. Dickson describes a situation in Africa where Bradley gathered the division commanders and staff together and said matter-of-factly that II Corps was beginning to lose its steam and fall behind schedule. He then opened the floor to the generals and asked what they proposed to do about it.

"The natural rivalry between units took hold and each speaker tried to be bolder and more aggressive than his predecessor," recalled Dickson.[50] Bradley ended the meeting by telling them that he would hold them to their plans; Dickson compared his strategy to Tom Sawyer's famous fence-painting ploy. He was soft-spoken where other generals might be loud, but the fact that he used few words was to his advantage—it gave what he did say more weight.

While Bradley often left the details of attacks to his subordinates, he was certainly capable of addressing those details. At key points, he ordered his artillery to open its barrages with synchronized firings, announcing the start of their attack with a thunderous and demoralizing crash.

While Bradley's preferred tactics called for containing strong points and flanking them, as a general rule he was not an advocate of simply bypassing enemy strongpoints as he rushed toward a further objective. He tended to see them as dangerous launchpoints for attacks against *his* flank. And while he was willing to put off assaults on heavily defended objectives—Brest in France would be an example later on—he often found that he had to pay a price for this; the delays almost always helped the Germans, who would prove to be impressive fighters when holed up.

There were only a few times when he concluded that moving head on (or nearly head on) against strong defenses was his only option—but as those proved to be major battles, most notably in breaking out of the Normandy beachhead and in crossing the German West Wall defenses, they are the fights that are sometimes used to characterize his overall thinking. The campaigns in Tunisia and Sicily give a much broader view of his thinking.

Bradley did not equate sheer speed with aggressiveness, nor did he necessarily measure success in a battle by ground gained. For him, aggressiveness was found in contact with the enemy. He tended to see the destruction of the enemy army, not the conquest of territory, as the object of battle.

★ ★ ★ ★

Bradley chose William "Bill" Benjamin Kean as his chief of staff, otherwise keeping the rest of II Corps staff in place. Kean, a 1919 graduate of West Point, had served Bradley as chief of staff at the 28th Infantry Division back in the States, and would remain with him through Africa, Sicily, and into northern Europe.

In many ways, Kean was Bradley's alter ego, the bad cop to Bradley's good cop. "Bad cop" doesn't do him justice—Kean was extremely efficient, and excelled at his job. He was under no illusions that he should be liked; if anything, he seemed to pride himself on terrorizing the incompetent. His demanding style made it much easier for Bradley to be easygoing and reasonable.

Bradley set out to make II Corps his own. He amended Patton's clothing and helmet restrictions, a move that won him considerable good will. But the real test, the only test that counted, would come in combat.

The Allied plan to take northern Tunisia involved some 300,000 men and twenty divisions.

The Eighth Army with six divisions under Montgomery would come up from the south through Enfidaville. It would move along the coast in the direction of Tunis, aiming to cut off an escape to the Cap Bon peninsula.

The British First Army under Anderson would come from the west, pushing directly toward Tunis. Anderson would have six British and three French divisions to make the attack. Operating under Anderson, II Corps and three French battalions (the Corps Franc d'Afrique), would move north and attack through the coastal hills to Bizerte, cutting off that route of escape.

The plan was similar to the one Bradley had proposed earlier. Initially it stripped about half the 1st Armored Division and gave it directly to Anderson. Bradley succeeded in changing that by telling Anderson that rather than putting the unit under Anderson's direct command, he would move it under his orders to clear Anderson's roads at the start of the campaign. That left it free for Bradley to use later on.[51]

Bradley's first major accomplishment of the campaign came before it began. Turning roads into one-way thoroughfares, pressing tactical vehicles into service as supply trucks, and lifting blackout restrictions to facilitate travel by night, the Americans were able to move roughly twice the supplies the British estimated possible. Granted, it wasn't combat, but it was a telling demonstration of military efficiency.

II Corps' objective, Bizerte, lay on the northern coast, tucked beyond Lake Bizerte (actually a protected bay off the Mediterranean). The city of Mateur sat about halfway between the American force and Bizerte, at the end of the Djoumine and Tine River valleys. Mateur was at a crossroads; the terrain beyond it was relatively flat, giving a clear passage to Bizerte. Control the city, and the rest of plain was yours.

II Corps' route toward Mateur, however, lay through a succession of hills not all that different from the ridges and passes it had found so murderous to the south. They were the problem, not Bizerte. Bradley studied the maps but kept his plans tentative until he had a chance to see the terrain first hand.

He had a sufficient understanding from the topographic maps to disregard Eisenhower's suggestion April 16 that he send the 1st Armored Division spearheading through the Tine valley, an area the intelligence officers had already derisively named Mousetrap Valley. Bradley filed the suggestion—worded as an "expectation"[52]—away, disregarding what would have been a ruinous order. Instead, he decided to launch his strike with infantry. Once they overcame German defenses guarding the valley, he would unleash his armor northwards in a concentrated strike against Bizerte.

It was a reversal of the usual doctrine, which called for armor to spearhead an attack, exactly as Eisenhower had suggested. (And Patton had done previously.) Bradley never made a very big deal of reversing the conventional wisdom in the attack—to him it was a matter of common sense and bitter experience that the high ground here should be taken so his armor could be "sprung" forward in the second phase of assault. His plan also made use of an important American asset, its artillery, which was deployed against German gun positions as well as the dug-in defenders on the front lines.

Bradley arranged his three infantry divisions along a line in the hills. The 9th Infantry, led by Manson Eddy, started in the north, immediately west of Bald and Green Hills. The 1st Division was aimed at Tine River Valley in the south. The battered 34th Division, barely saved from the recycling pile by Bradley, sat in the middle. The way the defenses were arranged and Bradley's strategy lined up, the 34th had the easiest sector. He clearly had low expectations for the division.

Now commanded by Ernie Harmon, the 1st Armored Division was held back in the Tine River Valley, waiting for the breakthrough. (By not committing the division, Bradley also kept open the option of using it further north if circumstances dictated, though this was not in his original plans.)

To put Bradley's plans in perspective, neither the drive by the British First Army nor Montgomery's Eighth Army push showed any particular flare. Anderson's British First Army, to the right of II Corps, was launching a wide-angle attack eastward, aiming at Choulgul, Tabourba, Djedeida, and finally Tunis itself. Anderson's idea was to overwhelm the Germans with multiple attacks; running short on supplies, the Germans were unlikely to be able to meet all the challenges.

Montgomery roundly denounced the plan, among other things calling it a "partridge drive."[53] By splitting up his forces over so wide an area, Montgomery predicted that Anderson would be unable to muster enough of an advantage anywhere to break through the stiffening Axis line—and he was correct. But Montgomery's own plans in the south didn't fare well either. Armed with intelligence that the hills he faced were lightly defended, he still bogged down as he tried to battle his way across them. Having fought its way across the desert, the Eighth Army had trouble adapting to the new challenges in terrain.

★ ★ ★ ★

II Corps' attack got underway the night of April 21 with a blistering artillery barrage. In the heat of the northern hills, the artillerymen soon stripped to the waists as they sent shell after shell against the enemy. At dawn the next day—Good Friday—the 1st Infantry Division stepped off against targets in the Mousetrap, seizing a number of hills but then stalling against fierce resistance. Further to the north, the 9th Division also met with mixed success, pushing back defenders but stalling before Green Hill, a critical position on the road to Mateur. It was the same spot where the British had failed in the winter.

The first reports were slow coming in. Bradley, feeling the strain of combat, was irritable and nervous. Finally Hansen, his aide, suggested they go for a walk. Bradley took his rifle and they hiked over a nearby hill. With all the wildlife gone, he had his escort toss rocks in the air while he blasted away at them.[54]

Back at his command post, Bradley had his radio tuned to the general frequencies, trying to follow the battle through snatches of conversation. The radio crackled with dialogue from British pilots in Spitfires, chasing a Messerschmitt 109.

"God damn it," barked one of the pilots. "Get out of the way and let me get a crack at him."[55]

That was a spirit Bradley could admire.[56]

On Easter Sunday, with the 1st Infantry Division moving slowly forward, Bradley took a quick drive north to check on the 9th and his French troops near the coast. While the Americans had accomplished much in shifting their units northwards, Bradley was worried about supply problems for the French units. The French units, which included Africans and even some anti-Fascist Spaniards, wore a ragtag collection of American and British uniforms and were equipped with a wide range of motor vehicles from both countries, along with horses.

Knowing how difficult the British had found the defenses at Bald and Green Hills, Ninth Division commander Manton Eddy had planned a flanking maneuver that would take his units around them. It was a good theory, but the reality was that there were no roads that could be used to make the turn. To get through, the units had to hack their way through brush five feet high. Supplies were walked through on narrow trails to the lead units. Progress was understandably slow.

But it was progress, especially compared to the British units to the south and east. With little other option, Bradley urged Eddy onward.

Back at his command post, Bradley began facing up to a difficult problem at the northern edge of the 1st Infantry Division's attack. Crack German troops held a high ridge that they could use to survey the entire countryside. Dubbed Hill 609 (from the metric height on a topo map), the long wall was more like a castle, with nearly sheer walls and strong defenses. Worse, it was ringed by hills just a little lower that guarded its approach.

Hill 609 was now the key to springing the Mousetrap. It lay along the border between the 1st Infantry Division and the 34th, in the 34th Division sector. It was a formidable obstacle—more formidable than Bradley had foreseen. The 1st Infantry Division, advancing to the southeast, drew up close enough to the positions to take fire on its flank, but was not in a position to launch an assault.[57]

Before a plan to deal with it could be drawn up, Anderson called Bradley's deputy commander and asked for an infantry regiment to help his own stalled attack. As for Hill 609, added the British commander, just go around it.

Bradley grabbed his maps and headed south to 1st Division headquarters, where Anderson met him. There he proceeded to give the British general a quick lesson in topography and tactics—there was simply no way to leave the hill in place without getting pummeled.

As for lending him the regiment—which would have represented a substantial portion of Bradley's forces and put a serious crimp in his plans to attack—Bradley told Anderson that he would agree only if ordered by Eisenhower.

Eisenhower soon backed him up, but the problem of Hill 609 remained. The Big Red One had neither the tactical position nor the resources to take on the defenders there; the logical choice was the 34th. Its recent history hung over it, however.

In *A Soldier's Story*, Bradley says he decided to use the 34th Division because he had promised Alexander that the unit would redeem itself. The account is even briefer in *A General's Life,* consisting primarily of his command and promise to General Ryder: "Get me that hill, and no one will ever again doubt the toughness of your division."[58]

Surely those accounts leave out quite a bit of soul-searching. Bradley admits that on hearing Ryder's plan, he worried that Ryder's first objectives—taking some of the outer strong points in a simultaneous attack—were too ambitious. The route the attacking units would have to take was so close to the Germans that it hadn't even been scouted.

A heavy artillery barrage helped clear the way, and elements of the 34th made it to the face of Hill 609. And there they stalled.

Ryder proposed an attack from the hill's flank and rear. Bradley, realizing the defenses at the back of the hill were as strong as those at the front, believed the attack couldn't succeed without a heavy bombardment against the dug-in positions. But there was no way to get artillery there.

Unless they used tanks. He ordered seventeen of them to provide covering fire for the assault on the morning of April 29. That move, swinging the armor around to the enemy's rear, caught the German defenders by surprise. Units of the 34th Infantry Division began pushing up the slopes.

The same night, a battalion from the 16th Regiment of the 1st Infantry Division launched an attack on Hill 523, which lay a mile to the east of 609. Taking the hill with a bluffed bayonet charge, the battalion cut off the enemy's best route to reinforce Hill 609.

A vicious fight ensued, and the Americans who initially took Hill 523 were overrun.[59] But the tactical momentum now had shifted, and despite the heavy losses, the 34th took part of Hill 609 on April 30. After even more fierce fighting, all resistance there ended the next day. The 1st Division troops that had been caught by the hill's guns were now free to clear out the rest of the Mousetrap. The reversal put the Americans on the high ground, and when rumors came May 1 that the German forces were gathering for a counterattack, Bradley smiled at his G-2 and said, "Let 'em come. We want to kill Germans."[60]

Later that night, Bradley sat in his command tent looking over his map. His staff had mounted a large map of the campaign and covered it with a sheet of acetate allowing it to be drawn on repeatedly. Marking out the defensive position and the offensive possibilities with red and blue crayons, Bradley considered his options.

By now, the 9th Infantry Division had made good progress in the north, and Bradley realized that by moving units north, he might score a coup with a quick run to Bizerte.

It was a risky move. He would have to weaken his drive in the south, leaving the divisions there vulnerable to a strong counterattack. Worse, if the intelligence was wrong and his northward thrust broke down on some as-yet unscouted hill—a la 609 or 523—the entire sweep might stall. The combat team would be itself vulnerable to counterattack, perhaps fatally so.

Bradley decided not to take the risk. The 1st Armored Division was launched through the now defanged Mousetrap, rumbling into Mateur May 3. From there, it sprinted toward Ferryville and Protville, reaching them by May 7 and 8 respectively, and cutting off the possibility of a German retreat northwards from Tunis.

★ ★ ★ ★

Bradley's strategy clearly worked, but the reasons he gave to his staff to avoid the splashier but riskier northern bolt are instructive. Bradley believed that what was at stake in Tunisia was not simply victory over the German force—that was almost foreordained. What he worried about was further damage to the Americans' prestige. The defeat at Kasserine and stumbling after El Guettar had made a victory important, and the avoidance of a setback critical.[61]

Bradley's assessment was based partly on his suspicion that the Germans would not simply collapse as they were pressed toward the sea; counterattacks and reversals were still very much a possibility in his mind. But the decision also indicates that he was looking at the battle from a strategic point of view. Combined with his earlier insistence on keeping the 34th Infantry Division in the battle, it is a strong argument that his understanding of the war was not merely limited to tactical objectives or even strategic military objectives. He was looking long term, and considering the impact of the war on the home front as well as on his troops. This understanding led him to make a conservative choice in this case, just as it had led him to make a riskier decision—keeping the 34th on the line—earlier.

Of course, he would also have seen what effect a reversal in the field, or even a stalled drive, could have on a general's career.

Bradley's attitude toward the 1st Infantry Division and its commander, Terry Allen, eroded during the final stages of the Tunisia battle. He seems to have made allowances for the division, which had suffered severely in the fighting, but he also believed it was not well disciplined. He laid most of the blame on its commanding general.

Allen was known for aggressive leadership and a personal devil-may-care style that inspired his men. His assistant commander Ted Roosevelt, President Theodore Roosevelt's son, was cut from the same mold. But Bradley thought the commander and his division too independent. One event that seems to have cemented his opinion came on May 6, as Bradley's forces were heading toward Bizerte. The 1st Division was assigned to hold a defensive line north of Chouigui on Bradley's right. Allen, perhaps thinking that the Germans had completely collapsed, pushed his force into the Chouigui foothills. A heavy Axis counterattack the next day pushed the Americans back with heavy losses. Bradley personally intervened, moving units around and bringing up a combat team from the recently arrived 3rd Infantry Division into place to prevent further damage.[62]

Bradley seems never to have forgiven Allen for undertaking the attack without authorization. However, both Allen and Roosevelt remained in place.

★ ★ ★ ★

The 1ˢᵗ Armored Division sprinted down the Tyne Valley to Mateur, the key crossroads town in the II Corps sector, reaching it with minimal resistance May 3. With the objective taken, division commander Ernie Harmon paused to realign his unit for the final push against the Germans.

The division was still in some disorder, despite Harmon's efforts to reshape it. His gruff ways did not sit well with many of his officers, and he was especially at odds with Brigadier General Paul Robinett, the leader of the division's Combat Command B.[63] On May 4, General Anderson sent an observer to Harmon's command post for a firsthand look at his battle plans. The British were apparently surprised to learn that Harmon intended to spend the next day and a half regrouping instead of pushing forward and drawing the Germans away from Anderson's front. Anderson wanted Harmon to move forward immediately.

When Bradley arrived later that day, Harmon braced himself for the order, mustering arguments on why he needed the time. But Bradley, familiar with the division's state, agreed to the extra time. Worried about a line of hills to the north, where the Axis defenders had mounted anti-tank weapons, the two men worked out a flanking attack that would skirt the worst positions and still allow the division to drive toward Ferryville and Tunis, a two-pronged fork into the enemy's backside.

Finally satisfied with the plan, Bradley paused and asked Harmon if he really thought he could do it.

Yes, said the commander. But it would cost fifty tanks—and the lives that went with them.

"Do it then," said Bradley. It would be less expensive in the long run.[64]

Resistance was already teetering throughout northern Tunisia. The 34ᵗʰ Infantry Division, swinging south through the 1ˢᵗ Infantry Division's sector, took Chouigui May 7. The 9ᵗʰ Division arrived in Bizerte the same day. The defenses around Tunis were breached around the same time. The 1ˢᵗ Armored Division cut the road between Tunis and Bizerte May 8, isolating the German forces.

The Germans began surrendering in droves.

Bradley rose early May 9 and, after his customary phone calls, went out of his tent to watch the sun rise over the nearby hills. It was a beautiful, awesome sight, the bleak rock surfaces glimmering with the new dawn.

Victory was only a few hours away. A little past eleven, Harmon called to tell him that Major General Fritz Krause, commander of Afrika Korps, wanted to surrender.

It was the commanding general's prerogative to accept such surrenders in person, but Bradley had no need for the honor or its satisfaction. He had come to despise Germans, and wouldn't even meet with the enemy officers personally. He told Harmon the surrender was to be unconditional, and left it to him.

The battle was over. Tunisia had been won.

The accepted historical wisdom on the northern African campaign is that the American Army came of age there. An army that was almost childlike went into battle and, in Bradley's words, learned to walk.

But the maturing of the American Army was a complicated process. The metaphor suggests a steady progression; that wasn't the case at all. Lessons learned in Africa needed to be relearned and revisited in the years that passed, and while the Americans became more professional, the battlefield itself continued to evolve. Veterans died; replacements learned all over again. Veterans made amateur mistakes in the heat of battle.

Nor was the evolution simply a matter of "blooding the troops" as the British often put it. The American Army had to transition from a small peacetime force to one engaged in the most ferocious and wide-ranging war the world has ever known. The transition didn't mean only that it had to grow; it had to change much of the way it did things. It had to get new equipment and learn to use what it had.

And it had to learn to kill. This was a lesson Bradley brought home time and again. The Americans had shown a disturbing tendency to surrender early in battles. He blamed this on war games where referees often called an end to fights prematurely. Hard fighting could often turn a battle when an army was outnumbered, as the Germans had shown countless times. American soldiers had yet to fully embrace this.

There was one other thing that had been learned in Africa, this one rarely mentioned by anyone: their commanders had to be willing to accept losses in battle. They needed to make cold calculations—fifty tanks now versus a hundred and fifty later—and do so without hesitation.

It was a difficult, even terrible lesson, a necessity of war. If Bradley ever spoke of it, it seems not to have been recorded. But it was a lesson he clearly had learned.

Summing up the Tunisian campaign in *A Soldier's Story*, Bradley recalls Eisenhower's one-dimensional advice to him on taking command, noting that Ike had wanted him to be tough with his division commanders. But simply being tough, Bradley noted, wouldn't have gotten the job done. From Bradley's point of view, the corps could only succeed if the division commanders were supported—in his words, "The corps commander must know his division commanders, he must thoroughly understand their problems, respect their judgment, and be tolerant of their limitations."[65] He speaks of bolstering their self-confidence as well as their judgment.

Even allowing for the grand sentences one tends to write in memoirs, Bradley's statement is unique. He's laying out the corps commander's job as one of coach, helper, and facilitator—not the sort of thing one would look for in Clausewitz, or expect to hear from Napoleon or even Pershing. It is a thoroughly modern approach to warfare, and as much a recognition of the complexities of fighting across a wide front with a wide range of weapons and masses of men. Yet at its heart it is also personal, as Bradley says success depends on knowing each commander and his respective strengths and weaknesses.

The Army came far in those months, but no farther than Bradley himself traveled. In three months, he rose from a portfolio-less observer to the ranking American general on the battlefield. His stint in command made him the most successful corps commander in the Army.

Personally, he had not only seen combat for the first time, but had managed to escape death on three occasions, by his count. The three months had tested and in many cases vindicated what he had learned and what he believed.

He remained outwardly more or less the man he had been at the beginning of his time in the war—quietly confident, willing to solicit opinions from others, a tactician. He had a nationalist streak in him, and a prickly pride where it touched on the American Army, even though privately he was realistic when assessing it. He did not obey orders blindly, especially when they came from British generals; in fairness, he was probably less cooperative with Anderson than he was with any other commander, British or American, through the rest of the war.

Inwardly, it was hard to say what changes the months in combat had wrought. Bradley certainly couldn't.

Three months. It was the longest he'd ever been away from his wife and daughter.

And the war had really only just begun.

CHAPTER 3

Husky

Everywhere he looked, there were airplanes. P-38 Lightnings, their silver wings and torsos shimmering in the sun, sat wingtip to wingtip across from the Algiers runway where Bradley had dodged mud puddles in the C-47 a few months before. They were new additions to the war, replacements for the beat-up, under-powered P-40s that had flown over the American troops during their first campaigns.

Things had changed in three months.

Bradley stepped down from the C-47 at Maison Blanche Airfield in Algiers and walked to the car that had come to take him to see Eisenhower at his headquarters in the St. George Hotel. It was May 14, 1943.

The command post buzzed with activity, aides passing through the halls. British and American officers conferred in hushed tones. Eisenhower greeted Bradley warmly and took him into his office, asking first about the prisoners of war II Corps had taken.

The Germans, Bradley told Ike, were "still cocky."[1] The POWs were worried only that their submarines would sink them on the long passage back to the United States, where they were to be interred. The best thing about the prisoners was their numbers—the roads were choked with them.

Congratulatory exchanges over, both men fell silent. Eisenhower got up from his desk and went to the wall, where a curtain hid a map. He pulled the fabric away, revealing the plans for their next task, the conquest of Sicily.

The plans were approved yesterday, Ike told Bradley. D-Day for Operation Husky was eight weeks away.

The Allied invasion of Sicily is mostly treated as a footnote in the war. Sandwiched between the northern African campaigns and the invasion of Italy, it lacked the psychological significance of either. Relatively short, it lacked set-piece battles or daring tactical charges. While there were certainly casualties, no one battle was large enough to rack up the mind-numbing figures seen later in Italy or France.

The invasion was the logical extension of a strategy the American command really didn't want. To many, including President Roosevelt and General Marshall, it was a distraction from the main goal of subduing Germany, a distraction that had actually begun with Torch. From an immediate strategic point of view, taking the island made a great deal of sense. It intruded into both the Axis and Allied lines, a natural forward operating area for airplanes and Navy vessels. Given its location near Africa, it was relatively easy to supply—and conversely, well-positioned to use as a jumping off point for an invasion.

On the other hand, it was not necessarily an easy target. Troops there were within easy reach of better protected bases on the Italian peninsula. Supplying both the invasion and subsequent operations would be complicated. And then there was the fact that, since it was part of Italy, it was likely to be well-defended.

The operation, most especially its planning, was among the most contentious of the Allied campaign. There were bitter divisions among the Allied commanders. Part of the difficulty stemmed from the fact that the British did not believe the American Army was capable of much. But the island's difficult geography, the fact that seaborne invasions were still a new science, and poor staff work added to the problems.

While Eisenhower was in overall command of Husky, once again the service chiefs beneath him were all British—Admiral Sir Andrew Cunningham, Air Chief Marshal Arthur Tedder, and General Sir Harold Alexander. Montgomery once again headed the British Eighth Army; Patton was in charge of the American Seventh Army.

Sicily is often described as a football about to be kicked by the Italian boot, but the Allied campaign may be easier to visualize by thinking of the island as a long and slightly off-center isosceles triangle that begins on the right near the Italian mainland and tapers down to the left. Much of the population lives along the coastlines. At the top of the triangle, the city of Messina sits in the corner of the island closest to the mainland. Below it is the city of Catania; lower, Syracuse sits not quite at the base. Palermo, the largest city on the island, lies on the northwest coast.

Much of the inland area is mountainous, and the northeast is dominated by Mount Etna, an active volcano. The geography made it virtually impossible to fight a large-scale battle in the center of the island, and equally difficult to move large forces through all but the coastal areas.

As originally conceived, the Allies were to strike on two of the three sides of the Sicilian triangle—the British Eighth Army on the east and south below Syracuse, the American Seventh Army on the northwest near Palermo. Montgomery felt that the plan left his forces vulnerable to attacks on the flank and gave him too much ground to cover and protect. He suggested a series of changes; most were adopted by Alexander and approved by Eisenhower. These called for the Americans to invade on the southern coast to the left of his attack, then move north into the mountains to guard his flank. His plan also left them without a major port for supply.

Patton objected on several grounds, most prominently the fact that he'd been given a 47-mile beachfront, outrageously long given the size of his force. The plan asked the Americans to take objectives that Montgomery, with a much larger force, had declared he couldn't secure. And, once ashore, the Americans would have a secondary role in the overall battle.

But Patton did not press his objections. His acquiescence is a continuing puzzle to historians.[2]

Bradley's II Corps was the major component of Seventh Army. It would land with the 1st Infantry Division and the 45th Infantry Division. The 1st Division would land near and take Gela. The 45th Infantry Division would land near Scoglitti.

The 82nd Airborne would jump inland near Gela in a move designed to keep Axis reinforcements from reaching the city and the beaches below. Also attached to II Corps was Force X, composed of the 1st and 4th Ranger Battalions; they were assigned to seize Gela. Almost universally known as Darby's Rangers, the elite infantry units were personally led by Lieutenant Colonel William Darby, who had selected and trained the men himself.[3] In addition, II Corps had some artillery and medium tank units, as well as assorted support elements assigned for the landing phase of the operations. Three key airfields were included in II Corps' early objectives: Ponte Olivi, Comiso, and Biscari. II Corps would then move on to secure the Vizzini-Caltagirone Road, vital to protecting the British flank. The road would also give II Corps access to routes north, but no other objectives were specified in the initial plan.

Patton's Seventh Army also included Joss Force, the 3rd Infantry Division (Reinforced) under Lucian Truscott. Additional armor and artillery were attached to 3rd for the assault. Patton's floating reserve included Combat Command B from the 2nd Armored Division, as well as the 18th Infantry Regiment (part of the 1st Infantry Division).

"That's spreading us pretty thin," Bradley said when he saw the II Corps landing plan.[4] But at least from the records, that was his only objection, and in any event, it was too late to change the overall plan.[5]

Though Montgomery and Patton were media favorites, Bradley gradually began to garner some notice in the press after Eisenhower publicly credited him with leading America's troops to victory in Tunisia.[6] The resulting stories tended to be necessarily shallow, but the image of Bradley they presented would inform descriptions of him well after the war.

Somewhat typical was an article by *Newsweek* published in the May 17, 1943, edition. The first paragraph is dedicated to the news of Bradley's takeover from Patton, indicating that it had been embargoed until Tunis was won. Patton is called a "mobile warfare expert" in parentheses, identifying him for the reader—and at the same time subtly implying a difference from Bradley. A little further on, Patton is again identified as one of the "noisiest and toughest" men in the Army. Bradley is then defined, in contrast, as one of the "shyest."

The brief sketch gives Bradley's West Point pedigree, emphasizing his participation in baseball and football, but then claiming that he made "little impression" in the classroom. He is said to have made a "standard tour" of military posts, have a good bridge game, and an impressive knowledge of military history, especially strategy. (Strategy here is probably meant for what Bradley and other military men would call tactics.) After comparing him to Patton once more—both are strict disciplinarians, says the writer—he is contrasted as the rare officer who does not raise his voice. Mentioning his stint at Fort Benning prior to the war, the writer credits him with getting Benning ready for the conflict, but spends more time talking about how Bradley loved to hunt, and notes especially that he loved to kill water moccasins, allegedly putting on his old football shin guards and shooting them every Sunday morning. The image allows the writer to end with a quip that Bradley was still known around Benning as St. Patrick. The water moccasin story is clever and cute, even if it is hard to imagine the forty-something Bradley donning thirty-year-old football gear to wade into streams for pests.[7]

The details the reporter chooses for the story are revealing—if not of Bradley, certainly of the intended audience. Bradley was actually a good student at West Point, finishing in the top third of his class. The writer's point is obvious, if mistaken: Bradley is a regular guy when it comes to intellect, and just about everything else. Anything that would contradict this is left out or glossed over. His stint as a mathematics professor—an unusual detail for a general officer—could easily have been mentioned in connection with West Point, but it's not.

By contrast, Bradley's prowess as an athlete some thirty years before is mentioned more than once, and the story ends with an emphasis on his hunting skills, real or imagined. The not-so-subtle message that emerges is that the Army's leader is quiet, athletic, a *real* man, and, like you and me, reader, just a regular guy when it comes to the intellect department.

Other reporters emphasized the "regular guy" aspects of Bradley's character. What is notably lacking from the stories is any information on what the role of a corps commander is. The few discussions of military strategy seem particularly wrong-headed. A *New York Times* writer implied that Patton took over II Corps because there was a need to use armor in the first phase of the battle, and Bradley came in because infantry dominated in the second.[8]

My purpose here is not to pick on the reporters, but to point out how their sketches, incomplete and in many respects inaccurate, formed the basis of popular conceptions of Bradley. He's a regular guy, somewhat soft-spoken and definitely shy. He's not overly intelligent. He's not Patton—which means he must not be a mobile warfare expert. At least he's a good shot. As for what he does in the war and why he was in charge of the American Army when it won its first real battles in Tunisia. . .those details are simply missing from the stories.

Bradley obviously can't be faulted for the misconceptions about the campaign and his role in it, but it must be said that his diminished media image stems partly from his own neglect. Unlike Patton or Montgomery—or Fredendall, for that matter—Bradley did not attempt to court reporters or garner media attention. He had no press camp or office at his headquarters until very late in the war. Bradley is often said to have been shy, and it's tempting to say that this extended into his relations with reporters. But one can't be *too* shy and become a five-star general. True, he clearly was reticent and self-consciousness when meeting people for the first time. But the overwhelming reason he didn't cultivate a media image seems to be one of values: his upbringing had taught him to perceive outward self-promotion as bragging and wrong, and as far as he was concerned, that's what news stories were.

Photos of Bradley around the time he visited Algiers show a middle aged man with a face still relatively smooth. He wore round, wire-rimmed glasses, and as always kept his mouth pressed together with only the hint of a smile.

Most likely he opened his mouth in a full grin June 10, though the cameras were nowhere to be found. A TWX arrived at his headquarters telling him he had been promoted to lieutenant general, giving him a third star. It was a temporary promotion; he was still only a lieutenant colonel on the permanent ranks.

Bradley's arrival in his new corps headquarters was less than auspicious; the welcoming committee consisted of a swarm of bugs. Appropriate, since the name—Relizane—meant City of Flies.[9]

There were other reasons to dislike the spot. The hot, dusty town was thirty miles inland from Mostaganem, where Patton had established

Seventh Army headquarters. Bradley wanted to move up to Mostaganem, where his staff had originally recommended a seaside location. But Patton refused, claiming it would be a tempting target for German commandos. The only respite at Relizane was the pool of a local Frenchman. Bradley rarely found time to use it.

The complexity of the Sicily operation that Bradley was prepping for is evident in the numbers it involved. First, there was the sheer length of the beachhead, which involved forty-seven miles. There were 80,000 troops assigned to make the assault or directly support it; some 45,000 of them were either in II Corps or were responsible for helping them land. Bradley's corps had 4,800 vehicles; 125 tanks were included in the landing plans.

The 1st Infantry Division had gained valuable landing experience in Torch, and though it had been tired and depleted toward the end of the African campaign, it had been given a critical role in the Sicily plans. Bradley continued to have reservations about Terry Allen and the division's discipline, and the time off between campaigns did nothing to assuage those doubts.

After the division's units were pulled back and given leave, a number of incidents were reported concerning crimes by Big Red One soldiers, including the looting of local stores. Soldiers shot at Arabs without provocation, apparently for entertainment. And conflicts between soldiers who had been at the front and those who remained behind the lines boiled into fistfights and out and out riots.

In Oran, troops assigned to the occupying force closed down clubs and other facilities ahead of the division's arrival, either trying to forestall trouble or to avoid sharing with the "outsiders," depending on your point of view. This didn't sit too well with the returning 1st Division men, who began taking out their frustrations on anyone in a khaki uniform. (The summer khakis had not been issued to combat troops, and thus were easily associated with the men who had stayed behind the lines.) The fights were so serious that Bradley was warned to put an end to them. He had the units sent back to camps, their free time severely restricted.

In *A Soldier's Story*, Bradley takes some blame for the situation, saying that he should have provided a better rest area for the combat-worn forces. But it's clear that most of his wrath at the time was directed at Terry Allen. In Bradley's view, Allen simply didn't believe in discipline. To Bradley, he was a rebel who went against the proper rules of conduct, and therefore encouraged or at least allowed his men to do the same. Bradley complains that the men in the division would strut about how tough they were, but at the same time flaunt rules that were meant to apply to all. Those two Bradley peeves—bragging (especially when it wasn't warranted) and injustice—were sure to set him off.

Bradley had other complaints against Allen, ranging from siphoning off supplies for the division that had been earmarked for other units[10] to a careless, even reckless radio call back in Tunisia taunting the Germans before an attack. The radio call inadvertently gave away the fact that Americans had broken German codes, depriving them of intelligence for weeks.[11]

Bradley spoke to Eisenhower about removing Allen, and Eisenhower agreed to return him to the States, recommending him as a corps commander. But Bradley says that Patton wanted to keep him at least through the first part of the Sicily operation; all Bradley could get him to do was tone down a commendation.

While he certainly had limits, Bradley was not a strict disciplinarian, or even beyond winking at the rules. Discussing the Rangers' stay in camp before the Sicilian invasion, Bradley writes admiringly in *A Soldier's Story* about how the 1st Battalion bargained with local merchants to trade war souvenirs for beer. This wasn't exactly in keeping with military regulations, but was far from rioting and obviously within the acceptable bounds of behavior from his point of view.

The other division making the assault landing was the 45th Infantry Division. The division had not yet seen combat.

A National Guard unit originally from Oklahoma and Texas, the 45th Division was commanded by Troy Middleton, who had received two battlefield promotions during World War I. Retiring from the Army in 1937, he had worked as a dean at Louisiana State University before being recalled to duty.

The division had a reputation as one of the finest in the United States. But it was handicapped by a switch in the naval units that were supporting it; practice assault runs were not encouraging. Two of the 45th's three regiments landed several miles off target on a dry run on June 23. (The 1st Division also missed its target, though by only half a mile.) The problem wasn't just the sheer number of troops that had to be landed in the operation, or the fact that it would take some 2,590 vessels to get them there safely. Many of the landing craft were entirely new types. Among the most imposing was the immense Landing Ship Tank—a large seagoing vessel capable of depositing as many as twenty tanks ashore. Besides tanks, the LSTs carried trucks and smaller landing craft, and were generally equipped with machine guns, the number and caliber varying from vessel to vessel throughout the war. But the ramps the LSTs featured at their bows were useless here: sandbars made it impossible for them to make it all the way to the beach. To get around this, some carried pontoons that could be strung out like long bridges to shore. Most had to rely on a variety of smaller vessels to pick up and ferry men and gear to land.

And yet, even with all these vessels, there weren't actually enough to get Bradley's supplies ashore as quickly as he wanted. The plan called for three successive waves of supplies and vehicles to hit the beach over a twelve-day period. The first few days would see him very tight on supplies. Bradley's plans called for 4,500 vehicles (about 600 of which were towed artillery pieces) to land in Sicily on D-Day.

That sounds like a lot, but it was a small portion of what the division commanders thought they needed. Some idea of the problems Bradley faced can be seen in the request by the Army air corps that space be found for 660 of its own vehicles, needed to prepare the airfields Bradley was supposed to secure.

Impossible, said Bradley.

After a brief debate with the colonel making the request, Bradley lost his patience and told him that the air corps could change places with the assault teams. You clear the beaches, he said, and the soldiers could come in the next wave.

The air corps complained to Patton, who backed Bradley. Eventually the request was dropped to about a third, which Bradley agreed to.

Bradley moved to Oran at the end of June. He stalked through a requisitioned house near the ocean, occasionally looking out to sea, restless and anxious, worried and excited at the same time. Finished planning, he was anxious to get on with the battle.

The highlight of his week came when his staff managed to find a few cases of Coke from one of the supply units in the port.

On July 4, the 45th Division thronged through the town, turning Oran into a crowded lot of confusion. Navy chiefs snarled orders at puzzled dogfaces. Tanks and trucks loaded with supplies were backed into place on the landing vessels.

Somehow, everything came together. Bradley's headquarters truck, packed with K-rations and ten gallons of water, was loaded onto the USS *Ancon*, a converted ocean liner that would serve as his floating command and the flagship for the ninety-six vessels tasked with delivering the 45th Division and its attachments (dubbed Cent Force) ashore.

Later on, Bradley would be surprised to find that his K rations were missing, apparently stolen by the sailors. That surprised him greatly—in his opinion, the worst food aboard ship was better than the best K ration.

One food in particular pleased him. When Rear Admiral Alan R. Kirk told him he could have anything aboard, Bradley asked for a dish of ice cream.[12]

The American troops embarked from three major ports, Oran (45th Infantry Division), Algiers (1st Division), and Bizerte (3rd Infantry Division). The ships moved in a slow convoy west to east toward Sicily, a distance over eight hundred miles. Instead of heading straight across to Sicily, they sailed westwards, hoping to convince the Axis that their true target was Greece or Crete.

The diversion and the difficulty of organizing and coordinating such a large invasion force meant that most of the troops would be aboard ships for days before the assault began. Bradley, having boarded on July 4, had an entire week to wait for D-Day, scheduled for the morning of July 10. For most, including the general, it was a tedious, monotonous, and nervous wait.

Sicily's defense was managed by a combined force of Italians and Germans. These were two separate armies in every sense of the word.

Italian General d'Armata (general of the army) Alfredo Guzzoni commanded six coastal divisions and another four mobile divisions in his Sixth Army. The units were hopelessly undermanned, the men underfed and under-equipped. As a general rule, the Italians lacked good officers and were poorly trained. Their morale was horrible. There were individual exceptions—the units in and around Gela, especially the 429th Coastal Battalion which fought the Rangers, would prove tenacious fighters. For the most part, though, the Italian troops on Sicily were even worse than those the Allies had encountered in Africa.

The Germans had only recently arrived, but as usual they were well organized and well led. Two divisions were on Sicily: the Hermann Goering Panzer Division and the 15th Panzer Grenadier Division. The 29th Panzer Grenadier Division would join the battle soon after the invasion.

Bradley watched from the bridge of the *Ancon* July 8 as the flotilla approached the ships carrying the British troops. They had debarked from ports as far east as Haifa and Beirut, a massive armada slowly accumulating its members. Every so often he turned his eyes to the sky, scanning for German aircraft. He expected to be spotted; he feared a massive aerial attack. But the enemy never appeared.

Frogmen and submarines sent to survey the invasion beaches under cover of darkness returned with disturbing news—sand bars in the 45th landing area meant the approach to the beach was shallower than expected. The plan for getting most men to shore aboard LCVPs would have to be altered.[13]

Admiral Kirk rounded up rubber rafts for the assault vessels, but it was at best a partial solution. Unable to come up with something better, Bradley turned in that night and had a restless sleep. A few days before, he and Patton had agreed they had a fifty-fifty chance of dying during Husky. Tonight it was not so much his own death as that of others that kept him awake.[14]

The weather presented a foreboding glimpse of disaster the morning of July 9. Less than twenty-four hours before the planned assault, the waves rose as thirty-five mile an hour winds whipped the ocean into a white-frothed frenzy. Stomachs heaved, Bradley's among them. The forecasters had promised the weather would clear by the next morning. It was a good thing: Bradley believed the operation was too far gone to be canceled for anything short of a hurricane.

The long and slow passage was nearly over, but for Bradley the time at sea had been literally a pain in the backside—he developed a severe case of hemorrhoids. With the pain increasing the morning of July 9, he went to the ship's doctor to see if could get some relief. The doctor decided to remove them, and Bradley found himself confined to his rack (or ship's bed), where the rolling waves quickly made him seasick.[15]

Around 1:00 a.m., Navy aides came and woke Bradley and his staff. The ship was in the Gulf of Gela, off the southwestern shore of Sicily, and the invasion force was just organizing for the run into the beaches. Up on the bridge, the officers could see searchlights peeking out from the land. Bradley's aide Chet Hansen felt a stab of tension as one came toward the ship. Then suddenly it flicked off. The night was quiet.

It remained that way for another two hours. Finally, gunfire rocked the stillness: the support ships in the invasion fleet began bombarding the shore defenses. The attack was deafening.

H-Hour had been set for 0245, or 2:45 a.m., in full darkness and full tide. The sandbars and the usual confusion of war set back the timetable slightly, but Ranger Force X swarmed ashore in Gela around 0300. A blast from rockets aboard one of their landing craft hit an ammo dump, causing an explosion that could be seen from Bradley's ship. Running a gamut of pillboxes and minefields, the Rangers took the town, storming a group of Italians in the cathedral. Force X would repel counterattacks from Italian and German tank units through the daylight hours, holding firmly to the strategic spot.

The first units from the 1st Infantry Division landed east of the town a little past 3:30 a.m. The division found light resistance at first, though the men had to contend with mines and other obstructions before moving off the beach. Their most difficult enemy was confusion, as the long shallow approach to land made for a complicated improvisation between the large and small landing craft. But by daylight the division was well on its way to its first day objective.

Things were more difficult further to the east near Scoglitti, the right hand of II Corps assault. The 45th Infantry Division was bedeviled by mistakes. The first landing craft hit the wrong beaches. The sandbars, the waves, smoke from the shipboard guns—the assault was a typhoon of chaos. Troops were landed in the wrong place. Beachmasters closed beaches to new troops, directing the landing craft to hastily scouted alternatives. Units were split up, plans changed, rechanged, then changed again. Fortunately, the defenders were as confused as the invaders. Many fled, cowed by the big guns of the support fleet. The landing succeeded with a minimum of casualties.

As confused as the seaborne invasion was, the parachute assault was even more bedeviled. The 82nd Airborne Division, under Patton's direct command, had been tasked to land some 3,000 paratroopers around Piano Lupo north of Gela, cutting off any counterattacks and efforts to reinforce the forces near the beachhead. It was the first nighttime combat jump in American military history, which made it difficult enough. The troops jumped into a wind estimated at thirty-five miles an hour, which made it even harder. And the fleet of C-47s got lost soon after takeoff, which made the mission impossible.

Only one out of six paratroopers landed close to where he was supposed to.[16] About 200 managed to reach Piano Lupo. Another 275 were scattered around the area where the 1st Infantry Division was attacking. The rest were distributed around the island in small, vulnerable knots. The paratroopers spent much of their time on that first night and the next day getting their bearings and organizing themselves. However, their dispersion had a silver lining: they were able to harass the enemy in small groups, contributing to the Axis forces' confusion.

By far the best experience of the invasion belonged to the 3rd Infantry Division. The troops took Licata in a virtually unopposed textbook landing. Marching inland, they were greeted by children who flashed the V sign.[17]

Bradley spent a fitful day aboard ship, sorting through the messages with his staff. It's likely that he had been planning on going ashore by the first afternoon, but the hemorrhoid operation made that impossible.[18] Instead, he had to content himself with reading the different dispatches from the units and speaking to his commanders by radio and messenger.

The overall picture seemed promising, but the distance from ship to land made everything feel unreal. Hansen, working at the general's side most of the day, said the ship felt unnaturally safe.[19] It was as if the war only truly existed on shore.

The Navy bombardment continued throughout the day. It was so intense Bradley could feel the pounding beneath his feet as he walked on the deck, even though his ship had no guns to fire. He kept pacing the wardroom that had been turned into his temporary command post, wanting to get ashore.

He finally sent Hansen in his place. The young aide was amazed by the confusion and baffled when he saw that many of the houses had somehow survived the bombardment without being damaged. But the overall impression he came away with was positive—the beachhead had been firmly established.

Coming back to the ship to report, Hansen started across a hastily positioned gangplank. He missed his footing in the dark. Falling, he managed to grab onto the Jacob's ladder—a flexible ladder at the side of the vessel hanging down for just such emergencies. He got a full bath nonetheless, and made his report "wringing wet."

General, he said, *I recommend you spend the night ashore.*

Why, wondered Bradley.

It's much safer. The ships are sure to be bombed.

Bradley laughed, and told him not to worry.[20]

Bradley made it ashore early the next morning, July 11, riding first on an LCVP, then transferring to a DUKW that took him into Scoglitti. He had to sit on a life preserver to spare his still wounded backside.

The DUKWs would prove to be one of the most invaluable vehicles of the war. They were also the strangest looking. They might be best described as a boat with a truck chassis built into the bottom. Manufactured by General Motors, the "Duck" measured thirty-one feet long and about eight feet wide. The pressure in the tires could be adjusted from inside the open cabin, a first. Trundling from the soft sand of the beach to the hard road, the DUKW driver would adjust the tire pressure, allowing the ungainly looking amphibious vehicle to drive on the road nearly as well as a truck. The vehicle was slow in the water, and not particularly speedy on land, but its versatility was unmatched.

Bradley found the Cent Force beach a confusing and "dismal"[21] sight. Lifebelts and other discarded paraphernalia were scattered in the surf and sand. But confident that the light resistance would allow the division to pull itself together without too much trouble, he made his way west to Gela where the 1st Infantry Division had landed.

The scene became grimmer as he went. Dead bodies and burned out trucks lined the road. The Luftwaffe, though vastly outnumbered, attempted to attack the invaders and their ships, buzzing dangerously overhead.[22]

Bradley arrived at the division command post just as the Hermann Goering Panzer Division was making a counterattack, trying to shove the Big Red One back into the sea. The division, short of artillery and anti-tank units, faced an assault by two different elements of German Panzers.

General Allen had rallied every available truck to help haul artillery pieces off the landing craft so they could be used for defense. Meanwhile, the infantrymen dug in above the beach, ducking as the German tanks literally rolled over them. Then they rose and began firing at the German infantrymen coming behind the armor. Shells flew from the ships at sea.

Bradley discovered that Patton had ordered one of the division's units to move out of position, exposing Allen's flank. Bradley solved the problem by shifting part of the 2nd Armored Division against the position, plugging a potentially disastrous hole.

After a tenacious fight, the enemy was halted about a mile and a half from the beach. Bradley credited Allen and the 1st Infantry Division with an incredible job on the beach, saying in *A Soldier's Story* that "only the perverse Big Red One with its no less perverse commander was both hard and experienced enough to take that assault in stride."[23]

What Bradley did not do in the memoir was express his anger at how Patton had helped jeopardize the division.

Patton had visited earlier in the day, before the German counterattack. He complained bitterly about Allen's alleged slow pace. The division at that point had failed to take the airfield that was its first day objective; he wanted it taken. In the process, Patton countermanded Bradley's directions that Allen hold a position that covered the gap between the two landing areas. Patton's directions essentially had the division go around opposition and leave some of its area lightly defended in an attempt to get further inland. Left uncorrected, the move would have given the German attackers a way not just to hit the 1st Division flank, but to split the entire landing force, jeopardizing the 45th Division as well.

Patton had ignored the chain of command; any order of that magnitude should have gone to Bradley, who would have been in a better position to focus on its overall effect. This always angered Bradley, who was as jealous of his prerogatives as commander as any general. But in this case, Bradley saw the command as particularly ruinous, given the potential consequences. Given how the battle went, it's difficult to argue against Bradley.

Bradley later complained to Patton, who apologized. But at some point afterwards, Patton told Eisenhower that Bradley had not been aggressive enough, using the situation on the beach as an example. The criticism—clearly unfair—has generally been accepted without analysis by historians and used to argue that Bradley was an overly cautious general. One can only wonder what the verdict would have been and who would have gotten the blame if Allen's troops had been routed from the beach.

One last thing was characteristic of the incident—Bradley did not mention it in *A Soldier's Story*, and it seems only to have been added to *A General's Life* because his co-author deemed it important.[24]

With things under control and the counterattacks repulsed, Bradley got back in his DUKW and rode back to Scoglitti. In town, he took his carbine with him as he looked over several hundred Italian POWs. Approaching the prisoners, he handed the rifle to Hansen.

As the aide grabbed the gun, he somehow managed to get his finger into position to fire. A shot rang out; someone yelled "sniper!" and everyone scurried for cover.

Except Bradley.

"Chet," he growled as the others dusted themselves off. "Be careful with that damned thing, please."[25]

The 45th Division took Comiso airfield on July 11. The enemy was so confused that three German aircraft landed there a few hours later without realizing the airfield was under American control. They were all promptly captured.

But confusion on the American side that same night led to one of the worst friendly fire incidents of the war.

A little past 10:30 p.m., a group of C-47s began crossing in over the fleet, headed toward land. They were the vanguard of a 144-plane fleet filled with 82nd Airborne paratroopers headed toward Farello airdrome, where after landing they were to be stationed as reserves. Orders had been issued warning Navy and ground units that the planes were coming.

Watching from the village of Scoglitti, Bradley could hear the planes approaching. Suddenly the night sky turned white with exploding shells. The Navy and the units on shore had mistaken the airplanes for enemy attackers. Though he knew what was happening, there was little he could do. Within moments, roughly half the force was damaged, with twenty-three planes shot down. A total of 410 men would be officially counted dead in the fiasco.[26]

An investigation later showed that many of the units, both Army and Navy, had not received the orders about the airborne units. It was never clear whether the Navy or the Army fired first. Paratroopers and the crews who crash-landed faced fire from the foot soldiers on shore as well.

Despite such costly screw-ups, II Corps made rapid gains after the first wave of Axis counterattacks were repulsed. On the night of the 11th, Bradley sat working in his mobile command post, checking his maps and transposing the squiggles to his understanding of the terrain. His intelligence officer climbed up into the truck and told him that an Italian soldier had just been grabbed nearby. He was wearing civilian clothes.

A spy? Bradley asked Dickson.

Just a soldier who'd been home on leave when the attack began, replied the intelligence officer. Most of the Italian soldiers in the nearby front who were Sicilian had no will to fight, Dickson added. They were scared and would just as soon go home.

Maybe we should let them, suggested Bradley.

Dickson suggested they start rumors to that effect; Bradley laughed and told him to go ahead.[27]

It wasn't an idle idea. Dickson's intelligence showed that the Sicilians hated the Germans, and he correctly surmised that they would present no danger to the American forces if they were simply allowed to desert and go back to their farms. The fact that it was harvest time on the island gave them added incentive. Meanwhile, just letting them go would solve a lot of problems for the Americans. Processing and holding the prisoners had consumed considerable manpower and resources in North Africa.

Bradley was turned down when he tried to get official approval for his plan. Regardless, Dickson's campaign proceeded, not only through agents spreading rumors, but with leaflets. Assured clemency or not, Italian soldiers deserted by the bushel. There were so many in fact, that the Allied Command finally authorized "parole" for Sicilian prisoners of war on July 28. Some 33,000 Sicilian prisoners were allowed to return to their farms.

The populace itself had turned bitterly anti-Fascist, and especially anti-German. In an unpublished memoir, Dickson wrote that "the Germans had sowed another crop in Sicily—hatred.... The harvest began with the nocturnal stabbing of German soldiers found singly or in pairs and it did not end with the assassination of a colonel by a hand grenade tossed by an Italian soldier."[28]

Fragging and desertion was part of the general disintegration of the Italian armed forces and, ultimately, the Fascist regime. On July 25, Mussolini was removed by the Italian king; kept under guard, he would be rescued by the Germans and restored to power in what was essentially a puppet government later that fall. In the meantime, the war would continue in Italy through the spring of 1945, as ferocious as ever.

The initial plan called for II Corps to take the Vizzini-Caltagirone road about twenty-five miles from the beaches. By July 14, troops from the 45th Division had the road within artillery range; the objective would soon fall. Patton, onshore in Gela, called Bradley in for a consultation.

The road gave Bradley's divisions access to routes north. Bradley must have expected that they were going to talk about the next stage of the assault. Using the road, II Corps could have moved up the island and attempted to flank the Germans opposing Montgomery near the coast.

But when Bradley arrived and found Patton in the middle of a thick cloud of cigar smoke, he heard news he hadn't expected:

Alexander had just ordered the Americans to vacate the Vizzini-Caltagirone road so Montgomery could use it.

Bradley was incredulous. The order meant that II Corps would have to halt its advance. Its role in the attack, paltry to begin with, had just been reduced to bystander.

Looking at Patton's map, Bradley's first thought was that he could move the 45th Division to the west along the road, ceding the area to the British while still making some use of their gains. With the 1st Infantry Division still moving northward, this would leave him in position to take Enna and a strategic road area to its south known as The Hub. But the orders from Alexander were clear—the 45th Infantry Division had to be kept completely off the road. Bradley was being instructed to take the division back to the southwest, passing below his 1st Division in the process.

In short, the division was to return to the beachhead, giving up its gains completely.

The orders were galling for many reasons, not the least of which must have been Bradley's knowledge that Montgomery's forces were making slow progress. A quick attack by Bradley on the German flank would undoubtedly relieve the pressure—but Montgomery wanted to make that attack himself. (And in fact, he had already given orders to his units to do so.)

Bradley saw this as a slap in the face of the American Army. But what really bothered him was that Patton would not protest the orders.

The decision changed the tenor of what might have been a fast drive northwards. The delay caused by the exchange—or rather replacement—helped the Germans regroup at a point when speed was exactly what was needed. It's not surprising that Bradley viewed the orders as an example of Montgomery's ego going out of control, and Alexander's acquiescence as an example of both distrust in the Americans' ability and a determination to favor the British no matter what.

Bradley pressed Patton, but Patton refused to question the orders, indicating they were a *fait accompli* and he must comply quickly. Various historians and biographers have expressed confusion over Patton's passivity. Some hypothesize that Patton felt he was about to be relieved by Eisenhower, and thus was in no position to question anything.[29] There are various other theories, including the supposition that the road directive was supposed to be a suggestion from Alexander rather than an order—an outlandish theory given that Montgomery was already moving his troops. The simple explanation here seems the best: Alexander didn't trust the Americans and made an extremely poor tactical decision based on this mistrust and perhaps a lack of information. Patton didn't push it, because Patton never pushed issues like this with his commanders unless they actively solicited his advice.[30]

Bradley had no option but to carry out his orders. His displeasure was obvious to his staff, but characteristically he displayed it by acting more controlled and growing even quieter than normal.

With the 45th Division gone, the Canadian 1st Division moved forward on the road. Immediately it ran into heavy resistance. Ironically, some commentators have criticized Bradley for the abruptness of his withdrawal, saying that he did not coordinate with the Canadians and failed to provide artillery support which would have helped them. The artillery, of course, had been pulled back to accommodate the general withdrawal, a fact that the critics don't seem to have grasped.

During the "side-slip" as Bradley called it, he decided to relieve the commander of 180th Regimental Combat Team, part of the 45th Division. He asked Patton to name Lieutenant Colonel Darby to the command.

It was an impeccable choice. Darby's accomplishments creating and training the Rangers were well-known before the invasion. His personal courage was beyond question. During the battle for Gela, the colonel had grabbed an anti-tank gun and personally led an attack against the marauding armor. He was a natural choice for the job, which entailed a promotion to full colonel.[31]

Patton approved the promotion, but instead of simply putting orders through, he decided to talk to him about it. Patton was awarding Darby with a DSC for his bravery at Gela,[32] and Bradley went along to congratulate him.

Take the job, Patton told Darby, and you'll be a colonel in the morning. He added that a thousand colonels would love to be in his position.

Darby looked over at Bradley and asked if he actually had a choice—something he noted was unusual in the Army.

Patton told him he did.

"Thanks anyhow," Darby answered, "but I think I'd better stick with my boys."[33]

Even turned down, Bradley admired the colonel and his Rangers' *esprit de corps*. He had a similarly high opinion of the 82nd Airborne's paratroopers. In his memoir, Bradley writes with some admiration of stopping during a drive to the 45th Division command post to pick up a hitchhiker from the 82nd Airborne. The soldier, it turned out, had gone AWOL from a hospital and was trying to get back to the fight.[34]

Bradley let him go on his way after giving him a lift, though making sure to take his name first so he would be removed from the missing rolls.[35]

The commander of the 180th Regiment whom Bradley was considering removing was Colonel Forest E. Cookson. Bradley had several good reasons to replace him. His personal manner tended to make people think him nervous and indecisive. On D-Day, he had been left off on the wrong beach and failed to reach his unit for thirty hours.

The regiment had other problems demonstrating a lack of military discipline and, in Bradley's eyes, leadership. At some point on July 14, after Bradley had been turned down by Darby, one of the companies under the 180th command was involved in a massacre of enemy POWs.

Sergeant Horace T. West was supervising a group of forty-six prisoners, marching them behind the lines. Nine were to be interrogated; the others were simply to be processed as prisoners of war. Suddenly West separated out the nine designated for interrogation, borrowed a Thompson submachine gun and ammo from the company first sergeant, and gunned the others down. He reloaded and continued firing, walking among all of the prisoners until he was sure they were dead.

A second massacre of prisoners took place later that day, this time under orders from Captain John Travers Compton. Thirty-six men were killed by an ad hoc firing squad ordered by Travers.[36]

News of the massacres traveled quickly; among those who would soon bear witness were a 45th Division chaplain and two war correspondents. Bradley heard of the incident involving Travers and was so appalled he drove to Patton's headquarters to tell him about it. Patton at first didn't believe it was true, thinking it must be an exaggeration. He was willing to cover it up—in fact, he suggested that Bradley have the captain "certify the dead men were snipers or had attempted to escape or something."[37]

Bradley would have none of that. He was outraged by the injustice, the violation of basic soldiering, and the fact that an officer had been involved. After an investigation conducted by the 45th Division inspector general determined that the men had been killed in cold blood, Bradley pressed Patton to try the men responsible. Patton eventually agreed.[38]

The defense in the captain's case argued that Travers had merely carried out Patton's general order to kill snipers. The prosecution didn't bother to cross-examine the captain, who never had to explain why he thought prisoners who were stripped to the waist were snipers. He was acquitted, but died in action in Italy that November.

Sergeant West, though convicted and sentenced to life imprisonment, was granted clemency in November 1944 on the grounds that the crime had been committed during temporary insanity.[39]

Bradley put morality and justice at the forefront of his soldier's code, and he was furious when these virtues were violated by his own army or others. He complained bitterly about the Germans' indiscriminate use of mines—not just to cover their retreats, where there was a military purpose, but promiscuously in places where civilians were likely to encounter them. Bradley correctly predicted that they would be a problem long after the war ended.[40]

The Germans, in Bradley's view, fought with a savagery that caused needless deaths to both sides. He was especially angered by episodes where German soldiers, pretending to surrender, lured Americans to their deaths. But rather than suggesting revenge, or using these crimes to excuse his own troops, Bradley held his men to a higher standard. His childhood home may not have been overtly religious, but Bradley believed a soldier had to be a moral—even a righteous—man.

Shortly after the landing, Bradley's staff set up his command post around a large truck that Bradley used as a combination office and bedroom.

While many commanders took over vacated houses, Bradley liked more flexibility. He spent a large portion of his day—at least five hours— traveling to his division command posts, with visits to a variety of subcommands along the way. Part of this was necessity, as the mountains and hills of Sicily made it difficult for the radios of the time to communicate, securely or otherwise. But he also liked to see the men he spoke to, and insisted on visiting the terrain he was fighting in firsthand. With his army advancing, his command post had to keep up.

The rear of his two and a half-ton Army truck had been converted into a sort of travel trailer including a primitive toilet and sink. There was just enough room for Bradley's bed, a small table that functioned as his desk, and a campaign map of II Corps' area. Bradley would stare at the map for literally hours at night, unable to sleep, thinking about what tactics should be used the next day.

The intense circumstances under which he lived and worked drew him close to the people around him, not just his staff officers but his driver and orderly as well. Given his rank and age, Bradley became something of a surrogate father to them. His driver, Sergeant Alex Stout, confessed to reporter Ernie Pyle that the general even helped him out with small loans.[41]

Stout was a 23-year-old Cajun who had started driving for Bradley back in the States. Like many NCOs who work for high-ranking officers, the sergeant could be something of a mother hen at times, even to the point of insisting that Bradley take a half-hour or hour "off" by driving to some secluded but peaceful spot in the countryside. His jeep was outfitted with a box for food, and he added a special cushion salvaged from a German tank to make the seat more comfortable on the general's still ginger backside. Bradley trusted Stout's driving implicitly, valuing the sergeant's ability to drive quickly even in blackout conditions on the hairpin roads.[42]

When the distances were too great or time too precious, Bradley turned to a small Piper Cub flown by Captain Delbert L. Bristol, a fellow Missourian who hailed from Kansas City. The pilot had christened the plane Missouri Mule II; Missouri Mule I had flown in Tunisia, where it was so battered that it had to be abandoned.

The Piper Cub was an impressive aircraft, versatile and able to land in relatively short distances, a real asset in Sicily where the roads rarely had long straight-aways. But it was primitive even by the standards of 1943. Designed as a trainer, the aircraft sat two, a pilot and a passenger, one behind the other in an extremely narrow cockpit. Each place had duplicate controls. Starting the plane was a two-man operation—inside the plane, Bradley would pull open the throttle and toe down on the brake while Bristol turned over the prop.

All this travel made Bradley somewhat vulnerable to the enemy, and while he was usually far enough behind the lines to avoid being a target of rifle fire, he was used to being under shellfire. Nor was that the only danger from the enemy.

One afternoon while visiting Terry Allen, an alert sounded that forced him and the others to jump into a nearby slit trench. Bradley looked up in disbelief as a group of American A-36s strafed the headquarters area.

As soon as they left, he grabbed the phone and called Patton.

"Who told you they're our planes?" asked Patton. "Maybe they were German."

"General, I just climbed out of a ditch," replied Bradley. "They're A-36's all right."[43]

★ ★ ★ ★

While Bradley was rearranging his divisions and preparing to move northwards, the 3rd Infantry Division operating directly under Patton took Agrigento and Porto Empedocle. On the 17th, Alexander sent orders formally dividing the island and making clear that the American Seventh Army was to simply sit and protect Montgomery's Eighth Army.

Patton sprang into action. He visited Alexander and mapped out his vision of a dash around to Palermo. Intelligence had made it clear that the Germans had decided to pull their units back into the eastern portion of the island. With the Italian divisions disintegrating, Patton told Alexander that he would have an easy time getting to Palermo.

Taking Palermo would give the Americans a large port to funnel supplies through, obviating the need to use Syracuse. Alexander agreed.

Momentarily, at least. On July 19, he sent orders telling Patton that Seventh Army was to drive northwards and cut Sicily in half *before* taking Palermo. But Patton's chief of staff decided to lose the half of the orders commanding Patton not to set out for Palermo, claiming they had arrived garbled. By the time they were resent, it was too late to stop the drive without a major disruption.[44]

Meanwhile, Bradley had completed his sidestep and was moving north toward Enna. Still bringing in supplies over the beaches, he had trouble keeping his troops adequately stocked with bullets and food. The Seventh Army headquarters, theoretically in charge of supplies, was of little help. Bradley's frustration grew as he struggled to deal with such mundane problems as the lack of adequate maintenance depots. He had to appeal directly to Patton after complaints from his own supply and engineer corps; inevitably, Patton would brush him off, referring him to his staff for logistics matters.

Bradley would remember these problems when he planned for Normandy. But at the time, the experience was extremely frustrating. II Corps eventually began directing much of the supply itself.

Alexander's division of the island left Enna in the British sector. The 1st Canadian Division made slow progress toward it. Having trouble on the main road, the Canadians detoured eastward, seemingly maneuvering to bypass the walled Sicilian city, which was perched in the mountains.

In theory, the movement left Bradley's right flank exposed; he explains this at some length in *A Soldier's Story*, claiming that he was unwilling to risk the possibility of a raid.[45] Bradley may have been overstating the threat; the Axis soldiers held a strong defensive position, but it is far from clear that they could have launched an offense from there. In any event, he seized the chance to take Enna, launching two regiments from the 1st Division against it over the Canadian roads.

The battle was short: the Germans, realizing they could be easily cut off and surrounded, fled. The city belonged to the Allies, and the commander of the Canadian division sent Bradley two bottles of Scotch. Later, the BBC announced that the British and Montgomery had captured the city—a report so ironic that Bradley remembered it wryly years after the war. It was hardly the last time the British—and Montgomery specifically—would be credited with a victory Bradley's troops had won.

Meanwhile, Patton was racing around the western half of Sicily with the 82nd Airborne, 3rd Infantry, and 2nd Armored Divisions, aiming toward Palermo.

Bradley thought the plan foolish. A charge north by those units along the route Bradley was taking or a little to the west would have put the bulk of Seventh Army in place for a strike against Messina much more quickly. Given that ample intelligence showed that the Germans were determined to escape toward Messina and get their army across to the mainland if necessary, Bradley's objections made enormous strategic sense. His troops were in Caltanissetta on July 18; that was about halfway to the northern shore, or a little under forty miles as the crow flies. The round-about approach to Palermo wasn't necessarily the best way there, either: elements of the 45th were near the city July 22 when the 3rd Infantry arrived.[46]

With Montgomery moving much slower up the coast than anticipated—or the Americans moving faster, depending on the perspective—Alexander once again changed his orders, finally authorizing the Seventh Army to press against the Germans. But he was vague with the details, seemingly leaving them to the two army commanders to work out.[47] Patton flew to Syracuse July 25 to meet Montgomery and discuss plans for the final phase of the campaign.

There shouldn't have been much doubt on what these would be. The location of the forces and the geography of the island dictated strategy. Mount Etna and the nearby mountains squeezed both the north and eastern approaches to Messina. Montgomery, already on the coast, needed to proceed north while protecting his flank in the hills to the west. Patton could attack along the northern coast, but would also have to protect his flank to the south. This meant taking Highway 113 hugging the coast, and Route 120, which ran along Mount Etna's flank, taking a twisting route in the foothills.[48]

This end game was essentially what had been recommended in the plan Montgomery rejected before the campaign. Apparently realizing he couldn't reach Messina without additional pressure on the Germans from the north, he suggested it now, somewhat to Patton's amusement.

Bradley, already on the northern coast of the island, had been getting ready for a right turn since at least July 22.[49] The overall outline of his plan was simple—the 45th Division would go along the coast, and 1st Division would move through the interior, using the road and feeders that ran between Mount Pelaot and Etna. Among the major towns fortified in the area were Nicosia and Troina.

Strengthened with troops from the 9th Infantry Division arriving through the port of Palermo, the 1st Division pushed on. The twisting roads and sharp valleys made it hard for the attackers to mass quickly. The altitude and soil made for little vegetation, which meant little cover. Still, the Big Red One made steady progress.

The German positions in front of Montgomery's Eighth Army were anchored by a defensive line in the valley that the Americans were storming into. If the Americans broke through, the Germans would be forced to retreat on Montgomery's front as well. Troina, controlling the road east, held the key.

The area was defended by the 15th Panzer Grenadier Division, which stiffened as the Americans moved forward. The division was flanked on the north by parts of the 29th Panzer Grenadier Division; to the south, elements of the Herman Goering Division held the hills.

The Big Red One took Nicosia on July 28 and began looking eastward toward Troina. Heavy rains July 29 enraged the mountainside streams, adding local flooding and mud to the usual demons of mines and machine-guns. Intelligence reports indicated that the Germans were preparing to retreat. Dickson, Bradley's G-2, predicted that Troina would only be lightly held as the enemy moved through it. The 1st Division also believed that the German morale was low, and the defenders would scatter if pressed.

On July 31, Allen sent forces to take Cerami, a small town and a nearby hilltop to the west of Troina. There was resistance, but the attack went well and the objectives were taken. Bradley came out to the command post of the 39th Infantry Regiment (a 9th Division unit attached to the 1st Division) to see what was going on. Allen's plans called for the regiment to take Troina by itself. Bradley thought this would be adequate. Like everyone else, he assumed that the town was lightly held, and in fact was making plans to exchange the 1st Division with the 9th once the town was taken.[50]

The commander of the 39th was Colonel Harry A. "Paddy" Flint. Flint was a character in the best sense of the word.

Bradley had met Flint in Africa, and recommended him to 9th Division General Manton Eddy to "spark up" the 39th. Flint had imbued the regiment with his personal motto: "Anything Anytime Anywhere, Bar

Nothing." The colonel chalked it as AAA on his helmet—a uniform violation Bradley pretended not to see, even when Eddy pointed it out.[51]

It was hardly the only uniform violation Flint was guilty of—he would reportedly strip off his shirt and, wearing pants and scarf, visit his men topless near the front, daring Nazi sharpshooters to hit him.[52]

Flint's leadership and moxie were both tested as soon as the Germans counterattacked that night and threw his unit off a key hill to the west. The counterattack was so fierce and decisive that Allen had to change his plans for taking Troina.

On the afternoon of August 2, Bradley drove to Allen's command post at Cerami, roughly five miles as the crow flies from Troina. He was amused to see that the Fascist slogans still covered the walls. The artillery had started to lash the German positions in the hills, and the gunfire was so intense that it drowned out the generals' conversation. Bradley finally looked at Allen and suggested wryly that the artillery fire over the school, not through it.

Both Bradley and Allen still thought taking the town itself would be relatively easy. But their men were already realizing the situation was much more serious. At the 26th Regiment, Colonel John Bowen warned Allen when he got the orders for a new attack that the Germans were well dug in and would be able to strike at the assault as it launched the attack. He also said that there was a considerable enemy force in the hills—not the token defenders that earlier intelligence had predicted.

By the end of the day, the colonel had been proven right—the new attacks faltered under withering defensive artillery fire. Attacks on August 3 took the 1st Division closer to its goal, but left Troina still out of reach. A fifty-minute air and artillery bombardment on August 4 battered the Germans. Bradley watched the raid from a turn in the road near Cerami. He counted thirty-six light bombers—A-36's laden with 500-pound bombs—and watched as they dropped their weapons, producing an immense cloud of gray dust over the city. But at the end of the day, the Germans still held their ground.

The battle was finally turned by the 60th Regiment, arriving from the 9th Infantry Division. The regiment, with engineers to help it make the

steep passage, was sent along a dirt road in the direction of Mount Camo-
lato. The move allowed the unit to threaten the Troina defenses with its
artillery. Worse, the maneuver would make it possible for the Americans
to swing around and take Cesaro in the German rear; this would cut off
all possibility of retreat. On August 5, the German commander began a
withdrawal. American troops entered Troina without resistance at noon
August 6. It was a battered wreck.

Before those troops entered the city, Terry Allen received word that
he was being relieved as division commander; Roosevelt was also relieved.
The timing and circumstances were peculiar, and while Bradley says it
was his decision to relieve them, what exactly happened remains a matter of conjecture and controversy. Because the full story has never been
told, it's become something of a *Rashomon* for interpretations of Bradley's treatment of commanders during the war.

While disappointed with Allen's performance in Africa, Patton and
Bradley had agreed to keep Allen with the division through the Sicilian
campaign, at least until a good time came to change commanders. That
was where matters stood until July 25, when Major General Clarence
Huebner, who'd been posted as an American liaison to Alexander, was
dismissed from Alexander's staff.

That same day, Bradley was preparing to move the 1st Infantry Division off the line, removing it for rest—and eventual retraining. The division, he told Eisenhower, was battle weary. Then he added, in his
handwritten note, that the problem was more Allen and Roosevelt than
the division itself, suggesting that they be replaced.[53]

Right around this time, Patton heard of Huebner's dismissal. He'd
always had a high opinion of him, and either on his own or after speaking to Bradley decided he would be a perfect leader for the 1st Division.
Patton wrote a letter to Eisenhower asking that Huebner be named to
replace Allen. (Patton definitely spoke to Bradley about the matter; it's
just not clear how to divvy up "credit" for the decision, if such a thing
can be divided.)

Major General Lucas hand delivered the letter to Ike July 28. Eisenhower immediately agreed, informing Marshall the same day. Patton then discussed the matter personally with Eisenhower on July 29, insisting that the moves be made without prejudice. (Removing Allen or Roosevelt *with* prejudice would strongly imply that they had been unfit, and would essentially have ended their careers. Even so, removing them without ready assignments would hardly be perceived as a promotion.)[54]

What happened next remains unclear. With the battle for Troina still raging, Allen and Roosevelt were informed that they were to be removed.[55] Yet they were told that it wasn't for cause, and indeed were kept on until the battle ended.

The consensus theory on how this happened was developed by historian Carlo D'Este in his book *Bitter Victory*. In essence, D'Este blames it on something that has plagued armies forever—a bureaucratic screwup. (D'Este also implies Patton and Eisenhower were responsible, not Bradley, a point that is somewhat more contentious.)[56]

According to D'Este's theory, the decision to replace Allen and Roosevelt had been made before the battle. (The 1st Division, battered by combat, was to be removed from the line after Troina, which would have made the end of that battle a natural point to inform the commanders.) Rather than being held back until the end of the battle as they should have been, the orders for the changeover were delivered by error in a routine pouch sent from II Corps to 1st Division.

Once received, the orders were passed to Allen, who called Bradley; Bradley, says D'Este, "lamely replied that he had had the orders for some time and was awaiting a time when the 1st Division was out of line before making the changeover. There had been a foul-up when the orders were sent via regular Adjutant General channels, he said. Then, 'Carry on, we'll sort this out later.'"[57]

Later that night, Patton called Allen and reiterated that he was still in charge.

It seems possible that the orders had been prepared without a date, awaiting the right time to be presented; somehow they were moved from one desk to another, and the process began erroneously. On the other hand, these were not routine orders covering movement of troops or the re-stocking of food supplies. A personnel change of that magnitude would ordinarily receive careful attention by staff. Mistakes, especially during times of stress, cannot be ruled out of course, but this would seem a very unusual one.

The biggest problem with the theory, though, is that Bradley never mentioned such a snafu. In fact, his published version of the affair is very different.

But it's clearly not true.

Bradley doesn't mention the availability of Huebner as a factor in Allen's replacement, and he more or less skips over the question of timing. Nor is there a mention of a bureaucratic snafu. According to *A Soldier's Story*, Bradley gave Allen and Roosevelt the news of their relief personally. He also doesn't mention that he essentially took over planning the tactics toward the end of the campaign there.

What he does say is that he decided to "break the news as gently as I could—for I knew it would shock them both."[58] He recalls that he called them to his command post in Nicosia, and as they were en route, they were stopped by MPs and ticketed for failing to wear their helmets.

As a punch line to the episode, Bradley says Allen remarked, "We get along a helluva lot better with the Krauts up front than we do with your people back here in the rear."[59]

It's an amusing bit of comic relief. But while it's certainly possible that Allen and Roosevelt were stopped at *some* point for not wearing their helmets, the incident's placement in the book seems highly suspicious. The story comes after two pages of justification for letting Allen and Roosevelt go, and seems more a character portrait lifted from somewhere else than a true recounting of events. The two certainly appear more than a little carefree for men about to be relieved in the midst of battle.

Perhaps the incredible timing of the incident with the MPs was true, just one of those odd things that happen in life and war. Or perhaps it was interposed by the cowriter trying to keep the story interesting and amusing. It does illustrate the point that Allen didn't take kindly to Bradley's (and Patton's) rules.

But what to make of the insistence by Bradley that he called them to his command post to break the news, when all of the evidence is to the contrary?

A lot is clearly missing, not just in Bradley's version, but in most historical retellings. The account in *A Soldier's Story* is an exception to the book's overall candor. Interestingly, Bradley doesn't run from the responsibility of firing Allen, who was an extremely popular commander. He does just the opposite.

So what was he hiding?

In Terrible Terry Allen, Allen's biographer Gerald Astor blames the firing largely on Allen's independent attitude toward discipline and his maverick attitudes. He believes, however, that alcohol and/or fatigue may have had a role.[60] Astor theorizes that the stress "could well have driven him to the bottle."[61] But he can't supply any evidence from the records one way or the other.

This isn't exactly surprising. Few fitness reports from the era refer to excessive drinking, though surely there must have been some. As Astor points out, American attitudes toward drinking at this point were ambivalent. But Allen's drinking was of a much higher magnitude than normal. There were plenty of rumors of his performance suffering from fatigue on Sicily, including ones that he was indisposed during battle—so much so that even Alexander mentioned he was sick.[62]

In the midst of the Troina battle, war correspondent Quentin Reynolds recorded an odd moment at Allen's headquarters. According to the account in Astor's book, Reynolds was present the night of August 1–2 during a briefing between Allen and his subcommanders. At some point in the middle of giving orders, Allen rose and asked to be excused. His officers and the reporters waited. Two of the correspondents finally went to look for Allen and found him in a grove a hundred yards away, kneeling in prayer.[63]

Reynolds' story has been taken at face value and cited in many works without the slightest hint of a raised eyebrow. But surely few commanders leave off giving orders in the middle of a briefing to go and pray. Even assuming a call of nature was involved, the way the reporter writes about the incident makes it clear that it was highly unusual. It begs speculation, especially given the more ample evidence that Allen had a drinking problem throughout his life, his somewhat questionable performance in battle that day and next—and the fact that he was notified that he was no longer going to command the 1st Infantry Division a few days later.[64]

If alcohol were involved, it's not surprising that Bradley wouldn't mention it. It's exactly the sort of thing he would be discreet about, considering it a moral failure rather than a professional one.[65]

Discussing the sacking of Allen, Bradley has sometimes been implicitly criticized by historians who suggest that the decision was based merely on a personality clash between the two men. Further, these arguments are often accompanied by descriptions of both generals that, perhaps unconsciously, make Bradley seem imperious and intolerant. The fact that he did not drink until he was well into his thirties (by his account) is often rolled out as an exhibit against him, as if temperance were a handicap.

But the criticism is unfair. Patton as well as Bradley wanted Allen removed. Allen's performance at Troina probably made Bradley act sooner rather than later. Whether Allen's performance was hampered by personal matters will simply never be known.

Bradley does seem to have had a nuanced view of Allen, Roosevelt, and the 1st Division. He believed that part of the discipline problems in the division stemmed from the fact that Allen and Roosevelt were too similar in their disdain for regulations. If one had been more of a stickler, Bradley said, as a pair they might have done much better. It was a variation on a strong Bradley theme—balance. In choosing Kean as his chief of staff, Bradley was consciously setting up a similar yin and yang, with himself as the more affable man in charge, and Kean the hard-liner.

The Big Red One was taken from the line for rest and retraining. It would return to action in France under Huebner and play a critical role in the conquest of Europe. Terry Allen and Ted Roosevelt would also play important roles in the rest of the war, Allen as division commander of 104th Division, and Roosevelt on the beaches of Normandy, where he landed in the first wave. Roosevelt died of a heart attack in July 1944; he was posthumously awarded a Medal of Honor for his bravery on D-Day.

Around the time the 1st Division was starting toward Troina, Chet Hansen came into Bradley's trailer and asked to speak with him. Bradley knew his young aide well enough by now to know that he had something unusual on his mind, but what Hansen said surprised him nonetheless.

Ernie Pyle wants to travel with you a few days, Hansen told him. *What about it?*

Bradley didn't hesitate:

No way.

Before the war, Ernie Pyle had been a successful newspaper columnist. His six-day-a-week column ran in the Scripps-Howard newspapers, a chain of twenty-four dailies, including the *Washington Daily News.* Pyle traveled across the country writing human interest stories on a variety of subjects, from off-beat personalities to the vagaries of living out of a suitcase. The columns were popular, giving Pyle a national following, but it wasn't until the war that he became a true journalistic superstar.

Pyle's portraits of the war in Europe, generally seen from the grunt's level, were among the best-read features in the newspapers, and even today are celebrated for their precision and authenticity. Pyle wrote in a deceptively simple style that elevated seemingly mundane details to touchstones of truth. By focusing on "ordinary" individuals—from workers caught in the London Blitz to privates on the line in Africa—he made the war personal in an era long before blogs and YouTube postings. Pyle's emphasis on the common man was revolutionary at the time; while there were instances of reporting on individual soldiers, for the most part war correspondents focused on the "big picture" of battle. Profiles, when they did them, tended to be on the generals leading the war.

Pyle reversed that, and in fact had not profiled a general until he approached Bradley.[66] Bradley of course knew who Pyle was, but if he understood the significance of the request, he wasn't flattered by it.

Hansen tried to convince Bradley to agree to give Pyle access by arguing that the families and friends of the 80,000 or so men entrusted to his care would like to know who the hell was watching over them.

Bradley laughed at Hansen's argument.

When does he want to start? he asked.

Pyle spent three days with Bradley, beginning each morning with a breakfast of powdered eggs and soybean cereal in the general's little mess tent across from the truck. Pyle then clambered into the jeep with Bradley and went with him to the division headquarters. They ate lunch together on the road, and on at least one occasion barely escaped a German dive-bombing together.

"I make no bones about the fact that I am a tremendous admirer of General Bradley," Pyle later wrote. "I don't believe I have ever known a person to be so unanimously loved and respected by the men around him."[67]

Bradley confesses that they were both somewhat wary of each other when they started, but the time together mellowed Bradley enough for him to open up publicly for one of the very few moments in his life. Surveying a German-held town—it's not mentioned which one it was, but from the time and circumstances it was probably Troina or one nearby—Pyle mentioned to Bradley that he could never do the general's job. He didn't want the responsibility of having to kill people.

Bradley admitted it was difficult—he didn't sleep well, he told the reporter. But though he hated ordering that a city be bombed—as he was going to here—it had to be done to win the war. He spoke of trying to wage his assaults to minimize the loss of his troops, though he admitted that this was not always possible. And then Bradley told the reporter that, as difficult as it was to give such orders, he'd spent his whole life preparing to do so, and it was surely easier for him than it would be for younger men.[68]

Pyle was notorious for going without his helmet in the battle zone, but at Bradley's insistence he wore it while he was with him. (Though he admitted they were uncomfortable, Bradley felt they prevented serious injury and death, and saw them as critical to discipline.) Bradley convinced him to wear it so the soldiers who saw him would as well, noting that if they traveled together they'd be near the front lines where it would most likely come in handy.

"It got to be a game with us," Bradley noted after the war. "He was almost swallowed up by his big steel helmet. It looked uncomfortable on him and it was uncomfortable. But so great was his heart that he never complained. But he never wore the helmet either except when I was around."[69]

A small but telling difference in the way Bradley and Pyle tell the story of their acquaintanceship illustrates another facet of Bradley's character.

Bradley claims in passing that he shared a small drink with Pyle each evening they were together. Pyle says there wasn't much liquor available and Bradley, being not much of a drinker to begin with, only treated his guests. (It may or may not have helped that Bradley preferred bourbon if he drank at all.) When writing *A Soldier's Story,* Bradley characteristically downplayed details or incidents that would make him appear more virtuous than the average man. One can search both his books in vain for a note about his giving his cigarettes away, or his lending money and advice to his driver; both are prominent parts of Pyle's columns about him, and by all testimony common occurrences during the war.

What attracted Pyle was the same thing that attracted many of the people who spent time with Bradley—he was truly a three-star general with a genuine democratic touch. In many ways, he still related to people the way he had watched his father relate to them in those long, chilly days back in Missouri.

★ ★ ★ ★

While the battle for Troina raged, the 3rd Infantry Division replaced the 45th in the north. Patton and Bradley had discussed the possibility of using amphibious landings to encircle German strongpoints and capture retreating units. As the Germans slowly retreated toward Messina, Patton decided that the 29th Grenadier Division in front of the 3rd Division was a candidate for just such an operation. He told Bradley and 3rd Division commander Lucian Truscott to plan a landing behind the village of San Fratello, where German guns on the high ground had slowed his attack. Bradley saw this as a problem—if the landing force was too small, it might be shredded by the Germans, even if they retreated. Truscott solved the problem by maneuvering his main body into a position to break through once the landing took place. The assault landed August 8 without opposition; the possibility of the rear envelopment helped force the Germans back—and led to the capture of 1,500 prisoners.

So far, so good. But then Patton called Bradley and directed that there be another assault, this one on August 11. General Truscott balked at the timing—he felt he needed another day.

Patton refused to allow the delay. Bradley drove to Patton's command post to personally push the request, sure that the landing would be too risky if the bulk of Truscott's force wasn't in position for a quick strike. By this time, Bradley had realized that Patton's primary goal on Sicily was not destroying the German Army, but rather reaching Messina ahead of the British. While these were closely related, they were not the same thing.

Bradley's patience with Patton was wearing thin. From the episode at Gela to the decision to divert to Palermo to a dozen minor instances that put ego ahead of military objectives, Bradley felt that Patton was not exercising good judgment in the campaign.

In Africa, Bradley had found Patton could generally be moved by reason. On Sicily, this was not always the case. It certainly wasn't in this instance, where Bradley's arguments were met with the blunt insistence that the assault move ahead. Patton himself visited Truscott, driving in a rush to the division commander's headquarters and threatening to replace him if he didn't carry out the attack on time.

The attack went ahead. It was a disaster. The self-propelled artillery and tanks got stuck in drainage ditches and found themselves unable to cross stone walls to support the assault on the town. Stuck near the beach, they were pounded by German artillery and tanks. The infantry companies that had landed held out desperately on a nearby hill, taking heavy casualties as their ammunition ran low.

Truscott had to push against the teeth of the enemy defenses in front of him to break the German lines and rescue his men. Relief finally found them the next morning.

The incident was one more sign to Bradley that Patton had lost touch with the proper role of an army commander. His theatrics had always nettled, but what was alarming on Sicily was his impetuousness. Patton was uselessly costing lives.

In some cases, Patton's unwillingness to listen bordered on the absurd. When he ordered an amphibious assault on Spadafora, Truscott and Bradley both pointed out that the 3rd Infantry Division's thrust was moving so fast the ground troops would reach the area before the boats could. Patton was so angry that he threatened to bust both men to colonel if they wouldn't carry out his orders.

"This, naturally, settled the matter," write Samuel W. Mitcham Jr. and Friedrich von Stauffenberg in their study of the Sicilian campaign, *The Battle of Sicily.*[70] The invasion went ahead on August 16—and, as Bradley had predicted, troops were on the beach waiting to greet those arriving from the sea.

It would have been one thing if the rush along the coast could have stopped the Germans from escaping to the mainland. But by this time it was obvious that the Germans were going to get off the island no matter what the Americans did.

Bradley was sitting in his truck August 12 when his chief of staff, William Kean, came in with a worried look on his face. Behind Kean was the corps surgeon, who had received a letter from the commander of the

93rd Evacuation Hospital. The letter detailed a visit Patton had made two days before. While at the hospital, Patton had encountered a soldier with no visible wounds. When the soldier was asked what was wrong with him, he replied that his nerves were shot.

Patton slapped him and yelled at him, called him a coward, and told him to get back to the front.

Bradley already knew about the incident, at least vaguely—Patton had told him about it that day, explaining why he had been late in his visit to Bradley's command post. In Patton's version, it was a single slap. In the report Bradley read now, the general had hit the man at least twice, striking him so hard a second time that his helmet flew off.

Bradley looked at the doctor.

Anyone else see this? he asked.

The doctor said no.

With the doctor dismissed, Bradley told Kean to take the report, seal it in an envelope marked for their eyes only, and lock it away in Bradley's safe.

Bradley would later claim that he could not have sent the report on to Eisenhower, since protocol dictated it go to Seventh Army command—Patton, in other words. But that claim is nonsense. Clearly he was covering up for Patton. As angry as he may have been with him—and there is ample evidence of his anger and disappointment in his memoirs—he was not interested in destroying Patton's career.

It's possible that on some level Bradley agreed, if not with the severity of Patton's actions, at least with the overall notion and intent. Battle fatigue and other combat-related stress ailments were poorly understood at the time, even by psychiatric professionals. While Bradley might have been compassionate on a personal level, he was also a soldier. His assessment in Africa was that the Army wasn't tough enough, wasn't bloodthirsty enough.

In *A Soldier's Story*, he says that he didn't think Patton was being brutal. It is war that is brutal. By yelling at the man and even hitting him, Patton simply took to an extreme what Bradley himself did when telling men they had to engage the enemy.

But regardless of what anyone believed about battle fatigue and stress, even in 1943 an officer's striking a soldier was a punishable crime. The fact that the commanding general of the Seventh Army did it in a hospital made it even more spectacular.

Bradley said later that he felt Patton was too important to be felled by the incident. He may have been protecting the Army as much as Patton. In any event, his actions didn't save Patton. Word of the incident rapidly spread through Sicily, and Eisenhower was soon informed. The incident remained secret for months, but it severely damaged Eisenhower's relationship with Patton.

Bradley's own relationship with Patton wasn't exactly soaring. The successful retreat by the Germans and their tattered Italian allies to mainland Italy left Messina open. Men from the 3rd Infantry Division reached the outskirts of the city on the evening of August 16. Patton decided he would enter Messina himself the next morning, and told Bradley that Truscott's units were not to go in until he arrived.

He also invited Bradley to join in a parade that would greet the British, rubbing the fact that the Americans had beaten them in Montgomery's face.

For Bradley, the whole matter was the latest sign of Patton's megalomania. Bradley claims in *A General's Life* that he was tempted to go into the city himself that night. That way he'd be standing on a street corner ready to greet him when he arrived.

More seriously, Bradley felt the delay cost the 3rd Division one last chance to kill Germans, which was after all their business on Sicily. He turned down the invitation.

Patton rode into Messina around 10:00 a.m. His car beat the first British unit by about an hour.[71]

The cost of the 38-day battle to take Sicily was fierce: the United States lost 2,237 men killed, and another 6,544 wounded or captured. The British, who had slugged away at the hills in the east, lost 2,721 dead, and another 10,122 wounded or captured. Axis casualties included 29,000 killed or wounded, with another 140,000 captured.[72]

But the bulk of those casualties were Italian, and most of those captured had given themselves up freely.

The Axis' successful evacuation across the channel between the island and the mainland meant that some 100,000 enemy soldiers and 10,000 vehicles remained in the war. They had not left in rout, but in an organized withdrawal that allowed them to preserve their gear and a good portion of their fighting spirit. The Allies would have to deal with them soon.

For Bradley, the campaign had been a long and arduous one. He had predicted beforehand that it would last forty days; he was off by two days. But there were many things he couldn't have predicted, and maybe wouldn't even have believed.

Africa had been an affirmation of everything he had worked toward for over thirty years. Commanding troops in combat for the first time, firing a weapon at the enemy for the first time, even learning to hate—it was all new, all excitement, all exhilaration.

Sicily was harder. It was a more complicated campaign, a longer one. It wore him down physically—if the photos at the end of the African campaign show him as a relatively youthful man of fifty, those at the end of Sicily, barely four months later, reveal a man who seems to have aged a decade. A lot of this might have been due to the lack of sleep, but heavy combat affected everyone.

That, and the necessity of ordering young men to their deaths, as Bradley had hinted to Pyle. Bradley may have held onto his reputation for calmness and rational thought, but that outer shell must have been hard won.

In Sicily, Bradley confronted many demons. He saw Patton's worst side, and had to face up to the fact that American soldiers—*his* soldiers, *his* officers—were capable of murder. And he saw proof that the reality of war—the mundane and the terrifying—would continue for a long time.

Was Bradley disillusioned by what he had seen in Sicily? There are hints in his memoir that he may have been: a note about Patton being brought low, remarks about Montgomery's ego. But if he was disillusioned, he never let on to his staff. It was not in his character to do so.

The remarkable thing about Bradley is not that he confronted war without breaking; other men, from privates to generals, have withstood such crucibles. What is remarkable about him is that he remained, to his peers, the same man. The ideals he began the war with—that there was a proper way for an officer to act, that there was a morality above war, above PR, and above the good of the Army—remained bedrock beliefs.

This is not to say that he could not be petty—he could snark about General Mark Clark and his abilities readily enough, for example. Nor should we elevate Bradley into an improbable stick figure of virtue. But it is a testament to the character that had been bred into him over the course of many long walks to and from school some forty years before. Bradley's command of tactics, his ability to organize logistics, and his knack for getting subordinates to do their jobs were all certainly important characteristics, all critical qualifications for his job as a general. His steadiness was apart from these. It was an intangible characteristic that led people—from his aides to Eisenhower—to say that he could be counted on.

And in war as in life, that is sometimes the most difficult quality to find in a man.

By the time Sicily fell, Eisenhower had recommended a plan to the Allied Command for the invasion of the Italian mainland. The plan called for Mark Clark to lead the Fifth Army in a landing at Salerno; the British Eighth Army under Montgomery would land at Taranto. Eisenhower tapped Bradley to serve as Clark's understudy—he would replace him if anything happened to Clark before the invasion. With Sicily now in

Allied hands, Bradley flew to Mostaganem in northern Africa to examine the invasion plans.

Planning for the campaign in southern Italy was as confused as that for Sicily, with the added uncertainty of political intrigue. The arrest of Mussolini brought a government that wanted desperately to surrender, and kicked off a separate intrigue as the Italian government sent feelers to the Allies indicating they wanted to surrender. Maxwell Taylor went secretly to Rome to discuss this possibility. An agreement was reached, but the Italians attempted to back out at the last minute. When Eisenhower tried to force their hand by announcing the agreement, the Germans moved quickly to formally take control of the country.

Arriving in Mostaganem August 25, Bradley discovered that Clark's Fifth Army would have two corps—one almost entirely British, the other American. He immediately felt uneasy over the mixing of the two nationalities in the same army structure. It hadn't worked well in Africa, and he couldn't see how it would work well now.

Worse, the invasion by the American corps was being spearheaded by the 36th Infantry Division, which had not yet seen action.

Bradley would hardly have time to brood on the deficiencies, much less do anything about them. The day he learned the outline of the plans for Italy, Marshall sent a cable to Eisenhower saying he wanted Bradley to command the American Army landings in France the following summer. Eisenhower balked—a long communication to Marshall August 27 seems to indicate that he wanted to substitute Bradley for Clark in Italy—but by the next day he had changed his mind and definitely settled on Bradley.[73] All that remained was to tell him.

CHAPTER 4

Overlord

Bradley shifted on his feet, watching as the photographers scrambled to take pictures of Montgomery and Eisenhower. Ike, all smiles, had a U.S. Army Legion of Merit badge in his hand. Flashbulbs exploded as he held it toward Montgomery's chest.

It was Sunday, August 29, 1943. Bradley, Patton, and Truscott, along with some of the Seventh Army staff, were at Catania in Sicily to watch Eisenhower award the medal to Montgomery. Bradley had never met Montgomery, but he had heard more than enough to prepare him for the general's conceit. The British commander seemed to positively preen before the cameras.

Patton, by contrast, was subdued. He was quiet at the grand lunch that followed the ceremony; later, Bradley learned that he had brought a handwritten apology to Eisenhower for the slapping incident.

The conquest of Sicily over, the generals were enjoying a brief respite from the fighting. There were no plans yet to use Seventh Army or

II Corps in the Italian invasion; the Allies lacked enough assault craft to do so. But any extended campaign in Italy would call for more troops, and the Seventh Army seemed a likely source. In the meantime, while Bradley struggled to bring himself up to speed on the Italian operation, his men were busy with occupation duties—sorting out Italian prisoners of war, and clearing away mountains of rubble and debris.

Lunch was an elegant affair, as it always was after a grand victory. Oliver Leese, the British general who headed Montgomery's XXX Corps, befriended Bradley, inviting him to watch his artillery provide support for the landing on the Italian mainland, planned for September 3. Bradley accepted, though the role of observer didn't particularly thrill him.

Lunch dragged on. Aside from a quick greeting, Eisenhower barely spoke to Bradley. Nor did he spend much time with Patton or the other Americans; today was Montgomery's day. His attentions confirmed what the American generals already believed—their boss was thoroughly in awe of the Brits. All of them, but especially Montgomery.

Who, if they had been asked for an opinion, had taken a *damn* long time getting north on the island despite having more resources than the Americans did and following a plan entirely his own.

Finally, Eisenhower rose. So did Montgomery. The British general was going to take Ike on a victory lap through Messina.

If ever there was a cue to go, that was it. Bradley, who in contrast to the subdued Patton confined his brooding to his truck and his maps, smiled, shook hands, and went back to Palermo.

He took off just in time. A few minutes after he was in the air, two German aircraft strafed the field.[1]

Over the next few days, Bradley brought himself up to speed on Clark's plans while juggling his responsibilities as II Corps commander. Early on the morning of September 2, his standby role now all but over, he set out to watch the invasion he had been understudying. It was a long drive from the other side of the island, and he was only a little past Brolo on the coast, still a good hour away, when a small airplane buzzed the jeeps.

Bradley recognized the plane as a Piper Cub. His first thought was that it was lost. But a second swoop revealed it as Missouri Mule II, his plane. One of his aides was looking for him.

Go on ahead, he told his driver. *If they're looking for us, they'll find a straightaway somewhere ahead.*

A short distance away, past the curves that hugged the hillside above the coast, Bradley saw Chet Hansen waving to him.

Patton wants to see you right away, Hansen told him. *It's important.*

Bradley reluctantly climbed aboard the aircraft and flew back to Palermo. There he telephoned Patton and asked what was up.

Patton claimed he didn't know, exactly, only that Eisenhower wanted to see Bradley personally the next day in Algiers. He offered his C-47, and told him to stop by for breakfast.

Breakfast was at 0700, but Bradley turned up at 0615, not wanting to be late for the temperamental commander. To kill time, he walked through the town, surprising the anti-aircraft crews on duty. It was a brilliant Sicilian morning, the sky azure and the sun not yet steaming hot. But the natural beauty of the island could not induce anyone, Bradley especially, to forget the war—the streets where Bradley walked were strewn with rubble and the broken remains of battle.

Passing a phalanx of tanks, he crossed a large piazza into the mansion Patton had appropriated for his headquarters. The musty interior was cluttered with baroque flourishes—thick drapes and marble statuary that to Bradley and his aide looked like the cheap plaster casts one would find in a five and dime.

Patton was in his usual expansive mood, joking, cursing, and teasing. He picked up Bradley's holstered Colt—a weapon that had accompanied him for some thirty years—and told him he needed a smaller gun as a personal weapon; a "social gun,"[2] Patton called it, a weapon that would be less cumbersome in non-combat situations. Besides his ivory-handled pistol, Patton had a small .32 he carried in a shoulder holster; he promised Bradley he would get him one.

By now Bradley suspected Eisenhower had a new job for him, but Patton claimed to have no hint of what it would be. Before they were scheduled to take off, word came that Ike was headed for Alexander's headquarters in Cassibile near Syracuse; Bradley was to meet him there rather than Algiers.

When Bradley arrived, Eisenhower and his staff were working over the final arrangements for Italy's surrender. Bedell Smith, bleary-eyed, brought him up to speed on the negotiations and assured him Eisenhower would talk to him soon. General Alexander then came over and told Bradley about Montgomery's landing in Italy. There had been no opposition, and things were moving as well as anyone could hope. Good news, but Bradley thought Italy's terrain meant the fight would be long, drawn out, and vicious.[3]

The trio of generals was interrupted by Eisenhower, who unlike the others seemed charged up by the long hours he'd been spending on the negotiations.

There you are, Brad, he said. *Come and talk.*

Bradley followed him into the tent Eisenhower was using as an office. A long wooden table split it in half; except for the table, some chairs, and a collection of cigarette butts filling old C-ration cans, it was empty.

Eisenhower got right to the point.

I have orders for you. You're going to command an army in the invasion of France.

Bradley pressed his lips together, trying not to show surprise, trying to seem nonchalant.

When do I leave? he asked.[4]

Bradley was characteristically reticent about what would turn out to be the most important assignment of his life. His staff surmised that he had been given some sort of promotion when he emerged from the tent— why else had he been called over?—but Bradley himself showed little emotion. Nor did he supply any details until the end of the day, when they were back aboard the plane and halfway to their command post.

"Well, Chet," he told Hansen, "I guess they're giving me an army."[5]

The job assignment was actually a double one, at least for the moment. Bradley was named to head both an army and an army group, the main American land component of the invasion of France. At that point, the First Army Group and its First Army existed largely on paper; Bradley would transform them into premier military units in less than a year's time.[6]

At this point, the Allies hadn't so much planned for the invasion as *planned* to plan. A supreme commander for the invasion hadn't even been appointed. British Lieutenant General Sir Frederick E. Morgan was acting chief of staff for the unnamed commander. His primary task was to put together a planning staff to determine what would be needed for a 1944 invasion.

If that sounds confusing and tentative, it was. When Morgan got to work, the Allies weren't even sure which army would supply the top commander. The United States and Great Britain had agreed earlier that he would come from whichever country mustered the most troops for the invasion. As the size of the invasion grew, it became obvious that would mean an American would take the leadership post. But it wasn't until Churchill met with Roosevelt in August 1943 that the two nations formally decided an American would be in command.

That commander had not been named when Bradley was tabbed for his job. Most assumed that Marshall would get the job, with Eisenhower returning to the States to take over as Chief of Staff.

Bradley's double assignment as army and army group commander was considered a temporary expedient. At some point as the planning progressed, he would step aside from the army group—the higher post— and concentrate on the army command. Three senior generals—Jacob Devers, Lesley J. McNair, and Courtney Hodges—were considered in line for army group commander. Rumors at the time put McNair in the lead, followed by Devers.

★ ★ ★ ★

While not overly controversial, Bradley's selection does have to be explained, given that, by rank and time in service, he was relatively junior for the job. In a sentence, his major qualifications—experience, ability, and temperament—outshone any other possible candidate.

From Marshall and Eisenhower's point of view, there were three logical choices to plan and head the invasion of France: Patton, Clark, and Bradley. Each had garnered considerable experience over the past year, and each had his own strengths and weaknesses.

As described in the previous chapter, Marshall favored Bradley, and on August 25 he cabled Eisenhower asking that Bradley be "released" to begin the assignment. Eisenhower hesitated, sending a response that mentioned Clark's experience at planning amphibious operations, and saying that he would have Bradley take over the Italian campaign. By the next morning, however, he had changed his mind, fully endorsing Bradley.[7]

If the decision had been made at the very start of the Sicily campaign, Patton might have been the leading candidate. He had commanded a corps and an army in battle, was an aggressive combat leader, and had stature and reputation enough to impress the English. (The last was an important though unstated qualification.) His reputation for abrasiveness would have been his major negative; most likely that would have been discounted, as it had in the past.

But Patton's behavior during the Sicilian campaign raised serious doubts about his leadership. His passivity when the U.S. forces were given a secondary role and his decision to launch a dubious drive westward when that role was further reduced were hardly the characteristics anyone would want in the general leading the invasion of France. Nor had Patton displayed any particular tactical or strategic brilliance in either Tunisia or Sicily. His high-handed treatment of subordinates might be just the thing to get a division moving, but it would bode poorly at a higher level where cooperation between different services and nationalities was mandatory. Then of course there were the slapping incidents and their complications.

Again, had the selection been made before Sicily, Clark would have been a clear choice over Bradley. Eisenhower extolled Clark's strengths as an amphibious operations planner, an area in which Bradley had no experience before Sicily. Clark had a reputation for being difficult at times, and for having a large, over-riding ego, but not to the extent that Patton did.

But Sicily raised Bradley's standing considerably. He now had experience as a combat commander at the corps level in two successful campaigns, and had demonstrated a superior grasp of logistics as well as tactics.

Bradley's real asset, however, was his personality. It was perfectly suited to situations where persuasion was more important than simply bulling ahead. While he had shown that he could carry out difficult orders and make hard decisions when necessary, he was easily a more conciliatory figure than either Patton or Clark. From the start, he was someone both Eisenhower and Marshall felt they could trust; his performance in Sicily showed that his other qualifications were at least a match for the older generals.

In short, his selection was a no-brainer.

As for army group commander, at the moment Bradley wasn't really in the running.

Returning to II Corps headquarters, Bradley quickly pulled up his stakes. He'd been given permission to recruit a staff and take whomever he needed from the corps, and he did so, stripping some of its most experienced and able men. A total of twenty-five were immediately transferred, including Bill Kean and Monk Dickson, his G-3 officer Tubby Thorson, and his G-4 Bob Wilson. All assumed similar roles at First Army. His personal aides Hansen and Bridges also came along.

A few days later, on September 7, Bradley drove over to Patton's command post to say good-bye. He found Patton deeply depressed—"near suicidal" are the words used in *A General's Life*.[8]

Patton's initial reaction to Bradley's promotion had been positive and buoyant, at least externally. But the day before Bradley was to leave, Patton learned that the Seventh Army was being stripped of its divisions. This left it, in effect, a toothless tiger, and left Patton without an important job. His biographers and historians speculate that until this point he assumed that he would have an important role in the invasion of France; it was also possible that he would be sent to Italy. Marshall told Patton that he would get another assignment—Eisenhower wanted him to take an army into Normandy alongside Bradley—but the lack of specifics at this point convinced him he wasn't going to get the sort of job he really wanted. He was still in Eisenhower's dog house because of the slapping incident. He wrote in his diary that the news was "heartbreaking."

Bradley was in a difficult position. As frustrated and angry as he had been with Patton during the campaign, he nonetheless respected him as a soldier. He recognized the intangible qualities that made Patton such a great military leader, even as he deplored Patton's excesses. Bradley's own triumph made him feel awkward and embarrassed by Patton's present difficulties.

He listened politely as the senior general gave him advice about the invasion. They must also have talked about the Italian campaign, which neither man thought very well planned. Patton was still brooding over Clark's nonplussed response when he pointed out a massive gap in the British and American lines that was sure to be exploited. Bradley had numerous "misgivings"[9] about the plan, starting with the commanding general himself.

While Bradley may have felt bad for Patton, he wasn't the sort of person to let someone else's mood infect him. After a moving ceremony at II Corps the next morning—the troops sent him off with a rendition of "Auld Lang Syne"—he flew to Tunisia for another meeting with Eisenhower. Once more, Ike was preoccupied with the Italians, who had backed out of their surrender agreement and forced a change in Allied plans. Bradley told himself he was glad to be missing the Italian campaign; it already seemed star-crossed.

That afternoon, he began his journey to England. Flying from Algiers, he shared a flight with French pilots being ferried to Marrakesh. There was also a woman aboard who was having trouble with airsickness. When Bradley, ever the gentleman, checked on her, she threw up all over him.

Told that he could have a "plush" plane for his flight from Marrakesh to England if he was willing to wait a day, the general instead chose to fly right away in an older C-54. The small, hard seats provided slim comfort on the nine-hour flight, but as always Bradley was more concerned with getting where he was going quickly. He shared the cabin with a number of other passengers, including a group of airmen being shuttled back to England. Part of the cabin had been turned into an air-ambulance for an injured British corps commander. His three stars did entitle him to one small perk: he snagged three whole seats, which would allow him at least a small chance at sleeping on the long flight. But they were bucket seats; twisting his body around the arms he managed to doze off for a while, his trench coat providing some warmth in the chilly cabin.

The aircraft arrived in Scotland early the next morning. Waiting for another flight to London, Bradley breakfasted on fried tomatoes and bacon—a decision he made by accident when he couldn't understand the waitress's thick accent. The alternative turned out to be grilled kippers; he considered his choice a good one.[10]

General Devers met his plane in London. Devers probably figured that he had the inside track for the army group command, and had first met Bradley at West Point, where he had coached baseball. But unknown to Devers, Bradley did not have a very good opinion of his former mentor. He viewed Devers as "egotistical, shallow, intolerant, not very smart, and much too inclined to rush off half-cocked."[11] Eisenhower had, if anything, an even worse opinion of Devers. The two had had a serious conflict over the allocation of heavy bombers for Mediterranean operations. Bradley knew about the dispute, and probably resented Devers for it, believing that Devers had harmed the Sicilian operations by blocking the aircraft's use.

Devers drove Bradley to the Dorchester Hotel, where he would stay for the next few months. The Dorchester Hotel was located in the West End of London. Built in 1931, it was a large, modern building at the edge of Hyde Park, not far from Buckingham Palace in central London. To use the British term, it was a "posh" and well-appointed hotel. What impressed Bradley, though, was the roof, said to be substantial enough to withstand damage from German bombings. With that assurance he would often remain in his bed during air raids.

Another plus for the Dorchester—it was across the street from an American mess where he could eat. No more grilled tomatoes or fish for breakfast.

Soon after seeing his room, Bradley set off for Bristol on the English Channel, where the First Army was to have its headquarters. It was a three-hour drive by car, but Bradley was fascinated by the countryside, largely untouched by the war. The city itself was overrun by soldiers; there were so many that Bradley had trouble later securing hotel space.

In Bristol, Bradley met an old friend, Major General Leonard T. Gerow, the commander of V Corps. While the invasion plans were still extremely tentative, V Corps was the senior American command in Britain, and its 29th Division had been tabbed for the initial assault. Gerow had already become involved in the planning. Known as "Gee," he would stay on and become one of Bradley's corps and then army commanders in France.

After an overnight stay and some powdered eggs in the morning, Bradley returned to London. Strolling through Hyde Park Sunday evening, he was amused to hear a speaker near Marble Arch haranguing the crowd about the need for a second front in the war.

Whirlwind orientation over, Bradley returned home. He arrived in Washington on September 14 after a hopscotch flight that included stops in Iceland, Maine, and New York. His wife and daughter were waiting for him on the tarmac, a surprise arranged by a Pentagon officer.

It must have been an emotional reunion, but Bradley was character-istically terse describing it in *A Soldier's Story*. The actual celebration was subdued, if characteristic: after reporting to the Pentagon, which had been dedicated less than a year before, he took his family out for ice cream.

He ate an entire quart.

By now, his daughter Elizabeth was engaged to Hal Beukema, who was due to graduate the following spring. Mother and daughter were excited about the wedding, telling Bradley it was planned for June.

Bradley knew he wouldn't be able to make it; if the invasion stayed on schedule, he'd be in the thick of the fighting. But he said nothing.

Bradley spent two weeks in the States, most of it working. He man-aged a weekend visit to West Point, where his wife was living in the Thayer Hotel; they went down to New York City and took in a produc-tion of *Oklahoma*. With three stars and Pyle's newspaper columns behind him, Bradley could have been a celebrity in the city, wined and dined wherever he went. But that wasn't his style, and while he'd had a good experience with Pyle, he continued to shy away from newspaper correspondents or anything that smacked of self-promotion. He came and went without the fanfare a conquering hero might easily have gener-ated.

Even his visit to West Point and the New York area was connected with business—the First Army[12] had established a headquarters com-mand at Governor's Island in New York harbor, and he spent some time there, meeting men whom he would mostly replace. Back in Washington, Bradley spent considerable time combing personnel folders for eligible officers to fill the 361-man staff.

While his focus at that point was primarily on First Army, Bradley also had to organize 1st Army Group. Marshall had selected General Levan Allen to serve as his chief of staff. Allen had replaced Bradley at Benning when he left, and the two men knew each other well. Allen was an easy-going and personable officer, able to deal with what would turn out to be a somewhat high-strung First Army staff below him, to say nothing of Montgomery and his people.

General Marshall's schedule was so packed that the only way he could spend extended time with Bradley was by inviting him along on an airplane flight to Omaha to address the national convention of the America Legion. En route, they spoke about Sicily. Marshall had already seen the reports on the operation and was able to surprise Bradley with details of what had happened. If Marshall was thinking about the invasion in France—which at that point he was still planning to lead—he didn't let on.

Bradley spoke briefly at the American Legion convention, then returned to Washington, still working to round up a staff. He was surprised one day when he got a call from the White House asking if he would brief the president personally on what had happened on Sicily.

Somewhat nervous and ill at ease, Bradley made his way to the White House the next morning. He'd met the president only once, and then briefly. He wasn't even sure whether he was supposed to salute.

Roosevelt smiled and waved him into the office, instantly putting him at ease. Bradley launched into a brief spiel about how the troops had done. Roosevelt asked a few questions and then commented on how difficult it could be to lead men in the field.

Suddenly, his voice lost its usual bounce. In grave tones, Roosevelt told Bradley about a new weapon the Americans were working on—one that he feared the Germans might beat them to: the atom bomb.

Bradley was awed by the information, and in fact somewhat uncomfortable hearing it. He would remember it later—when the V-1 and V-2 weapons were falling in Europe. Then, one of his worst fears was that the Germans would fit them with what today would be called dirty weapons: radiological bombs that would spew their poisonous material indiscriminately.[13]

Bradley left home October 1, saying goodbye to his wife and daughter, sure that he wouldn't see them again until the war was over. But he'd always kept a tight rein on his emotions, and if he felt sad at the prospect of the long separation, it wasn't evident to anyone with him.

He had plenty of other things to brood about. Besides creating the First Army and the 1st Army Group, he had to consider the plan for their use.

★ ★ ★ ★

Lieutenant General Sir Frederick Morgan's official title was Chief of Staff to the Supreme Allied Commander (designate). From his initials, he and his staff became known as COSSAC. The name came to be applied to the initial plan for the invasion of France as well.

COSSAC called for three divisions to land in Normandy near Caen; an airborne assault would take Caen itself. The invaders would establish a front from Vierville-sur-Mer to Lion-sur-Mer. From there they would move south. Cherbourg was to be taken within two weeks of the invasion. That would give the Allies a port for supply and bringing in more troops. It was expected that upwards of eighteen divisions would be operating in the Normandy area by that point. A breakout from the peninsula would depend on the exact plans of the enemy.

Of the three divisions that would take part in the initial assault, only one was American—the division on the right side of the attack front, to the west. The other two divisions were British. The COSSAC plan called for the divisions to be organized as a British army group. The assault would be under British command until an American army group was brought ashore; this would mean several months.

There were a number of problems with COSSAC, starting with the small size of the invasion force. Morgan was working under many constraints; chief among these was the charge that he come up with a plan that could be carried out with the resources available in Britain. At the time, the Allies simply couldn't move more than three divisions across the English Channel. Then, again, Germany did not have a large number of forces or defenses in northern France, so it's possible that the COSSAC plan might have worked if initiated in the early summer months of 1943 when it was first drawn up.

COSSAC was clearly a rough draft, and was always treated as such. But it *did* decide a number of important issues, and in many ways it remained the backbone of the eventual invasion plan. Most critically, it selected Normandy as the landing area. If this seems obvious to us now, it wasn't in 1943, or in 1944 for that matter.

Bradley immediately realized that if the COSSAC plan was implemented as written, he would be supplying one division to the initial attack. Who would the unit answer to? Who would Bradley answer to? The supreme commander? Or to a ground commander, as Patton had on Sicily?

The issues remained unresolved as Bradley worked to form First Army. He decided he would split the command physically, taking a small number of staff back to London with him while leaving the bulk of the headquarters personnel near the troops in Bristol.

The command picture began to clear in late fall, when Roosevelt nominated Eisenhower as supreme commander, passing over Marshall, whom he decided was too valuable to him in Washington. Eisenhower's appointment was announced December 6, 1943. With an American at the head, the British would supply the ground commander; after a bit of indecision—Churchill initially wanted Alexander, while Sir Alan Brooke (the head of the general staff) wanted Montgomery—Montgomery was named to the command.

Bradley would have preferred Alexander, whose personality was much closer to his own. But he wasn't particularly disturbed; he didn't realize at the time just how much he would come to regret Montgomery's selection.

Meanwhile, there was the question of who would command the army group over him. Devers was by now the logical candidate, but Eisenhower didn't want him. He managed to convince Marshall to send Devers to the Mediterranean, in effect a demotion. Even before pushing Devers out, Ike recommended Bradley assume the job permanently.[14]

Marshall countered by proposing Lesley McNair or Devers. The man who wasn't chosen, Marshall suggested, would command another army alongside Bradley. Eisenhower argued for Patton as the other army commander, and stuck to Bradley as the army group commander. Ike eventually got his way on both. In Bradley's case, he succeeded by letting things simmer. The decision came as more a gradual drift toward the obvious than a sustained argument. As the months went by, Bradley knew more about the invasion, its plans, its needs, its strategy, than anyone else. The only difficulty would be replacing him as army commander, but that was a problem for the future.

In the meantime, Bradley handled both jobs with his usual efficiency.

If there was a great deal of logic to Bradley's selection to head the army group, Eisenhower's insistence on Patton ran in the opposite direction.

Even in civilian life, few superiors are ever comfortable when they have to turn around and work for someone who had once worked for them. This was true in the military as well, where promotions and the seniority system generally prevented this. The special circumstances of the war and Bradley's rapid rise made for exceptions. But none of them were as unusual as appointing Patton to serve under Bradley.

Bradley himself objected. His primary excuse to Eisenhower was his expectation that Patton would be uncomfortable acting as his subordinate. But Bradley also had a long list of complaints against Patton, whom he felt had been acting far too emotionally and even irrationally.

Bradley's objections also touched on Patton's competence as an army commander, at least in his choice and supervision of staff. II Corps had had a myriad of problems with the Seventh Army staff. The Seventh Army supply organization had been so bad, Bradley noted, that II Corps stepped in and took over the functions usually overseen by Army staff.

Eisenhower usually accepted Bradley's advice for personnel, but not when it came to Patton. Why not?

Historians have tended to look at just one half of the equation: Patton. They note that few other generals were as imaginative on the battlefield, or as good at getting their men to reach an objective. Eisenhower and Bradley made both points themselves.

But the other half of the equation was just as critical to Eisenhower's decision. He wanted Bradley as army group commander. He wanted Bradley to work with Patton. That combination, Eisenhower realized, was worth something to the war. Bradley, in today's parlance, was a no-maintenance achiever; Patton was a sparkplug who never lost the ability to engage the enemy and fight viciously. It wasn't just that Bradley could keep Patton's worst impulses in check; it was that he could get more out of Patton than anyone else.

In the letter he sent to Marshall about the possibility of appointing Clark rather than Bradley to head the invasion, Eisenhower noted Bradley's ability to "absorb...part of the burdens that otherwise fall directly on me."[15] This was an unusual statement to make about a corps commander. But it is clear that Eisenhower had an extraordinary level of trust in Bradley and believed that he could deal with Patton. Bradley himself later said something along these lines to his staff, noting that he knew Patton's "foibles," and was confident he could use him.

He said that to his staff. To Eisenhower, he made it clear he thought the arrangement wasn't going to work.

But Eisenhower got his way.

One solution to the problem of replacing Bradley as army commander was to bring in a deputy and train him to take over the job. Eisenhower, perhaps at Bradley's suggestion, floated the germ of the idea out to Marshall. Near the end of December, the two men agreed that Courtney Hodges would join Bradley as a deputy commander.

Marshall had other thoughts—he suggested Hodges take over as army group commander and leave Bradley in place. Eisenhower essentially ignored the solution, continuing to let the momentum build for Bradley.

There were other critical slots to fill. Bradley suggested Lucian Truscott as a corps commander. Eisenhower agreed immediately. But getting him was another matter. Truscott had become indispensable to the Italian campaign. Jake Devers, still smarting over Eisenhower's move to banish him from Overlord, was now Truscott's superior, and he simply refused to let him go. Eisenhower tried several times to get Marshall to release him, offering to send anyone but Gerow in his place. But Truscott was simply too valuable. In the end Bradley settled for General J. Lawton "Lightning Joe" Collins. Collins, who would later rise to Army Chief of Staff, had already served in the Pacific, seeing action on Guadalcanal, where he commanded the 25th Infantry Division and earned the nickname "Lightning Joe," before coming to Europe as the VII Corps commander.[16] He would play an important role in Europe as one of Bradley's most trusted lieutenants.

Named to lead the Allies onto the beaches, Montgomery found much to object to in the COSSAC plan. As soon as he arrived in London that January he went to work amending it. (When it came time to write his memoirs, Montgomery not only claimed credit for revising the plan, but made it sound as if he was the only one who had the foresight to see its problems. It was a characteristic overreach, exactly the sort of thing that annoyed Bradley and most of the other Americans who had to work with him.)

Montgomery presented the outline of his ideas at a meeting on January 21. The outline was considerably better than COSSAC. Montgomery's revisions recognized that the key point of the initial landing must be to establish a beachhead strong enough to support a rapid buildup of troops. He also pointed out that the key moment for the invaders would come when the Germans used their mobile reserves. He proposed a five-division front, with another division's worth of airborne during the assault phase. There would be two armies, one British and one American. Their dividing line was the Bayeux River. East to the Orne would be held by the British; the Americans were to the west.

The Americans' primary objectives were to take Cherbourg and secure the peninsula. From there they would move south and west. The British Army would take Caen and Nantes, moving south. The main job of the British as the beachhead was secured would be to take on any German troops attempting to attack from the east. Given the general deployment of the German forces, this was the most likely direction for a counterattack.

Caen was to be taken on the first day, setting the stage for the immediate consolidation of the beaches and opening the way for a drive eastward. Besides being the hub of good roads east, south, and westward, the open ground around Caen gave an army room to maneuver, something it would lack close to the beaches and in the tiny checkerboards of the bocage area that dotted most of Normandy. A key component of Montgomery's overall scheme was the use of armored spearheads to make rapid advances; these thrusts would be key to taking strategic points before the Germans could reinforce them.

This rapid thrust and maneuver appealed to Bradley, who was impressed with Montgomery's plan and presentation almost in spite of himself. It was not perfect, and a number of its flaws were recognized immediately. Among them was the lack of concentration of forces—they were spread out along a wide front—and the subsequent small size of the force (relatively speaking) taking Caen. But there was no arguing that the plan itself was considerably better than COSSAC. It also gave the Americans—and therefore Bradley—a much larger role.

Over the next several months, Bradley and Montgomery met often, working out details for the invasion. For Bradley, these meetings were always difficult. "These meetings were invariably stiff, almost formal," declares A General's Life. "Monty was usually coolly aloof, almost withdrawn, and not readily open to suggestions. There was no 'chemistry'; our personalities simply did not mesh. He left me with the feeling that I was a poor country cousin whom he had to tolerate."[17]

Bradley did get along with Montgomery's chief of staff, Freddie de Guingand, which made things easier. But the conflict he had with Montgomery was a small part of the friction and the political maneuverings in the Allied high command.

Bradley disagreed with Montgomery's assessment that the defenses on the beaches and the areas just behind them would be light. He also seems to have thought Montgomery was hopelessly optimistic about reaching his objectives—the ground commander predicted to Bradley that his tanks would reach Falaise on D-Day.

As the winter moved on, Bradley continued to split his time between London and Bristol, overseeing the buildup and training of his forces while continuing to refine the plans for their use. Bradley tried to keep regular hours, knocking off each evening at five. He knew if he stayed late, his staff would feel obliged to do the same, and he wanted them to catch up on their rest now. They wouldn't have much time in the future.

Inevitably, though, there were late nights, and Bradley often broke his five o'clock rule. But he did keep his quarters separate from his office, something he hadn't done in Africa or Sicily. For a few months at least, there was no large campaign map to stare at when he couldn't sleep in the long hours before dawn. With the heavy reinforced concrete roof far over his head, he even managed to stay in his bed through a number of air raids.

Being in London gave Bradley considerably more access to Eisenhower, and the two men spent more time together than ever before, mostly at work, though occasionally after hours. Eisenhower's insatiable love of bridge saw them facing off against each other often. Eisenhower paired with Kay Summersby, his driver and companion. Eisenhower was quietly intense as he played, and according to Summersby did not like chatter or conversation to distract him.[18] He usually won.

"I found General Bradley a peaceful, charming, alert companion," wrote Summersby in her first memoir after the war, *Eisenhower Was My Boss*. "Speaking in a quiet tone which belied a fighter's heart, he endeared himself to all of us in the official family."[19]

Bradley exuded an understated dignity in social situations, and could be quite charming one on one, though in larger groups he still tended to stray toward the sidelines, out of the spotlight. He had a slightly mocking wit that was disarming in the context of his personality. He joked with Eisenhower about Summersby being his "shadow,"[20] something few others would have been able to get away with.

The relationship between the two men grew ever warmer and more comfortable, despite the stress of war. Their days at West Point were a particular bond. The pair would occasionally recall old games, boring others to tears as they critiqued players and scoring drives.[21] On a professional level, Eisenhower valued Bradley's abilities as a tactician. He also appreciated the fact that he was, to use a phrase common today, very low maintenance. Bradley was agreeable and cooperative, certainly in comparison to generals like Montgomery who had different visions for the war and were icy and aloof as well. And unlike the emotional Patton, whom Eisenhower had been close to for years, Bradley kept his mouth shut, avoiding publicity and controversy.

The two men got along like brothers, Summersby noted years later, looking back on a dinner in France.[22] The personal and professional realms mixed well in their relationship, aided no doubt in equal measures by Bradley's personality and, at least at this juncture, their similar views about how the war should be conducted.

"I cannot approve of your plan."

Air Chief Marshall Sir Trafford Leigh-Mallory frowned and briefly—very briefly—fixed Bradley with a stare.

"It is much too hazardous an undertaking. Your losses will be excessive."

Bradley tried to keep his cool. He was sitting in Montgomery's office at St. Paul's School, discussing his latest plans for the invasion, now just three months away. While the general outline had been agreed on, there were myriad details still to be worked out. One of them was the use of airborne troops, which Bradley saw as essential to success on Utah Beach.

Leigh-Mallory had a different view.

The British commander was in charge of the air operations for D-Day, which put him in charge of the aircraft dropping the airborne troops. But this was a gray area—once parachuted in, the troops were essentially no different than ground forces, and were under Bradley's command.

"The assault on Utah Beach can't go forward without an airborne landing," said Bradley simply. "It's essential."

Always cool, the air in the conference room had turned several degrees frostier. Bradley was used to dealing with the British generals by now, and used to the attitude many seemed to exude: defensive superiority, alternating with compulsive arrogance.

Leigh-Mallory turned to Montgomery and repeated his objections. The aircraft dropping the troops would be under heavy fire; the hedgerows in Normandy would make it difficult for the gliders to land.

Let me make it clear, said Leigh-Mallory, his tone growing even more arrogant than normal. "If you insist upon this airborne operation, you'll do it in spite of my opposition."

"I always take responsibility," Bradley replied. "No problem there."

"That's unnecessary," said Montgomery finally. "I shall assume full responsibility for the operation."[23]

The beaches Bradley was assigned had different tactical pluses and minuses. Utah Beach, on the Cotentin peninsula northwest of Cherbourg, would be especially vulnerable if the Germans were able to send reinforcements to the beachhead. With only a few exits from the landing area, strong German concentrations could stall the invasion and even collapse it with a strong counterattack.

To deal with this, Bradley proposed drops by two airborne divisions. The operation was much larger than what had originally been in Montgomery's plan.

The 101st Airborne would land behind the beach, securing several causeways that came out of the marsh. The 101st would then charge south to hook up with units landing at Omaha.

Meanwhile, the 82nd Airborne would drop further inland, landing near Ste. Mere Eglise, Carentan, and La Hay Du Puits, cutting off the

German forces at the far end of the peninsula, choking off their connection to the rest of France.

Montgomery's decision to approve the plan did not end the matter for Leigh-Mallory. The air marshal took the matter directly to Eisenhower, and the controversy continued. Bradley refused to budge. He conceded the plan was risky, especially for the 82nd, which was dropping too far from the beach to expect reinforcement or help during the initial phase of the assault. But the airborne operation, Bradley insisted, was essential. The assault on Utah could not succeed, and would not proceed, without the drops.

Eisenhower agreed. He would continue fending Leigh-Mallory off nearly until D-Day.[24]

Omaha beach presented its own problems. A low escarpment guarded the sand, giving defenders a curtain of heights to fire from. Along the roughly five miles that the Americans would attack, there were only five areas where vehicles could exit. The Germans had begun adding a range of obstructions, pillboxes, mines, and defensive positions to the beach and the ground beyond. The combination made Omaha a terrible place for a landing, but it had to be attacked and held. It was the only usable beach between the British armies and Utah Beach. If it weren't taken, there would be a large gap between the British and American beachheads. The Germans could use that space to roll up the invaders, knocking them back to the sea.

Bradley asked for a British reconnaissance team to assess the Omaha Beach. An engineer and a member of the Special Boat Section swam in one night with an augur and took samples of dirt below the beach. The scout reported to Bradley the next day at Norfolk House in St. James Square. He told Bradley the sand there could hold tanks; that assuaged Bradley's fears that he wouldn't be able to land enough firepower to punch past the waterline. But the commando added that the beach would be difficult to assault even with tanks along.

"I hope you don't mind my saying it," said the captain, Scott-Bowden. "But this beach is a very formidable proposition indeed and there are bound to be tremendous casualties."

Bradley clamped him on the captain's shoulder and said he knew.[25]

The beach was originally scheduled to be assaulted by V Corps' 29th and 4th Infantry Divisions. But Bradley brought in the 1st Infantry Division, exchanging it for the 4th Division. The Big Red One was the most experienced unit available, and had undergone extensive retraining since Sicily.

For Bradley, it was a difficult decision. The division had already seen considerable action and suffered a large number of casualties. Omaha was clearly going to be a hard fight. After the war, Bradley said giving Omaha to the 1st Infantry division was an injustice, but a necessary one.

Bradley's plan at Omaha was to take the flanks of the beach in the first wave, filling in the middle as the assault continued. The 16th Infantry Regiment would land on the left, in front of the village of Colleville-Sur-Mer. The 116th Infantry Regiment from the 29th Infantry Division would land to its right. Also critical to the plan was an assault by the 2nd Ranger Battalion at Pointe du Hoc, where German guns covered the assault area.[26]

Bradley decided to beef up the attack by adding Sherman tanks in the first wave. The tanks were equipped with gear allowing them to "swim." Two battalions of the waterproof tanks—called DD or duplex-drive tanks—were included in the initial assault. American Sherman tanks, the DDs had been fitted with a British kit that would keep them waterproof and allow them to travel through the water. The plan called for them to launch from about five thousand yards out, "swim" to the beach, and help the infantry attack pillboxes and other strongpoints.[27]

Bradley knew that many men would die during the invasion, and he never shied away from that fact. But when he heard some of the rumors about the numbers of casualties expected, he began telling the officers and non-coms he met that fears were being exaggerated. He cited the casualty figures in the Mediterranean, especially Sicily, where for the most part the numbers were modest. In one speech to the 29th Infantry

Division, he admitted that "some of you won't come back—but it'll be very few."[28]

The remarks were reported in *Stars and Stripes*, then repeated by the press in the United States. At a time when Roosevelt and Marshall had been trying to prepare the country as it confronted what would be the biggest day of the war, Bradley's words seemed incongruously optimistic. Afterwards, he was at pains to point out that American casualties were under 10 percent, with about a third of that killed—a great deal of men, to be sure, but numbers that he considered acceptable, given the importance and difficulty of the operation.

Despite a flare-up of negative publicity in the States over the slapping incidents, Eisenhower managed to get Marshall's approval for Patton's appointment. Patton arrived in England in late January.

Eisenhower told him he would take command of the Third Army, which would go into France following the invasion. In the meantime, Patton would help the Allies mount a diversion, drawing German attention away from their actual plans. Patton of course wanted a larger role, but this was far better than exile.

For his part, Bradley reminded himself that Third Army was not yet part of the 1st Army Group, and therefore Patton was Eisenhower's problem, not his.

If relations between the two men were strained, they nonetheless acted properly toward each other. Patton had congratulated Bradley on his appointment, and went out of his way to be cordial. Bradley was generally as proper as he was reticent, and at times despite his doubts clearly enjoyed being around Patton, who could be charming as well as highly entertaining. The two men shared a suspicion of Montgomery, unsure whether he would be bold enough after the landings; Patton's concern was more pronounced, at least to judge from his letters to his wife.[29]

Somewhat solicitously, Bradley asked Patton to come to London from his headquarters in central England to share ideas on improving the organization of American armor. He agreed Patton could have Hugh

Gaffney as his chief of staff, allowing Gaffney to give up command of the 2nd Armored Division.[30]

The controversy about the slapping incident had gradually died down, and Patton seemed poised to return to everyone's good graces. For a moment it even appeared he would be dispatched to Italy to help rescue the situation at Anzio. But Patton was Patton, and his mouth was always more dangerous than a dozen enemy machine guns.

So perhaps it's not surprising that in April he blundered into another controversy, this time by making some offhand comments about Great Britain, America, and Russia ruling the world after the war. The comments were made to a small group of mostly women who formed the Welcome Club for American GIs in Knutsford, a local group with a similar mission to the U.S.O.

Patton, who was clearly trying to joke, hadn't realized that there was a reporter present, nor had he expected that the comment—most often without the Russians included, a tacit snub—would be news in Great Britain.

And even bigger news in the United States.

It was a minor incident, in Bradley's opinion—something that would have blown over if anyone other than Patton had said it. But Eisenhower complained to Bradley that Patton was becoming a bigger headache than he was worth.

"If have to apologize publicly for George once more, I'm going to have to let him go," complained Eisenhower. "I'm getting sick and tired of having to protect him. Life's too short to put up with any more of it."[31]

Bradley recorded the incident in *A Soldier's Story*. Unfortunately, he doesn't say in his memoir whether he rolled his eyes or not.

Eisenhower wavered for several days, telling Marshall he would probably send Patton home, and considered moving Hodges over to the Third Army. In the end, Marshall told Eisenhower the decision was entirely his. Ike bawled Patton out, let him know that he was considering "washing his hands" of him (Patton's phrase). He let Patton twist in the wind for a few more days before telling him he was keeping him on as army commander.

Eisenhower spoke to Bradley during the days between his meeting with Patton and his final decision to keep him on. In the version of the story in *A General's Life,* Bradley says that Eisenhower had decided to send Patton home, but then backed away for several reasons, chief among them—according to the book—the fact that they could not get Truscott to replace him. Moving Hodges over (Bradley's other suggestion) would leave a hole in Bradley's command.[32]

What did Patton think of Bradley?

His January 18, 1944, diary entry is often quoted as his ultimate statement on Bradley. It is not particularly charitable:

> Sgt Meeks told me after breakfast that he heard on the radio last night that General Bradley has been made commander of all the ground troops in England. I suppose that this means that he will command the American army group. I had thought that possibly I might get this command....
>
> Bradley is a man of great mediocrity. At Benning in command, he failed to get discipline. At Gafsam when it looked as though the Germans might turn our right flank...he suggested that we withdraw corps headquarters to Feriana. I refused to move. In Sicily, when the 45th Division approached Cefalu, he halted them for fear of a possible German landing east of Termini. I had to order him to move and told him that I would be responsible for his rear, and that his timidity had lost us one day. He tried to stop the landing operation #2 east of Cap d'Orlando because he thought it was too dangerous....Finally, on the night of August 16-17, he asked me to call off the landing east of Milazzo for fear our troops might shoot at each other. He also failed to get word to all units of the II Corps on the second paratroop landing.

On the other hand Bradley has many of the attributes which are considered desirable in a general. He wears glasses, has a strong jaw, talks profoundly and says little, and is a shoot companion of the Chief of Staff. Also a loyal man. I consider him among our better generals.[33]

It undoubtedly represents Patton's actual feelings at the moment he was writing, but how fair is it to take the passage as an actual assessment of Bradley?

First and foremost, it's clear that the outburst is being fueled by his disappointment at missing the job of army group commander (which technically Bradley had not yet been given). The comments about discipline are easily dismissed; Patton never had any trouble with Bradley's "getting discipline" on Sicily or in Tunisia. The combat incidents Patton mentions are all instances where Bradley was objectively more cautious than Patton, but they are obviously highly colored by Patton's take on events. The first two involve a perception of a tactical situation where the enemy could have easily gained the upper hand. The danger Bradley saw existed; it's just that Patton assessed its likelihood differently. His critique is more along the lines of: *Bradley is more cautious than I am, and to be a great general, you can't be cautious. You have to take risks. That's how you become great.*

That's an excellent point, one that many commentators miss. And certainly a case could be made that Patton was more willing to take those risks than Bradley—even if Bradley was himself a measured risk taker.

The trouble with Patton's criticism is that it misstates the situation in *every* incident. Not to mention the fact that Bradley's assessments were proven correct by what actually happened.

It's highly unlikely that Bradley halted the advance at Cefalu because of a possible German landing; Patton's diary is the *only* place that possibility is even mentioned. This was at a point where Patton was racing to Palermo, and a landing on the flank of the 45th's advance could have presented a danger. But Bradley had already sent advance units toward Palermo further west, and from his perspective his real goal was to the east. So it's very likely that he simply saw no need for it. Especially given the paucity of amphibious resources, something Patton doesn't mention.

In the second incident, Bradley was supporting Truscott's position. Events proved that their assessment was the correct one.

As for the last incident, Patton simply misstates Bradley's actual objection to a landing that he saw had no purpose.

Bradley's corps *was* slow in getting the message out on the paratroop landing, but it did get it out. A detailed investigation following the incident recommended changes in procedure but did not condemn Bradley, or II Corps for that matter. Even units who had received the warning fired anyway. Eisenhower severely criticized Patton for the incident, unfairly, but that's no excuse to blame Bradley. Still, this is probably the most accurate charge in the list, though ironically it is the one generally dismissed or ignored by historians using the passage to critique Bradley.

Patton's turn at the end of the passage—starting out sarcastic and then coming around in what appears to be a statement without irony about Bradley's loyalty—is as typical of Patton as the criticism. The emphasis on loyalty is not surprising: clearly it was true, given that Bradley had tried to protect him in the slapping incident (something Patton probably didn't know). It was also a quality Patton valued highly.

Taking that remark at face value implies the next should be taken genuinely as well. Patton almost surely *did* think Bradley was one of the country's better generals—it's just that none were in Patton's league. At least not in his mind.

One can see Patton's mind working as he writes—the first rush of emotion, the list of complaints, then the reconsideration, however slight it might be.

Unfortunately for both men, the passage is usually lifted out of context to "prove" that Patton hated Bradley, or as evidence that Bradley was an overly cautious general. The actual incidents that Patton refers to are never assessed on their own.

The reality is that Patton's attitude toward Bradley was as complex as Patton was. That negative passage is balanced in many places in his diary and other papers by much more positive statements. Surely in comparing Bradley to himself, Patton found Bradley deficient. But Patton found *everyone* deficient. He was the last person whose words should be used as evidence of *anyone's* abilities, especially when he was blowing off steam in his diary or complaining to his wife.

It is hard to believe that Patton, given his ego and uncontrollable, nasty temper, could have performed so well in the awkward position of Bradley's subordinate, unless he respected Bradley at a deep level. In fact we know he did. Patton gave his appraisal of Bradley in a 12 September 1943 Efficiency Report:[34]

1. **Name and grade of General Officer reported on:**
   Omar N. Bradley, 03807, Lieutenant General (Inf.)
2. **Period covered by report:**
   1 July 1943 to 8 September 1943—2 Months, 8 Days
3. **a. Duties performed during period:**
   Commanding General, II Corps, 1 July 1943 to
   8 September 1943
   b. Manner of performance:
   Superior
4. **Physical activity:**
   Superior
5. **Physical endurance:**
   Superior
6. **Knowledge of his profession:**
   Superior
7. **For what command or duty would you specially recommend him?**
   An Army
8. **What opportunities have you had for observing him during period covered?**
   Intimate daily contact
9. **Does he render willing and generous support to plans of superiors regardless of personal views in the matter?**
   Yes

10. **Of all general officers of his grade personally known to you, what number would you give him on this list and how many comprise your list?**
Number 1. I know all of them.
Further remarks deemed necessary.
None

G.S. Patton, Jr.
Lieut. General, U.S. Army,
Commanding

As important as the Normandy landings were, they could not command all of the Allies' resources or personnel. Most critical was the lack of landing craft, which reduced the size of the initial assault, delayed it a month, and eventually forced the postponement of Anvil, the landing in southern France. (Though controversial, Bradley advocated Anvil as a way of tying down German divisions and providing more reliable seaports for the campaign across France.)

Fighting in Italy occupied the 82nd Airborne's 504th Regiment until April 22; and it was so badly mauled in Italy that Matthew Ridgway, the commanding general, held it out of the battle as a reserve. An entire replacement regiment had to be inserted in its place.[35]

With the invasion approaching, Bradley visited the divisions, checking on their training. He looked the part of "the soldier's general." His pants were rolled into a pair of high-top paratroop boots; he wore a battered trench coat against the cold British weather. Even reporters out to flatter him used words like "plain" and "homely."[36]

Gene Ford, an Army photographer, remembered after the war that Bradley would go up to privates and question them on how well their shoes fit and how the food was. And he was still shy about getting his picture taken.

"Once while trying to line him up in the forefront pinning a medal on a sergeant," remembered the photographer, "he turned to me and said, 'Son, play up the sergeant. He's much better looking than me.'"[37]

Bradley tried to be unobtrusive, ordering the division commanders not to alter their training schedules to accommodate him: he wanted to see actual training, not carefully orchestrated displays. One battalion commander made the mistake of failing to follow these orders. Bradley recognized a rehearsed maneuver when he saw one and promptly had the commander sacked.

Bradley was only one of several distractions for the men training for the biggest moment of their lives. All manner of VIPs visited the troops, partly to raise their morale, partly to see what was going on. That spring, Bradley found himself accompanying Prime Minister Winston Churchill on an inspection tour of the U.S. divisions scheduled to take part in the invasion. This was a three-day affair, with Churchill's train hauling the prime minister, Bradley, and Eisenhower across much of southern and central England. Churchill held court each evening in his car, sounding off on what Bradley called the "perfidies of war."[38] At one stop, the prime minister expressed an interest in the M-1 carbine, then newly being issued to the troops. The 9th Division set up a demonstration, handing carbines to Bradley, Eisenhower, and Churchill.

Bradley's targets were at seventy-five yards. Eisenhower's fifty. Churchill's twenty-five.

They had at it.

Bradley should have done fairly well, but he never found out.

"Manton Eddy wisely hustled us away before we could inspect the targets," he quipped afterwards.[39]

Bradley doesn't seem to have been overly enthused about spending time with Churchill or other VIPs. He spent many social occasions saying relatively little, and it seems likely his mind was wandering toward more pressing matters, whether they were of the many administrative snafus that had to be straightened out or the upcoming battle in France. One night he was invited with several other top officers to attend dinner at Churchill's residence at 10 Downing Street. Bradley was not looking forward to it, but duty called. He took some solace in the fact that his invitation noted the King was likely to attend.

Maybe that would mean an early evening, Bradley told Eisenhower.

No such luck. The King stayed until 1:30 a.m., making it impossible for Bradley to go until after he left.

Bradley was habitually an early riser, and most of his staff followed his example. This could make for problems when working with the British, who tended to start much later in the morning. The different schedules and styles increased the tension between the two staffs. Tempers grew testier as the date for the invasion drew closer.

Even Bradley's legendary calm was tested. At a meeting of senior commanders at Montgomery headquarters April 7, Bradley nearly exploded when Montgomery presented the invasion plan with a series of what he called "phase lines"—time delineated objectives that went from the beaches to the Seine River, where the Allies were supposed to be on D+90, or ninety days after the landing.

Bradley had objected to the phase lines earlier, feeling they were much too rigid and would inevitably limit the commanders as they sought to move forward. The extensive network of boundaries would implicitly argue against exploiting unforeseen developments and at the same time provide a ready means of criticism should the armies fall behind schedule. He thought he had gotten Montgomery to agree, but here they were again.

Bradley argued strongly—one of the few times anyone witnessed him showing real emotion about the Overlord plan in public. Montgomery finally agreed to remove the phase lines from the American portions of the plan.[40]

He would probably have done better to remove them entirely, as those in the British sector would prove to be extremely optimistic.

Heading back one night from Torquay on the coast to his quarters in London, Bradley saw two young American women serving with the Army trying to hitch a ride. He ordered his driver to stop his Cadillac staff car, and he and Hansen squeezed over to give them room. The girls were shocked that a general had stopped, but it wasn't out of character; Hansen could cite a number of instances when he'd picked up stragglers, including once in Washington, D.C., where Bradley gave a lift to an astounded corporal.

While Bradley's kindness needed no special prompting, it may have been that he was thinking of his daughter—she was getting married soon. He told Hansen that she had written about purchasing dresses for the bridesmaids and herself.

"Two things I wanted to do," the general confessed, opening his emotions up briefly to his closest aide. "One to see her graduated and the other to see her married. Now I'm missing both."[41]

The Germans, meanwhile, raced to fortify France. In November 1943, there were forty-six German divisions in the country; by June there would be fifty-five. A number were poorly trained, but that still left a substantial force. Subtracting sub-par units and those created to hold specific dug-in positions, historian John Keegan in *Six Armies in Normandy* estimates that there were thirty German infantry divisions in France,[42] considerably more than the Allies could initially commit to battle. About a dozen were stationed along the Channel coast. These were studded with combat veterans and had a strong backbone of experienced officers and NCOs. Nine Panzer divisions, including one panzergrenadier division, were in reserve nearby.

The placement and utilization of this reserve was a bone of contention between the German commanders. Field Marshal Erwin Rommel commanded Army Group B, which had the responsibility for Normandy; he was subordinate to Field Marshal Gerd von Runstedt, who was Supreme Commander West. Rommel believed the Allies had to be stopped at the beaches. He had ordered a massive expansion of the coastal defenses, and wanted his units placed as close to the projected battle areas as possible. Von Runstedt, on the other hand, believed that the armor would be best deployed in a massive counterattack once the main Allied forces were ashore.

Their conflict was never entirely resolved. Rommel was able to move some of the armored divisions close to the beach areas, but not as close as he wanted.

Montgomery had faced Rommel's forces in Africa, and Bradley was impressed by how well the British field marshal seemed to know his opposite number. (Rommel had left Africa by the time Bradley commanded II Corps.) Montgomery predicted that Rommel would attempt an immediate counterattack, committing his reserves quickly. Allied strategy was arranged to exploit this if possible, hoping to benefit from a piecemeal addition of units to the German line.

The Allies had a tremendous advantage in intelligence. The Germans knew there was a large buildup in England, and that an assault was coming soon. But Allied dominance of the skies severely limited aerial reconnaissance, and a massive disinformation campaign kept the Germans guessing where the invasion would come. The Allied deception plan convinced them that the landing would be in the Calais area.

Meanwhile, fresh intelligence reports arrived at Bradley's G-2 section every day. Monk Dickson was practically ecstatic, examining nine inch by nine inch photos of the projected battlefield. These were remarkably detailed, especially compared to the smaller and blurrier images the intelligence officer had had in Sicily.[43]

Some of what Bradley saw alarmed him, most especially new launching platforms for V-1 and V-2 rockets. Their discovery siphoned off some of the pre-invasion bombing missions. But that was not the only concern. Bradley was thinking of the weapon Roosevelt had mentioned to him; obliquely, he discussed the possibility of new high explosives with Hansen without actually saying anything about the atom bomb.[44]

Bradley was also worried that the Germans would attempt to drop radioactive material on the Allies, aiming to use radiation poisoning to stunt their advance.

"We thought at the time the Germans were ahead of us and might drop some of their radioactive waste material into England," Bradley told West Point cadets after the war. "We put out the order that if anyone got sick after being near a rocket to report it. It seems there were only three of us in England who knew what this was about."

The rocket reference, presumably, was to V-1s. The weapons were known to Allied intelligence prior to their becoming operational following the invasion of France.[45]

In addition, there was the possibility that the Germans would use poison gas during the invasion. This fear necessitated the inclusion of masks and protective clothing that added to supply problems as well as the weight individual soldiers had to carry.

A more tangible headache was improvements in the Germans' defenses. Poles fitted with mines were sown in fields behind the beaches where they would disrupt glider landings. Teller mines—plate-shaped devices activated by weight or other pressure—were placed liberally around potential battlefields. In late May, intelligence reported a shift in the enemy defenses that made the original drop plans for the 82nd Airborne too dangerous. Bradley moved the forces closer to the beach, altering his plans for the initial assault as well as the drive across the peninsula.

As part of the lead-up to the invasion, Bradley granted longer interviews aimed at telling the folks back home who was leading their "boys." A *Time* magazine cover story on May 1 intimated that the time for the invasion was drawing near. The reporter called Bradley "Lincolnesque." The story he wrote was clearly the result of traveling at least for a short while with Bradley. Some of the characteristics Pyle had noted were now a stock part of the Bradley media persona, sure to be highlighted by anyone who wrote about him: he was a kind of everyman, quiet, unassuming, but also smart and even "calculative," the word used in his school yearbook. (There it had probably been meant as a pun on his math ability, though the reporter didn't seem to realize that.) Bradley was also given credit for the attack plan in the Mousetrap, its uniqueness recognized for the first (and perhaps only) time.[46]

In *A General's Life*, Bradley remarks he regretted that the torrent of publicity transformed him into a semi-celebrity. It was inevitable, he admitted; the people in America demanded to know who their soldiers were fighting under. The one consolation, he added, was that they would know he had not sent them into battle recklessly.[47]

Patton visited Bradley's headquarters in Bristol on May 31. There was still great resentment toward Patton on Bradley's staff, but Bradley made sure he was treated properly, even providing a motorcycle escort—a directive that caused one of his aides to quip that perhaps the drivers should be wearing boxing gloves.[48] The following morning at breakfast, Bradley went over his plans for the invasion with his former boss. He was in a good mood—Patton had thought he was depressed earlier in the month, but now told his diary that Bradley seemed cheerful.[49]

That afternoon, the two men flew to Portsmouth to join Montgomery. The Allies had tea, then closeted themselves in Montgomery's office to go over the plans. Montgomery suggested that Patton come in when the assault reached the stage where Brittany and Rennes were to be attacked. Bradley, as always, said little—he had already made plans to have Patton and his army engaged by then.

Later at dinner, Montgomery took bets on when the war would be over. He wagered five pounds that it would be done by November 1.

Too optimistic, said Bradley. He took the bet, though he hoped he would lose.

On June 2, Bradley received word he had been promoted to permanent brigadier general. (His war time status remained lieutenant general.) The promotion was the cause of a few smirks. It was post-dated to September 1, 1943, which meant that it officially came before Bradley was awarded his permanent status as a colonel—October 1, 1943. He quipped that he wasn't sure whether he was going backward or forward. At least, he said, he'd have one star when he was buried in Arlington.[50]

The next day, Bradley got into his battered Packard with Hansen. The front seat was filled with their gear—gas masks, guns, helmets. Hansen sat in the back with Bradley. He had an aluminum tube filled with the invasion maps propped between his legs.

In an expansive mood, Bradley's mind stretched back to 1918, and he told his aides about a baseball game he'd played in. He'd pitched a two hitter and batted in two runs.

A short time later, Bradley reached Plymouth. A small boat was waiting to take him and staff to the USS *Augusta,* the heavy cruiser that would serve as his flagship—or, in Army terms, floating command post—during the initial stage of the battle. The bulk of the First Army headquarters staff was aboard a second ship, the USS *Achernar,* manning a war room there.

On the way out to the ship, Bradley picked up his helmet and slipped it over his head. He snugged the chinstrap, ready to return to battle.[51]

CHAPTER 5

The Longest Days

T he numbers spewed fast and furious, detail layered on detail, all from memory:

800 tons of carpet bombs

8,000 rockets on Omaha

5,000 on Utah

64 tanks to swim ashore

Bradley spoke to the news correspondents as if he were back at West Point, delivering a math lecture. It was June 3, two days before the expected landing. The reporters had many questions. The first few were to settle curiosity—they'd never heard tanks could swim before. Then came more pointed queries.

"How soon do you expect to take Cherbourg?" asked one reporter.

Bradley glanced at the map, where the city was circled in red. The map declared it would be taken by D+8.

"I'm going to have to stick my neck out," Bradley told him. "But as of this moment, I'd gladly sell out for D plus 15—yes, or even D plus 20. The D plus 8 estimate you see here on the map is probably much better than we can do."

It was a sober and telling moment. Press briefings like this were often rah-rah-rah affairs, the speaker full of confidence and optimism. Bradley was considerably more realistic than most. The Germans had been reinforcing the Normandy area at a frantic pace, he told the reporters.

The latest intelligence showed that the Americans were going to be facing more and better units on Omaha than they had expected. Bradley's intelligence chief "Monk" Dickson estimated that as many as seven enemy divisions might be in position to reach the beaches during the invasion. Properly used, they could overwhelm any of the beaches. Bradley didn't give the reporters these specifics, but he did outline the hurdles his men faced. There would be three critical moments:

- The initial landing, which he felt would be achieved without too many complications;
- A counterattack from the Germans around day six or day seven;
- The Allied attempt at a breakout, which would follow the counterattack.

Satisfied, the reporters went back to their cabins to write their stories, which would be embargoed until after the invasion. The real question was one they couldn't bring themselves to ask: would the invasion succeed?

Bradley took a quick turn around the deck. The sky was clear—a surprise, since the meteorologists were talking about an approaching storm. Back in his quarters, the captain's cabin, Bradley tried fitfully to get some sleep. His chief of staff Bill Kean had a cot at the side; other staff members were sprawled out in the map room, curled up on coats to cushion the deck. Bradley's aide Chet Hansen was in the gangway. No one slept very well.[1]

★ ★ ★ ★

The assault was planned for June 5, but the approaching bad weather caused a 24-hour cancellation. Heavy rains and high seas weren't just a problem for the ships and small craft making the crossing; bad weather would prevent protective air cover, a critical element of the plan. Because of the tides, the assault window extended only to June 7. A cancellation beyond that would mean waiting another two weeks—and the likelihood of a security lapse, an immense drain on morale, and untold logistical problems.

But there was nothing to be done about the weather. Ironically, June 4 dawned bright and clear. Bradley spent some of the morning in his war room, a specially constructed two hundred square foot sheet metal hut built on the deck where the *Augusta*'s spotter aircraft were normally kept. A map table filled the center of the room; on its surface was a map of the beaches and their defenses. Maps and charts were taped along the walls; there was a map showing the enemy's coastal guns, another showing the beach terrains.

There was also a pinup of a girl lounging on a beach that would have been considerably more fun to land at.

Bradley was restless. He fretted about the delay, worried about the likely result of trying to sequester 140,000 men for two weeks...or maybe four if the weather didn't cooperate again.

He tried to relax by reading *A Bell for Adano*, John Hersey's novel about an American officer on Sicily.[2] He couldn't concentrate on the book. He picked up a day-old *Stars and Stripes* and read the baseball scores, lingering over the account of a 16-inning game between the Detroit Tigers and the New York Yankees.

Nothing tempered his restlessness. And it got worse—that afternoon, Bradley headed ashore for a conference on the delay. By now, the weather had risen; Bradley didn't need a meteorologist to tell him that yet another postponement was imminent.

Rear Admiral Alan Kirk, the naval commander of the Western Task Force carrying the U.S. troops, reviewed the situation and what the storm would mean—a two-day postponement, a possible daylight landing, two weeks or more of delay.

It was a long, frustrating meeting that arrived at a conclusion no one wanted—if they couldn't land June 6, they'd land June 8, with the bad tides, full daylight, and staggered beach times. It was the worst possible plan for an invasion—but it was better than calling everything off for two weeks.

Bradley headed back to the ship. By the time he reached it, it was midnight, and word had already come from Eisenhower: the invasion was on. June 6 was the day.[3]

Bradley spent much of June 5 waiting for an air attack that never came. The German Luftwaffe, reduced because of the demands of the Eastern front and depleted by combat with the Allies, had grounded most reconnaissance flights because of the weather. The German navy didn't send out its usual patrols that night either, expecting that the bad weather would make it too difficult for an invasion force to sail. Rommel, after checking forecasts that predicted the weather would not favor an invasion until at least June 10, had returned to Germany to celebrate his wife's birthday. He was also planning to visit Hitler and ask for two more panzer divisions.

Bradley had a boil on his nose lanced, and then discovered he'd have to wear a huge bandage; he banned anyone from taking his photo.

As darkness fell, the armada crept forward. The *Augusta*'s 8-inch guns were formidable, but they were dwarfed by those on the seven battleships and two British monitors (essentially floating gun platforms). There were more than twenty cruisers in the support fleet, with just under a hundred destroyers and an assortment of other combat vessels. Landing ships and small craft totaled well over 4,000. Ferried aboard larger vessels were 2,583 DUKWs and another 514 DD tanks.

Meanwhile, 1,300 RAF bombers were readied for takeoff. Twin-engined Mosquito nightfighters swept the sky over the Channel and northern France, hunting for anything that would challenge the ships.

Bradley left Kirk on the bridge around eleven that night and turned in. Taking off only his life jacket, he went to bed in his clothes and Moberly infantry boots.

At 0335, a loud bell roused him from sleep. *Battle stations!*

By the time Bradley reached the bridge, tracers were flaring from the shoreline. A bomber fell out of the sky, swooped in their direction, then leveled off before exploding behind the ship. The shore was on fire, bright orange flames licking the sky.

The *Augusta* sailed slowly toward the coast. Clouds hung low over the water; it was cold and the wind was stiff, but there was no rain. B-17 Flying Fortresses and B-24 Liberators passed overhead—329 of them to be exact. But the thick cloud cover was a formidable opponent for the bombardiers. Worried about killing their own men, they pickled their payloads too far from the German defenses to do any good. Bradley counted that among the key early disappointments on Omaha beach.

A little before 6:00 a.m., one of the sailors gave Bradley a wad of cotton for his ears. The *Augusta* trained her guns on the shore batteries and defenses. Until now, the howling wind had blocked most sounds; even the airplane crash had been silent. But the salvo of the big guns was a roar from hell.

Or maybe the shout of a hundred thousand men come to take back the continent. The force of the guns pushed the large ship down in the water, the vessel shuddering under the weight of the strike. Again and again she fired. Black shells sped upwards in the night, their high arc visible from the bridge.

"I missed the Fourth of July last year," Bradley told the captain and the others on the bridge. "I'm making up for it this morning."[4]

His aides thought he was confident, even optimistic, ready for battle. He was still able to make easy jokes more than an hour later in the operations room, waiting for the first reports. Meanwhile, he kept track of the timeline in his head, seeing each unit in his mind as the time came for it to launch—the Rangers climbing Point du Hoc, the 1st Infantry Division touching the sand.

But then came the inevitable lull, the low point when, after being teased by the promise and optimism of the terse first reports—

We've made the beach!—the lack of information and good hard intelligence began to wear. The staff grew tense. Bradley grew quieter. There was little anyone in the war room could do about the battle now; the privates and corporals and sergeants on the beach, their lieutenants and captains—the men being shot at in the waves and on the sand would determine Bradley's next moves.

Needing to know how effective his ship's fire was, Kirk asked Bradley if he could send someone from his staff to help a naval gunnery officer make the assessment. Bradley agreed; Hansen volunteered.

A PT boat came alongside the cruiser. Compared to the *Augusta*, she was a tiny vessel, little more than a speedboat with guns. But that was in her favor: she zigzagged toward shore, slipping between the armada of cruisers and destroyers. Two sailors lay belly-flat on the bow of the PT, trying to spot mines in the high waves.

Landing craft were jammed near the water's edge. The safe channels to shore were narrow, bordered by German obstructions and the hulks of wrecked vessels.

The PT threaded along the shoreline, the gunnery officer and Hansen training binoculars on the land. As ferocious as the shelling was, there was still plenty of life in the German defenses.

Back on the Augusta, the fragmentary reports reaching Bradley got him worried. The plan for the invasion had called for the Americans on Omaha to reach a road just beyond the beach by 0830. The time came and went without a single report from the two regiments making the assault.

Returning soaked and cold from his scouting mission, Hansen reported that the troops he'd seen in the 1st Division area were stalled at a sea wall not far from the water's edge. Meanwhile, the landing craft behind them, unable to get through the choked water lanes, were diverting to another beach.

The Americans were ashore, but things were not going as well as planned.

★ ★ ★ ★

The failure of the heavy bombers' attack on Omaha upset a crucial part of Bradley's plan for the beach. Compounding the problem were troubles with the DD tanks. Many struggled to get ashore, most because they were released far too early. Only five of the thirty-two Shermans in the 741st Tank Battalion reached land safely, two because they were taken right into the beach by their LCT. In addition, fewer infantry were on shore because of the jam up on the beaches.

But the biggest problem on Omaha was the ferocity of the German resistance. The bombardment from the ships was like a massive, frightening earthquake, yet the Germans rallied effectively, raining down fire on the beaches. The initial assault force was not small: 34,000 troops with 3,300 vehicles. But Omaha would prove the most difficult beach to take.[5]

As noon approached, Bradley got word from V Corps that the troops on Omaha were pinned down and the routes off the beach were heavily defended. The reports troubled him deeply. His main concern was to rapidly build up the units on shore, bringing in enough men and supplies to repulse any counterattack. His second wave for Omaha consisted of 25,000 men and 4,400 vehicles, all due to start landing at noon. But he couldn't send them in if the beach had not been secured. Nor could he leave them off-shore, where they would be useless in battle and ripe targets for the Luftwaffe.

Bradley considered sending the men to the other beaches, both Utah and those in the British sector. It was a critical decision—sending them to another beach would have an important impact on the battle plan. If Omaha was abandoned, it would leave a massive gap in the Allied lines. Just the failure to advance from the beach would present a tactical dilemma for the rest of the invasion.[6]

Facing a decision that could have potentially changed the course of the war, Bradley sent his chief of staff General Kean to gather first-hand information. Together with Colonel Truman Thorson (Bradley's G-3) and Hansen, Kean took a picket boat over to *Achernar* to see if they had better information on what was going on. The wind and waves tossed the little boat severely; so Kean and the others had to leap for a rope ladder and hoist themselves onto the command ship. But for all his trouble, Kean found little that he didn't already know. The sum total was chaos and simply ignorance about what was going on ashore. When Kean returned to the *Augusta*, Bradley told him to go to the beach—there was simply no other way to find out what was happening.

Kean had a dangerous task, and the fact that Bradley sent him is one sign of his desperation for reliable information. (Bradley couldn't go himself, not just because his loss would have left the force without a leader, but because it would have put him out of touch with his commanders.)

A Snelling PT boat took Kean and Hansen about 2,000 yards from shore, well within range of the shore batteries. From there they boarded an LCVP, a small landing craft. So many obstacles blocked the way that the coxswain let them off in four feet of water.

As they waded to shore, they saw bodies in the surf, wrecked boats in the water, rubble piled everywhere. As Hansen put it:

> All over the beach lay hundreds of gas masks and packs, and all the equipment that men throw overboard quickly. Floating in the shallow water there lay rolls of film, thousands of discarded life belts, rations, smashed portions of landing craft. Floating nearby in the water we saw one body with a leg blown off. There was evidence that several boats had hit the mines....The beachmaster...was a young captain who reported that his CO had been wounded or killed....Cases of ammunition were scattered about. There was complete disorder on the beach....
>
> As we talked to the captain, an enemy artillery shell landed in a concentration of the LCTs off to our left. Troops were scrambling ashore quickly in the waist-deep water. Wounded lay in shell holes near the bank....Another shell landed nearby,

hit a truck and threw a soldier's body thirty feet into the air where it hung for a moment, turned over, and fell lifelessly to the ground.[7]

And yet—the beach had been cleared of small arms fire, and the troops were moving up to the exits and beyond.

They were moving. Omaha could be secured.

Kean frantically searched for a boat back to the *Augusta*.

Bradley ordered the second wave in. Things remained dicey. They needed bulldozers to clear the debris, more men to rush past the initial lines of defense.

And most importantly, they needed more leadership ashore. Kean's report made it clear that the battle had already taken a significant toll on commanders at the platoon level and above. The division commanders had not yet gone ashore, and much of the fight was being led by junior officers and NCOs.[8]

Feeling more confident, but still considering changes to the overall plan, Bradley found his own boat and made his way over to the USS *Ancon,* where General Leonard Gerow, commander of V Corps, and General Clarence Huebner, commander of the 1st Infantry Division, had established their headquarters. There he discovered that the 16th Infantry Regiment had called for support; Bradley ordered the 18th in as reinforcements as quickly as possible. Large elements of the 116th had initially landed in the wrong area and moved laterally across the beach toward its objectives. Along the way they had left pockets of resistance, which now had to be cleaned up.

But these were relatively minor adjustments. Gerow's map showed that the defenses had clearly been pierced. There was no need to dramatically alter the invasion plans. What they needed to do now was push men ashore, to try and get the situation as stable as possible before the Germans were able to move in their reinforcements.

Difficult, but doable.

As he admits in *A Soldier's Story*, Bradley went to the ship partly because he was worried about the effect of the battle on Gerow and

Huebner, who had never seen combat as senior commanders before. While Bradley doesn't say so directly, he intended to get Gerow and Huebner ashore to help make up for the loss of the senior regimental commanders. It was a critical moment, with a leadership vacuum on the beach.

Huebner needed no prodding—he already had plans to get ashore by evening, only a few hours away when Bradley arrived. Gerow said he was going in the morning, when communications could be set up.

"To hell with your communications," said Bradley. "The division needs you. Get ashore."

Gerow changed his plans.[9] Bradley left to check on things at Utah.

The VII Corps headquarters ship was the USS *Bayfield,* an attack transport that had carried members of the 8th Infantry Regiment to the battle and was doubling as a hospital ship. Bradley met with "Lightning Joe" Collins, the corps commander, and Raymond Barton, the commander of the 4th Infantry Division.

Certainly compared to Omaha, things were going well on Utah. The battle there had begun with parachute drops inland not long after midnight. Hundreds of C-47s dipped low over the water, braving sudden barrages of flak and struggling to stay on the courses indicated by teams of pathfinders, whose radar beacons were not always on target. The ground fire made the pilots fly faster than planned, and added jinks and jives never encountered in training. Paratroopers went out in groups of sixteen and eighteen from the planes, jumping past arcing tracers. The heavy wind pulled sharply at their canopies; flooded fields waited to drown many below.

The 82nd Airborne had been tasked with taking Sainte Mere Eglise, about six miles from the coastline. There it would cut the road and a rail link to Cherbourg. The division was also assigned to capture bridges over the Merderet River, another half mile or so beyond the train tracks. The

101st Airborne Division, dropping farther south, was to hold the causeways leading to the beaches, as well as bridges that crossed the Douve River.

The drops were not as scattered as that over Sicily, but they were still night drops, and chaos was a bigger threat than the enemy. The 82nd Airborne took Sainte Mere Eglise within an hour of the jump, as several platoons were able to converge on the town center after landing in and around it. (One soldier snagged his parachute on the steeple in the center of town. He hung there helplessly, pretending to be dead while watching the German defenders firing at his comrades.)

The village became a rallying point for the Americans, who formed small groups and began making their way to their other objectives. Gliders with more troops and heavy equipment crash landed in the fields nearby. The landings were even more chaotic than the parachuting, with many men killed and equipment lost. The assistant division commander of the 101st died when the glider he was in crashed into a tree; a jeep in the cargo compartment jerked free and crushed him.

Despite the confusion and losses, the airborne assaults achieved most of their first-night and early morning objectives. Casualties were lower than expected—only 21 of the 850 C-47s were destroyed, far fewer than Leigh-Mallory had predicted. (The British commander, in fact, wrote an apology to Eisenhower for opposing the plan.)

The Allied bombers that attacked the German defenses at Utah were more accurate than those at Omaha, but still not very effective. The ships' guns did better, and the naval shelling helped clear mines from the beach. The DD tanks assigned to Utah were able to land without a single loss, and the beaches were secured within an hour of the landing.

Troops began pouring through the exits. Teddy Roosevelt Jr.—whom Bradley had removed from the Big Red One—waded ashore with the 4th Infantry Division. The ranking general officer on the beach, he put together an attack that secured one of the crucial exit routes, allowing troops to move inland. Tanks and men from the 4th Infantry Division hooked up with the 101st Airborne Division by the time Bradley arrived aboard the *Bayfield*.

With night approaching, the admiral in charge of the landing craft on Utah wanted to suspend the unloading of men and supplies. He'd lost several small boats and, Bradley implied later, was losing his nerve. Bradley hadn't lost his. He knew he needed more men, more ammo, more everything delivered to the beaches. He insisted that the unloading continue. It did.

Supply was critical on D-Day and in the days that followed. It was a problem never completely solved. Ammunition was critically short at several points in the campaign, materially affecting the drive into Germany and arguably prolonging the struggle at the Bulge and elsewhere.

The reasons were myriad and began back in the States, where the procedure for organizing and transporting supplies itself was disorganized. A seemingly mundane matter such as the order in which supplies were loaded into a ship could have vast consequences on the battlefield; a delay in taking a certain type of ammo off a vessel was multiplied by shortages or scheduling snafus affecting the smaller craft needed to ferry it ashore. More disastrous was the lack of manifests indicating which ships were carrying what supplies. Their failure to arrive, despite a number of pleadings, requests, and orders, turned much of the operation into guesswork. Manpower problems—and union work orders among the Merchant Marine—would give Bradley headaches for the remainder of the war.

On D-Day, the difficulties on Omaha created a backlog of their own, in effect putting the supply chain nearly a day behind as the battle began. And the Navy's caution, both in bringing supply transports near the beaches and in committing combat vessels to dangerous areas would become a continuing source of irritation for Bradley over the next several days.

"These people have the idea that it's criminal to lose a ship," he complained. "They just won't take any chances with it…instead of using them and making them work, taking whatever losses they have."[10]

As far as Bradley was concerned, they could pave the bottom of the Channel with ships as long as they had enough forces on the beach to withstand the German counterattacks.

★ ★ ★ ★

Bradley went over the side of the *Bayfield* as dusk fell. He had a difficult time climbing down to his PT boat on the rope ladder, and finally jumped the last few feet. A sailor at the bow, trying to hold the small vessel steady against the rocking transport ship, fell into the water and was nearly crushed between the two.

They headed back to the *Augusta* in the dark. In the darkness, it was difficult to get any bearings, and the little PT boat swung through the throng of blacked-out ships. Warnings that the Germans might try and attack with E Boats—small craft similar to PTs—meant Bradley's vessel was constantly challenged, despite blinking a recognition light.

They were still hunting for the *Augusta* when guns began firing all around them. Tracers lit the night. The bullets crescendoed upwards, fending off a Luftwaffe attack—whether real or imaginary, Bradley never knew.

The crew finally spotted the *Augusta* and pulled up alongside.

"Permission to come aboard!" shouted the PT skipper through his megahorn.

"Lie off!" yelled a crewman from above.

"We have passengers!"

"Lie off!"

The tiny ship bobbed up and down as the gunfire continued. Something burned out in the Channel—a downed aircraft or an unlucky ship?

Finally the gunfire slowed, and the patrol boat closed with the cruiser. Bradley grabbed the rope ladder and hoisted himself upwards.

"Where are the prisoners?" asked a sailor as he came on deck. The crew pushed forward behind him. The shout of "passengers" had been misheard as "prisoners," and the crew was anxious to see the first trophies of war.

"Oh hell," said a sailor. "It's just General Bradley.[11]

Back aboard his command ship, Bradley made his way to the operations room. He stayed there well past midnight, poring over the reports and assessing the situation on his two beaches. Casualties were relatively light—only about 200 at Utah and 2,000 on the first day at Omaha, but the situation remained dangerous.

Fortunately, the fears that the Germans would use poison gas proved unfounded. Most of the gas masks the troops had carried ashore now lay discarded in the sand. While rumors of "secret gases" would continue until the end of the war, none were ever used.[12]

On Sicily, Bradley had reacted angrily to atrocities involving POWs when the incidents were reported to him. But while those incidents offended his sense of justice—the men had surrendered and were in American care, under the charge of an officer or NCO—Bradley's outrage had particular limits.

In Normandy, atrocities were committed on both sides, though apparently never as blatantly as the incidents he had insisted be prosecuted. There were scattered instances of soldiers on both sides being gunned down after they had surrendered, or as they tried to surrender. At different points in the battle, the Americans, especially paratroopers, did not stop to take prisoners, whether the enemy was willing to surrender or not. The same seems to have been true on the German side. On the other hand, a large portion of enemy prisoners of war were processed, most without incident.

One of the things that truly angered the Americans was the wiring of their dead with explosives, which not only killed a second or third man, but also mutilated the dead in what seemed an obscene and sacrilegious gesture. For their part, Germans reacted angrily when they captured prisoners who had looted personal equipment—guns mostly—as souvenirs from their own dead.

Bradley's attitude was brutally realistic. Told by someone that Germans had lured Americans close by pretending to surrender and then shot at them, Bradley's reply was, "That should make them mad."[13]

Bradley spent the next few days going back and forth between his ship and the beachhead, growing increasingly frustrated about the fact that his command post was still back on the *Augusta*, yet refusing to divert the resources it would have taken to move him. Establishing the Army headquarters on land required considerable equipment, which in turn meant diverting some of the craft ferrying supplies to the soldiers. Bradley was obsessed with getting artillery and tanks ashore, expecting a major counterattack, and kept reiterating his priorities.

It wasn't as if nothing was getting ashore. On the contrary, the beaches were jammed with supplies and soldiers. Bradley had conferences every day trying to smooth the flow. Kean, his chief of staff, devoted most of June 8 and the early morning hours of June 9 to trying to straighten out the developing chaos. The Germans were dropping mines and sending E boats to raid the flotilla; in retrospect the losses would come to seem fairly light, but in the sheer anxiety of the moment every small attack might signal the start of something larger.

★ ★ ★ ★

On D-Day-plus three, Bradley and Dickson sat in their jeep, watching MPs direct an army of vehicles across the causeways at Utah. A young soldier stood at the entrance to the causeway, waving traffic across in just his bare undershirt. The wind kicked off the waves in gusts, and the young man was shivering.

Bradley got out of the jeep. Dickson scrambled to follow.

"Son, you look mighty cold to me," Bradley told the soldier. "Where's your coat?"

"Lost it, sir," replied the soldier.

"Well here, you take mine," said Bradley, stripping off his tanker's jacket. "I can get another one easier than you."[14]

On June 10, Bradley's aides finally established his command post on shore near Pointe du Hoc. In the meantime, a pair of cars arrived to take Bradley to Montgomery's headquarters. He was surprised to find the waiting vehicles weren't staff cars as he had expected, but armored cars.

Bradley demurred—what kind of leader was too scared to move around the country except in an armored vehicle?

"They've been trying to get me in one of those things for years," he groused, referring to his security people. The British weren't going to succeed now. He found a jeep instead.[15]

DUKWs were everywhere near the beachhead, heavily laden with ammo and other supplies. The soldiers the general passed were starting to show signs of fatigue; even the freshest arrivals hadn't shaved for a few days. They were tired, their uniforms dirty. Bradley's own clothes had taken a beating. Usually he arrived from the ship soaked from having to wade through the water, but today he had worn a pair of oilskin trousers—wading pants that kept him dry as he came in from the boat.

En route to Montgomery, Bradley's small coterie of vehicles stopped for a funeral procession in a village. The parish priest led a line of women clad in black down the road. On each side, ruined houses smoldered with fire, wisps of smoke curling through the dank air. Dead cattle littered the fields beyond the wrecked buildings. Stiff legs pointed skyward from their bloated bodies. Here and there a French tricolor flapped from a window. A woman saw the jeep and formed her fingers into a V as Bradley passed.

The rest of the villagers went on with their business, clearing the rubble, grieving the dead, trying to pull the shards of their lives back into something coherent—praying that the Germans were gone for good. They had nearly as much to fear from a counterattack as the Allied troops did.

Montgomery's plans for taking Caen on D-Day had stalled; this failure would plague him and become a point of irritation for the entire Allied command. At this point, the immediate problem was that the failure to take Caen left open a path for a German counterattack. Bradley had to adapt his forces to that possibility.

The British commander met Bradley in the yard in front of a stucco house. He spread a map on the hood of his car and began reviewing the situation. Dressed in a floppy gabardine jacket and his trademark corduroy trousers, Montgomery looked more like a hunter out on a country jaunt than the Allied ground commander trying to pull together his line. All in all, Montgomery told Bradley, he was pleased with his progress.

Bradley smiled and admitted that things were far better than they had been during the opening hours of D-Day. "Someday I'll tell General Eisenhower just how close it was in those first hours," he said.[16]

Two days later, Bradley broke out a fresh uniform, helmet, and boots for another meeting ashore, this one with General Marshall. The chief of staff had traveled from America to see the European bridgehead himself. By now, the beach had been cleared and organized. The world had changed dramatically in less than a week.

Marshall, in his dress "pinks," parceled out few smiles. For a moment, Bradley seemed a junior officer again, overly deferential and soft-spoken. "Very glad to see you sir," was his greeting to Marshall.

Eisenhower, Montgomery, and other Allied commanders accompanied them as they drove over to Isigny in the elbow between the two American beachheads. The battle wounds were fresh. Bullet and shell holes pockmarked the church; houses still smoldered with smoke and fire. Leading the way back to the beach so they could go back out to the ships, Bradley found the way jammed with traffic. He got out of the jeep, strode over to the line of vehicles, and played traffic cop, shunting the supply trucks to one side so the VIPs could squeeze past.

Earlier that morning, the 101st Airborne had taken Carentan. Some five miles inland, the city connected to the coast via a narrow channel. Receiving Ultra intelligence that a counterattack was planned, Bradley brought Maurice Rose's 2nd Armored combat command into the town to reinforce it, setting the stage for a ferocious firefight the next morning.

The Germans began at 5:30 with an advance by the 37th SS Panzergrenadier-Regiment under cover of an artillery barrage. The mobile infantry appeared at first to be making good progress as they sped toward the city near the Carentan-Domville road. But the trees and hedgerows that lined the road and separated the small fields were excellent cover for snipers, machine guns, and small knots of soldiers. The Germans soon found themselves in a harassing crossfire. The attack slowed.

Suddenly a phalanx of Shermans burst against the right wing of the German attack. The tanks mauled the infantrymen, who had advanced without support against what they thought were lightly armed troops. The counterattack was broken.

The victory meant Bradley had stitched his two fronts firmly together. The drive across the Cotentin Peninsula could proceed.

Bradley valued Collins and his VII Corps very highly, but the Corps had its share of problems. Coming on shore soon after the initial assaults, the 90th Infantry Division stalled in combat, failing to take what Bradley believed were easy objectives. Within days it had been tagged as a "problem division."

Collins recommended that its commander, Brigadier General Jay W. MacKelvie, be relieved. Bradley reluctantly agreed, deciding that MacKelvie was not aggressive enough with his men—"not enough of a driver to be a good division commander,"[17] recorded Hansen at the time.

Collins' VII Corps deputy, Gene Landrum, was given the command. But he was put on a very short leash, and when the division continued to falter after three weeks, he too was cashiered, replaced with Brigadier General Raymond S. McLain, a National Guard general whom Bradley had been impressed with in Sicily.

The division's failures included the capture by the Germans of two companies, and a retreat from a key position that left the rest of the line in the lurch. In its commanders' defense, the green troops were fighting in one of the most difficult offensive environments possible. But for Bradley, the issue of the division's performance was a reflection of its senior officer corps. When he cited Landrum's failure, he said he had failed because he had not thoroughly cleaned house. For all his humanity toward the troops and his soft voice, Bradley could be brutal when it came to dealing with his subcommanders.

(Under McLain, the division went on to have a successful record. McLain's efforts were rewarded when he was promoted to corps commander in October.)

Because of its problems, the 90th was replaced by the 9th Infantry Division, which began its drive across the Cotentin beginning June 14. By nightfall on June 17, the peninsula had been cut, sealing Cherbourg's fate. But getting enough ammunition to the troops was becoming a major headache. Artillery played a critical role in Bradley's strategy and in basic Army doctrine—it wasn't called an infantryman's best friend for nothing. The guns or "tubes" were getting ashore, but their ammunition wasn't. One corps was limited to twenty-five rounds of 155 mm shells per day.

That would soon seem generous.

Two days after the peninsula was cut off, the weather rose on the Channel. Rain poured and winds howled. The immediate affect was to give the Germans a respite from Allied air power, which was making it difficult for the Nazis to move reinforcements as well as supplies up to the front lines.

The storm grew. The cold front ushering it in was so severe the temperature became almost winter-like. The heater in the truck Bradley used as his command post gave out. He refused to order a new one, deciding to his staff's chagrin that he could easily do without it.

The storm battered the Mulberry artificial harbors and tore through the beaches, doing far more damage than the Luftwaffe. The flow of supplies and new troops stopped.

The effects of the storm are generally measured only by the delay in getting supplies to the men, but the bad weather also slowed VII Corps' drive on Cherbourg and indirectly delayed the breakout from the peninsula.

Before the storm, Bradley hoped to take Cherbourg by June 21.[18] That timetable would have allowed for a hard push south shortly thereafter. The storm-induced delay of about five days was critical for the Germans, allowing them to reorganize and stiffen defenses in an area that naturally favored defense. Meanwhile, the ammunition drought became so severe that an airlift was arranged and the Army tapped the emergency ammo dump Bradley had brought in by barge at the start of the campaign. Personnel were instructed not to mention the ammunition problem even tangentially over the radio, lest the Germans realize that a concerted attack might rout the Allies because of it.

Hitler had ordered that Cherbourg be defended to the end. The commander of its garrison dutifully complied until his men were able to sabotage the port facilities. He and about 800 of his troops surrendered June 26. By that time, between the sabotage and bombing and naval gunfire, much of the city lay in ruins.

The German general refused to broadcast an order for the rest of his men to surrender. Holdouts had to be systematically engaged and hunted down over the next few days, adding to Bradley's bitterness. He refused the German commander's request to dine with him; the general ended up eating K rations instead.

Bradley's attitude probably wasn't helped by reports that the Germans had booby-trapped and mined much of the city. Destruction of the port facilities and buildings was extensive and obvious; it would be many long weeks before the Allies could dependably use the port. But there were also rumors that the Germans had planted time bombs throughout the port area. Dickson and his men spent considerable time interviewing captured German engineers, trying to figure out if the rumors were true. The Navy took the claims very seriously, and Bradley finally ordered Dickson to tell them they weren't true—a point Dickson believed but couldn't prove. He followed orders, then sweated it out, hoping nothing would happen, until the twenty-one days were up and no bombs had gone off.[19]

When Cherbourg fell, a dozen German Army nurses were taken as prisoners. Acting on Dickson's advice, Bradley arranged for the nurses to tour the American hospital facilities before they were transferred to the German front lines without demanding a prisoner exchange.

"The gesture paid off," Dickson recalled later. "We got three deserters that night...and all along our course we heard repercussions of the discouraging takes these girls told of our equipment and might."[20]

Bradley did not ride triumphantly into Cherbourg when VII Corps took the city, nor did he stage a triumphant review once it was secure. It was in sharp contrast to what other Allied army commanders had done in Africa and Sicily, and at a press conference several days after the city's capture, he was asked why. Bradley surely had a host of reasons—he was busy planning the turn south, had other battles to worry about, and was getting ready to transition from army to army group commander. But the one reason he singled out was typical Bradley: "I gave General Collins the job to take that city. He did his job. It was General Collins' party and I prefer that he take the honors."[21]

Decisions like this have sometimes been interpreted as signs of Bradley's shyness, but there's more going on here. Bradley at times was almost militantly modest, and it's not surprising that he wasn't very big on processional marches. But clearly he recognized that there was value in the parade, even if it was only personal. And he saw more value to the war effort if the honors (and publicity) accrued to Collins rather than him. It was invaluable motivation.

The fact that Bradley was willing to cede such honors to subordinates is certainly one reason they tended to admire him. But there was a price to pay to posterity. Army commander Patton is given credit for taking

Messina. Corps commander Collins is given credit for taking Cherbourg. They're in the pictures and prominent in the news reports from the time. Bradley made both victories possible, yet he missed the triumphant parades—and the photographs that remain today. That's one reason he's been miscast as a back bencher in many historical accounts.

In writing in his diary about the press conference, Hansen directly contrasted Bradley's decision to let Collins enter Cherbourg with Patton's decision to take Messina himself. [22] This was not an idle parallel. As army commander, Bradley seems to have been trying to correct the wrongs Patton committed toward him and his staff on Sicily. Certainly his staff was anxious to correct those mistakes.

In this instance, it had a trivial effect on the war. But Bradley's attempts not to be dictatorial toward his corps commanders, his attempt not to interfere, to treat people as he wanted to be treated—in short, to be not-Patton—could lead him to giving them more leeway to meet an objective than he might otherwise have desired.

That may have extended the next phase of his campaign on the Cotentin Peninsula, as he endeavored to let his commanders follow through on their plans with minimal interference. It may also have been one reason why he was so quick to dismiss leaders he felt had failed—if he couldn't trust them to get results, they didn't fit into his way of doing things.

The capture of Cherbourg resulted in one non-military bonus.

The Germans had stocked the city with an incredible amount of fine wines and brandy. There was so much, in fact, that Bradley wasn't sure what exactly to do with it. Finally, with Eisenhower's approval, he ordered it evenly divided among the divisions in France.

He got a half case of champagne for himself, keeping it until his grandson was christened some years later.

Montgomery had planned on taking Caen on D-Day. Had that happened, he would have maneuvered a large army into position for a drive east, threatening Le Havre, Rouen, and the entire northern eastern coast of France. With that drive underway, an American breakthrough south to Avranches would not have had to worry about German reinforcements, let alone an attack on its flanks. Brittany, very lightly defended, would be clear; a drive south of the Loire would be easy.

But Caen had not been taken, and Montgomery's failure was frustrating Eisenhower and the rest of the Allied high command. What must have been particularly infuriating was Montgomery's habit of telling Eisenhower one thing—assuring him that Caen would soon be taken, for example—while privately telling his generals something else. British 7th Armoured Division leader Major General George Erskine was told not to worry about taking Caen in late June, because the goal was just to tie Germans down.[23]

They completely misstated Caen's importance to the overall plan. It wasn't just a city on the Allied front. It sat at the head of a plain that the Allies believed would lead them through northern France and eventually into Germany. Montgomery himself had outlined a lightning strike across Europe, and the place where it was to have been launched was at Caen. So the failure to take the city threatened the entire plan for winning the war.

Bradley did not approve of Montgomery's personal style or like the way he treated Americans, but given that the field marshal seems to have deferred for the most part to Bradley on matters concerning the First Army, their relationship at this point was, at worst, professional. But following a meeting June 29, Bradley became convinced that Montgomery wanted to revise the post-invasion plans and retain control of the American First Army, incorporating it into an attack east to Pas de Calais. The area had suddenly gained importance with the launch of the new German V-1 rockets, the pilotless "buzz bombs" that were striking southern England.

Bradley objected on two grounds. First, while the rockets were important psychological weapons, they were not causing much damage to military assets; in effect, they were being wasted, at least tactically.

And Montgomery's plan would keep the Americans—and Bradley—under his thumb. Bradley opposed the plan. With the British stalled in front of Caen, the idea of attacking into Pas de Calais was moot. But Bradley's suspicions must have colored his perception of Montgomery's proposal to use the American 3rd Armored Division in his fight against Caen during Operation Epson, a failed attempt to get into and through Caen at the end of June.

With the Germans threatening his western flank, Montgomery wanted to move the American division in against a pack of German armor. Bradley wanted to use the armored division for his own drive off the Cotentin Peninsula. Eventually Bradley came up with a compromise—he would take over a portion of the British front to his left, allowing Montgomery to use British units for his attack.

But forging the compromise wasn't easy. Tensions between the two commanders rose to the extent that Bradley's staff seemed to be watching their normally calm commander for a blowout by the end of the month.

"Do you want me to give you a baseball bat?" quipped Kean before Bradley went to talk to Montgomery about the shift.

Bradley laughed and told him he wouldn't need it—he was coming back either "bloody or out of a job."

Baseball bat or no, Bradley parried Montgomery's arguments that afternoon and retained the division for his own use. At one point during tea, Montgomery suddenly switched the conversation to the topic of Bradley's aides—he'd brought Hansen with him.

"I say, do you have a major for your aide de camp?" asked Montgomery, pointing to Hansen's insignia. "Simply a dog body, you know. A whipping boy. I would not have an aide de camp who is more than a captain."

"What are all these lieutenant colonels I see around here?" snapped Bradley.

"Oh they are simply my MA and PA (assistants), part of my personal cabinet, so to speak," answered Montgomery.

If someone is good enough to work as an aide, retorted Bradley, *he will do well in another job.* He saw the position as a training step for future ranks.

"Messenger boys, simply messenger boys," sniffed Montgomery.[24]

★ ★ ★ ★

One afternoon while Bradley surveyed the supply operations on the beach, a correspondent from NBC approached him with a cable from the States. It was a copy of a news story reporting the wedding of Bradley's daughter Elizabeth to Henry S. Beukema. They had married in the chapel at West Point on June 8.

★ ★ ★ ★

With Cherbourg taken, Bradley's next goal was to move off the peninsula, breaking out of the Normandy beachhead to seize ports in Brittany and to sweep south in the direction of Orleans and eventually on toward Paris. The Brittany ports were critical objectives, because they were removed from the fierce Channel storms, and were easily accessible from the United States.[25]

But the drive south would not be a simple one. The peninsula's rivers, bogs, and topography basically left three routes southwards, all well defended. In theory, the best area would have been in the vicinity of St.-Lo and Coutances; this was the thick middle of the peninsula, a stretch of some seventeen miles that ran along a good road between the two towns. Depending on where the German line was breached, the attackers would have their choice of small but parallel roads that could be used to push farther south.

But the Germans undoubtedly realized this as well, and dug in deeply at St.-Lo. Given the strength of the resistance, Bradley felt there was no way to come across the line and mount the attack without a head-on assault, which he wanted to avoid.

The terrain to the east was extremely boggy, and while Bradley eyed Carentan as a jump-off point, he feared that cutting across the marshes would take too long. Then, too, he would have to deal with the defenses at St.-Lo, which would either sit in his way or be a powerful nest of hornets in his side.

His third choice was to slash down the west coast from La Haye du Puits to Coutances. Again, he would have to deal with marshes, but

Bradley thought it was the best alternative. Even before Cherbourg was taken, he directed Middleton to organize the attack. Collins' corps, meanwhile, was to swing back from Cherbourg, engaging the enemy in front of Carentan.

Bradley's usual daily routine was to meet with his corps commanders and division generals in the field and then check in on the supply situation on the beach. He occasionally became involved in discussions with soldiers and field grade officers about small group tactics and even weapons; when told by tank officers about problems of dealing with the thickly armored German Panther tanks (*Panzerkampfwagen V Panther*), he suggested using 90 mm anti-aircraft guns against them. (The idea was a good one, though it took time to work out tactics.)

He incessantly studied his maps and the local terrain. Meanwhile, the Germans were reinforcing their units. Since the invasion, the German forces had shuttled most of their reinforcements to Caen. But now the Germans were moving more and better units to fight the Americans, hoping to fence them in. Toward the end of June, a patrol from the 90th Infantry Division captured prisoners from the 2nd SS Panzer Division, which had been shifted from Montgomery's sector to Bradley's.

On the morning of July 3, Bradley held a press conference at his command post. He started with a prepared statement on the capture of Cherbourg. It was the usual military public relations brief—accurate in its generalities and boringly predictable in its lack of particulars. Then he stepped over to a map and began lecturing on the new operation.

"This is off the record,"[26] he told the correspondents, before diving into a briefing of his attack plans. It was a performance worthy of his days as a tactical instructor, detailing for the correspondents how each corps was going to move and what the timetable was. The reporters were naturally interested in St.-Lo, the biggest city in that part of the peninsula. Bradley was cagey, not saying directly that he wasn't interested in taking it—but letting on that he intended to cut off and isolate the city, at which point the Germans would probably retreat. If they didn't, the city would be far more vulnerable than it was now.

The reporters pressed. When would it be taken?

"I'd guess six days," he said. "Depending on how long it takes to break through the crust and get rolling."

The operation had actually begun a few hours before. VIII Corps was already on the road toward Coutances.

The weather failed to cooperate; it was an unusually stormy and wet stretch for summer in France, and the rain made the already soggy ground even soggier. Still, the early progress was cause for optimism.

On July 4, American artillery across the entire front fired what was estimated as a 1,600-gun salute at high noon—a thunderous roar meant to celebrate not only American Independence but the beginning of the end for Germany's.

But what looked so good on Bradley's map proved in real life to be next to impossible. Middleton stalled. Progress was soon measured in yards rather than miles. By July 9, his troops moved only a few miles. Even "Lightnin' Joe" wasn't able to live up to his nickname—the bogs in front of Carentan slowed him to a point where progress was painful and excruciatingly slow.

Minefields, bogs, and most of all the bocage helped the outnumbered German defenders grind the offensive to a halt. The use of new troops on the American side, both wholesale—in VII Corps, the 83rd Division had come into the line for the 101st—and as replacements—VII Corps' 4th Division counted some 4,400 replacements in its ranks since D-Day—was also a factor. The inexperienced Americans had to learn to fight. Meanwhile, the Germans fought stubbornly well, brought in blooded reinforcements, and managed to blunt the Americans with a counterattack. The Panzer Lehr Division proved an especially tough opponent, taking a heavy toll with its Mark IV and Mark V tanks.

The Americans were wearing the Germans down, but Bradley hadn't planned on a battle of attrition. On July 14, he called the offensive to a halt. By any measure it had been a bloody bust.

★ ★ ★ ★

The area Bradley's troops were fighting in is known as the "bocage" to the French. The word is sometimes translated into English as "hedgerow," itself not a particularly well-known word to most Americans. The dictionary definition of a hedgerow is simply a row of trees or hedges separating one field from another. The word and the definition do little justice to what the Americans faced.

The land in Normandy had been farmed for centuries, and was broken into a patchwork of fields owned by different families. To mark off the fields, farmers had built walls and dirt mounds, planted trees and thick bushes. Over the years earth and vegetation had grown up, so that each field was separated by a natural wall.

The thickness and height of these walls varied greatly. In some places, dirt mounded up six or eight feet high; at the top a row of trees and thick vegetation might add an impenetrable layer anywhere from six to twenty feet high. In other spots, the fields were relatively open, separated by well-spaced trees. Some of the barriers were as thick as one-lane roads.

Added to the rolling countryside, the bocage presented a daunting barrier to a mechanized army. Even without digging in, they gave a defender several advantages—he would be difficult to spot, he would have some height over his opponent, and he would have a decent amount of natural cover. The network of narrow roads that ran through the area gave the defender another advantage. He could get from one position to another without exposing himself to enemy fire, he could move without being seen, and he could slip into other positions quickly and easily.

Using the narrow roads to launch attacks or even travel was dangerous. They twisted and turned, providing many points for ambush. Cutting across a field was problematic as well, since there was always the potential for multiple defensive positions. Depending on the location, interlocking fire could be mounted from three sides, practically encircling any troops entering a field. German machine-gun tactics and the weapons themselves were perfectly tailored for such situations.

Then there was the problem of climbing the bocage walls. A man might scramble up the steeper ones, but a vehicle would have trouble making the grade. Tanks had to expose their undersides as they climbed, while leaving their guns generally useless. Explosives and bulldozers, though vulnerable to enemy fire, were used to cut holes in the bocage when available, but the latter were in short supply. In some places the vegetation was so thick even a bulldozer had a tough time pushing through. Soldiers who fought in the bocage compared it to jungle fighting; Collins called it worse than Guadalcanal.

If this was an area made for a defender, it was also a place where typical American infantry tactics made for an extremely slow advance. American foot soldiers generally learned to hold and maneuver against an enemy. In simplest form, that meant part of a company would engage an enemy strongpoint, catching the enemy's attention and holding it in place. Meanwhile, another part of the company would move on the position from the flanks.

In theory, this was an effective and simple technique, avoiding the slaughter of a head-on attack. The problem in the bocage, however, was that the enemy could pin down the attackers more easily than the attackers could pin them down. It was often impossible to flank the enemy, since the flank was as strongly defended as the nominal forward position. The small fields and heavy undergrowth tended to break the battle into many small firefights. Maneuvering through them was time-consuming, and meant a plethora of hard-fought, small-scale engagements.

"Green" troops also had to resist the natural response to drop when first shot at. Stopping during a battle can be the most dangerous thing to do, since it makes a soldier an easier target. Yet this is a natural reaction, and one that must be unlearned, often only under fire. The reaction was especially dangerous in the bocage, where one or two defenders could stop a rush by a force ten times their number with a few shots, then pick off individual soldiers as they lay on the ground. The learning curve was steep and vicious.

Clearing a single field could take hours. It also called for a considerable amount of ammunition—one thing the Americans greatly lacked. They also lacked a weapon that could answer the German squad-level machine guns. Lightly armed (by comparison), American squads and companies could not match German units on a one-on-one basis, yet that was how they generally had to fight. The terrain made it difficult to mass an attack, and there were plenty of places for mines and anti-tank weapons to be hidden. The sound of the Shermans provided advance warning that the tanks were on their way, lessening the possibility of surprise.

The German tanks had the same problems as the Americans, and as offensive weapons their role was limited. But on defense, the tanks could provide enviable fire power, and were more than a match for any of the tanks the Americans brought in. Bradley liked to say that once dug in, a tank lost much of its value; but even so, bocage-concealed panzers were still formidable weapons.

The most effective American anti-tank weapon available to an infantry squad was the bazooka. But to count on a good hit—not necessarily a kill—it had to be fired at point-blank range, which generally meant exposing yourself to the enemy. Only gradually and through bitter experience did the Americans learn how best to use the weapon, targeting the rear of the tank where its armor was weakest and covering fire least likely.

Artillery fire might have helped give the U.S. assault more punch, but between the storm and other supply problems, shells were in short supply. As the battle moved inland from the beaches, the Army lost the off-shore guns of the vessels that had supported them since D-Day, further limiting the force available to overcome the enemy.[27]

The bocage battle was a slow, plodding affair, one that went against most of what Bradley believed about how a battle should be fought. He couldn't use speed and simply outmaneuver his enemy. He found himself in a head-on slugging match, the last thing he wanted. Armor was of such little use during the early stages of battle that he told his staff he had decided that the proper ration of infantry to armor divisions was three to one—not just a step down from Africa, but also from Sicily.

The decision to fight in Normandy wasn't Bradley's, but once it was made, he had to make the best of it. Clearly, he (and everyone else) underestimated the difficulty of fighting in the bocage. Bradley knew there were hedgerows, of course, and there had been exercises in the English countryside where the terrain was thought to be similar. But the checkerboard bocage in Normandy were considerably thicker, higher, stronger, and ultimately more perplexing. The American preparation—Bradley's preparation—was inadequate to deal with them.

In his unpublished memoir of the war, Dickson recalled that he had interviewed several British officers who had fought in the area during the German invasion of France. They spoke primarily about the swamps, missing what would become the truly important aspect of the geography. In Dickson's opinion, the defensive advantages of the area came as a surprise to the Germans as well as the Americans; if so, it was a surprise the Germans certainly made the most of.[28]

It also has to be said that the quality of the individual German soldiers in actual combat turned out to be higher than was predicted. This was a pattern repeated throughout the war, from the very first battle that Americans were engaged in—Dieppe—until the end. The German soldier was well-trained, well-armed, and very disciplined. He was a formidable foe.

The original Allied plan would have avoided much of the bocage by wheeling southeastwards in the area of Caen, where there were more and better roads as well as wider fields. But Montgomery did not take Caen.

Bradley realized that if he couldn't break past the German defenses soon, he might never be able to do so. With the Germans rapidly reinforcing their lines, a terrible possibility loomed: a return to the trench warfare of World War I.

Already the fighting had produced an enormous number of casualties. Allied divisions suffered an average of 2,000 casualties a month in Normandy; the Germans lost 2,300. In contrast, historian Anthony Beevor calculates losses on the Eastern Front at about the same time as 1,000 per month per German division, and 1,500 per month for Russian.[29] Normandy was one of the most consistently bloody campaigns of the war, with most of the casualties occurring after the beaches were stormed.

A stalemate and trench warfare would be even worse. Bradley had to contemplate not just the death toll, but the prospect that a long delay in breaking through the German lines might greatly lengthen the war—or even alter its course for the worst. The winter would certainly bring more storms, perhaps much more devastating than the one in mid-June. If Cherbourg remained the Allies' only port, their supply problems would multiply. A sharp German counterattack striking at the seam of the Allied front could easily drive them all back into the sea.

Suddenly stopped of momentum, desperate for a solution, Bradley had a massive map erected in a mess tent across from his command truck. He sat in the tent, alone with the map, searching for a way out of the bocage.

CHAPTER 6

Breakthrough

Bradley stared at the map for two nights, walking up and down the planked wooden floor of the tent. He made notes and alterations, drew lines, marked the disposition of troops, changed his mind.

By July 10, the outline of a plan had formed. It was called Cobra, and like the poisonous snake, it relied on a quick but devastating strike against the enemy.

Cobra was deceptively simple. He aimed to punch a hole in the German line just west of St.-Lo. Through that hole, he would pour as much of five divisions as would fit. (The plan eventually added another division.) While part of the force held the sides, an infantry division would swing down to Coutances, cutting off the German defenders to the north. Meanwhile, an armored spearhead would stream southwestwards toward Brittany.

Bradley needed overwhelming force to punch his five-mile gap in the line. He also needed a patch of ground dry and stable enough to move through. He found one west of St.-Lo, where there were enough passable roads and fields to allow a rapid advance. But to get through, he'd have to apply much more force much more rapidly than he'd been using until now. His idea wasn't so much to push against the Germans as to turn them into dust: Bradley marked a 3 ½- by 1 ½-mile-wide space for aerial bombardment to begin the campaign—one of the first uses of carpet bombing as a tactical weapon in battle.

Using heavy bombers on the battlefield was rare but not entirely unprecedented; Montgomery had recently tried something similar against Caen. But the earlier missions were flown, in theory at least, against specific targets; here the target would be simply a wide swath of land. (Given the technology of the day, there was little actual difference, except in concept.) The bombers would also be much more tightly coordinated with the ground attack than in any previous campaign.

The bombers' use is sometimes compared to the way artillery was employed at the start of an attack. The metaphor is limited. Possibly the shortage of artillery ammunition led Bradley to the idea, but if so (and it's not clear from his writings that this was actually the case), his notion quickly became something more. Aircraft were capable of delivering a considerably larger blow than the best artillery currently ashore. Additionally, the raid presented an intimidation value that was substantial and integral to the plan. And rather than substituting for artillery, the effect was intended to substitute for extended combat by ground units.

To use a modern concept, Bradley saw the bombers as a way to fast forward the action, achieving in a few hours what would have taken weeks. The attack would leave the enemy unprepared, just as a tank charge through a thinly held line created momentum impossible to stop. His divisions would speed through the mile and a half depth where the enemy had been obliterated, skipping past several layers of machine-guns, mines, tanks, and other dug-in defenses, launching into a battle of speed and maneuver.

Bradley specified that the bombs would be dropped very close to the front line—eight hundred yards was his original suggestion, or a little less than a half-mile. Given the technology of the day, that was almost suicidally close. (In the final plan, the troops were about 1,200 yards from the designated bombing area.) Looking to mitigate the danger to his men, he chose a start point for the assault along Periers Road, an east-west road easily visible from the air. Bradley felt this would give the bombers a clear demarcation of the bombing zone—critical at a time when bombing runs relied on a navigator sighting through the nose of the plane.

Mindful that bomb craters had made battlefields impassable in other places, Bradley also wanted only small bombs to be used—100 pounders were his preferred weapon. He calculated that 4,000 tons were needed, and was counting on an average crater pattern of one hole every sixteen feet.

Given how badly the bombing had missed its targets at Omaha, the plan reflected a remarkable trust in airpower. One measure of how radical Bradley's concept was can be seen in the fact that the air force failed to completely understand its elements. Their misunderstanding resulted in changes ranging from the bomb size (too big) to the direction of the bombers' approach (ninety degrees off), alterations that had as much effect on the actual implementation as the limits of the technology. Bradley learned of most of the changes too late to effectively protest or alter his plans to accommodate them.

While the air strike would generate the most controversy, both at the time and afterwards, there were several other risky elements to Cobra. One was the narrow front, which presented logistical problems in organizing the assault force. In *A Soldier's Story*, Bradley says there were two main roads and several unimproved roads in the area heading south. But even the main roads would be considered narrow farm lanes to most Americans today, and the ground here was as clogged with bocage and bogs as anywhere else. Moving through the area was a logistical puzzle.

Further, in order to make the push, Bradley had to commit everything he had to the battle; his entire reserve would be one untested battalion. Given the danger a German counterattack presented, that was cutting things extremely close.

Some historians have been flummoxed by Bradley's offhand description of how he planned Cobra—find a soft spot and drive through it. The statement is classic Bradley in its modesty, but it's not accurate. He wasn't attacking a weak spot. He was creating one. The spot he chose was not soft, even by comparison with other parts of the line. The Germans held the high ground near St.-Lo, and the main force of the German Seventh Army was deployed in the area. He was aiming to smack the snake hard in the head so that it couldn't quickly respond.[1]

Dickson's intelligence, which gave a fairly accurate picture of the German deployments, played an important role in shaping Bradley's specifics.[2] The Allied buildup of men and supplies aided Bradley as well. He now had four corps in the American sector: Collins' VII Corps, Gerow's V Corps, Middleton's VIII Corps, and Charles Corlett's XIX Corps. XIX Corps had filled between Collins and Middleton in the area east of the Vire River.

Bradley started talking with his staff members about his new concept the first week in July. By that point, he had chosen the general area and probably settled on how he was going to deliver the massive force he needed to start. The first person he discussed it with was Courtney Hodges, his deputy commander. Then Kean, Thorson, and Dickson. It was Thorson, the operations officer, who dubbed it Cobra.

The sector where Bradley planned the breakthrough was in front of VII Corps, which was neither surprising nor a coincidence of geography. Besides containing some of his best troops, it was led by "Lightning Joe" Collins, who had quickly become Bradley's favorite corps commander. All of First Army would contribute by engaging and pressuring the enemy, but the main thrust and exploitation would be led by Collins, and he played a key role in reviewing the plan. Lightning Joe had his first look July 12; over the next few days, he reviewed it with his staff. Then he and Bradley began making refinements, working in Bradley's makeshift map tent.[3]

As outlined by Bradley and Collins, the 9th and 30th Infantry Divisions would make the initial assault following the bombing attack. They would then step aside to hold the flanks. Part of the 83rd Division would help protect the west flank. The 1st Division would swing toward Coustances, with help from Combat Command B of the 3rd Armored Division. The rest of the 3rd Armored Division would swing farther south to protect that force's southern flank. The 2nd Armored Division would push deeper, protecting the flank and preparing for the drive toward Brittany.

Bradley called a conference with his division and the corps commanders to discuss the plan as it neared completion. Never shy, Ninth Infantry Division commander Lieutenant General Monton Eddy protested that the breakthrough was too wide for the now battered 9th and 30th Infantry Divisions.

"The carpet's too wide for two divisions," said Eddy.

"Very well then," said Bradley, turning to Collins. "You can have the Fourth Division."

Tubby Thorson, Bradley's G-3, looked worried—not only had Bradley just given away his only reserve for the offensive, but shifting the division into position would be difficult.

Bradley just laughed, confident the logistics problems could be overcome. He noted that as a corps commander in Tunisia he had never had the luxury of operating with a full division in reserve; holding it back was too cautious. Finally, he turned back to Collins.

"Anything else we can give you?" Bradley asked, referring to the different attachments and varied units he'd added to Collins' infantry divisions. "You've got everything now but my pistol."

Collins held out his hand.[4]

The story is an amusing anecdote, but it illustrates a deeper point: Bradley, and the U.S. Army as a whole, were extremely flexible in adapting tactics and forces to the conditions of the battlefield.

The U.S. Army is sometimes criticized for emphasizing mobility rather than firepower during the war; some historians have claimed that the triangular structure of American infantry divisions deprived them of sufficient force. But infantry divisions rarely if ever fought in isolation, at least under Bradley. The orders of battle in Africa, Sicily, and northern Europe all show an enormous flexibility and an integration of force.

Bradley's flexibility went beyond simply shifting a regiment here and there. First Army entered the bocage without tactics or experience to properly deal with the situation. Those tactics were developed at the company and squad level over the course of several weeks.[5] Soldiers had to learn to coordinate infantry, armor, and artillery in very specific ways; their commanders, up to and including Bradley, had to arrange their forces and adjust plans accordingly. This is often taken for granted in historical accounts, but the U.S. Army's flexibility was much higher, and in most cases more effective, than any other army's during the war. Its performance in France and later Germany is in direct contrast with Montgomery's army in France, and Bradley should receive a good portion of the credit. Bradley's willingness to shift the available parts around was a key part of the battle.

Bradley's command post was shelled July 14. Fragments from a 170 mm artillery shell blew through the side of his truck. Bradley himself wasn't there at the time.[6] Throughout First Army, deaths continued at an alarming pace. Among those who died was Ted Roosevelt Jr.—though ironically perhaps, the irrepressible brigadier general was felled not by a German bullet but by a heart attack.

Bradley got the news just after suggesting that Eisenhower appoint Roosevelt to head the 90th Infantry Division; the division had faltered once more, and Bradley was convinced that he needed a sparkplug to get it going. He aimed to pair Roosevelt with "a thick-skinned disciplinarian" and expected the division would be in shape within weeks of Roosevelt's arrival. Eisenhower approved Roosevelt's appointment a few hours after his death just before midnight on July 13, not having yet heard the news.

"Roosevelt had earned a division command as few men have but we had waited too long," wrote Bradley after the war. "He braved death with an indifference that destroyed its terror for thousands upon thousands of younger men. I have never known a braver man nor a more devoted soldier."[7]

On July 19, Bradley and his aides boarded a battered C-78 Cessna and flew over the Channel to talk to Leigh-Mallory about the plan.

The aircraft had been knocked around in the battle for Normandy; stitches on its fabric skin bore testimony to its hard service. An easy target for the Luftwaffe, the aircraft was generally considered too dangerous for someone of Bradley's rank to use. More critically, it was making the trip across the Channel without an escort. But the C-78 was all that was immediately available, and Bradley needed to be in England to explain his plans for Cobra. When his aides suggested that he wait for a bigger (and safer) plane, Bradley brushed them off. He interpreted such suggestions as a matter of luxury and vanity. The plane was there, he had a meeting to get to—there was no question in his mind that he should use it.[8]

Strapped into the copilot's seat, his plans in an aluminum tube between his legs, Bradley waited patiently through the half hour flight for the plane to reach Northolt Field near London. From there he drove to Leigh-Mallory's headquarters to explain Cobra. Unfurling his maps, he emphasized the Periers Road boundary marker, even suggesting how the bombers could use the sun to their advantage. He got a good reception, and was in an excellent mood when he left at 5:00 p.m., joking with Hansen.

As Bradley tells it in *A Soldier's Story*, Leigh-Mallory was extremely enthusiastic about the overall concept. According to Bradley, he was told that RAF bombers could not be used for the attack because of the small size of the bombs—apparently they lacked the proper rails—but he came away with a pledge of an Allied force of 1,500 heavy bombers, 396 mediums, and 350 fighter bombers for the operation. The main force would consist of American B-24s and B-17s, each carrying 4,100-pound bombs. The attacks would start exactly eighty minutes before the jump off, or "H-Hour." The last would take off seventy-five minutes after the assault troops began moving forward. A small portion of the attack was to be launched against strong points north of the Periers Road by fighter-bombers, whose attacks were believed to be more accurate than the others, but the vast number of bombs would fall south of the road.

Fighter-bombers were also to fly with the tank and infantry columns, working together as closely as possible. This was possible thanks to ground controllers who would communicate with the fighters via radios. Bradley had them placed in tanks so they would stay with the advanced columns, and to lessen the danger to them as they sped across the enemy lines. Assigning the tanks to the air force, which was responsible for the controllers, caused a rare bit of humor in the otherwise serious preparations.

The contributions of Major General Elwood R. "Pete" Quesada, the man largely responsible for the close air support, is one of the lesser told stories of Cobra. Quesada joined Bradley's team before D-Day as the head of IX Tactical Air Command, which was assigned to support First Army. At that point, "air support" was a new and somewhat nebulous concept. Nor was it universally accepted: many air force officers saw little glory in "ground pounding," while the commanders on the ground didn't see much value in the work of "flyboys."

Quesada, with Bradley's enthusiastic support and encouragement, proved both wrong. He was committed to the idea that commanders should be able to deploy air power as part of an attack, integrating the force as they would coordinate infantry, artillery, and armor.

There were three different elements to air support in the Normandy campaign. Two had been used throughout the earlier campaigns, though they were tweaked here. The first element consisted of assigned bombing and strafing missions, with pre-flight targets screened and approved by a group of air and ground officers working together. Other targets were designated during the battle itself, via radios that communicated to a central ground control center. These were ordered by a local commander, who had to go through several communications layers as well as a chain of command before a request for air power could be answered.

Quesada also assigned some of his fighter-bombers to specific ground units and had them communicate directly with each other over VHF radio. P-47 Thunderbolts—rugged fighters that were invaluable as attack aircraft—would work with lead columns of tanks in the 2nd and 3rd Armored Divisions in a way that had never been done on a large scale before. The aircraft provided reconnaissance information as well as firepower. Equipped with machine guns, 500-pound bombs, and in some cases napalm, they sortied every thirty minutes, a constant umbrella over the tanks. This close support would play a critical role in the breakout and the battles that followed.

Bradley was a strong advocate of air power, though his collaboration with Quesada has gone largely unremarked. (Today, Quesada is generally remembered—if at all—as the pilot who gave Eisenhower a joy ride over the Normandy battlefield in a Mustang P-51, defying General Marshall's orders.) Quesada's headquarters were adjacent to Bradley's (itself an innovation), and they were often together. Bradley speaks admirably of him in *A Soldier's Story,* calling him among other things "a young and imaginative man unencumbered by the prejudices and theories of so many of his seniors" and "brilliant, hard, and daring."[9] Quesada accompanied Bradley to the initial planning meeting with Leigh-Mallory, and was a strong advocate of every phase of the air plan.[10]

The story of Cobra would not be complete without the invention of Curtis G. Culin Jr., a New York City sergeant who had the idea of welding a tusk-like plow onto the front of tanks.

In mid-July, Bradley got a call from an excited General Gerow, who insisted he bring his ordinance officer, Lieutenant Colonel John Bruce Medaris, to see something special.

What the officers saw was odd, rather than special—a light tank with what looked like four prong-like plows welded onto the front. Whatever

Bradley might have thought at first glimpse was quickly superseded when the tank charged forward into a thick hedgerow, not stopping until it came out the other side in a haze of dust and vegetation. The prongs allowed the tank to force the barriers out of the way, rather than simply rising over them.

It was a simple but powerful idea. Within hours, Medaris had every ordinance unit in First Army working on a version of the rhinoceros, as Culin's invention was called. By the time Cobra began, Bradley estimated the tusks were on three out of five tanks in the operation.[11]

The "rhino" and similar inventions were a good example of American innovation, and they loom large in many accounts of the Normandy campaign. They're easy examples of American ingenuity solving an apparently intractable problem. Their actual contribution to the campaign, and specifically to Cobra, is, however, difficult to assess. By the time the inventions appeared, a variety of tactics had emerged for taking the bocage fields. The rhinos lessened the tank crews' exposure and possibly shortened the time needed for penetrating individual hedgerows, but that still left the interlocking defenses and stubborn fighting of the Germans. Nor did the invention render the tanks invulnerable or remove their need to work closely with a large number of infantry; and roads remained the main arteries of the advance.

Bradley drew up Cobra without knowing the rhinos existed, and there is no evidence that they altered the course of the battle. Yet in *A Soldier's Story*, he gives the invention equal billing with his own planning and is extremely generous in crediting the rhinos with the campaign's success.[12]

More than Bradley's modesty is at play here. He was clearly taken by the inventiveness and initiative of the soldier. Just as important—perhaps more so—the invention came from a "regular guy," a quick-thinking joe from Brooklyn, New York. The story is of a piece with Bradley's bedrock beliefs about the importance and worth of the common man. The same convictions that led him to expand and champion the officers training program for enlisted men convinced him to emphasize the invention when he talked about the campaign.

Of course, giving so much credit to the invention shifts the historical attention away from the planning of the operation itself. Many popular accounts of the campaign focus on the rhino, at least partly thanks to Bradley's own description. Intentionally or not, he once again diminished his own standing in the popular mind, and the historical record, by telling it.

Montgomery approved Cobra on July 19. The attack was initially scheduled to start on the morning of July 21, but rain forced its cancellation. The same thing happened the next day and the next, as bad weather dogged the coast. The aerial bombing, a critical part of the plan, held it back. In the meantime, the Germans reinforced their line.

On July 20, Bradley was working in his truck command post when Eisenhower arrived for a visit. Bradley brought him to the large campaign map and took him step by step over the plan for Cobra and the drive he expected to follow. Coustances would fall quickly, Bradley predicted; he was already planning to deal with a large number of prisoners. He marked the map boldly, showing the slashing lines.

Eisenhower concentrated more on the problems Bradley would face than the possibilities of success, at least if his later comments to Montgomery indicate his feelings.[13] But Bradley was confident and in a good mood as he ended the briefing. Outside the tent, Gerow and Collins waited. Bradley had sent for them so Eisenhower could present them with medals honoring their contributions on D-Day. A small crowd of staff and other soldiers from the headquarters area gathered for the impromptu ceremony after Eisenhower and Bradley emerged from the Cobra briefing.

"When General Marshall visited the assault areas and saw the great devastation that marked the beaches where our troops landed, he himself directed that DSMs [Distinguished Service Medals] be submitted for the corps commanders in charge of those operations," declared Eisenhower. "For the troops were not only great in the assault but they were led by great commanders."[14]

Eisenhower joked that the medals would remind them they were expected to do even more in the future. Then he pulled out another medal and presented it to Bradley. Bradley turned red, embarrassed—he had asked that he not be included in the ceremony, wanting his corps commanders to have the spotlight to themselves.

The rain canceled the start of Cobra the next day as well. Bradley continued refining the plan, making small adjustments and working out a feint with Gerow intended to hold the Germans away from the main attack. (The strategy was similar to the "spoiling attacks" the Germans had employed against him in Africa.) By now, Bradley was optimistic enough to be thinking not only of what would follow Cobra, but of the organization of the 12th Army Group once the breakout was achieved. The establishment of the army group was not quite what he wanted or had hoped for—rather than being independent of Montgomery, Eisenhower had directed that the 12th Army Group continue to serve under Montgomery's 21st Group command until he moved his headquarters to the continent.

Bradley's accession meant that Hodges would take over First Army. It also meant that Patton, who had been champing at the bit to join the action, would finally come to Europe as the head of the Third Army.

The breakout plan was still roughly the same as it had been before Overlord began: Third Army would drive to Rennes and then Brittany. (The Atlantic ports were a prime objective, meant to ensure better supply routes ahead of the expected winter storms.) Meanwhile, First Army would move south, holding against the Germans along the east with the aim of creating a pocket between the Americans and the British.

The dynamic at First Army changed somewhat after Bradley moved up, and the changes demonstrate what sort of effect Bradley must have had when he was there. His chief of staff Bill Kean, a strict taskmaster used mostly for routine staff work, became much more prominent in tactical planning. That presumably had something of an effect on the corps commanders, who were dealing with a very different personality when discussing tactics than they had been during Bradley's tenure.

Courtney Hodges took over as commander of First Army. Hodges was quiet by nature, and if that is something often said of Bradley as well, men who worked under both saw a difference. Hansen gave a blunt description of Hodges at one point in his diary: "A brittle, impersonal general to the bulk of his staff....subordinates suggest that his grasp is not as great as that of Bradley."[15]

The rest of the staff remained in place. Bradley commented that the First Army staff was emotional and high-strung; some assessments by outsiders, notably Bedell Smith, were harsher. What seems clear is that the First Army staff performed less well, though not badly, without Bradley's quietly effective leadership.

The failed assassination attempt July 20 on Hitler had no impact on Bradley's plans, but it did cheer morale. The staff gossiped about the potential impact, with the intelligence officers suggesting that the German high command was anxious to quit the fight.

Among the rumors that reached Normandy in the wake of the attack was the announcement that Heinrich Himmler, head of the SS, was now in charge of the troops in Germany.

"That's good," said Bradley. "He ought to be easy to lick."[16]

A gray mist drifted from the hills as dawn broke Monday, July 24. The attack was now set for that afternoon—provided the weather cooperated. Bradley talked with the air commanders; the weathermen predicted the clouds would lift by noon, just in time for the bombardment to begin. But as the hours passed, it became increasingly clear that the cover wouldn't dissipate in time for the heavy bombers to make their attack. The operation was called off at 11:30 a.m.

Bradley, at Collins' headquarters, drove back to his command post a short time later. Colonel Truman Thorson, Bradley's operations officer, was waiting for him with a concerned look on his face.

Not all the bombers had heard the signal to come back. Worse, a group of them had dropped their bombs a mile short, hitting an ammo dump and other targets inside the 30th Infantry Division.

While the damage and casualties were light, Bradley was angry when he learned the details. The bombers had come in perpendicular to the Periers Road, not parallel to it. That meant a vital part of the attack plan had been changed without his knowledge.

Leigh-Mallory soon arrived at Bradley's command post, but the air commander had as little information as Bradley. Much later that night, Mallory called and told Bradley that the plan had always been to fly perpendicular to the Periers Road. The air force planners apparently felt that it would take too long for the bombers to fly parallel to the road. They had made the change without contacting Bradley.

Bradley was livid. In his mind, the entire plan was predicated on the opening air attack. Using the road as a clear boundary and thus missing the American forces was critical, he thought, not only to the safety of his men but to the plan's success. But now it was too late to change the plan. It would have to proceed as the airmen dictated. Further safety measures were taken—some of the units were moved a little further back—and the offensive was rescheduled for the next day.

The fighter-bombers were the heralds, diving from the stubborn clouds to spit bullets and bombs into the hedgerows and road positions where the Germans were dug in. Yellow smoke furled from the American positions as the aircraft dove, tangling with the black fingers from nearby explosions. Black and yellow dissolved in the gray wisps of low clouds and drizzle as the fighters banked away.

Then came the heavies, first one, then two, pathfinders tiptoeing toward the battlefield. Suddenly the sky was filled with aircraft wingtip to wingtip, low and loud. Their bombs landed with such force that the ground seemed to rise to meet them. The sound was terrible, drowning out the shrieks of the dead and dying. It was as if Judgment Day had begun.

The pounding continued for an hour. It was so severe that even when it ended, many of the American troops couldn't move forward. A few hundred had been caught by short-falling bombs, but many were simply in shock at the terror that been unleashed from the sky.

It was 0936, 25 July 1944. Cobra was underway.

Bradley spent the day fretting. Collins' advance got off to a slow start in some areas because of bombs that fell on American troops. The bombers caused heavy casualties in the 30th division—61 dead, 50 missing, and another 374 injured. In II Corps as a whole, total casualties included 108 dead and 472 hurt.[17]

Among the causalities was Lieutenant General Lesley McNair.[18] The general had decided to watch the beginning of the assault from a slit trench with a battalion at the front line.

The friendly fire deaths were so severe that Bradley resorted to a device he rarely bothered with—a memorandum for the file documenting the original bombing plan and how he felt the air command had screwed up and lied.

Meanwhile, the battle raged. Artillery and mortar shells, husbanded over the past few days, rained heavily on the Germans, who responded with their own artillery.

As devastating as the aerial bombing seemed, it missed many of the defenders. Resistance was stiff as the Americans began moving southwards, their timetable delayed slightly by their friendly fire casualties. In some areas, the Germans were able to take advantage of the delay, moving up to set more mines, making progress even slower.

Progress on the roads was slowed not only by enemy fire and mines, but by craters caused by large bombs—despite Bradley's instructions and the apparent agreement of the air commanders, bombs as large as five hundred pounds had been used. Among the roads particularly hard hit were those near Marigny, which was a critical objective between St.-Lo and Coutances.

On a historical map, Cobra looks like an American arrow with a sharp head poking through a thick German line. Up close it looked very different. It was a thousand battles, viciously fought. One road saw troops sweep through; another field saw progress nearly as slow as the weeks before. A lucky shot here, a missed mine there—each life turned on a point of fate, and on those lives the direction of the battle rested.

By midnight on the first day, the 30th Infantry Division had taken Hebecrevon, holding the high ground to the west of St.-Lo. The 4th Division had penetrated far enough south to open a good gap in the German line. The 9th Division, stymied in its objective of Marigny[19] north of the road between St.-Lo and Coutances, had nonetheless battered the Panzer Lehr Division to a point of exhaustion, threatening a devastating breakthrough.

Attacks by the rest of First Army were holding the enemy units there in place. The situation was tense for the Americans, but the cracks were everywhere in the German wall.

By morning, the Germans had committed all of their reserves to the fight. Dickson predicted that, if the crust of the defense was broken, the Americans might go a long way.

Collins held back the 1st Division and its attached armor (Combat Command B of 3rd Armored) during the first day of the assault while waiting for the breakthrough. On July 26, with the German lines stretched but not yet completely broken, and all their reserves committed to the fight, he decided it was time to unleash them. He sent the force funneling through a narrow gap toward Marigny. It reached the outskirts of the town by nightfall.

Just to the east, the 2nd Armored Division plunged southward into Saint Gilles and then beyond, moving southwards with increasing speed.

The dam burst July 27. But the break came so quickly that the Allies almost missed it.

The plan for Middleton's VIII Corps had been merely to hold the Germans there in place while Collins' arrow plunged through the German line. But Middleton's troops found the Germans in front of them were retreating—quickly.

Bradley realized the Germans were afraid of being trapped, which in turn meant that their communication lines and deeper rings of defense were threatened, even wiped out. He altered his plans to take advantage of it. Rather than trying to create a pocket around Coutances, Bradley decided to push the offensive farther south—and to widen the gap in the German lines. He switched assignments to allow this. VIII Corps was given goals that had belonged to VII Corps, which was told to shove deeper south. He pushed XIX Corps to move faster, applying pressure on the other side of the line. The 2nd Armored Division was thrown forward. Bradley pried the opening wider to give himself more room to maneuver.[20]

Coutances fell on the third day—a few hours later than Bradley had predicted, but close enough to be encouraging. The first phase of Cobra was now a clear success. So long as the many disparate units could be properly managed, the next phase would be, too. In fact, things were going so well that Bradley began reconsidering his objectives and timetable.

By the morning of July 28, Coutances had fallen, and the road to Brittany looked reasonably clear. Bradley shared with Hansen—in deepest confidence, or "not for publication" as he liked to say—that things were going extremely well. Very possibly they would be at Rennes in two weeks; if so, Brittany would fall soon after that.

Bradley expanded on his thoughts, one of the rare times he went so deeply into overall strategy with his aide. They were to keep moving quickly, not give the Germans a chance to regroup or rest. They would have no chance to dig in.

A lightning quick drive would make the end result obvious. He suspected that Germany would attempt to negotiate surrender, and that the air war would halt. If so, they would push on regardless. As far as Bradley was concerned, there should be no terms—surrender must be complete and absolute.

He was expansive, confident...and deeply drained.

Yet oddly, he was unable to sleep. Bradley surprised Hansen by asking him to get some sleeping pills to help him get rest at night. He'd had a small bottle in England but had used them all.

"When I go to bed I find myself thinking ahead on this thing and I cannot get to sleep without planning my mind throughout half the night," Bradley told his aide. "Where to go, and how to do it. Then when I try to get some sleep in the [early] morning, the AA starts firing."[21]

Bradley's original plan to trap a large portion of the German defenders in the eastern sweep was thwarted by the strong defense of the Germans against the VII Corps' armor and their successful retreat,[22] but as Bradley's ruminations made clear, it didn't matter. The German retreat invited a rapid movement against the German Seventh Army. Bradley was using speed now as a weapon, as the enemy simply couldn't recover quickly enough to defend itself. Meanwhile, he pushed XIX Corps south as the British launched Operation Bluecoat, a drive in their sector designed to link with the American advances and exploit them.

The 2nd Armored Division galloped south, successfully splitting the German 7th Army's two corps at a weak seam. The division was literally on a roll; for the first time in Europe, American tanks and the mechanized infantry that accompanied them were able to move and maneuver freely. The division became a sharp knife slicing through the tender meat of the German Army, splitting it in two.

On July 30, the 2ⁿᵈ Armored Division, with the 702ⁿᵈ Tank Destroyer Battalion, began a furious thirteen-hour tank battle with the 2ⁿᵈ Panzer and 116ᵗʰ Panzer Divisions. It was a wide-ranging, freeform affair, a multi-fronted confrontation comparable to the best encounters on the open plains of Africa. Aided by mobile artillery and fighter-bombers in close support, the Americans blunted the Germans' hope of a counterattack. The division's victory marked the end of Cobra. The Allies could no longer be confined to Normandy, or any part of northern France for that matter.

Cobra broke the Americans from the Normandy peninsula, helped the British get out of their box above Caen, and primed the pump for an electrifying drive across central France that liberated Paris and brought Bradley to the German frontier in a month's time.

Yet Bradley rarely gets much credit for it.

This has partly to do with the way many modern histories are written, with the focus on the individuals at the front—a reaction and balance, it should be said, to an earlier over-emphasis on the great generals.

But even when the focus is on the generals, Bradley seems oddly left out. The fact that Collins made alterations to the plan is often emphasized, though with little analysis of those contributions or any attempt to place them in the perspective of the overall plan. Collins certainly deserves credit for Cobra's execution, but his role in the battle was one any corps commander would take, formulating specifics from the broad outline and objectives. Collins never claimed that he designed Cobra, and in fact praised Bradley for his tactical skills.

Then there's Montgomery. In his memoirs, Montgomery turned the entire plan for the assault around, as well as the actual tactical situation, claiming that the Americans were always supposed to make the breakthrough, and that the British "capture" of Caen set the stage for Cobra. This, he said, was because it took divisions away from Bradley's front.[23]

In actual fact, Montgomery had only part of Caen under control when Cobra started, and the Germans were moving from his sector to Bradley's. Nor had the field marshal envisioned Cobra as the set-piece of the Allied attack eastward; Caen was in fact the perfect spot for that, as it would have opened the way for the northern drive he continually propounded.

In fairness, Montgomery in his memoirs does not take credit for giving Bradley the idea for Cobra, as some commentators have alleged. But his tendency to revise history with spray paint rather than an airbrush does invite such overstatements.

One of the reasons for Bradley's neglect is the fact that Cobra is often discussed only at the tail end of D-Day accounts or sandwiched between descriptions of the landing and the battle at Falaise Pocket. This is understandable. On the one hand, D-Day is well known and is obvious as a beginning. Falaise, the biggest killing field of the war, clinches the campaign for northern France and is a logical ending. Then, too, describing the purpose and flow of Cobra is more difficult than either D-Day or Falaise. Though simple in outline, the breakout was more complicated than either battle. And the fact that its nature changed midway—the 2nd Armored Division's plunge was designed more as a protective ring for VII Corps rather than a spearhead of the attack—complicates the telling, even if it demonstrates Bradley's flexibility.

Some authors have gone so far as to suggest that Cobra wasn't a real breakout from Normandy but rather a stage-setter for it, suggesting that the breakout happened afterwards, when Patton arrived and the armies were moving across France. Some have even claimed that it wasn't seen as a breakout at the time.

The first point is tied up in views of the war that give Patton the lion's share of the credit for victory in France. He was the head of the army that dashed across France (under Bradley, though of course that's not often mentioned). If you're writing about Patton, then obviously what he does is going to be your focus. His achievements will be brought to the foreground and, intentionally or not, the achievements of others pushed back. Clearly that's a subjective choice, and even Patton's own testimony that his dash was set up by Cobra won't convince those who want to see Patton as the unmatchable hero of the war.

But the second argument is simply wrong. It implies, subtly perhaps, that Bradley was surprised by the success of the battle, somehow didn't grasp the strategic importance of what he was doing, or had no real notion of what he wanted to achieve. All of those implications are far off base.

Bradley clearly saw Cobra as the way to get off the peninsula and into the rest of France. He explicitly told Hansen this. He didn't stand up at a press conference and tell reporters that, of course. He wouldn't have. Even a general more attuned to public relations would never have done something so foolish as to predicate the future of the war on one operation. But everyone knew they were trying to do something big with the offensive.

Ernie Pyle said that before the operation began, officers told him, "This is it. This is the big break-through."[24] Pyle's column was printed after the fact due to censorship, but there's no reason to think that he was adding that gloss after the operation's success.

James Jay Carafano in *After D-Day*, a major reconsideration of the battle, notes that, to some extent, historical analysis of Cobra has suffered from the first wave of historical accounts, which were handicapped by concerns over inter-Allied and inter-service rivalries and sensitivities. The attention paid to such dramatic developments as the rhino tanks and air power also tended to take attention from the plan itself. (Although in my opinion, the role of air power in the battle has been greatly deemphasized in most recent accounts.)

Carafano also notes, in very polite language, that historians generally failed to thoroughly examine the battle, often accepting at face value statements that were little more than truisms and generalizations.[25]

Some of those impressions might have come from the initial reporting of the overall battle. Many of the news stories at the time seemed to focus largely on the slow going movement of the Allies after the initial invasion. Commentators implied that the Allies were not being aggressive enough. Bradley's staff was angered by these reports, though he tended to dismiss them as understandable due to the commentator's lack of knowledge of Allied operations and planning.

"We must grin and bear it," Bradley told Montgomery about the criticism from the press.[26]

The Cobra plan has all the characteristics of Bradley's best work. Relatively simple in overall design, it combined massive firepower and masterful logistics. It was truly a combined arms effort—not strictly an infantry smash or an armored drive. It took the terrain as a starting point, and sought to think about the army and air force in both conventional ways and ways that had not been tried before carpet bombing, the fighter-bombers. It's not surprising that the latter depended very much on communication and cooperation, hallmarks of Bradley's management style. Nor is it shocking that it exhibited confidence in his commanders and sub-commanders—from logistics and supply, where large units were moved quickly across a highly chaotic space in range of enemy fire, to the corps and division leaders, who had to motivate their juniors to launch and sustain a difficult battle.

The plan was also flexible enough, and Bradley open-minded enough, to withstand a major alteration midway as the German opposition collapsed, capitalizing on new opportunities. In many ways, it was the key battle of 1944, nearly as important as the landings themselves. Without Cobra, the Allies might have had to rely on a static, head-on battle plan similar to those of World War I; stiff German defenses could have extracted a heavy toll. Cobra paved the way for the victories that followed.

The carpet bombing that opened Cobra remains controversial some six decades later.

Deaths by friendly fire seem even more tragic than others, underlining the terrible costs of war. Bradley was certainly sensitive to this, and clearly the toll bothered him following the war. In his mind, he had sought to decrease the possibility of such deaths by finding the road to be used as a marker, and then directing that the attackers approach parallel to it. To Bradley—and probably Quesada, who was his close advisor and an air-man—these were reasonable steps in a radical and risky plan.

Bradley blamed the friendly fire deaths, including that of General McNair, largely if not solely on the air force's decision to fly perpendicular to the Periers Road rather than parallel to it. Bradley raged about this at the time, and was still fuming when he wrote *A Soldier's Story*.

It's not clear why the air commanders changed the approach and, more importantly, didn't inform him of the change. After the fact, some of the officers contended that there was no agreement. Judging from Hansen's diary, the reaction of Quesada, and the actions of other air force officers, this seems to be either typical shifting of blame, or perhaps miscommunication down the line.

Why was the direction of the bombers changed?

The reason given to Bradley (and put in the official investigation afterwards) was that a parallel approach would have stretched the bombing operation to two and a half hours rather than one.[27] It's difficult now to see if that is actually correct; bombing timetables can be complicated by a number of factors. On its face, however, the answer seems, at best, an oversimplification. It appears to have been derived by multiplying the dimensions of the target area, estimating that flights of heavy bombers would cross over in similar waves and fly over the entire area in the same direction and patterns, whether parallel or perpendicular. In such a case, it would take about twice as long to bomb a space little more than twice as wide (perpendicular to the road).

Such an approach to the bombing raid would have been unimaginative, at best. What the estimate really implies is that no real attempt was made to plot the routes and timetables that would have made Bradley's suggestion work.

Flying perpendicular routes across the road would have exposed individual bombers to less ground fire than parallel approaches, even if those approaches did not run the entire length of the battle area. The planners charged with drawing up the air mission most certainly would have realized that. As their job was to minimize their losses, they would have used that as their first step in designing the bombing plan.[28]

But why did the airmen go ahead with the plan without notifying Bradley?

The simplest explanation is that they did not understand how critical their role was to the plan. They were working in a system that did not allow for the very close integration of air and ground power. They did not realize that the close proximity of the ground troops was a necessary component of Cobra, nor did they fully appreciate how Bradley intended to incorporate what today is called "shock and awe" into his opening drive.

Bradley wanted the bombers for more than just their explosive power. While radical in its employment of strategic bombers, Cobra was not unlike other Bradley plans that took psychological aspects of battle into account. Psychology is in fact a critical component of any battle where speed is used as a weapon. When Bradley spoke to Hansen about the potential collapse of the German Army because of his ability to move quickly through its lines, he had in mind the psychological effects of defeat as surely as logistics. His use of propaganda as a weapon on Sicily, encouraging Italian soldiers to defect, would fit easily in a modern PsyOp war plan, and was in fact employed during the first and second Gulf Wars. And Bradley's efforts in North Africa to keep Americans under American command and winning their own victories was pure psychology as well.

In short, even the most controversial aspect of Cobra demonstrates Bradley's mastery of what we consider modern techniques. The fact that others weren't always on board with his thinking should be interpreted as their failure, not his.

★ ★ ★ ★

None of this means that using the road as a line of demarcation would have resulted in no friendly fire deaths, or even fewer deaths. The technology of the day limited accuracy, even when the skies were completely clear.

"Blue on blue" fatalities by air were a fact of life throughout the war, as Bradley knew from his own personal experiences in Africa and Sicily. Clearly, he was willing to accept some risk. He originally planned on moving his men back only eight hundred yards (a little under half a mile) from the road; the air commanders suggested nearly three miles, then three thousand yards. Three thousand was much too far to use the attack as the springboard for his assault, and he eventually compromised on twelve hundred, with a fifteen hundred-yard buffer for the closest heavy bomber target.

The road was an obvious marker, visible in good weather under the best conditions—but battle rarely provides those, and Cobra certainly did not. Using the road as a parallel marker was no more a guarantee of safety than flying perpendicular to it; if anything, a mistake on a parallel route could be even more deadly.

Even believing that the parallel line would diminish his troops' exposure, Bradley must have known there could be casualties.

"We work in objectives and the winning of the war," Bradley once told his aides. "You can't win wars without losing lives. That fact you must face."[29]

With Cobra successful, Bradley left his post as First Army commander to become head of the 12th Army Group. Courtney Hodges, who'd been Bradley's deputy, took over as the head of First Army. Patton came in as the head of the Third Army, with Middleton's VIII Corps going to Patton in a reshuffle.

There were now twenty-one American divisions in France. First Army had a total of twelve divisions, while Third Army had nine. Bradley jump-started the transition by having Patton work "unofficially" with

VIII Corps late on July 28. This facilitated the drive toward Avranches, spearheaded by the 4th and 6th Armored Divisions. The early appointment seems to have surprised Patton, though he quickly made the most of it.

If things had gone according to plan, the American 12th Army Group should have functioned as a coequal with Montgomery's 21st Army Group. Bradley should have answered directly to Eisenhower. But Eisenhower was still in England. The Americans remained under Montgomery.

In practice, Bradley said later, this was not a major problem. He noted that Montgomery's authority was largely limited to setting the lines between the two Army groups. Though not inconsequential, this was hardly complete control. And, said Bradley, Montgomery "neither limited our authority nor [gave]…us directives that might have caused us to chafe."[30]

But Bradley's rather benign statement misses the animosity and resentment his First Army staff felt towards Montgomery. It also fails to highlight American frustration with Montgomery's slow progress. And it skips over the rather obvious fact that Eisenhower was just as far from Montgomery as he was from Bradley. The inescapable conclusion is that Bradley—and the Americans under him—were treated as junior partners in the alliance despite their achievements.

From Bradley's point of view, the British were guilty of bruised egos. The more attention the Americans got, the more jealous the British were. Meanwhile, British newspapers fanned the controversy by continuing to award Montgomery and his army lavish headlines at odds with the facts on the ground. Bradley says that Montgomery encouraged some of the carping, especially later on, by claiming that he would have done far better than Eisenhower in running the overall war.

There certainly was ego involved—large doses of it—but Montgomery and Bradley had somewhat different concepts of how the war should be waged, and those differences were much more important in the end than Montgomery's or Bradley's personal foibles.

Bradley, with some justification, prided himself on his ability to get along professionally with practically anyone; that proposition would eventually meet its test with Montgomery, as the trajectory of their relationship from this point would be strictly downward.

By contrast, Bradley warmed to Patton, so much so that he regretted his hesitation in accepting Patton as an army commander. Patton had a tendency to flatter superiors to their faces, then complain about them privately. He did that to some extent with Bradley, but the overall tone of their relationship was positive, far better than it had been in Sicily. Patton was deferential, but so was Bradley, who despite everything continued to respect Patton and his abilities.

Some commentators have suggested that Patton flattered Bradley by making him believe that he, Bradley, came up with ideas that Patton had himself invented. That's a misunderstanding of both men. Bradley did not need to be the author of an idea to be convinced that it was a good one, nor was he foolish enough not to realize when he was being flattered. And at least in dealing with Bradley, Patton had no need for such games. If he employed them, he would not have been bashful about recording this fact, and his diary and letters would be crammed with such accounts. They're not.

Bradley's general method was to give Patton the outline of a plan and ask for his input; he then altered the plan or not, based on those suggestions. He did this with everyone, not just Patton. And he did it from the very start of his tour in Africa to the very end of the war in Germany.[31] He expected his commanders to offer their ideas, and certainly in the case of Patton would have been shocked if he had not. While Bradley believed he had to keep a check on Patton's tendency toward high-risk aggressiveness, overall he approved of his tactics and thinking, certainly in northern Europe.

Bradley felt that Patton was a different man in Continental Europe than he had been on Sicily. He credited the "slap" and its aftermath. For Bradley, the incident tempered Patton's personality just enough to take the edge off its more egotistical elements. In fact, in *A Soldier's Story*, Bradley says the private who had been hit did more to win the war than any other private in the Army.[32]

There's certainly truth in that. Still, it does leave out credit for Bradley, who surely deserves some.

Patton had always acted differently toward those above him than to those below him. He was a different man to Bradley because Bradley was in a different position. But more importantly, for the first time Patton was working directly under a commander who valued his abilities and expected him to take an important role in the war. He wasn't shunted off to the side where his only way of proving himself was to engage in a tactically foolish race for an arbitrary objective. He was treated, if not as an equal, certainly as a respected commander by his immediate superior.

And when he presented his plans, he couldn't get away with nebulous descriptions—Bradley would have seen through a Palermo diversion instantly. Patton had to justify his moves, thinking them through a little more fully. That made them better.

The collaboration benefited Bradley because Patton was one of the Army's best tactical leaders in the war. But it also benefited Patton. Patton got far more support from the 12th Army Group than he had from Montgomery or Alexander—or Eisenhower, for that matter.

There were still negatives and occasional friction between the two men. Patton periodically groused about Bradley not being aggressive or not seeing things the way he did. More serious, a leak from Patton's staff nearly gave away the plan for Cobra before it was launched. Patton, chastened, promised to fire the aide responsible, though he delayed until another issue brought matters to a head.

Hodges might not have been the exact opposite of Patton, but he nonetheless provided a sharp contrast. Even Bradley described him as quiet. Bradley tended to be quietly gregarious; the First Army staff worried that Hodges lacked that warmth. This was a problem as he dealt with the division commanders, especially when he tried to follow Bradley's methods of consensus building.

More of a problem was that Hodges did not have Bradley's tactical skills. Kean took a greater role in the tactical planning for First Army, and in general assumed a higher profile than he had under Bradley. But Kean's personality tended toward the abrasive; without Bradley to balance it, the effect was even harsher.

★ ★ ★ ★

Bradley's promotion came at an extremely fluid point in the campaign. Unlike his move from Corps commander, he could not afford to raid First Army for the bulk of his staff. He left Kean and most of his staff at First Army, taking only his personnel officer (G-1, Joseph "Red" O'Hare, who finished the war as a brigadier general), his two personal aides (Chet Hansen and Lewis Bridges), and Sergeant Richard Dudley, who arranged Bradley's mess and took care of his "household."

Twelfth Army Group chief of staff Major General Lev Allen had already established a forward base in Normandy when Bradley moved up full-time. The command unit was so large that Bradley claims to have been dismayed when he surveyed the tent city north of Coutances. Code-named "Eagle," the 12th Army Group was divided into three parts, with the core portion—Bradley, an engineering section, G-2, G-3, and G-4 sections, and a small support team—organized and equipped for rapid movement, or at least as rapid as a headquarters unit could be. Dubbed Eagle Tac, this forward group traveled by truck and trailer; it consisted of sixty-five officers, with about twice as many enlisted men. The size would double by the end of the war.

Eagle Tac changed its location ten times in the months that followed, endeavoring to keep Bradley as close to the front as possible. The rest of the headquarters—broken into Main and Rear groupings—moved somewhat less often.

To this point in the war, Bradley had used the back of a truck as his command post. There were certain advantages, starting with the fact that it was highly mobile. He had never been much for personal comfort in the field; Hansen's diary is filled with references to his boss's roughing it with the troops. These references undergo an interesting transition as the war goes on. They start out highly approving. To Hansen, Bradley's inattention to his uniform and his willingness to eat K rations are seen as positive, even macho, achievements. Hansen often compares other generals unfavorably to this account.

Gradually, however, the aide seems to have grown tired of this rough and tumble approach to army life. While some of this may be laid to normal military grousing, it was also a realization that Bradley was no longer a "mere" field commander. What he viewed as luxuries were signifiers of his importance. They were also reflections of his different responsibilities, in a sense, tools to help him do his job: Bradley was already hosting a veritable tag team of VIPs, and that would greatly increase as the summer turned to fall.

Bradley's preference for a Spartan existence could easily be interpreted as false modesty. Worse, coupled with his laid-back manner, it could undercut the image of authority that a high-ranking general must present.

At Hansen's urging, Bradley ordered the creation of a trailer to serve as his roving Army Group headquarters. Based on the trailer Montgomery used, Hansen had drawings prepared to guide its construction. It featured a sleeping area and enough room for small conferences, but the main luxuries were a small shower and a commode area—items that Hansen did not go out of his way to explain to Bradley, fearing he would veto them as frivolous.

"Will go ahead on it without his knowledge," noted Hansen in his diary.[33] He later flew to Great Britain to oversee the trailer's construction and was quite proud of it.

"The trailer was so ornate that I often felt it necessary to apologize for the comfort it provided," said Bradley in *A Soldier's Story*.[34] The unit had skylights, mahogany panels, and carpet—a far cry from the steel floor of a truck or the muddy boards of a converted mess tent.

★ ★ ★ ★

The war had changed dramatically in just a few days. Even the French seemed to sense it—in Normandy, they had been cautious, staying inside their homes and rarely even daring to greet the Americans. Now as Bradley traveled through the countryside south of the peninsula, people lined the roadway, cheering.

It was August 2, 1944, a Wednesday and Bradley's first full day as commander of the 12th Army Group. The staff meeting had been almost a shock—different people, different location. He still made his rounds, though, and one of his stops was Patton's command post in Beauchamps. As they approached Granville, Army engineers halted him so they could safely blow away an old bridge and widen the route. Bradley and his aides got out of the jeep, posing for a photographer who took a picture of him with a local gendarme. Nearby, little girls held flowers for their liberators.

Bradley eyed the engineers' supplies critically, noticing coils of barbed wire.

"Where are they going with that stuff?" he asked Hansen. "That's for defensive battle."[35]

Back on the road and headed toward Middleton's headquarters, Bradley checked his watch and had the driver pull off the road for a quick lunch of K rations—crackers, according to Hansen. "I hate to run in on people at noontime," he said. "Better to come there at 1230 and be able to say we have already eaten."[36]

Bradley's armies were on the offensive, but he still had to worry about sudden reversals. At Middleton's headquarters, he discovered the general unsure what to do about Fougeres, a crossroads city south of Avranches. The city provided a way for the Germans to wedge into the American advance into Brittany, cutting it off the way a tourniquet cuts off circulation to a limb.

Middleton said he was unable to get in touch with Patton to see what he wanted him to do; failing to get Patton himself, Bradley ordered Middleton to send the 79th Infantry Division to the city, protecting the flank of the Third Army.[37]

Bradley found Patton later and apologized for issuing the order—it was a breach of the chain of command. Patton shrugged it off, telling Bradley it was the right thing to have done. In his diary, Patton claimed he had told Bradley he was in danger of catching the "British complex of over-caution."[38] But Bradley's expectations of a counter-strike would soon prove warranted.

250 OMAR BRADLEY: GENERAL AT WAR

★ ★ ★ ★

Confusion reigned in the German lines as the Americans poured out of Normandy. The failure of the counterattack by the 2nd and 116th Panzer Divisions worsened the catastrophe for the Germans. Vast columns of prisoners were taken; First Army collected some twenty thousand in less than a week of fighting.

The pre-invasion plan had called for the seizure of the Brittany ports as the Americans' primary goal after breaking out of the peninsula, but other opportunities loomed. Bradley kept adapting his plans. Probably by July 30, and certainly no later than August 3, he realized the dramatic advances had changed the situation in northern France to the point where Brittany could be taken with far less forces than originally planned. He also decided that the ports should no longer be his top priority. For if the destruction of the German Army was completed rapidly, there was a real potential that Antwerp and other nearby ports could be taken. This would shorten the supply lines to the German frontier. With Montgomery's approval, he issued new orders that turned much of Third Army around, directing Patton to swing most though not all of his forces back eastward.[39]

If Cobra was the critical battle of the Normandy breakout, the decision to turn was the critical strategic move in the war to liberate France.[40]

But it was not without tradeoffs or considerable risk. Finally with the room to maneuver—and the army commander to do it—Bradley also had to remember that the Germans had a large army in France. He expected that the Germans would use that army in a counterattack, trying to blunt the advance.

It came August 7.

The German drive came through Mortain toward Avranches. The idea was to cleave the American forces in two. But the Germans simply weren't strong enough to do so. The First Army's 30th Infantry Division, with help from fighter-bombers, blunted and then stopped the attack. The German counterstroke failed even to alter American plans. With a substantial reserve near the sector in case they were needed, the Third Army continued its sweep eastward.

Even as the battle raged, Bradley saw a new opportunity: an encircling movement that would trap a substantial portion of the German Army in the Argentan-Falaise area

Before the German counterattack, Bradley had begun acting on the idea that the Germans would withdraw in the face of the American push eastward. He developed a master plan to sweep below Paris, bypassing it so that he could maintain a steady sprint toward Germany. He envisioned a massive pincer movement that would catch as many as twenty-six German divisions in northern France and the Low Countries.

A withdrawal by the Germans would have been a logical move—as the Third Army swept southwards it was in effect drawing a big noose around its enemy. Bradley had already begun planning how he would close the noose with the help of airborne troops and a sea assault;[41] he clearly saw the need for a much deeper penetration, which would have been logical if the Germans were moving quickly. But the stubbornness of the German defense suggested a quicker and just as decisive battle if he could push his army northwards faster, well short of Paris.

One of the things that seems to have surprised Bradley in France was the slowness of the Germans to react. Judging from Hansen's diary,[42] he expected that they would realize that they were in danger of being trapped after his turn and would quickly pull away. A glance at the map indicates that they had only one route eastwards in the Falaise area, an extremely dangerous situation given the speed at which Third Army was traveling. At the same time, the heavy engagement by the First Army at the north and central portions of the German line should have indicated that there was little hope of holding out, let alone breaking through the American line. The Allied forces were like a set of jaws poised to snap around the Germans, whether at Falaise or farther east.

With access to Ultra, Bradley knew that orders from Hitler not to retreat were influencing German actions. Still, their situation seemed so untenable that he was surprised the orders were obeyed.

When Bradley misread his enemy, he tended to do so in one of two ways, both related. He thought they would read and react to tactical situations more quickly than they did. And he also generally felt that, seeing the tactical situation on defense was hopeless, they would not continue to fight in it, favoring strategic retreat or surrender.

These are the prejudices of an offense-minded general, one who seeks to fight a war of maneuver—Sherman rather than Grant, to dramatically over-simplify those Civil War generals' approaches. (There is an American prejudice to value offense higher than defense, but to the extent possible the terms should be considered neutral here.) Even Bradley's caution rises from those prejudices. If he saw something in his own lines that he would exploit were he the enemy, it had to be dealt with before making his attack. He was particularly aware of the danger of attacks on the flank or breakthroughs to his rear because those were exactly the sort of attacks he wished to make.

These prejudices, amply demonstrated here as well as in his earlier battles, are in direct contrast to criticisms sometimes leveled against Bradley that he favored straight ahead "plodding" infantry advances.

Circumstances determined that Bradley's task would be overwhelmingly offense oriented, but it is striking that even the few battles where his troops were on the defensive—Mortain, the Bulge later on—were from his perspective offensive opportunities. Both were turned fairly quickly into offensives. In each case, Bradley saw that his enemy was presenting him with an opportunity, and to some degree was surprised that they were so willing to do so.

It's tempting to wonder how much Bradley's views were shaped by his earliest experiences in Africa, where for a while the Germans seemed to anticipate every move by the Allies. There the Americans were up against Rommel (at least at first; he left by the time Bradley took over as corps commander). There were few equals in either army, and in a way, few better teachers—even if you are learning from the other side of the lines.

Interpreting the situation was only part of the problem for Bradley. He had then to deal with the practical aspects of exploiting it. While thinking of what would happen across the Seine, he was still trying to overcome the problems of supply that had plagued the Allies since the landing. As his armies moved out from the beaches, they faced a second difficulty—that of getting ammunition, gasoline, and other necessities across the battered landscape to their men.

Patton initially wanted to continue farther east before making the turn to capture the German Army, but whatever argument he offered to Bradley failed to convince him. Bradley called Montgomery, suggesting that Patton's rapid turn from the area of Le Mans northward to Alencon would cut off the Germans.

The Canadian First Army had begun attacking south that morning. Bradley and Montgomery decided that the Canadian attack would form the northern jaw snapping down on the German pocket. The two army groups would meet at Argentan, below Falaise, trapping perhaps as many as fifty thousand Germans and killing another ten thousand.[43]

The operations looked easy on paper, but the rapid series of maneuvers caused problems for Patton's army, which had to swing through a relatively narrow area in a short period of time. As always for the Americans in Europe, supplies were dear. Patton also worried, uncharacteristically, about his flank below Alencon, seeing a hole from St. Hilaire to Mayenee. But Bradley told him not to worry; Third Army was moving so rapidly that the Germans would not be able to exploit the gaps.

What they could and did do was fight ferociously in the pocket, slowing the Canadian advance from the north. Part of Patton's XV Corps drove to Argentan and then closed to within seven miles of Falaise by the evening of August 12; Patton offered to move north to Falaise and meet the Canadians. But Bradley stopped him.

Bradley's decision would be second-guessed after the war, by no less an authority than Bradley himself. He came to feel that he had missed an opportunity by allowing the Germans to escape. Unfortunately, what exactly he was thinking has become obscured by a number of writings, including those in *A General's Life*, where the details of the operation are overlaid with interpretations from historians long after the fact.

First of all, it's important to remember that the Falaise pocket was a tremendous victory for the Allies and a catastrophe for the Germans; that fact can get lost in the analysis of what-might-have-beens.

In establishing the plans for the Allied advance on the pocket, Bradley and Montgomery placed the Americans along a line at Argentan, to the south of Falaise. The Americans actually crossed the line as they established their position on the southern side of the pocket (the Argentan shoulder). Bradley feared a friendly fire incident if they continued into the Canadian sector.[44]

Judging from the sources at the time and the actual moves that Bradley made, he seems to have believed that the Canadian Army would meet its goal of Falaise without too much trouble. But regardless, his orders suggest that rather than completely blocking off the escape of whatever forces were trapped, he was intent that the Americans hold what he called a firm shoulder against the pocket. At no point did he move or plan to move a large force in the way of the German retreat.

Bradley says as much in *A Soldier's Story*, noting that he was afraid whatever Patton could put in the way of the retreating Germans would have been overwhelmed by a ferocious German attack. Patton's units would certainly have been outnumbered, even taking the most conservative estimate of the German forces.

This argument, however, would seem to hold true for the Canadians as well, who were already having trouble even pushing down on the shoulder. So why was the plan to close the gap made in the first place?

The likely explanation is either that Bradley (and Montgomery) thought the force in the pocket was much smaller than it actually was, or he believed it had already escaped.

That must have changed when the Canadians continued to have difficulty. But by that time, Bradley was faced with another choice. The Germans had practically no organized defenses between the main portion of Patton's army and the Seine. This was an enormous opportunity that presented the Army Group commander with a classic dilemma: destroy enemy forces, or take territory?

Bradley points out the choice in *A Soldier's Story*. There he admits that the "destruction of the enemy's army is the first objective of any force."[45] There are exceptions, though, and tactical advantage can be one. Was racing across the Seine a better play than closing the gap?

Supposedly so, though Bradley makes a very poor argument in *A Soldier's Story*.

There's a reason for that, though—Bradley never fully agreed.

"If Montgomery wants help in closing the gap, I thought, then let him ask for it," Bradley declares in *A Soldier's Story*,[46] justifying his decision to allow Patton to send two divisions eastward, in effect weakening the force available to close the gap. That sentence covers a monumental disagreement between Bradley and Montgomery, as a reading of Hansen's diary reveals. In actual fact, Bradley was arguing with Montgomery over the latter's contention that the primary objective must be to seize territory on the way to Paris.[47]

Despite what he says in *A Soldier's Story*, Bradley seems to have spent several days arguing that the pocket should be closed. By August 14, when it was apparent that Montgomery wasn't going to change his plans, he approved Patton's request, opting to leave the gap open and pound the escaping Germans from the shoulder.

After making that decision, Bradley seems to have had a host of second thoughts, worrying about Patton's flank. He expressed his concern to Patton the next day. Patton, now back to being characteristically optimistic, thought Bradley was being too conservative, and assured him that his forces would be able to hold.

In the meantime, the Germans were still fighting ferociously at Mortain completely oblivious, in Bradley's view, to the danger in their rear. Their continued reluctance to retreat gave the Allies a chance to reconsider the decision about closing the gap. On August 16, Montgomery decided that he would aim his northern forces at Chambois rather than Falaise. He asked if Bradley could send a force to meet him there. With the bulk of the Third Army no longer in position to close the gap, Bradley and Patton devised a plan to do so by fashioning a provisional corps under Gerow. This took some time, and it wasn't until August 19 that the Americans met the Canadians and elements of the Polish Armored Division around Chambois.[48]

In the end, roughly fifty thousand Germans were captured in the pocket. Another ten thousand were killed. Those who escaped did so without most of their equipment.

They also left behind any illusion that the German Army remained invincible.

Criticism of the Allies' "failure" at Falaise began immediately after the battle and has continued to the present day.[49] Most critics have centered their arguments on claims that up to 40,000 Germans were able to escape because of the delay. The historian Martin Blumenson (a stronger supporter of Bradley's actions at Falaise than Bradley himself) estimated that 20,000 to 40,000 Germans escaped.[50]

One thing that is not in dispute is that Falaise was a gauntlet of hell for the Germans; sometimes overlooked is the fact that the equipment of the entire German Army in Normandy was destroyed. The scene was hellish.

"Forty-eight hours after the closing of the gap I was conducted through it on foot, to encounter scenes that could be described only by Dante," wrote Eisenhower in *Crusade in Europe*. "It was literally possible to walk for hundreds of yards at a time, stepping on nothing but dead and decaying flesh."[51]

The differences over strategy between Montgomery and Bradley were at a very basic level. They help explain why Bradley was so anxious to get out from under the 21st Army Group. It was not simply a matter of egos or national pride; Bradley disagreed strongly with Montgomery's basic strategies in the war.

These disagreements would only grow as the war continued.[52]

CHAPTER 7

Rise and Fall

Eisenhower arrived at Eagle Forward on August 18 for a conference. Bradley wanted to talk about the push across the Seine and his plan to slide around Paris southward. Instead, Eisenhower spent much of the time complaining about British news stories implying that Montgomery was being pushed aside. The stories had appeared in the wake of Eisenhower's announcement that he was (finally) moving his headquarters to the continent.

Bradley, of course, wanted to get out from under Montgomery's command, and the sooner the better. But Eisenhower had decided to retain the present arrangement until the end of August; until then, Bradley still had to answer to Montgomery.

It was becoming increasingly obvious that Bradley's preferred strategy—striking east south of Paris—was far different than Montgomery's. When the three men discussed the strategy for the next stage of the war the next day, Bradley argued that he should be allowed to make a direct strike at Metz and the German border. In terms of sheer distance, this was a breath-taking ambition—Metz was some 175 miles from Paris.

Bradley wanted to send two armies in that direction, and had already been planning on how to supply them by air. He had also begun thinking of how he would situate the armies to occupy Germany. As described later, his plan would also have called for Montgomery to continue in the north, moving toward Calais. It was similar in general to the plan envisioned before D-Day, which had envisioned a British thrust on the north and an American thrust on the south.

Montgomery wanted to concentrate the entire force to the north. A few days before, he had unveiled a plan that would mass the Allied army against the German forces along the northern coast of France and in the Low Countries. There were sound reasons for attacking there: the main German Army was concentrated in that area, and more importantly for the British, it was also the launching spot for V-1 and V-2 weapons. Taking the area would also give the Allies ports on northern France to use to supply their army in a push to Germany.

The specifics of Montgomery's plan would have kept Montgomery in charge of the main Allied drive. It wasn't just Bradley who would have been affected. Montgomery was arguing to rewrite the pre-Normandy arrangement that called for Eisenhower to lead the attack. Placing everything under Montgomery would essentially make Eisenhower a figurehead as far as the ground war was concerned, with Montgomery making the real decisions.[1]

Bradley opposed the plan on a full range of grounds, from political—the Americans needed to be in control of their own troops, especially given the number—to tactical—Montgomery's plan had numerous flaws. Even leaving Allied politics aside, throwing everything north ignored what was happening on the battlefield, and implied a much longer war.

Concentrating the attack northwards would put a large part of the Allied army at the top of the Saar Valley and the Rhine, not just presupposing but dictating an attack there. (Montgomery in fact proposed this just a few weeks later.) The geography and fact that the force would face the bulk of the Germany army's strength suggested it would be a slow battle of might versus might.

Bradley's plan implied a mobile assault through the Lorraine into Germany below the Ardennes. Here the geography as well as the presently disorganized German defenses suggested a rapid assault. Patton's army was already galloping forward, not because (as the press and some later historians would have it) of Patton's personality, but because the conditions favored it. Add another army to it, and the momentum might be unstoppable. Once the West Wall was breached and the Rhine crossed, all Germany would lay open.[2]

Bradley engaged in a delicate series of discussions, in effect trying to negotiate a decision that would favor his plan, or at least a modified version. He agreed to "give" Montgomery a First Army corps and the XVII Airborne Corps (which included the 81st and 101st Airborne Divisions), while still retaining the bulk of the army and all of the Third for a drive into the Saar.

Eisenhower approved his plan on August 18, but Bradley must have sensed that Montgomery's resistance remained a problem. At some point that day or the next, he received information that elements of Patton's army had already reached the Seine. Furious, he called Patton's staff and told them he was on his way to the command post.

Bradley was angry because Patton had gone farther than instructed— farther, probably, than Bradley had told Eisenhower he would go. Bradley feared that Patton's aggressiveness would upset Montgomery and jeopardize Eisenhower's support for his offensive.

"For my sake," said Bradley, "stay put there now—don't advance any further across the river. I'll try to sell them on this."[3]

He failed. Eisenhower reserved a final decision, but in the meantime it was clear that, while he wouldn't give Montgomery everything he wanted, the northern thrust would have top priority and at least some of Bradley's forces. Any push by the remaining 12th Army forces would be secondary at best.

Bradley kept trying, perhaps hoping that the "facts on the ground" would convince Eisenhower to adopt his plan or some variation. He let

Patton proceed; by August 21 Patton predicted in his diary that he could be inside Germany within ten days if permitted to push to Metz and the surrounding area. His forward units had gone seventy miles that day. But Bradley was struggling on in a lost cause.

So was Montgomery, who wanted it all, not the British-leaning compromise that Eisenhower adopted.

Montgomery was so clueless that he flew to Bradley's headquarters August 23 to try and convince Bradley to support his original plan. Bradley, who'd just moved his command post to a barnyard near Chartres southwest of Paris, must have been shocked by Montgomery's deigning to visit him—it was the second time in a week—but there was no chance that he would change his mind. Bradley was less than cordial,[4] and Montgomery soon left.

When Patton went up to Chartres a short time later, he found Bradley fuming—the angriest he had ever seen him. Bradley told him that Eisenhower had rejected the latest variation on his plan, which would have allowed him to keep Patton and two corps from the First Army in motion eastward. Montgomery was to have full priority, with all of First Army supporting his flanks, and all of the airborne corps at his disposal.[5]

According to Patton, Bradley was mad enough to wonder aloud "what the Supreme Commander amounted to."[6]

Patton suggested that Eisenhower would be forced to change his mind if he, Bradley, and Hodges threatened to resign. But that sort of power play was abhorrent to Bradley, and he dismissed it.

Bradley modified the plan again, further reducing the force available to Patton. Patton suggested a plan to keep his army moving, and at least in his diary was enthusiastic about it. But Bradley must have realized that this was a poor substitute for what he had originally envisioned—sending overwhelming force into the weak point of the German line.

The debate over the plans for each stage of the war had myriad dimensions and consequences. As always, the reality of the Allies' long and limited supply network into France affected everything. Bradley understood that a hard thrust into Germany would need a strong supply network to support it; if Montgomery had the bulk of the forces, then he would get most of the supplies. Even if Patton made outrageous gains, the location of the forces as well as the logic of the overall strategy would dictate that he be stopped as soon as either supplies began to be strained or the northern attack ran into trouble.

Though his plan for a two-army drive in the south had been vetoed, Bradley continued to fight against Montgomery's plan to concentrate everything the Allies had to the north. He seems to have waged as much of a battle with Eisenhower as any with the Germans, relentless and unstinting, if polite and logical. The further Patton or Hodges went, the stronger his arguments were that equal weight be given to his drives. Bradley especially resisted anything that would bind his armies to Montgomery.

He told Eisenhower that while he certainly got along well with Montgomery personally (perhaps a little white lie), it was important for him to retain control over his own troops. Bradley used every argument he could think of, including an appeal to public relations. "We've got to make it clear to the American public that we are no longer under control of Monty's," he told his staff.[7]

Despite Bradley's continued campaign of persuasion, Eisenhower formalized his final decision in a letter to Montgomery on August 29, giving the weight of the drive to Montgomery. The First Army was to support Montgomery. He left Montgomery to "effect" coordination with Bradley, the details to be "left to the Commanders concerned." He did, at least, allow Bradley to keep pushing the Third Army in the south.[8]

Two days later, Eisenhower formally took over control of the Allied forces, in theory promoting Bradley out from under the 21st Army Group and placing him on an even footing with Montgomery. But it wasn't the elevation it seemed. Bradley had not only lost the argument on strategy, he had lost effective control of a major part of his army group, and he had lost the ability to determine the end game of the war. This was his reward for engineering the breakout from Normandy and destroying the largest German Army in western Europe.

The amazing thing is that Bradley did not become bitter about it. He continued to work not only with Eisenhower but with Montgomery. He supported the reduced-in-size Third Army drive as best he could. He never gave up hope that he would have an opportunity to regain the initiative Eisenhower's decision had cost him.

To use a metaphor he might have liked himself, he acted as if he were the coach of a baseball team that had given up five runs in the first inning—there was still plenty of time to mount a comeback.

It was a very Bradley thing to do.

Eisenhower's decision to concentrate on the drive north is usually discussed in terms of politics and personalities, Montgomery's above all. While this would have been largely Bradley's point of view, in fairness some perspective should be offered. SHAEF (Supreme Headquarters Allied Expeditionary Force)—and especially Eisenhower—believed that the Germans would collapse quickly once the main part of their army was defeated. Eisenhower's intelligence officers were arguing that a push against the main German Army in northern Europe would cause a quick collapse. If that happened, they argued, the push east into Germany would be easy.

The Allies also expected to face guerilla warfare once they occupied Germany. A lightning strike that was not followed up with sufficient force would be dangerous.

And finally, there was the matter of supply.

In his memoir on the war, *Crusade in Europe*, Eisenhower emphasizes the supply problems, noting that the Allies now had thirty-six divisions in France, with each requiring some 700 tons of supplies per day. At that point, the Allies had only two harbors functioning, Cherbourg which had just been repaired, and the British Mulberry. (The Mulberries were temporary harbors that had been hauled across the English Channel to Normandy. Marseilles in southern France had just been taken. The American Mulberry had been wrecked in the earlier storm.) As critical was the problem of getting these supplies off the water and to the men

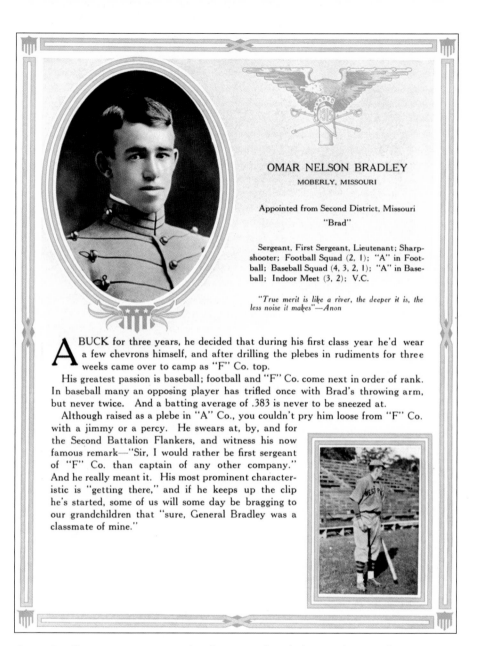

OMAR NELSON BRADLEY

MOBERLY, MISSOURI

Appointed from Second District, Missouri

"Brad"

Sergeant, First Sergeant, Lieutenant; Sharp-shooter; Football Squad (2, 1); "A" in Foot-ball; Baseball Squad (4, 3, 2, 1); "A" in Base-ball; Indoor Meet (3, 2); V.C.

"True merit is like a river, the deeper it is, the less noise it makes"—Anon

A BUCK for three years, he decided that during his first class year he'd wear a few chevrons himself, and after drilling the plebes in rudiments for three weeks came over to camp as "F" Co. top.

His greatest passion is baseball; football and "F" Co. come next in order of rank. In baseball many an opposing player has trifled once with Brad's throwing arm, but never twice. And a batting average of .383 is never to be sneezed at.

Although raised as a plebe in "A" Co., you couldn't pry him loose from "F" Co. with a jimmy or a percy. He swears at, by, and for the Second Battalion Flankers, and witness his now famous remark—"Sir, I would rather be first sergeant of "F" Co. than captain of any other company." And he really meant it. His most prominent character-istic is "getting there," and if he keeps up the clip he's started, some of us will some day be bragging to our grandchildren that "sure, General Bradley was a classmate of mine."

Omar Bradley's West Point yearbook page. Already he was known for quiet competence and perseverance.

Bradley at his desk, portraits of his wife and daughter close by. It was only in the later stages of the war that he gave up using his van as a command post, moving into buildings a few miles from the front. (Joseph Fansler Petit collection, West Point)

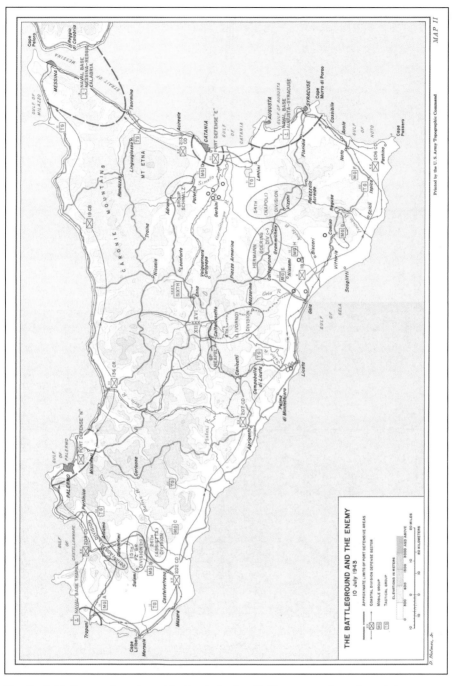

Bradley's II Corps played a critical role in the Sicilian campaign, though he found himself increasingly estranged from George Patton, the Seventh Army commander. (Joseph Fansler Petit collection, West Point)

Many of Bradley's key staff remained with him through most of the war. Among the key personnel were (left) William Kean, his chief of staff, and aide Chet Hansen. (Joseph Fansler Petit collection, West Point)

Bradley spent much of each day in the field. Here he talks with members of a tank company late in the war. (Joseph Fansler Petit collection, West Point)

Bradley with Bedell Smith, Eisenhower's chief of staff. (Joseph Fansler Petit collection, West Point)

Bradley inspecting a company bivouac in the field. While invented by the press as a story hook, the nickname "GI General" aptly described Bradley's genuine concern for the "regular joes" who fought the war. (Joseph Fansler Petit collection, West Point)

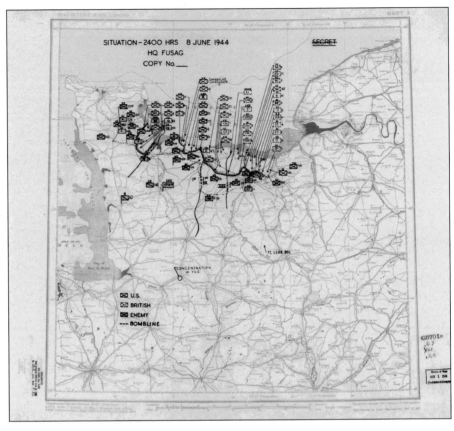

Last minute intelligence complicated D-Day plans, but by June 8, the Americans were firmly established on shore and had a reasonable estimate of the forces they were facing, as this 12th Army Group situation map shows. (Library of Congress)

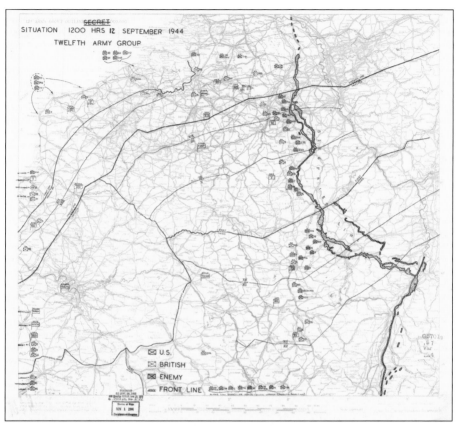

SITUATION 1200 HRS 12 SEPTEMBER 1944

TWELFTH ARMY GROUP

U.S.
BRITISH
ENEMY
FRONT LINE

By the end of the summer, the 12th Army Group was near Germany's borders. The next three months would be among the hardest and most frustrating of the war.

Bradley and George Patton were friends and antagonists—though much more the former than the latter. The pair was especially close in Europe, where Patton thrived on Bradley's praise as much as his advice.

William Simpson (right) headed Bradley's Ninth Army and was one of his steadiest lieutenants. (Joseph Fansler Petit collection, West Point)

Stalled by political infighting and slowed by the defenses of the German West Wall (top photo), the 12th Army Group had bogged down by the time snow arrived in November 1944.

The Army continued to innovate at all levels; above, some unidentified soldiers demonstrate a four-barreled machine-gun jury-rigged together. (Joseph Fansler Petit collection, West Point)

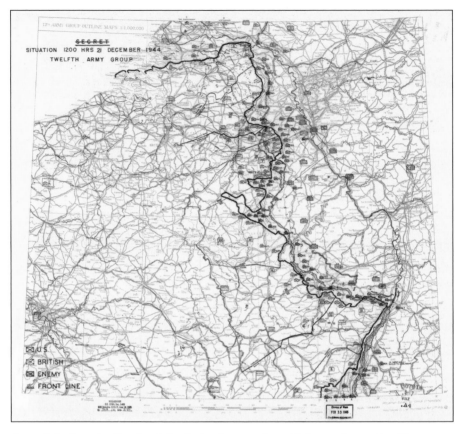

A week before the Battle of the Bulge began, the 12th Army Group intelligence had no idea of the size and location of the gathering German storm. This situation map shows two divisions in the Ardennes area—within a few days, upwards of two armies would smash through the line.

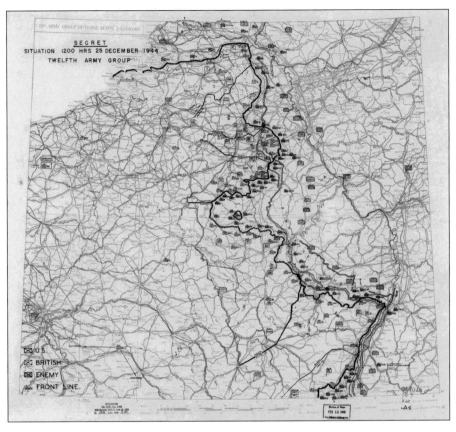

Despite the ferocity of the German attack, the 12th Army Group stabilized the front and held out at Bastogne, thanks to the heroism of countless soldiers. But Bradley lost command of two of his armies as Eisenhower misassessed the situation.

Bradley and Marlene Dietrich dined together a few days before the Battle of the Bulge. Their friendship appears to have been entirely platonic.

Bradley's relationship with Eisenhower was close, but they often clashed on strategy. (Joseph Fansler Petit collection, West Point)

Bradley celebrated his fifty-second birthday in Belgium with a small cake—then went back to work.

British Field Marshal Bernard Montgomery, seen here with Leland Hobbs, was Bradley's unacknowledged antagonist for most of the European campaign. (Joseph Fansler Petit collection, West Point)

The Bulge behind them, Bradley's armies closed in on Germany. Here Major General F. A. Keating explains the position of his 102nd Division to Bradley and, from far left, Generals Raymond McLain, Alvan C. Gillem, and William Simpson.

Bradley autographs a helmet for Private John Powell in February. Powell and his unit had finally gotten through the Hurtgen Forest. (Joseph Fansler Petit collection, West Point)

After Bradley's armies crossed the Rhine, Eisenhower was finally persuaded to change his strategy. Here Bradley, Eisenhower, Patton, and Hodges check a map on the eastern side of the river not long after the crossing.

Bradley's army commanders in March 1944. From left to right, Patton, Third Army; Hodges, First Army; Bradley; Simpson, Ninth Army; and Leonard Gerow, whose Fifteenth Army had just joined the line. (Joseph Fansler Petit collection, West Point)

Bradley at the end of the war. He'd aged considerably, but he still wore the shy, closed-mouth smile he'd had as a cadet.

at the front. The Allies were frantically repairing roads and railroads, but there was a severe shortage of intact bridges. Operating across the Seine magnified the problem.

By concentrating north, Montgomery's plan solved two problems. First was the destruction of the German Army, which was concentrated there. Second, the capture of Antwerp and the nearby Channel ports would cure most of the Allies' supply problems. Not only would this give Eisenhower an excellent port, but it would eliminate a considerable part of the road and railway problem, making the route to the armies significantly shorter.

What would have happened if Bradley's plan for a massive eastern offensive had been approved? Assuming that the initial thrust went well, could the American armies have reached Germany—and from there, gone to Berlin?

Clearly, they would have reached German soil. Probably, they would have been able to break through the West Wall defenses. Not only were these weakly defended at that point, but (as we know only in retrospect) the area where Patton would have made his thrust was one of the more antiquated and vulnerable portions of the line.

The question is what would have happened next.

The critical problem would have been supply. There were shortages of gasoline and ammunition, and such basics as winter clothing failed to reach many frontline troops before the cold weather set in. Even though Bradley's offensives were being given priority, at some point these shortages would have caught up with him. But it's not out of the question that this wouldn't have happened until Patton was well into Germany.

Even assuming the worst—that the Americans were stopped at a Rhine bridgehead in mid-fall, say—American occupation of southern Germany would have changed the complexion of post-war planning. The discussions at the Yalta Conference the following February would have been quite a bit different.[9]

Of course, none of this happened.

★ ★ ★ ★

Allied politics aside, there were other complications that Bradley had to deal with.

The first was the Brittany peninsula. While the rest of Patton's army was streaking eastward, Middleton was cleaning up the Brittany peninsula—or trying to. He launched an attack on Brest August 25 with three divisions, but failed to dislodge the enemy. Upwards of forty thousand Germans had piled into the city and hunkered down. Damage to the port facilities—to say nothing of the city itself—made taking the city less important, but as August went on without the Germans surrendering, Bradley understood that victory was a psychological necessity. As he told Patton, "We must take Brest in order to maintain the illusion that the U.S. Army cannot be beaten."[10]

The failure to take Brest quickly was at least partly a result of the eastward gamble, which was clearly worth taking. With the invasion of southern France, the Brittany area was now less important. Indeed, Brest itself was so damaged by the Germans and the fighting that the port was useless. But these were things that could not be easily explained in the media or even to political leaders, and not for the first time in the war, political and propaganda considerations drove military action.

Even so, it took until September 19 to free the city.

As psychologically important as Brest was, it paled in comparison to Paris. Militarily, the French capital was of little use to Bradley, and his plans essentially ignored it—he wanted to sweep south, keeping a good distance between the city and his armies. He wasn't afraid of German resistance there, or even of the damage that an extended battle would have done to the city's architectural and historic treasures. His reason for staying away was much more practical: he didn't have enough food to feed the people there.

Paris, Bradley reckoned, would require six thousand tons of food and other necessities a day. Even if the supplies were available, getting them there meant diverting resources that could have gone to the armies.

Bradley's hand was forced by growing chaos in the capital. Bradley met a self-appointed delegation of Frenchmen and at least one British spy and heard first-hand about the conditions in the city. The German commander had, in effect, offered to surrender it without a fight, but only to the Allied army, not the Resistance. Bradley ordered the French 2nd Armored Division—which was under his army group—to head toward Paris with the American 4th Division and take the city.[11]

Slowed by celebrating countrymen along the way—and at least according to rumors at Bradley's headquarters feeling the effect of premature liberation celebrations—the French armored division took its time. On August 24, Bradley told the 4th Division command that if the French were too slow, they should forge ahead of them. That got the French moving; elements of the 2nd Armored Division reached the city the next day and accepted the surrender of the German commander.

On Saturday, August 26, Eisenhower met Bradley at his headquarters trailer at Chartres and suggested they sneak into Paris early Sunday morning. With Kay Summersby driving Ike's sedan, they entered the city, escorted by a pair of armored cars and a jeep. They made their way to de Gaulle's headquarters, where Bradley met the French general for the first time.

Bradley found him cold and severe—a sharp contrast to the crowds that greeted the American generals later that day at the Arc de Triomphe. Eisenhower ordered the car to stop so he could get out and salute the tomb of France's unknown soldier. Immediately they were surrounded by a crowd. Eisenhower got a kiss from a huge Frenchman; Bradley fared somewhat better, getting a kiss from a young woman.

While Eisenhower and Summersby weaved their way through the adoring crowd, Bradley made his getaway in a jeep.

While the French people warmly welcomed the Americans, de Gaulle was already trying to establish his independence from them. But the real friction was between the British and Americans. The touchiness of the

Allies' relationship was evident a few days later, when the 28th Division marched down the Champs Élysées in a parade designed to impress the French that the Allies were in France to stay. (The impressive-looking parade took place as the unit marched to battle, Bradley modifying its route to the front to accommodate de Gaulle's request for a "division or two" to march through and show how strong the allies were.)[12] British newspapers implied somewhat tartly that the Americans were taking over the war.

In fact, quite the opposite was happening, at least as far as strategy was concerned. Eisenhower limited the supplies available to Bradley and to his armies; as Bradley had foreseen, this necessarily limited what he could do. By the end of August, the Third Army had been put on a 2,000 ton per day diet—barely enough to keep itself in place, let alone move forward.[13]

Bradley felt that Patton did not immediately understand the consequences of the priority shift and how limited his supplies really would be. If not, he did soon enough. Looking back with some amusement, Bradley told a story of Patton coasting into his command post area with a bone-dry gas tank, ordering his driver to make sure to fill it up from the group supply—he wasn't going to waste even an ounce of his "own."

Dragoon—the renamed Anvil invasion of southern France—got underway August 15. Marseilles was captured August 28, but this did not relieve the problems of supply farther north, where Antwerp remained the key prize.

Bradley's First Army, operating on Montgomery's right flank, charged ahead with VII Corps, crossing into Belgium at the beginning of September. German troops retreating from Normandy and the Pas de Calais stumbled into General Collins' troops at Mons. Thirty thousand were taken prisoner, and another two thousand killed. This battle—now generally forgotten—gave the First Army a path to Liege and Aachen.

Finally, Montgomery moved with uncharacteristic speed. In great contrast to his earlier campaigns, he covered some 250 miles in six days, freeing a swath of the Channel coast from German rule. He was now poised to take Antwerp.

From Montgomery's perspective, the road to Germany was open. All he had to do was sail down it.

On September 2, Bradley gathered his army commanders together in Chartres for a talk with Eisenhower. He sat patiently as the Supreme Commander spoke rather grandly about the future of the war, becoming more expansive by the moment.

Bradley glanced toward Patton as Eisenhower mentioned Clausewitz. Patton barely kept a sarcastic smile from his face. Hodges, at least, was his usual stoic self, emotionless. Either of the army commanders, to say nothing of Bradley himself, might have pointed out that they had not only commanded larger forces than Clausewitz, but had already done more with them than Clausewitz dreamed.

But there was no reason to cut Eisenhower off. He was in a good mood, and Bradley sensed that he was finally going to get his way.

Not entirely, but his plan would at least extend the gains Third Army was making in the south. If Eisenhower approved, Bradley's forces would be able to aim at Frankfurt, across the Siegfried Line. Once there, the entire future of the war would be determined.

Bradley made his pitch and encouraged his lieutenants to present their arguments in its favor. In the end, the trio convinced Eisenhower that the latest version of Bradley's plan made sense. He agreed to allocate more supplies for Third Army and allow Hodges' First Army to move one corps further south to support Patton. The objective was a quick dash across the Siegfried Line to seize Frankfurt. At the same time, the rest of 12th Army Group, now referred to by Eisenhower as the Central Group of Armies, would continue to support Montgomery and take Brest.[14]

It was similar to the plans Bradley had advocated earlier, and better than he had hoped for just a week before. It would set the pattern for strategy through the rest of the war: what came to be called a broad front strategy with separate prongs threatening Germany. The appeal to Eisenhower was that it gave him the option of backing whichever prong did well—as Bradley had argued earlier.

Later that day, news arrived at Bradley's headquarters that Eisenhower's plane had been forced down. It wasn't the catastrophe that everyone feared—the plane had made a soft landing on a beach, but Eisenhower hurt his knee helping to pull the plane away from the water. Because of his injury, Eisenhower couldn't explain his decision to Montgomery himself. Instead, he wanted Bradley to do it.

Bradley flew to Amiens the next day, September 3. He was surprised to find Montgomery friendly, and even more surprised—at least according to his statements later—that Montgomery did not object to the plan.

But Montgomery did object to the plan—strenuously. His forces entered Antwerp on September 4. The same day, he sent a message to Eisenhower saying that Eisenhower should (in effect) forget Bradley's ideas. Instead, he should put the weight of the Allied advance behind him and march straight down the Ruhr. And Montgomery told Eisenhower to come see him and discuss it; he was too busy himself to go to Eisenhower.

For once, Eisenhower was angered by Montgomery's impertinence. In a letter to his commanders, Eisenhower laid out the two-pronged strategy. Bradley had finally won that battle, even if the adopted strategy was far less than he had initially sought.

Montgomery's taking Antwerp did nothing to aid the supply situation. While the Germans had been unable to destroy Antwerp's port facilities, they still controlled the Schultz Estuary between the city and the sea. Those forces had to be eliminated before Antwerp could be used.

This was not an easy task. There were sixty miles' worth of islands and peninsula, dotted with German defenses. Montgomery had a choice: clear the peninsula and open the port, or move in the other direction toward the Rhine and the Ruhr.

Actually, the choice was Eisenhower's. Since sufficient supplies were critical to maintaining the double thrust, it might be expected that Eisenhower next ordered that Montgomery clear the way to Antwerp. But in fact he didn't. Instead, he approved a plan by Montgomery to strike across the Rhine in Arnhem.

It was a bold and ambitious plan and far too much of both, as it turned out.

As Bradley had been pointing out for weeks, Montgomery's army was operating in a landscape particularly unsuitable for a rapid drive. The Netherlands was crisscrossed by canals and waterways, which afforded plenty of defensive opportunities. Merely blowing up bridges could slow any advance to a crawl. But Montgomery nevertheless insisted he could move quickly there.

The British field marshal wanted to sidestep the main German opposition by turning north. Eying a 60-mile stretch of low land, he planned a series of parachute drops to capture key bridges to establish a route for his army. The areas secured by the paratroopers would be sewn together by his XXX Corps, led by the Guards Armored Division, considered one of 21ˢᵗ Army Group's best units.

Bradley only found out about the plan after it had been approved by Eisenhower, in what was itself a breach of protocol. This was not a small operation with no impact on the Americans. Montgomery was moving away from First Army, exposing the American flank.

Dumbfounded, he called Eisenhower and demanded an explanation. Eisenhower told him it was a worthwhile gamble; he was to realign First Army's corps to support it.

Bradley saw the offensive as yet another Montgomery move to take over First Army. Worse, shifting his army would undermine the offensive just as it was about to pay off. On September 13, First Army's 3rd Armored Division (part of VII Corps) had crossed the German border ten miles south of Aachen. Bradley was already inside Germany; why wait for the British?

He argued extensively but vainly, citing intelligence estimates that predicted further stiffening of the Siegfried Line if the Allies didn't move quickly. The First Army could move through Aachen; with proper support, Third Army would be through the Siegfried Line and across the Rhine in a matter of days.

Eisenhower was unmoved. His G-3, Major General Harold "Pinky" Bull, met Bradley at his command post to personally explain why he shouldn't be upset.

It was a hard job.

Bradley told Bull that his boss was too quick to side with Montgomery. Far too quick. Montgomery had always wanted First Army. This latest plan disrupted Bradley's already approved offensive; it was little more than a sidestepping way to get the Allies to follow his original plan, rather than the blueprint Eisenhower had approved.

"I won't have the tail wagging the dog," Bradley told Bull.[15]

All the SHAEF G-3 could do was to deny the obvious effects of Montgomery's plan.

Much of the conference devolved into an argument over supplies and resources, as Bradley tried vainly to keep the quotas needed for his own forces. The Third Army was fighting on a four-day supply of ammunition, with just enough fuel husbanded to get to the Rhine.[16] To keep going, both of his armies needed a minimum of 7,000 tons of supplies per day, and that wasn't going to continue if Montgomery had top priority.

Bradley vented much of his anger on the supply corps. He felt they could do a much better job getting supplies to the front lines. He cited the testimony of Wilson, who was still in First Army as its head of supply. Bull turned that back by saying that the supply command simply felt Wilson had no faith in them.

"Our ground forces have done the impossible," said Bradley, clearly running out of patience. "Let SOS [Service of Supply, the supply command] try the impossible for a while. I'm not convinced they're doing all that can be done."

"Hell, have 'em get off their asses and work the way our troops have," added Patton.

The argument went nowhere.

"God damn it, you kept the flag waving," Patton told Bradley after the meeting broke up. "I'm proud of you."[17]

Bradley had had enough. He told Eisenhower that if Montgomery was given XIX and VII Corps—in other words, the rest of First Army—he would resign.[18]

Eisenhower placated him by insisting he would retain control of First Army. And, added the SHAEF commander, there was no reason that Patton couldn't continue moving eastward.

No reason but the drain in supplies and the stiffening defense made possible by the delays.

Launched September 17, Market Garden would turn out to be Montgomery's most disastrous mistake of the war, and not just because some 7,500 British paratroopers were either killed or captured at Arnhem. The diversion of resources to 21st Army Group and, just as important, the decision to proceed with Market Garden rather than clear up the approach to Antwerp, fatally stalled the Allied advance into Germany. Before the operation jumped off, there was talk that the war would end by the New Year. It was soon obvious that talk was premature.

Bradley developed a new proposal to fit in with Market Garden, presenting it at a conference in Versailles, September 22.

The First Army would push toward a double envelopment of Cologne, meeting to the east of the city at Paderborn. Patton, meanwhile, would push north between Frankfurt and Mannheim, aiming for Kassel and central Germany. The British 21st Army Group would strike at Bremen and Hanover. The big prize was the Ruhr, Germany's industrial heartland. Bradley's plan was designed to seize the Ruhr while trapping and destroying a major part of the German Army.

Eisenhower's headquarters was the Trianon Palace, a hotel at the edge of the grounds of the famous nineteenth century palace. The contrast between Bradley's quarters and those of his commander was sharp. The elegant foyer reminded Hansen of the White House. Even Eisenhower felt the place was too grandiose, locating his office in an annex and blocking off part of it with plywood.

Bradley sensed the meeting was going to be worthless soon after he arrived, when staff gossip revealed Montgomery wasn't coming. The ostensible reason was Market Garden, which was reaching a critical stage. But nearly every American, including Bradley, read it as a slap to Eisenhower. Montgomery had sent his chief of staff, General Freddy de Guingand, as his representative, but de Guingand was not empowered to make any commitments for him.

Beyond the breach of protocol, Montgomery's absence meant nothing could be finalized. It didn't help that the reports about Market Garden were not good, and the failure to clear Antwerp's approach foretold a long winter.

The British predicted it would take until November to get the passage to Antwerp clear; there would be delays for minesweeping after that. Eisenhower stated the obvious—clearing the port was the top priority; without it, the Allies could not get enough supplies in to sustain a campaign in Germany.

Yet Eisenhower still would not direct Montgomery to clear the approach. Instead, he reaffirmed Market Garden as the Allies' main priority. He tightened Montgomery's front, which in theory would help him continue his offensive. Ike told Bradley to support the British with First Army, and directed that the rest of 12th Army Group sit tight until Montgomery had achieved his objectives. That ended, for the moment at least, Patton's drive in the south, as well as Bradley's plans for a double envelopment beyond Cologne.

But the thing that must have galled Bradley most of all was the fact that Eisenhower sent him to tell Montgomery what had been decided.

There were brief diversions during the conference. At one point, Bradley stopped in the lobby of the George V hotel, waiting to see some of his colleagues. A director and a performer for one of the troop entertainment shows began speaking to him; eventually they asked for his autograph, even though they didn't know who he was. Handing over the book, the director apologized because the only signatures in it belonged to a corporal and a private.

Bradley smiled. "They're plenty good enough for me," he said, brandishing a pen.[19]

Around noon on Sunday, September 24, Bradley found himself peering out the small window of his airplane, hunting in vain for the tip of the wing through the thick clouds. Despite the rain and heavy weather, he'd insisted on taking a plane rather than driving to Montgomery's headquarters; the drive would have taken at least eight hours each way, and he had no desire to prolong his ordeal. But the storm they were flying through proved more intense than predicted. They soon lost their way.

There wasn't a large margin for error—if they flew too far east or north, they would be over German territory.

Bradley got up out of his seat and went into the cockpit.

Calmly, he began navigating, looking out the window for landmarks. Finally he deduced enough from the roads and landscape to orient them toward Brussels.

Bourg is that way, he told the pilot, pointing. *The Germans are over there.*

They made it down without incident.[20]

The meeting was over more quickly than the plane ride. As usual, Bradley was correct and quiet. Montgomery was optimistic that he would soon have a victory.

Outside, the staff people grumbled that Montgomery was appropriating American equipment from First Army, then refusing to give it back. The Allies' relationship was borderline dysfunctional.

On October 9, Montgomery officially called off Market Garden. In the meantime, an offensive to clear the Scheldt had begun, with assistance from First Army. The first Allied convoy pulled into Antwerp November 26. By that time, the Germans had fully regrouped to the south, mustering as many as seventy divisions, albeit many of them undermanned and untrained.

Just before the end of September, Bradley returned from visiting Hodges at First Army with a present under his arm. It was a two-foot-high bronze bust of Hitler, with a note at the base:

> This ersatz bust was found in Nazi headquarters in Eupen, Germany. With seven units of fire and one additional division, 1st Army will deliver the original in thirty days.[21]

The estimate would prove more than a little optimistic.

Despite Eisenhower's orders and the problems of supply, Bradley's armies were not idle. He encouraged both Hodges and Patton to edge against the German defenses known as the West Wall or Siegfried Line.

Thick-walled pillboxes, extensive minefields, and deep rows of tank traps were coordinated with well-prepared artillery and geography to form an impressive defensive barrier to the Allies. Not only could the defenses be manned by a relatively small number of soldiers, but when combined with tactics such as spoiling counterattacks and aggressive fighting, they forced even a well-equipped foe to stop in his tracks.

Nowhere was this more apparent than in the First Army's battles in the Huertgen Forest, which exposed American weaknesses as surely as they demonstrated German strengths. Indeed, the battles are sometimes cited as America's greatest tactical failure of the war, a critique that by implication extends to Bradley, under whose command they were fought.

The battles extended over several months north of the Ardennes in the First Army area.

The Huertgen Forest—Hürtgenwald in German—is an area of some fifty square miles. Extending from Monschau in the south to Duren in the north, with the Rur (or Roer) River marking its eastern boundary, it is divided into three different forests and includes dams and the headwaters on the Rur. Much of the bloodiest fighting took place in a relatively small geographic area south of Aachen, in and along the Kall River Valley and the associated ridges, in small villages and a clearing in the general vicinity of Huertgen village, and near the town of Schmidt.

There were few roads in the area. Vehicles often could not travel off them because of the thick conifers and the hilly land in much of the forest. Even units on foot had trouble passing through some of the thickest tree stands. The fall's wet rains made travel even more complicated for tanks and other vehicles, though they did figure prominently in firefights when they were available.

German defenses in the area were webbed throughout the terrain, giving them the sort of advantage one would expect from native troops fighting on their own soil. Additionally, the heavy forest made it difficult for the American air force to support the ground troops.

With the exception of the last battle where the dams may have been recognized as a strategic goal, the area was of secondary importance in all of the battles. Hodges' primary concern for much of the fall and early winter was to prevent them from being used to attack his flank. This would have influenced not only his plans but the choice and strength of forces he devoted to the area.

★ ★ ★ ★

The first encounters in the forest came in September, after VII Corps, under Joe Collins, first breached the West Wall defenses. Over-extended because of a lack of fresh troops and supplies, Collins was unable to carry the attack when he encountered stiff German counter strokes. Attempting to straighten his lines, he assigned the 9th Infantry Division to seize a key road network near the villages of Huertgen and Kleinhau. Instead, the troops were badly mauled before falling back.

The 9th Infantry Division made a second round of attacks aimed at Schmidt in early October. The division found that the defenders had increased and their defenses improved. The drive ground to a halt October 16 short of its objective, after suffering heavy casualties.

Aachen fell on October 21, but only after a bloody, street by street gun battle. The capture of the city, the first of real size in Germany, presented the possibility of an avenue east, but it also increased the strategic importance of the forest, which could be used to screen German troops for a counteroffensive. The seven dams on the Rur were also of significant strategic value. With the rivers behind them filling as the fall rains continued, release of the waters they held back could flood the lower Rur Valley. This would make crossing the river more difficult, and possibly block the advance.

There is considerable historical debate about when the importance of the dams was actually realized. The best evidence suggests that it was not until sometime in November. Bradley seemed to be somewhat defensive about the dams after the war, telling historian Charles MacDonald that their significance was often discussed that autumn, regardless of whether the documents show it. *A General's Life* declares that they were the primary reason for Schmidt being targeted at the beginning of November. While this may be possible, it's not reflected in the orders for the operation. Nor are the dams mentioned in Hansen's diary.[22]

In any event, the key dam at Schwammenauel was eventually included in the goals for the 28th Division's drive in early November. Led by Major General Norman Cota, the division was part of Gerow's V Corps, and

Gerow was largely responsible for the planning of the assault. He had clearly studied the 9th Division's experiences in the forest, since he strengthened the 28th with extra mortar companies and tank destroyers, weapons that had proven useful against pillboxes in the earlier fights. He also added a large number of M29 Weasels, which were able to deal effectively with the rugged terrain. Gerow's plan generally followed the 9th Division's earlier lines, though with better provisions for supply, implying that he thought the earlier attacks had failed because they simply lacked sufficient force.

Bad weather, heavy concentrations of mines, and fierce counterattacks slowed the offensive. A small force managed to reach Schmidt on November 3, but they were thrown out the next day. A succession of errors and poor performance—most notably, the panic of an American battalion as it came under artillery fire—marred the operation, threatening to turn it into a rout for the Germans.

Alarmed by the poor performance of the division, Hodges chewed Cota out at a conference November 8 after meeting with Bradley. The division suffered so severely it had to withdraw not only from the area but from the battle.

The 4th Infantry Division attacked in roughly the same area later that month, and once again the battle was so fierce that both officers and men broke. This time, however, the Americans managed to take the villages of Huertgen and Kleinhaus; from there, they struck at the Brandernberg-Bergstein ridge, a key high point in the area. The battle was saved by the timely arrival of the 2nd Ranger Battalion, opening the way to the Rur River in the east.

The Rangers took severe casualties—19 dead, 107 wounded, 4 missing—which was about a quarter of their force. But their casualty rate was "light" compared to what some units in the 4th, 9th, and 28th Infantry Divisions suffered. A few were estimated to have sustained losses from 50 percent and higher.[23]

★ ★ ★ ★

In a way, the battles in the forest were merely a microcosm of the difficulties Allied armies faced all along the West Wall. Once the American drive literally ran out of fuel, the Germans regrouped. Fighting behind well-prepared defenses and protecting their homeland, even inexperienced troops did fairly well. The hills and forests amplified their defenses. The Americans found that bypassing German strong points didn't work well because German observation posts could direct devastating artillery almost anywhere.

But for all the advantages the Germans had on defense, the Americans also suffered from failures of leadership. When General James Gavin led his 82nd Airborne in the last battle to take Schmidt in February 1945, he saw the remains of a battle the 28th Division had fought—along with bodies of soldiers who'd fallen the previous fall and not been recovered. Gavin concluded that the division commander had lost touch with his units. He hadn't even realized where they were killed, or the bodies surely would have been recovered by now.

Gavin was outraged, and even more disturbed by the attitude of the present corps and division commanders in the sector, who despite all the experience of the previous battles, insisted on a strategy that had little to do with the actual terrain.[24] Gavin felt the commanders had "fought the battle on maps" without adequately familiarizing themselves with the terrain.[25]

The criticism seems hard to refute.

As army group commander, Bradley was not—and should not—have been concerned with the specifics of the attacks, leaving these to the lower commanders. And he would necessarily view action in the Forest as part of a larger whole. At some point, however, he could not have failed to notice that things were not going well in that area and ordered a change of plans.

There is, of course, a limit to how far the criticism should go. Some historians—the well-respected Russell Weigley is a prime example—have gone far overboard, claiming that the campaign illustrates excessive caution and lack of aggressiveness. He even claims that this caution cost the Americans victory in 1944.[26] That seems untenable.

Much of the historical criticism seems to stem from a misunderstanding of the purpose of the forest attacks—partly abetted by Bradley's claims that they were intended to take the dams from the very beginning. Bradley clearly did not see the dams as important until well into the campaign, and even then viewed the action in the forest as a sideshow. Using it as an example of his allegedly plodding approach to warfare is simply unfair.[27] It's just one more example of Bradley—and reality—being force-fitted into a preconceived conception of history by historians.

But that doesn't mean Bradley shouldn't be criticized.

Given the problems in the 28th Infantry Division,[28] it's possible that Bradley interpreted the failures in the forest as being caused by the division's leadership itself, not by any strategy. If so, he did not act as forcibly here as he had elsewhere. Cota remained in charge of the division, though it was removed from the line. Bradley may have felt that the error wasn't primarily Cota's, and that Cota should have either been given more support or, better, a different strategy or objective.[29]

In any event, Bradley seems to have concluded by the end of November that he had to change his plans in the face of all that had happened and was continuing to happen in Huertgen. Part of his thinking seems to have had to do with the dams and the belated recognition of their importance. Now realizing they would be extremely difficult to take on the ground, he began working to get the British RAF to attack the dams.[30] Some of the dams were attacked, but with no results. Events would interrupt further offensive action in the forest area; when they resumed, the defenses were the same but the army behind them much depleted.

The 4th Infantry Division reached Grosshau at the end of November. Depleted by battle, it was sent to a quiet sector to rest.

That sector was the Ardennes.

★ ★ ★ ★

Bradley had never had any illusions about waging war, but he was becoming more candid in his observations. To prevent war in the future, he thought, its horrors had to be driven home to everyone, civilian and soldier.

Germans especially. He told Harold Bull that every German town in their path should be bombed. Bull, shocked, said that was not the American way of waging war.

Patton cut in, suggesting they declare telephone switchboards a military objective, then bomb them.

October and much of November passed in anxious frustration. The failure of the Market Garden offensive and continued problems in supply dashed any hope of bursting through the German defenses.

With Montgomery's 21st Army Group finally concentrating on the approaches to Antwerp, Eisenhower directed Bradley to draw away a division to assist Montgomery, while continuing to apply pressure in the First Army area in hopes of drawing German troops away from the British.

This was an evolution back toward Bradley's two-thrust plan, eventually jelling as the so-called "broad front strategy." By the last week of October, Eisenhower formally directed Bradley to "strike with two armies [the First and the Ninth, moving toward the front] astride the Ruhr, while the Third Army will secure the Saar, cross the Rhine near Frankfurt and advance probably towards Kassel."[31] But the stiffening German defenses and the continuing problems with supplies and replacement troops blunted progress. Orders notwithstanding, the 12th Army Group was reduced to modest local attacks while it husbanded its resources for a major push, in effect giving the Germans more time to restore themselves.

Instead of getting better, the supply problems were worsening. The fall's stormy weather hit the coast, reducing the beaches' capacity. Cherbourg was only bringing in some 7,000 tons of supplies a day. By Bradley's estimate the supply situation was roughly where it had been D-Day plus sixty, but the Americans had as many men on the continent as they had expected three hundred days after the invasion. Artillery ammunition was in especially short supply. This directly affected strategy and progress; artillery was deeply integrated into American tactics, especially in an area like the German border where there were heavy defenses. The increasingly bad weather hampered aircraft operations and exacerbated the situation.

What Bradley called the "famine in supply" was getting worse for several reasons. One was simply bad weather. Another was Montgomery's failure to open Antwerp. A third was the decision to delay taking the Brittany ports. But the problems went beyond the ports. The Allied bombing campaign on the German transportation infrastructure inside France prior to and just after D-Day was now hurting the Allies. Bombing the railroad system was especially a double-edged sword—it made it difficult for the Germans to defend themselves, but it also made it difficult for the Allies once they advanced. Truck convoys and airlifts could not fully compensate for the blown railway lines, and using them created their own bottlenecks and shortages elsewhere.

Just as fundamental and far-reaching was the decision to limit the U.S. Army to ninety divisions, a decision made for political and practical reasons. In the popular imagination, support for the war was universal, and everyone in America was in the armed forces during the war. The reality was very different. In 1943, the Army failed to meet its draft quotas. Replacing troops lost due to casualties became a critical issue after D-Day. The manpower ceiling and the need to fight on two fronts put very real limits on the way the Army fought the war.

America's enemies and allies could only wish to have the limitations the U.S. suffered. But their effect on strategy as well as the conduct of the war were nonetheless real, and are often underappreciated, even by the men who fought it.

In mid-October, Bradley moved his command post from Verdun to Luxembourg, taking over the state railway building. It was a considerable upgrade from the tent and trailer existence the staff had gotten used to.

Among other things, the building was steam-heated, not an insignificant fact with winter coming on.

Bradley took quarters nearby in Hotel Alfa. A large, imposing building near the train station, the hotel was located a short distance from the medieval center of town. His bedroom had a window facing the street; he liked the view, dismissing concerns that he could be targeted by an assassin. While the building was the nicest by far that he had occupied to this point in the war, Bradley rarely made use of its elegant facilities. One of the few exceptions came on Eisenhower's birthday, when Bradley arranged a surprise party complete with champagne, orchestra, and what Kay Summersby called "a four-star cake."[32]

The city was only twelve miles from the front, and its selection would later become controversial. Bradley never explained why he chose to locate in the capital, whether it was a matter of geopolitics or logistics. Luxembourg was somewhat closer to Third Army headquarters than First or Ninth, keeping Bradley closer to Patton than Hodges, though in terms of travel by car or jeep the difference would have amounted to no more than an hour. (The city itself was in First Army territory.)[33]

The slow-down in the action left more time for the mundane affairs of command. Bradley answered letters, including a number from the mothers of wounded or missing servicemen. They were heart-rending. Bradley tried at times to soften the blow, changing the accurate but cruel details supplied by his staff. Rather than having been killed by a booby trap he hadn't seen, a soldier had been felled by a mine. It was a softening rather than a lie; a kindness, perhaps. But in the end, it hardly changed the real facts of war and loss.

Bradley visited Eisenhower's headquarters at the end of October. With Bedell Smith they took a day to go hunting and then spent much of the night playing bridge. It was a good visit: Bradley bagged seven pheasants, and more importantly got final approval for a November offensive.

The American buildup brought a third army, the Ninth Army, into Bradley's line. He planned to put it and the First Army in motion toward Düsseldorf and Cologne respectively. Patton's Third Army would proceed from Metz to Manheim. If the plan succeeded, it would put the Americans on the banks of the Rhine. Of the two thrusts, Bradley says he considered the one in the north more important.[34]

One of the most important parts of the plan was the location of the Ninth Army, which Bradley inserted next to the 21st Army Group, wedged between the British and First Army. Bradley figured he would lose some part of his army group to Montgomery if the latter finally moved forward, and he would rather do without the Ninth than the First. The Ninth was smaller and less seasoned, but Bradley also felt that its commander and staff would get along more easily with Montgomery. The First, he noted in his memoirs, tended to resent orders from above, even from someone like Bradley who had commanded it.

Though he had some twenty-two divisions, the long line of his front meant that Bradley had to weaken some portion of it for his offensive. The natural spot was in front of the Eifel—the hilly, heavily forested mid-section of his line. This was the Ardennes, straddling Luxembourg and Belgium. Bradley was content to let Hodges hold it with minimum force. It was a gamble, and one that he acknowledged readily after the war. But it was hardly the most dangerous he had taken. The Germans across the line were dug in, but did not appear to have a large enough force to mount an attack.

While the optimism that had ruled his headquarters early in the summer had dissipated, Bradley nonetheless felt that the war for the Germans henceforth would be primarily one of defense. They were low on fuel stocks. The Allied dominance of the air curtailed their mobility. At the same time, their defenses multiplied the power of their stricken army; it would be foolish to risk these by attacking.

As far as Bradley and the rest of the Allied command were concerned, the initiative rested entirely with them. Their main problem now was to punch through the German defenses and avoid a static war. Bradley estimated it would take thirty days to get to the Rhine, barring heavy resistance. If his offensive bogged down before the troops reached the river, they would be forced to bed in for the winter.

There would be one other consequence—if the 12th Army Group did not achieve a clear breakthrough, Eisenhower told Bradley, the initiative would pass entirely to Montgomery. Bradley would assume a supporting role in the Allied plans.[35]

The weather was already winterlike. Six inches of snow lay in parts of the northern Ardennes in early November.[36] Where there wasn't snow, streams and rivers were flooded with heavy rain. Roadways were washed out. The unusually cold and wet weather would continue to be a problem.

Though planned as a simultaneous two-pronged thrust, bad weather caused delays and changed the timing. Patton, leading the southern prong, got off first, braving rains that wiped out makeshift bridges across the Moselle. The mud and German defenses made for very slow going. General Walton Walker's XX Corps reached the outskirts of Metz November 9, but the city held out for nearly two weeks. Resistance in the area continued for several weeks beyond that.

The northern offensive began with an aerial bombardment. Originally planned along the lines of the Cobra carpet bombing, the results were less spectacular. The hard terrain and stubborn German defenses blunted both the Ninth and First Army spearheads.

It was during this campaign that the largest of the Huertgen Forest battles was waged.[37] But the entire Ninth and First Army front was full of rough fighting. Bradley's northern armies covered only seven miles in the first two weeks. By this point (if not sooner), Bradley had realized the danger posed by the Rur dams; with the ground offensive stalling, he began looking for a way to bomb them and eliminate their importance. In the meantime, the Siegfried line and German frontier provided exactly what he didn't want: a gruesome war of slow attrition.

In the south, Patton reached Saarbucken, a strongpoint on the Siegfried Line, on December 2. It was progress, though hardly the lightning strike for which Patton was known. Bradley kept looking for a breakthrough, hoping to put the weight of his attack behind whichever army could bull through. He found himself wishing that the Germans would come out of their defenses. He almost hoped that they would do something foolish, like stage a counterattack so he could destroy them in one fell swoop.[38]

With Eagle Tac in Luxembourg city, Bradley's headquarters became a convenient destination for visiting VIPs. Part of his job now included briefing them on the war. He generally avoided answering questions that he felt came too close to the vein of his situation, but he didn't cover up inconvenient facts. To a visiting delegation of businessmen in late November, he candidly admitted that they were having trouble getting enough ammunition. He was also frank about how much time it would take to win the war—six more months, he predicted.

The general was even more open with a visiting group of congressmen a few days later. But it was a discouraging experience. One of the congressmen was drunk, and the others seemed uninterested in what was going on at the front. While their attitudes may have been extreme, feelings at home were hardly as positive or supportive as later popular accounts make it seem. Bradley was constantly asked when the war would end by people anxious to get back to "regular" life. Complacency had settled over the United States following the rapid advance through France. Americans expected a quick end to the war, something Bradley knew wasn't possible.

Not all of the visitors to Bradley's headquarters were tiresome.

Around the middle of November, Bradley hosted Marlene Dietrich, who had come to Twelfth Army on an extended USO tour. Dietrich was a famous singer and movie star, and though born in Berlin, a virulent opponent of Nazism. Naturalized as an American citizen in 1939, she had begun helping War Bond drives immediately after Pearl Harbor.

For the first time in weeks, Bradley relaxed, laughing and smiling. In the middle of dinner, a phone call came. He excused himself.

General Simpson from the Ninth Army was calling. The 29th Division had managed to break through its line, and, now that it was dark, Simpson was unsure whether to keep it moving or pull back and dig in for a counterattack.

"Keep it going," said Bradley quickly. "Keep it going as far and as fast as you can."[39]

Bradley spent much of the last week of November and the first week of December shuttling back and forth between his bed, ordered there by a doctor as he fought a severe sinus infection and exhaustion. His staff plotted behind his back to prepare a "vacation" for him at Cannes, trying to line up old friends who would make him rest.

Patton reached Saarguemines on December 7. Constrained by the continuing ammunition shortages and weather which kept their aircraft grounded, the Allies were making slow progress against the difficult German defenses. More and more it appeared as if the future would be a difficult slog. Without some radical change, they might not be ready for a real drive into Germany until spring.

At First Army, Monk Dickson sifted through intelligence reports claiming that the German officer who had rescued Mussolini was now involved in a secret operation on their front. On November 20, Dickson had issued an estimate saying the Germans in front of First Army had no offensive capability. But within days, he realized he was wrong. Reports from the front lines turned up several German units he hadn't known were there. Some were SS formations.

Dickson began counting. By his estimate—admittedly now driven by the fear that he had made a grievous mistake—there were twenty-two German divisions across from First Army. They were well equipped with armor, and because they were SS divisions, could be expected to have priority on scarce German resources.

Dickson issued an estimate outlining the danger. There were four possibilities. The most likely was a counterattack with "air, armor, infantry and secret weapons at a selected focal point at a time of [the Germans'] ... choosing."[40]

Dickson's report alarmed Hodges, and on December 10, the First Army commander asked Bradley to move two divisions to reinforce VIII Corps in the Ardennes. But Bradley's G-2 countered Dickson's estimate, saying there was nothing to worry about; the German defenses were brittle and getting thinner all the time. They would soon snap. As for an offensive ... it wasn't going to happen.

Bradley did think the Germans were planning some sort of counterattack. But his interpretation of Dickson's report was that any offensive would come only after the Americans crossed the Rur River, when they would be most vulnerable. And it wouldn't be in the Ardennes. In Bradley's mind, it would come in the northern portion of First Army's area, possibly at Aachen. The conditions there would favor a German smash. The indications from the intelligence reports (backed up by the map plots he was looking at every day) showed a buildup of German units in that vicinity. In the meantime, small local attacks might be launched to boost enemy morale and divert American attention.[41]

Bradley turned down Hodges' request for more troops. Finding two extra divisions would have been difficult in any event. If he had them, Bradley would likely have used them to reinforce his offensives, rather than putting them into an area so quiet it was called "The Ghost Front."

"I felt very much alone in my opinions," remembered Dickson later. "But I remembered that General Anderson had called me a pessimist and an alarmist just before Kasserine. In any case, I was a lone heretic now."[42]

Bradley got up early December 16, his mind focused on a meeting scheduled for later that afternoon in Versailles. The weather was too heavy to fly; Hansen arranged a car instead. Faced with a four-hour drive, they got an early start, missing the morning briefing at Eagle Tac.

The meeting with Eisenhower and the SHAEF staff was about the need for infantry replacements. The matter was growing more critical and involved quality as well as quantity of troops. Eisenhower had begun scouring units for soldiers who could be transferred to combat, in some cases replacing those posted far behind the lines with civilian workers.

Bradley's G-1 or personnel officer, Joseph O'Hare, had been tasked to make a presentation on the issue in Washington, where he would press for more and better trained infantrymen. Bradley was accompanying him to Versailles, the first stop on O'Hare's itinerary.

They drove through Verdun, past the cemeteries and monuments of the last war. The morning was cold and the road covered with ice; the car nearly skidded into an oncoming vehicle at one point.

Paris, warmer but drenched in rain, seemed deserted when they arrived around lunchtime. They stopped at the Ritz, where the elegant dining room had been turned into an officer's mess. Eisenhower greeted Bradley at Versailles in a good mood. The day before, he had been promoted to five-star general, the country's highest rank.

Not needed, Hansen went off with some other aides. They would spend the afternoon and evening relaxing and drinking. Novelist and temporary war correspondent Ernest Hemingway was among those he partied with.

Soon after the conference started, a member of the SHAEF intelligence staff slipped into the room and put a piece of paper down in front of Major General Kenneth Strong, the G-2.

Bradley knew from Strong's expression there was trouble, but he couldn't have guessed what it was until Strong looked up.

The enemy, said Strong, had stormed into the area occupied by Middleton's VIII Corps in the Ardennes. Heavy fighting was reported, and communication with many forward units had been lost. The Battle of the Ardennes had begun.

★ ★ ★ ★

Bradley's first impression was that the attacks were spoiling attacks—strokes intended to trick the Americans into calling off their offensives. This was a familiar German strategy. It was not a reason to panic, or even to switch over to the defensive.

Bradley's interpretation was largely due to his belief that the Germans had a limited offensive capability. They were short of fuel, for one thing, and their dwindling manpower argued against taking risks. He also believed that the Ardennes would be the worst possible place for the Germans to strike. The road network was a twisted collection of scenic paths laid out among small towns. The roads were often constrained by bridges and hamlets where the central thoroughfare tightened to one lane. No highway went directly from east to west. Hills and ridges dominated most of the landscape. Thick forest alternated with cleared fields. At the western end, the Meuse River provided a natural barrier to recently liberated France.

True, the German Army had attacked through the Ardennes during the 1940 blitzkrieg. But the Americans were not the French. They controlled the air and had a modern, mobile army. More importantly, the Germans no longer possessed the army or the supplies they had in 1940.

There are only two goals for an offensive, Bradley wrote later: destroy hostile forces or take a terrain objective.[43] Neither could be achieved by attacking the Ardennes.

As the afternoon gave way to night, the reports showed the attacks were anything but a diversion. Eight German divisions that had not been identified before the battle were reported in the area, and the attacks were being made in several spots. Bradley, though still believing the assault was meant to bring Patton's southern offensive to a halt, reluctantly decided to shift the 7th Armored Division from the Ninth Army and the 10th Division from Patton's Third to help defend the area.

Knowing he would get an argument, Bradley called Patton himself to explain what was going on.

"That's no major threat up there," answered Patton. "Hell, it's probably nothing more than a spoiling attack to throw us off balance down here and make us stop this offensive."[44]

Bradley insisted. Elements of the division were soon en route to Bastogne.

Bradley spent the night getting information from his headquarters and the units involved, with timeouts for a toast to Eisenhower's five stars and five rubbers of bridge with Ike.[45] He also made a brief appearance at the wedding of Eisenhower's orderly and a WAC driver. When Hansen reported the next morning, he found the general haggard though apparently not deeply worried about the attack.

Bradley confessed he had lain awake in bed, considering the enemy's plans. At that point, he believed Liege, Belgium, was the Germans' most logical target. The offensive would aim to cut off a main supply line. Everything else, including the stiff attacks in Luxembourg, was aimed at either protecting that drive or taking attention away from it. Bradley estimated that fourteen German divisions were involved—far more than he would have considered possible just a few days before.

In actual fact, Bradley underestimated both the aim of the attack and its strength. Generalfildmarschall Gerd von Rundstedt had twenty-eight German divisions grouped in four armies poised for his drive. And the goal was much grander than Liege—Hitler had ordered von Rundstedt to take Antwerp.[46]

Bad weather protected the Germans from American aircraft attacks and hampered reconnaissance. It also made it impossible for Bradley to fly, so he took a car back to Luxembourg. A security detail met him in Verdun and told him there were rumors that German paratroopers had dropped behind the lines. Meanwhile, enemy divisions were pushing toward Luxembourg city itself.

Hansen asked Bradley if they should evacuate their headquarters.

"I will never move backwards with a headquarters," Bradley told him firmly. "There's too much prestige at stake."[47]

More importantly, Bradley saw no reason to be pessimistic. The attack was an opportunity.

"We may be able to stop it shortly and slam right back," he told Hansen.[48]

Still, Bradley was surprised when he reached his command post and saw the situation map.

"Pardon my French, but I think the situation justifies it," he told his staff. "But where in hell has this son of a bitch gotten all his strength?"[49]

Exacerbating the situation was the fact that Twelfth Army had no designated strategic reserves; having thrown everything into the attack on both sides of the Ardennes, Bradley had to reinforce the sector by taking units from the assault. Even SHAEF was low on forces—the sole reserves available to the Americans were the 82nd and 101st Airborne Divisions. Both had just returned from Montgomery's campaign in Holland and were due for a rest and refitting. Eisenhower committed both. The 82nd would end up on the northern end of the Bulge, while the 101st went to Bastogne and enduring fame.

A confused jumble of reports confronted Bradley. The German advance had pushed the Americans back in chaos. Many small units and individual soldiers were caught behind the lines. Some surrendered; others slipped through in small groups or fought their way to friendly lines. Bradley's intelligence officers had a hell of a time piecing information together.

Bradley worked until about ten that night. He got up early the next morning and, reassessing the German drive in light of the fresh reports, concluded, correctly, that the ultimate aim was possibly Antwerp. The ferocity and size of the assault were now obvious; reluctantly, he called off the First Army's offensive so its forces could reshuffle and hold the northern end of the bulge.

At Eisenhower's headquarters, the mood was grim. While Kay Summersby never claimed to be an expert on military matters, even she remarked later that "the more pessimistic staff members predicted a drive on Paris itself, plus a blitz through to the huge supply center at Liege [sic] and the key port of Antwerp."[50]

★ ★ ★ ★

The size and ferocity of the attack didn't just catch Bradley and the rest of the Allied command off guard; it caught the American public off guard. Not only had it appeared that the end of the war was in sight, but the recent news reports had given many the impression that American forces were invincible.

This was not just the result of propaganda or carefully managed reporting, though obviously both were at work. American forces had won incredible victories from Africa onward. Meanwhile, Soviet forces were making steady progress in the East.

The momentum seemed overwhelming. The Germans looked all but beaten, so when reports came of a massive German counterattack rolling up American forces, it was a shock to the American public.

Something similar happened to Allied intelligence officers. Having failed to realize that an attack was imminent, they panicked and saw things as being worse than they really were. Keeping a balanced perspective was the most difficult thing to do during the battle—aside from actually fighting.

By the time Bradley and the rest of his staff crowded into his war room at the railway building for the 0915 briefing on the third day of the German offensive, the map was covered with red markers. The Germans were moving through the center of the Ardennes with First Army holding either side of the Bulge—but there was no telling how long that would last.

First Army headquarters at Spa, Belgium, was threatened; the enemy was reported only a few miles away. Thirty tanks from the 1st and 12th SS Panzer Divisions had made it to a town nearby. General Edwin Sibert, chief of intelligence for 12th Army Group, who had been confident and even dismissive of German capabilities only a few days before, was now visibly shaken.

A soft hum rose in the room as the G-2 staff officers continued the report. Then one of Sibert's men told the story of American prisoners taken by the 12th Panzer Division. According to a witness who had managed to escape, some two hundred GIs had been lined up and machine-gunned. There were photos of the atrocity.

The room remained silent for a moment, the air knocked from each man's lungs.

Patton arrived in Luxembourg City later that afternoon. He immediately went into a conference with Bradley.

"I feel you won't like what we are going to do," Bradley told him. "But I fear it is necessary."[51]

Bradley showed him the positions on the map. Patton admitted that the situation looked worse than he had thought. He could halt the 4th Armored near Longwy, keeping it ready if needed. In the morning, he would get the 80th Infantry Division started for Luxembourg. Both units had been involved in his drive east. The 26th Infantry could be ready to move in another twenty-four hours.

Bradley emerged from the meeting confident. Patton's three divisions would be a powerful force to use against the German drive. But he was still thinking that the German assault proved they were close to a breakthrough in the south. If they could hold the attack—and presumably, if they didn't need to move more of Patton's divisions north into the Ardennes—the road would be clear to Frankfurt.[52]

Their meeting concluded around 2:30 p.m. Bradley traveled to Liege by air and then down to Spa to meet Hodges at the First Army headquarters. He had planned to drive directly to Spa, but the roads through the sector above Bastogne could no longer be trusted. The earlier rumors had proven true: German infiltrators in American uniforms had gone behind the lines and were raising havoc, though more so by rumor than effective action as it would turn out.

During the course of the battle, Bradley was stopped by GIs on nervous alert three times. He was asked to prove that he was an American with questions supposedly only an American would know—the capital of Illinois (which the MP got wrong), where the guard played on a football line, and who Betty Grable's latest husband was.[53]

He missed the Grable question, but managed to convince the soldier of his identity anyway.

Bradley wanted Hodges and First Army to mount a counterattack from the area of Malmedy toward St. Vith, which was still in American hands. Such an attack would have threatened the German forces on the northern side of the bulge, relieving the pressure on Spa. Taken with Patton's action, the drives from the south and north would threaten to pinch off the head of the German advance, capturing them in a noose. Reinforcements in Germany would have to be concentrated on the shoulders of this threat, rather than being used to push deeper into Allied territory.

But when he arrived at First Army, Bradley found the situation was worse than he'd thought. Hodges' forces were in no position to launch a counterattack. VII Corps, reinforced by the 82nd Airborne, was fighting desperately against advances south of Spa. V Corps had its hands full in the Stavelot and Malmedy sectors, where the German 6th SS Panzer Army was directing its blow.

Hodges kept shifting units piecemeal to stem the developing leaks in his front. While he agreed with Bradley's aim of meeting the attack with his own counterstroke, at the moment there was no way he could gather his units to mount it.

By the time he arrived back in Luxembourg city, Bradley realized there was no way he could let Third Army push farther into the Saar; the developing bulge in his lines had to be dealt with first. When Patton called to check in later that night, Bradley reluctantly told him he would have to get the divisions moving northwards as quickly as possible. He also told him to meet him the next day in Verdun for a meeting with Ike, Hodges, and Devers, who headed the 6th Army Group to the south. Still, this was a change in plans, not a disaster.

"I don't take too serious a view of it," Bradley insisted to Hansen, talking of the situation late in the day. "Although the others will not agree with me."[54]

★ ★ ★ ★

Bradley spent a few hours that evening working out plans and checking on developments. At some point either that night or early the next morning, he had the 4th Armored Combat Command B move north to reinforce General Middleton's VIII Corps on the southern side of the Bulge—a move that technically should have come from Patton, though perhaps surprisingly, Patton did not complain about his authority being usurped.[55]

The main phone connection to First Army had been cut, but they still had an auxiliary line open. In between monitoring the battle, Bradley found time to work on his Christmas message to the troops.

The news remained bad in the morning, with reports that the enemy had taken Houfalaize in the north and was still moving on Spa. It was difficult to get reliable information from the center of the bulge. At one point, there were reports that Bastogne had been taken, but news that the 101st was engaging enemy units there contradicted that.

Bradley told Middleton that Bastogne had to be held at all costs. Middleton had already come to that conclusion, and Bradley concurred with arrangements for the 101st Airborne and Combat Command B of the 10th Armored to defend the crossroads town, along with elements (and remnants) of the 9th and 28th Infantry Divisions.

While neither Middleton nor Bradley could have fully envisioned how the battle would develop there, both must have realized that the fight would be costly. Though an elite and experienced unit, the paratroopers were being asked to defend unfamiliar territory against armored divisions, not exactly a mission they had been trained for—but there were no other reserves available. It would prove a crucial move of the battle. The 82nd Airborne received a similar mission on the northern shoulder of the bulge, where it would fight just as valiantly, if not with as much fanfare.

To his staff, Bradley remained calm, confident that the enemy's drive could be stopped. But there were signs of stress—when their lead escort lagged on the way to Verdun, he curtly told his driver to pass them. The car raced ahead to France.

★ ★ ★ ★

In his memoirs, Eisenhower claimed that he began the Verdun meeting on a positive note:

"The present situation is to be regarded as one of opportunity for us and not of disaster," said Ike, in a statement that Bradley surely agreed with. "There will be only cheerful faces at this conference table."[56]

Patton, irrepressible as ever, cut in.

"Hell let's have the guts to let the [sons of bitches] go all the way to Paris."[57]

Given that Bradley and Patton were fairly optimistic and Devers was not directly involved in the Bulge, it's hard to know exactly who Eisenhower was bucking up with his comments, except for himself and his staff. They all had a much more pessimistic view of the situation than Bradley, let alone Patton. To SHAEF, the Meuse River was seriously threatened, and with it, Antwerp and the supply line for the entire Allied forces.

Bradley never saw the situation as that dire. If anything, he was overly optimistic, continuing to insist this was an opportunity, not a disaster. Even if the Germans reached the Meuse, breaching it required forces and supplies they simply did not have.

And Patton's joking exaggeration contained more than a nugget of truth. The farther the Germans advanced, the weaker they would become. They had neither the material nor the supplies to sustain a drive long-term. The thinner their line became, the easier it would be to cut them off.

Neither Bradley nor Patton said much during the early stages of the meeting, standard for Bradley, somewhat atypical for Patton. After Eisenhower's G-2 finished laying out the situation, Eisenhower said he wanted Patton to launch a counterattack with six divisions (counting those that were already involved under Middleton).[58] This was what Bradley and Patton had already worked out before the meeting.

The discussion turned to rearrangements of the front along the bulge and to the south, shifting sectors to free more divisions for the battle. Eisenhower then asked Patton when he could start the offensive.

"On December 22 with three divisions; the 4th Armored, the 26th, and the 80th."59

That was just forty-eight hours away—a hell of a trick under the best circumstances, let alone in an area with a limited road network and during poor weather. But Patton, who had lit a fresh cigar and was pointing at the map, was confident he could do it.

"This time the Kraut's stuck his head in a meat grinder," said Patton, turning his fist for emphasis. "And I've got hold of the handle."60

Back in Luxembourg, Bradley worked late into the night. First Army had abandoned Spa, but not before removing its forward fuel supply, which would have been a major catch for the Germans. On the southern shoulder, Middleton was more optimistic than he'd been to this point in the battle, telling Bradley he'd "shout for help" if he needed it.61

Bradley and his staff were annoyed when a telex from Eisenhower's headquarters told them to make sure no bridge over the Meuse was taken. It was an incredible directive, given the circumstances, an indication that Eisenhower and Bradley saw the situation from radically different perspectives.

As Bradley's chief of staff Lev Allen put it, "What the devil do they think we're doing? Starting back for the beaches?"62

But even that didn't prepare Bradley for what happened next. At some point that evening, Bedell Smith called and told Bradley that it had been suggested that the First and Ninth Armies be turned over to Montgomery.

Bradley, dumbfounded, began answering questions about how much he and his army commanders were in communication. A glance at the map showed that forty miles worth of Germans sat between him and Hodges; Bradley couldn't feel comfortable about that. Nonetheless, he still had intact communications—in fact, two telephone lines connected them. And the other headquarters could be reached by roads, albeit over a circuitous route.

Smith began arguing for the change.

"I'd question whether such a change-over is necessary," said Bradley finally. "When we go to drive him out of the bulge, it'd be easier to coordinate the attack from here."[63]

Finally Bradley admitted that there was some logic in a temporary arrangement.

A *temporary* arrangement.

He was in shock. Two of his armies were being taken from him—a stunning sign of a lack of confidence in his abilities, no matter what Smith or Eisenhower would say then or claim later. And it came just as his forces were turning the tide in the battle.

CHAPTER 8

Revival

Eisenhower decided to place the First and Ninth Armies under Montgomery for two reasons: arguments by the British that 12th Army Group was not in contact with First and Ninth Armies, and his belief that the situation was far worse than Bradley perceived.

Montgomery had called Eisenhower's staff earlier that day to suggest that all troops north of the salient be placed under his command. He convinced Jock Whitely, the deputy chief of operations at SHAEF, that this would be a good idea; Whitely in turn convinced General Strong, his boss. Both, not coincidentally, were British.

Given that Montgomery had been campaigning to have the entire American Army placed under his command over the past several months, it's not surprising that he would have seized this opportunity to make the argument again. What is surprising is that Smith and Eisenhower agreed. The only possible explanation is that Eisenhower thought the situation was far worse than it actually was.

There is more than ample evidence. His telegram to Bradley's headquarters regarding the bridges on the Meuse clearly indicates that he had an extreme view, regardless of what he might or might not have said at the morning meeting. Smith, when speaking to Bradley, apparently interpreted the downing of the main phone line between the commands as calamitous. Travel time to the northern army headquarters had been greatly increased by the German salient, but in truth Bradley knew First Army so well and vice versa there was little need for him to go there in person. Indeed, the army and corps commanders could—and would—function well on their own. Even if the staff was regarded as weak, as some have contended, it surely was not so weak that Bradley had to be in its command post every minute of every day; he hadn't been during the preceding battles.

Smith told Bradley another reason for the changeover was to make it easier to move bring up British reinforcements from 21st Army Group. The argument implied that Smith believed the situation was much more drastic than Bradley did. Of course, Bradley could have asked if those soldiers might not have performed just as well, or moved just as fast, under an American commander, or if the reinforcement could have been more easily accommodated under a sector shift. If he did make those arguments, it's not recorded. (The British corps Smith referred to ended up not being needed.)

There was more logic in attaching the Ninth Army to Montgomery. It was already operating adjacent to the British line and farthest from Bradley's command. But even there, the shift in command was necessary only if the Germans completely snapped the American communication lines, or if it was assumed that Bradley could not adequately supervise his forces. If communications were the problem, Eisenhower could have ordered Bradley to move his headquarters to a point behind the salient. That doesn't seem to have been discussed, and it's clear that Bradley had adequate contact with his armies.[1]

As jumbled as the intelligence reports may have been, Bradley had a reasonably accurate assessment of the forces he faced, their dispositions, the routes they were taking, and their objectives. He knew where his forces were. In short, he had a more cogent view and handle on the situation than Eisenhower or Montgomery did. More importantly, he already had a plan to deal with it—something neither Eisenhower nor Montgomery possessed.

Both Eisenhower and Bradley saw parallels between the Battle at Kasserine and the Battle of the Bulge. Bradley realized the differences and felt confident the German advance could be dealt with; Eisenhower saw disaster on an even grander scale.

Since moving his headquarters to the continent, Eisenhower had only known victories. His intelligence staff had been predicting Germany's imminent collapse for weeks. The Ardennes attack was a serious reversal in any event, but the disparity between the euphoria of late summer and the utter chaos as the battle began would have been enough to shake anyone's confidence. It didn't help that SHAEF security personnel practically screamed that enemy infiltrators were everywhere, seeming to believe every possible rumor.

Eisenhower called Bradley the next morning to confirm the changeover to Montgomery. Bradley argued against it vociferously, but Eisenhower's decision had been made. The best Bradley could do was get him to agree that it would be *temporary*.

"Temporary" was never defined.

From Bradley's point of view, this might have meant only until Patton's counter-offensive began—some forty-eight hours. It was to last far longer, much to his chagrin.

Patton, who moved his headquarters to Luxembourg City, was with Bradley when Eisenhower called. According to Patton, Eisenhower gave the lack of telephone communications as the main reason for the changeover; if that excuse was given, it was clearly incorrect, as Patton pointed out in his diary.

"It is either a case of having lost confidence in Bradley or having been forced to put Montgomery in through the machinations of the [British] Prime Minster," wrote Patton, who then added, "or with the hope that if he gives Monty operational control, he will get some of the British divisions in. Eisenhower is unwilling or unable to command Montgomery."[2]

★ ★ ★ ★

Eisenhower's decision *was* a direct slap at Bradley. Clearly Eisenhower realized this, since he tried the same day to soften the blow by writing Marshall and asking that he immediately get approval for Bradley's promotion to four-star general, which would put him officially on the same rank as Montgomery.

It was also a slap at generals Courtney Hodges (First Army), William Simpson (Ninth Army), and Joe Collins (VII Corps), and all of the Americans under them. By and large, they had done a reasonable job dealing with the situation.

Eisenhower had to make some judgment about how things would proceed, and it was his prerogative as overall commander both to plan for the worst and arrange his command as he saw fit. Very possibly he was trying to protect Bradley's feelings—and his own reputation later—by saying he still had the highest faith in him. It does seem remarkable, however, that he decided to entrust the two armies to the care of a general whose record in France was hardly a model of aggressive achievement.

Montgomery's failure to take Caen and then the approaches to Antwerp had put the Allies in this position to begin with. Market Garden had proven a dismal failure. There was no reason to believe that American troops would respond better to his command than to an American's. And Montgomery had been campaigning to usurp Eisenhower's authority for months.

In *A Soldier's Story*, Bradley claims that the change in commands would have made sense "if Monty's were an American command."[3] But the issue was not one of nationality or even personality; the question was, or should have been, whether Bradley could effectively control his troops. He was in touch with them, had laid additional lines to continue being in touch with them, and had a robust plan for dealing with the situation. This was not the first crisis Bradley had faced, though it was his first real reversal. As always, he reacted calmly and logically.

It was, however, the first real crisis Eisenhower had faced since Kasserine.

In *Crusade in Europe*, Eisenhower insisted the reason he gave the First and Ninth Armies to Montgomery was that Bradley needed "to give to the attack on the southern shoulder the attention that I desired."[4]

The statement is utter nonsense. Taken with his claim to have started the conference with an optimistic statement, it seems part of an effort to make himself seem much more the confident leader than he actually was at that moment. The reality is that Eisenhower panicked and made one of his worst decisions of the war.

Soon after assuming command, Montgomery sent a message to British Army commander Sir Alan Brooke filled with outrageous exaggerations if not outright lies. He had just visited Hodges's headquarters. "Morale was very low," he told Brooke. "They seemed delighted to have someone give them firm orders." As Bradley and his co-author put it with some understatement in *A General's Life*, it was "arrogantly self-serving."[5]

Montgomery's first action was to pull back the American forces on the north. This had been authorized by Eisenhower, one more indication that Ike and Bradley saw the battle in radically different terms. But when Montgomery recommended that Hodges be replaced—the Army commander, Montgomery said, looked as if he was in danger of having a heart attack—Eisenhower drew the line.

"I know you realize that Hodges is the quiet reticent type and does not appear as aggressive as he really is," Eisenhower wrote in his usual tactful way. "Unless he becomes exhausted he will always wage a good fight. However, you will of course keep in touch with your important subordinates and inform me instantly if any change needs to be made on [the] United States side."[6]

The withdrawals that Montgomery ordered were not popular among the American commanders. Members of the 82nd Airborne complained bitterly after the Bulge that they had withdrawn under protest.[7] Besides differences regarding strategy and tactics, the American commanders under Montgomery must also have chafed at his habit of issuing orders and *then* explaining them. Bradley worked in exactly the opposite manner, asking his commanders for their ideas first and then proceeding.[8]

The American forces took a tremendous beating in the four days of the German offensive. But by the morning of December 20 they had started to solidify their front. The struggle now centered around battles in three areas.

Bastogne is the most famous; it was located at a crossroads in the southern sector of the bulge. Just as critical was the battle on the northern shoulder near St. Vith, just over the German border in Belgium. The 2nd Panzer Regiment sprang north of the town, and by December 19 had threatened to cut if off from the rest of the American line. To the northeast, a German column had forged into the Ambleve River valley beyond Stavelot. This incursion threatened Spa, where the First Army had its forward headquarters.

In the center of the salient, the Germans were threatening Marche, but they failed to reach it, due largely to fuel shortages. (By the time their resupplies arrived on December 22, the Americans had reinforced the town. This forced the Germans to detour south, though they were still able to head towards the Meuse.)

Though it might not have been evident at the time, the German offensive had already failed in its primary goal. Antwerp was simply too far from the German lines, and the American forces were too strong to be simply brushed away. When they had the time and space to reorganize, the Germans were doomed—and would have been, even if they had had ample fuel supplies.

Hitler made a habit of comparing the Americans to the Italian Army; it was a severe miscalculation. Despite overwhelming odds and for the most part without elaborately prepared defensive positions, the Americans fought well. The ability of small groups and individuals to improvise and act on their own played an important role as small groups of soldiers coalesced and reformed after being initially overrun.

Under other circumstances—more weapons, more tanks, more men, more aircraft, more gasoline—the Germans might have reached the

Meuse and threatened the Allied supply line to Antwerp. This would have presented serious problems. But the Germans had never had the resources to do that. The offensive was a bold but ultimately doomed attempt at an impossible goal. All it did was hasten the Allied victory.

Even though he was no longer in command, Bradley kept in constant touch with both Hodges and Simpson, offering advice and keeping tabs on the situation. The heaviest fighting centered on Bastogne in the south, where Patton was rushing to the rescue, and Monschau in the north, where Hodges was shifting Collins' VII Corps to counterattack. Bradley realized that his bid to pinch off the Germans from north and south was still a possibility, and even though he wasn't in a position to order it, did everything he could to encourage it.

He was even optimistic about it until he received a call on December 21 from 21st Army Group telling him that the VII Corps' counterattack from the north had been called off. Instead, Montgomery was going to use the forces to "tidy up" his lines—a phrase and maneuver Bradley hated with all his soul. Rather than attacking, the Americans were to sit on the line.

Bradley seemed more frustrated than apprehensive as he waited for Patton's three-division offensive to get underway on December 22 in a mixture of fog and snow. The 4th Armored Division, moving from Arlon toward Bastogne, was on the western side of the advance. The 26th Infantry was at the center; the 80th was on the eastern flank, moving from Mersch toward Ettelbruck. (These divisions constituted III Corps. To the east, XII Corps was to move to the Sure River at the same time.)

Bradley was in no mood for paperwork, apologizing to his aides as it piled up on his desk. He thought about the battle almost exclusively. He talked to Hodges continually, chain of command be damned. He continued to emphasize that the German offensive must be contained with as few forces as possible. The rest would be saved and used for the counter-strike.

Patton had moved his command post to Luxembourg city, and he and Bradley were together so often that Bradley's staff began referring to them as "The George and Brad Show." They got along well, joking and even having their hair cut together. Between planning and checking on their troops, they'd watch movies and chat with VIPs. On December 22, the two generals spent time talking to visiting baseball players including New York Giants outfielder and future Hall of Famer Mel Ott. Patton felt left out of the conversation, and was uncharacteristically shy when it came time to pose for a picture.

On December 23 the weather cleared, and American aircraft were able to pound positions in and behind the Bulge. The Germans did not give ground easily. Near Merche, the repeater station used to boost radio signals between First Army and Bradley's headquarters came under attack by three tank columns which overwhelmed the eighteen men defending it. But land lines had already been laid, and Bradley remained in touch with his units—or Montgomery's, as they now technically were.

Bradley took time in the afternoon for a party for the children of the city, deciding it was important for morale. GIs had donated their candy rations for the children; Bradley had some fun passing them out. Later that night, Hansen went to his room to deliver a Christmas message from General Marshall. He found Bradley in his bathrobe, writing a note to his wife and daughter, wishing them a merry Christmas.

Christmas Eve was difficult. The stand at Bastogne by the 101st and attached armored units was being watched by everyone with a mixture of admiration and horror at the cost. Patton's forces were hit by strong resistance and remained a good distance away. The two generals spent much of the morning conferring. At one point, Bradley got down on his hands and knees to study the theater map and pick out road spots to be hit by artillery to disrupt the enemy's supply lines.

Bradley was frustrated by Montgomery's reluctance to launch a counterattack from the north. The British were rushing units to the Meuse and squirreling tanks there when the battle was miles to the east. The forces could either have been used for a counterattack, or at least as a relief for American units so they could go on the offensive.

There was no forgetting the danger of the situation, or the incongruities. German fighters buzzed the city that day, dropping down to spray the nearby street with machine-gun fire as the flak guns tried to ward them off. American tanks and trucks zipped past the building, headed toward the fighting arrayed with soldiers and odd improvisations—a mattress on a rooftop to protect against shrapnel, a trailer made from a captured German chassis. Meanwhile, Christmas carols filtered from the nearby cathedral.

Through it all, Bradley remained convinced the Allies were on the verge of a major victory—if he could just get the First Army to move.

The C-47, its wings heavy with snow, grumbled and groaned as it trundled down the short runway. The pilot jammed the throttles, urging the aircraft upwards, barely clearing the end of the runway.

Bradley, sitting in his heavy winter coat, looked impatiently out the window as the plane steadied itself just above the trees. The sky at least was clear; it would be a good day for bombing Germans.

And maybe a good day to attack them. Bradley, at Montgomery's invitation, was on his way to Eighth Army headquarters to discuss the situation.

Below, the roads were choked with vehicles rushing to the front. Bradley could see tanks, scout cars, and half-tracks. Near Brussels, a foggy haze reached up and folded itself around the fuselage, clouding the view. As they approached St. Trond, the clouds were so thick the pilot had to fly around twice before finding the runway.

When Bradley and Hansen—who'd been pressed into service as navigator on the flight—got out of the plane, they found no car waiting to pick them up.

A snafu? An oversight? Or a deliberate snub?

Bradley stewed silently.

"If there's no transportation," he told Hansen. "We'll climb in the plane and go back."[9]

Hansen found an officer from First Army headquarters on the other side of the field and asked if he would to take them to Montgomery.[10] On the way, Bradley chewed an apple, a belated lunch.

Bradley looked out the window as they drove through town, then turned back to Hansen. "Why is everyone dressed up?" he asked.

"It's Christmas," Hansen reminded him.

Bradley urged Montgomery to go on the offensive with First Army. Montgomery told him not only that he would not attack, but that he was preparing to order a further retreat. The field marshal claimed that the Germans had additional divisions and were saving them for a fresh blow.

The Germans have given us a real bloody nose, Montgomery told Bradley. *We can't turn this into a great victory. It's a proper defeat and we had better admit it*. Montgomery pinned the blame on Eisenhower, because he had refused to let Montgomery lead the Allied offensive east.[11]

Frustrated and undoubtedly angry, Bradley said little. He rushed back to the airport so they could return to his headquarters before it was too dark to land. They got lost on the way, but managed to take off by 4:15 p.m., the pilot ignoring a warning from the control tower that it was too late.

After they landed, Bradley's driver lost his way back to Luxembourg City. The general leapt out of the car impatiently, trying to figure out for himself where they'd missed their turn. It took quite a bit of sorting out before they found their way.

The next day, Bradley wrote an extraordinary letter to Hodges, emphasizing what he thought of Montgomery's order to retreat: Don't.

He strongly recommended that at least a corps be kept ready to attack. These were clearly things Hodges already agreed with—he still had Collins ready to attack. While Bradley was careful to say at the beginning of the letter that his advice did not have the force of an order, the letter itself was extreme and by some lights an insubordinate move.

Bradley called Eisenhower that evening, but with Ike out, spoke with Bedell Smith instead. Again, he urged a counterattack from the north.

It was a particularly good moment to do so—Patton's vanguard had finally hooked up with Bastogne. By Bradley's interpretation, the German advance had reached its high-water mark. Bradley told Smith that if Montgomery would allow the First Army to attack, they could catch the Germans in the pocket.

Smith's response summed up SHAEF's appraisal of the situation—the Germans were within forty-eight hours of establishing a bridgehead over the Meuse River.

This was pure Montgomery, or pure panic, or both. Bradley reacted angrily.

"Nuts," he told Smith, consciously appropriating General McAuliffe's already famous reply to the Germans earlier in the battle.[12]

Collins, whose VII Corps had played a critical role in breaking out of Normandy, had been urging a counterattack for days. Montgomery's plan, once the line was tidied up to his satisfaction, called for what Bradley termed derisively as "denting the nose" of the German advance—striking the Germans at their strength on the Marche Plain.[13] Collins argued vociferously that the attack should come further east, as Bradley had argued.

Indeed, at the very moment Bradley had been listening to Montgomery's lecture about how dire the situation was, the 2nd Armored Division had been attacking and trapping part of the 2nd Panzer Division in what would be known as the Celles Pocket. Though delayed by a succession of misunderstandings as well as by Montgomery's orders, the attack from the north side of the Bulge would eventually be as successful as the assault from the south, critical to turning the tide against the Germans.

★ ★ ★ ★

Bradley flew to Paris December 27 to meet with Eisenhower and discuss his latest plans to push the Germans back—roughly the same ones he'd been suggesting all along, an attack around the waist of the Bulge from north and south. When he arrived, Eisenhower was so excited over a surprise lunch of oyster stew that Bradley didn't bother to mention he was allergic to oysters.

On the way back east, Bradley played with an algebra problem in a magazine.

"I like to sit down and work out algebraic problems," he confessed to Hansen. "Or better yet, those in integral calculus. They help you to think. Keep you mentally alert."

Then he added, "But now I seldom find the time."[14]

Eisenhower met with Montgomery the next day. Montgomery was still expecting an all-out attack from the Germans. Eisenhower, not as pessimistic as Montgomery though still not converted to Bradley's view, believed that the Germans were going to bring in additional infantry to attempt to hold their gains. Montgomery said he would be ready to launch a counterstrike by January 1, assuming the Germans did not attack first. Eisenhower agreed. In a letter the next day, though, he emphasized that there must be an attack. He was finally coming around to Bradley's view.

"We must break [the German Army] up while he is out in the open,"[15] Eisenhower said, adding that the British 30th Corps be included in the attack.

In response, Eisenhower received a letter from Montgomery telling him that "coordination" between the two army groups was insufficient. What was needed was one commander—Montgomery—who would have control of the offensive going forward.

At the same time, Eisenhower and everyone else in the theater were reading accounts in the British press claiming that a supreme ground commander under Eisenhower had to be named—and suggesting, of course, that Montgomery should be that commander. British newspapers implied Montgomery had saved the Americans in the Battle of the Bulge, a gross misstatement of fact.

The reports caused considerable consternation in Bradley's headquarters—Hansen devoted nearly a page of his diary entry on December 26 refuting it—but the reaction was even more severe in Washington, where General Marshall read the reports and sent Eisenhower a cable on December 30 directing that under no circumstance should the bulk of American forces be placed under British command.

Finally, Eisenhower decided he had had enough. He finished formulating plans for the offensive—essentially the plan that Bradley had outlined a few days before—and wrote a letter December 31 informing Montgomery that the American divisions under Montgomery were to attack. When the northern and southern forks were joined, Eisenhower directed, Bradley would regain command of the First Army.

At that point, First and Third Army would move northeast to the Rhine. The American Ninth Army would remain attached to 21st Army Group, which would prepare for its own postponed attack at the north. The plan also gave 12th Army Group priority for U.S. replacements, and left Devers' 6th Army Group on the defensive in the south, basically holding the line there.

Eisenhower allowed Montgomery to coordinate the lines along the army group boundaries, both in detail and in emergencies, giving him the ultimate right of decision, an important concession. But at the same time, Eisenhower emphasized that all of the Allies must go on the attack and regain the initiative.

"The immediate thing is to give the enemy in the salient a good beating," wrote Eisenhower in a personal cover letter. Then he got to the heart of his letter.

"You know how greatly I've appreciated and depended upon your frank and friendly counsel," Eisenhower wrote, "but in your latest letter you disturb me by predictions of 'failure' unless your exact opinions in the matter of giving you command over Bradley are met in detail. I assure you that in this matter I can go no further."[16]

If Montgomery did not back down, Eisenhower added, he would refer the matter to the Combined Chiefs of Staff—and presumably ask for them to make a choice, Montgomery or Eisenhower.

The letter was a clear rebuke, even if the British commander was still being shown considerable deference. Montgomery finally backed down, convinced by his chief of staff Freddie de Guingand he would be cashiered if Eisenhower went to the Combined Chiefs.[17]

This was not quite the end of the matter—the field marshal gave a press conference January 7 awarding himself quite a bit more credit than he actually deserved for the battle, leaving any ordinary listener to believe that he and the British Army had bucked up those sorry lads in the American forces and gotten them through a tough row. The Germans, by now reeling under the weight of the Allied counterattacks, recognized the propaganda value of Montgomery's statements carried over BBC and issued an edited version highlighting his most egotistical remarks.

Bradley was given the report by his staff (which included Ralph Ingersoll, who back home was a well-known newspaperman). They demanded that he counter Montgomery's false impressions. With some reluctance (Bradley wrote in his memoirs that he didn't want his personal feelings toward Montgomery to color his decision, though one can only wonder why), he issued a statement explaining how the American Army had met the initial challenge in the bulge.

The statement emphasized that the shift had always been seen as a "temporary" arrangement, reciting Smith's original arguments in favor of it.[18] Bradley neglected to mention his opposition.

Montgomery's press conference had one positive effect on Bradley— it helped his staff convince him that he should have a press "camp" attached to his own headquarters. Reporters would not only be accredited but accommodated, with facilities, dedicated liaisons, and most of all access to the commanding general. Bradley finally saw that the media was important to his conduct of the war.

He was not a willing or enthusiastic convert.

Bradley doesn't seem to have mistrusted newsmen on a personal level. He liked Ernie Pyle—he was emotional when he heard he died in the

Pacific, as much a genuine tribute as any words he might have said—and he often trusted correspondents with embargoed information. But he surely did not recognize the value of holding regular press conferences, or see news stories as potential assets. He tended to view publicity with great disdain. Going out of his way to court the press and generate publicity, in his mind, was bragging, and he didn't like to brag. It made him uncomfortable.

It's telling that the arguments his staff used to encourage him to use the media were focused primarily on his men. He should spend time with Pyle, said Hansen, so the parents of his boys would know who they'd entrusted him to. He should give regular press conferences, said Hansen and Ingersoll, so American soldiers got their fair share of credit.

In today's media saturated world, Bradley's attitude seems more than a little quaint. It was also unusual at the time, at least among commanding generals. (Marshall, not coincidentally, was a critical exception.) But it was genuine.

Bradley never accepted that effective public relations translated into power and leverage behind the scenes. Yet Patton's notoriety as well as his skill surely influenced Eisenhower at different points, and Montgomery's status among the British public made him untouchable.

On the other hand, if Bradley had been more calculating in using the media, he wouldn't have been Bradley.

He rarely, if ever, criticized other Americans to reporters, and naturally would not give critical details. But he prided himself on being direct, and he appears to have been so when dealing with reporters, just as with everyone else. One newspaper did irk him—*Stars & Stripes*.

The semi-official Army newspaper's irreverent tone bothered quite a number of generals, including Patton, who took a special dislike to its cartoonist Bill Mauldin, once even threatening to throw him in jail. Bradley's displeasure was somewhat milder, though there are several references to it in his aide's diary. Bradley—or at least his aides—found fault with a number of comments in the paper, including one during the Bulge that said "it is presumed that Bradley continues to command the Twelfth Army Group which now consists of only the Third Army."

Patton told Bradley the paper had lengthened the war by six months.

"I shall not go as far as to say that," answered Bradley. "But you can be sure that if I become the theater commander, *Stars & Stripes* will undergo a major readjustment in its policy."[19]

In the popular imagination, the Battle of the Bulge ended with the relief of Bastogne by Patton's forces on December 26, 1944. In actual fact, the battle raged for weeks afterwards.

Rather than ordering a careful retreat as the tide turned, Hitler had his armies in the salient descend on Bastogne in an all-out effort to take the crossroads town. Fighting was bitter, hampered by ice, snow, fog, and freezing rain.

The First and Third Armies moved slowly toward each other, meeting January 16. Bradley regained First Army the next day. Even then, fighting in the Bulge was fierce. Patton launched an assault at the base of the Bulge—something he had long desired—on January 18, moving across the Sure River and up Skyline Drive. First Army pushed in from the face of the salient. By January 28, the Bulge campaign was officially over, and Bradley's armies prepared to resume their attack into Germany.

If Cobra was Bradley's high point, the Battle of Bulge is usually viewed as his low. In actual fact, his performance during the Bulge deserves to be reassessed more positively.

The fact that the German attack came as a surprise must be counted against him. While it's true that the rest of the Allied command was just as surprised, that doesn't exonerate Bradley.

Admittedly, the intelligence reports available to him were far from clear. The Germans took unusual steps to protect the secret of their buildup. But Bradley contributed to his own ignorance by believing, as the rest of the Allied command did, that the Germans were incapable of launching a strong offensive.

The greatest argument that Bradley could make in his defense was the fact that the attack was illogical. Given the resources available to Germany, it could not possibly succeed in changing the war. On the contrary, in Bradley's view (and in reality) it would weaken the defense of their homeland. While Bradley was correct, that cannot exonerate him, as no commander can ever expect an enemy to operate "logically."

While Bradley does point this out in *A Soldier's Story*, to his credit he does not attempt to take shelter behind the argument. He is relatively candid about what he expected—a counterattack beyond the Rur[20]—and thus admits his mistake. Grudgingly, perhaps, and certainly without dwelling on it, but he doesn't attempt to rewrite history in his favor.

Bradley told reporters and wrote later that his weakness in the Ardennes sector was a calculated risk, necessary in order to stay on the offensive north and south of the Ardennes. The alternative would have been either to keep Patton contained—the alternative generally mentioned—or to have left Hodges entirely on the defensive.

Framed in that context, the risk certainly seems justified.

Interestingly, Bradley has not come in for much criticism for taking a consistently optimistic view of the situation, one that was far at odds with Eisenhower's and Montgomery's. Perhaps this is due to the fact that his view was ultimately borne out by events.

On a personal level, Bradley remained calm and self-possessed throughout the battle. His most difficult achievement may have been presenting a calm front to his staff after the First and Ninth Armies were taken from him. Hansen never records Bradley saying a negative word about this in his diary. He took it, as the saying goes, like a soldier—though when it was over, he told Eisenhower that he would resign rather than serve under Montgomery in the future.

As always, Patton gets the lion's share of credit in many accounts of the battle. His remarkable achievement through his divisions and pushing them north should not be denigrated, but Bradley's role in this seems always to be forgotten. Also often glossed over is the fact that First Army did the bulk of the fighting. After the initial shock of the opening attacks, its leaders did a reasonable job under difficult circumstances, especially when one considers the numerical advantage the Germans had.[21]

Certainly the men on the ground deserve the lion's share of credit for what in the end was a critical victory. As historian Charles B. MacDonald put it in his in-depth study, *A Time for Trumpets:* "The victory in the Ardennes belonged to the American soldier, for he provided time to enable his commanders—for all their intelligence failure—to bring their mobility and their airpower to play. At that point the American soldier stopped everything the German Army threw at him."[22]

MacDonald, who served in the campaign, also wrote: "Did it really matter to the American soldier, fighting for his life in the harsh cold and snow of the Ardennes, who commanded him at the top? Who was this Montgomery? Who was Bradley? Who, even, was Hodges or Gerow, Collins, or Ridgway?"[23]

The historian implied that the answer was no—that when it came to the battlefield and the specific moment of decision, a soldier fought (or did not fight) for his friends and for himself. But while that is certainly true, in the larger sense it absolutely did matter who was in charge. Though the soldier might not exactly know who he was, the commander's decisions and conduct affected him directly. Montgomery's decisions in the north delaying the advance meant that the Americans near Bastogne felt the full force of the German attacks following Patton's linkup. The attacks certainly went on longer than they might have. And had Montgomery's instincts to retreat to the Meuse and dig in for the winter been followed, the American and British push the following spring would surely have been bloodier than it actually was. The Soviets could easily have met the Americans on the Rhine, rather than the Elbe.

The month-long battle in the Ardennes in the winter of 1944–45 is generally labeled as the most costly battle of the war for the Americans. As always, casualty figures vary, but the figures that Charles B. MacDonald gives in *A Time for Trumpets* are representative: 19,000 American soldiers killed, 15,000 captured, and another 47,000 wounded.[24] British casualties were about 200 killed, with another 1,400 wounded.

German casualty figures are even harder to pin down; these range from 60,000 to 100,000 total. MacDonald estimates that there were at least 100,000. The official German tally after the battle was 84,834.

As a point of reference, the North had 23,055 casualties at Gettysburg during the Civil War, with 3,155 known killed and 14,531 wounded. But this was out of a force just under 94,000. At the Bulge, MacDonald estimates that there were 600,000 Americans involved in the fighting.

A large portion of the casualties came after January 2, when the Americans were on the offensive. Over 6,000 of the American deaths occurred in this phase of the battle, with another 27,000 wounded and more than 6,000 missing or captured.[25] It should also be remembered that the assaults on the West Wall before and after the Bulge were bloody and difficult affairs. There would have been a substantial number of dead and wounded even without the Bulge, and while this does not justify the mistakes that were made, it does put them into a slightly different perspective.

"If our casualties were severe," Bradley said in *A Soldier's Story,* "the enemy's were even more critical. Moreover the proportion was better than we could have expected had he struck us on the plains of Cologne, better than if he had withheld his reserves until we reached the Rhine. In stalking us through the Ardennes, the enemy had been forced to expose himself to our fire."[26]

To sum up: Bradley *was* surprised by the offensive and its intensity. Once surprised, though, he dealt with the situation vigorously, attempting from the very beginning to turn it to his advantage. He had more faith in his soldiers and commanders than Eisenhower, let alone Montgomery. If he can be criticized for anything beyond the initial intelligence failure, it is that he was too optimistic too soon about its outcome.

With so many casualties during the winter of 1944–45, the replacement problems for the U.S. Army became even more acute. As part of the solution, Eisenhower increased his efforts to find combat troops among support units. One result was an order allowing more black soldiers to volunteer for combat duty.

Like the society it was drawn from, the U.S. Army during World War II was segregated. Black soldiers could qualify for combat, but could only serve in large segregated units, generally regiments, under mostly white commanders. While such famous units as the 9th and 10th cavalry regiments, which dated to the Civil War, had proven their worth, the restrictions in effect meant that most blacks could not qualify for combat; there simply weren't slots for them. They therefore found themselves in support units.

Eisenhower's orders did not have a large-scale impact. The terms for volunteering were difficult—a man already had to have received infantry training, a relative rarity for most black soldiers. Volunteers had to be privates. Still, about five thousand blacks volunteered, and about half were taken immediately.[27] They were placed in segregated platoons, which were then "integrated" into all-white units. Black and white platoons would share a number of facilities behind the lines as well as in combat, and this was considered radical at the time.

The soldiers' courage and performance under fire helped make the case for equality and eventual integration in the years that followed—which, as it happened, began during Bradley's term as Chairman of the Joint Chiefs of Staff.

While Bradley did praise black units and individuals,[28] he was not an advocate for integration during World War II or afterwards, nor was it his recommendation that more blacks be allowed in combat. Bradley shared the prejudices against blacks that were common in his day, though he was not a virulent racist by those standards. On a personal level, he seems to have acted with the same propriety he showed everyone: a news story covering his early military career talks of him playing fairly and with good sportsmanship against black players in a special football game.[29]

In his diary, Hansen describes a few instances when Bradley interacts with black soldiers; most are unremarkable. In one early entry, Hansen notes that Bradley did not believe blacks would be suitable fighters. This contrasts with positive comments by Bradley later; it's possible that his opinions evolved when presented with irrefutable facts.

Bradley expressed some concern about blacks' "place" in society during the war. [30] In July 1945, he recommended against continuing the "integrated" units, saying that the experiment had featured only above average soldiers who had seen limited combat and that there had been problems behind the lines. [31] After the war, Bradley made a number of statements about desegregation in the army, generally indicating that it should proceed slowly.

In *A General's Life*, Bradley says that these statements were misinterpreted to mean that he was against desegregation altogether. The book goes to some lengths to disassociate Bradley from some of the more racist support he received. It also takes pains to indicate his support of Army desegregation, which by the time the book was published was not only successful but one of the Army's greatest peacetime achievements, helping pave the way for society's acceptance of full civil rights for black Americans.

Bradley initially supported an Army plan that would have kept black enlistment at 10 percent or lower, and the service as a whole was slow to adopt procedures for implementing the integration order. The breakthrough came in January 1951—also during Bradley's term—when the Eighth Army in Korea began unofficially integrating combat units. By that March, all basic training in the country had been integrated; over the next few years, the last segregated units were gradually integrated or disbanded.

The frigid weather and overcast, threatening skies January 28, 1945, made Bastogne look every bit as wretched as it had been a month earlier. Though some of the December battle's worst horrors—the row of German bodies frozen in the barbed wire rolls at the outskirts—had been cleared away, the charred husks of tanks and burnt rubble of buildings made the war's sacrifices clear. Bradley surveyed the ruins with his customary silence, staring from the window of his car as his armed procession wound its way from Luxembourg toward his new command post at Namur, Belgium. From Bastogne they drove toward Marche, wending their way past fields and hills still heavy with death.

Bradley typically kept all of his feelings to himself, but none so much as those about the sacrifices his men made. He understood well the psychological toll death took—when Dwight Eisenhower's son John was assigned to his command, Bradley found him a post where the likelihood of his being injured was minimal, fearing the impact it would have on his father if he became a casualty of war.

Bradley drove through this sector often, and the changes the battle had wrought would stay with him for years afterwards. He was especially struck by the damage to small hamlets that had become momentarily important during the battle; their destruction seemed arbitrary and even capricious, lives and history flushed from existence for a moment's advantage in battle.

The signs of battle became less severe the farther Bradley went. His new command post was farther behind the lines than any of his others, set back in southern Belgium so he could be close to First Army.

In November, Eisenhower had said that if the 12th Army Group did not achieve a breakthrough during its November offensive, he would shift his attention to Montgomery and his plans for an offensive in the north. He now made good on that promise: the American Ninth Army would remain attached to the 21st Army Group for the foreseeable future, and the First Army would move in coordination with Montgomery.

The move put Bradley about an hour and a half from First Army. The Third Army, certainly not forgotten but with a low priority, was some three hours to the south. But Eisenhower wanted Bradley close to Montgomery. Regardless of Bradley's arguments that he would have to visit his army commanders more often than he visited Montgomery (or vice versa), Eisenhower would not yield. Ultimately, Bradley would see Montgomery in person all of three times over the next two months.

If Bradley's Luxembourg City headquarters were grand, his new command compound at Marche was more so. The command post was literally a chateau built on a high point protected by ancient embattlements.

Overlooking the Sambre and Meuse Rivers, the battlements stood across from the main part of the city. The day he arrived it was a gloomy place of gray stone. The stone wall of the old citadel stood over the late winter afternoon grayness as Bradley's vehicles wound their way up the hill.

The Chateau Namur,[32] the stately building at the summit of the for-tifications where Bradley lived and worked, was cold and dreary. Coal was hard to find, and thick blocks of the house seemed reluctant to let go of the damp. The red-brick, white-stone building had been ransacked by successive waves of occupiers, most recently Americans from the 29th Infantry Division. Bradley's staff had to beg the civilian authorities for furniture, augmenting their donations with material taken from homes confiscated from collaborators.

Bradley's office was placed in the governor's drawing room, his maps were hung over the frescoed walls, and his desk sat below a crystal chan-delier.

Bradley made one request—an ice cream machine.

The acetate on the map was soon covered with new lines and arrows, diagramming the push by Hodges and Patton to the original Ardennes lines. They aimed to roll up whatever was left of the German Army west of the Siegfried Line.

Bradley then wanted to break through the West Wall and march into Germany, but Eisenhower demurred. Instead, he directed Bradley to take several divisions from his armies to strengthen Montgomery and help Devers eliminate the Colmar Pocket in the south. Bradley was angry enough to put his objections on the record, charging in a memo that tactical decisions were being directed by national interests—a complaint squarely aimed at the British and Montgomery.

Bradley lost one division to Montgomery, but kept the four that would have gone to Devers. Patton happened to be present when Brad-ley argued over the phone with Bull that the 12th Army Group needed all of its divisions. "For the only time to my knowledge he lost his good humor," noted Patton in his diary later that day.[33]

★ ★ ★ ★

Montgomery's offensives, beginning with Veritable, were designed to open the path to the German heartland from the north. As Eisenhower told Marshall at a meeting on January 27, Montgomery's ultimate aim was Berlin via a drive across the Ruhr.

Veritable called for a push southwards into the area between the Maas and Rhine rivers. The Ninth Army would then come across the Rur near Düsseldorf, threatening to encircle the German forces in an operation dubbed Grenade. (The Maas runs toward the Rur, so that these two armies formed a pair of arms folding around the enemy.) The British Second Army would then punch through the German lines, striking over the Rhine.

The American First Army would protect the Ninth Army's flank. Once the Ninth was securely opposite Düsseldorf, First Army would then begin a drive toward Cologne and Bonn, moving on the western side of Rhine.

Until then, the Americans were supposed to sit and wait. At least that was how Montgomery saw it.

Eisenhower and Montgomery visited Bradley at the beginning of February to finalize details. Bradley was proper but cold toward Montgomery; Montgomery didn't seem to notice.

The German Army still had considerable strength, at least on paper. Eighty divisions faced the American and British Armies (they had seventy-one). Most of these, however, were undermanned and poorly trained. While the Germans had considerable fight left in them, as the Ardennes had proven, the enemy was appreciably weaker than it had been at the start of winter.

With the arrangements for Grenade out of the way, Bradley took Eisenhower on a tour of 12th Army Group, spending several days visiting various command posts. Where the roads weren't blocked by snow they were filled with mud; at one point Bradley and Eisenhower got out of Ike's Packard and helped push it from a mud hole.

Eisenhower's companion, Kay Summersby, had come to Belgium to be with Eisenhower during the conference. Summersby, by now an old friend of Bradley's staff, shared gossip and delighted Hansen by refusing to sit at Montgomery's table during dinner.

The personality clashes and power struggles had little impact on the troops on the front lines, and the Allied assault under Montgomery stepped off February 8. But once more, the weather and German defenses dogged the Allies. As always, the Huertgen Forest proved almost impenetrable. Operations there weren't helped by inadequate planning. When V Corps, under Huebner, finally got close to the Rur dams February 10, his men could not prevent the Germans from dynamiting them. Enhanced by the winter snows, water flooded the valley and made it impossible for the Americans to move through.[34]

Bradley was irked, pacing his headquarters like a frustrated ballplayer in a dugout waiting through an endless rain delay. He would note with annoyance in *A Soldier's Story* that had he not had to adjust his divisions to accommodate Montgomery, he would have continued through the Ardennes and been well inside Germany by then.

On Monday, February 12, Bradley returned to the chateau around 5:00 p.m. There were endless visitors, countless rounds of visits to his commanders, the usual mound of paperwork. The problems of simultaneously keeping in touch with his armies, SHAEF, and Command Z (the supply corps) continued to grow.

Bradley sat in his sitting room upstairs, tired, then looked up as Hansen and some of his staff entered. There were several girls in the small group, tipsy from having shared the headquarters scotch.

A small group downstairs began to play a song—"Happy Birthday."

Bradley was surprised, apparently having forgotten it was his birthday.

At dinner, some of Bradley's staffers teased him about his "dates" with Marlene Dietrich. Bradley relaxed; after the dinner he danced with the young women, joking with them easily.

For a few hours, at least, the war seemed very far away.

The next day, Eisenhower showed up at Bradley's headquarters with a bruised ego. The campaign by the British for a new ground commander had resulted in a compromise worked by Marshall to replace Eisenhower's deputy commander, Lord Arthur Tedder, with Sir Harold Alexander. While Eisenhower had been in favor of the move earlier, Marshall had made the arrangement without consulting him. Worse was the timing, coming so close after the Bulge and at a point when the papers were once more filled with glorious stories about the kickoff of Montgomery's offensive. The press would make it seem that the British were once again riding to the Americans' rescue.

In Eisenhower's view, it was another plan hatched by Montgomery to enhance his political position. He viewed it as yet the latest ploy to usurp his authority.

Bradley left no record of the conversation or what he told Eisenhower, but given his antipathy toward Montgomery, it's not hard to imagine that his first reaction must have been along the lines of *You're just figuring that out now?*

Regardless of whether he was so pointed, the next morning he loaned Hansen and his car to Eisenhower. The supreme commander drove up to have it out with Montgomery. Hansen, outside the room where Eisenhower and Montgomery spoke, reported some "table thumping" during the brief session.

The matter of a ground commander was dropped, once and for all.

But there was still a price to pay. Bradley was harangued by Eisenhower's staff, who kept insisting that the 12th Army Group stop *all* forward movement, as well as hand over reserve divisions and resources to 21ˢᵗ for its push.

Bradley's troops began engaging in an "aggressive defense"—which looked a heck of a lot like a series of local, small-scale offensives.

Patton and Hodges saw no reason that they should take a backseat to the British. Bradley clearly agreed with them. And while he continued to hear criticism from SHAEF, it seems that he was actively pushing the army commanders along.

Bradley "let" Patton take Trier, advising him to reach it by February 28 or else be ordered to stop his advance—an incentive to Patton equivalent of offering an oasis to a man in a desert. Then when Patton had taken it, Bradley told him he should keep going until someone called Bradley to order him to stop.

And I won't be listening for the phone, he added.[35]

Bradley's relations with SHAEF, Eisenhower, and his generals during February 1945 are fascinating. Clearly he was disobeying at least the form of the written orders telling him to stay on the defensive. The question is to what extent Eisenhower was actually endorsing it.

Bradley wasn't just arguing with SHAEF over the content (and use) of the reserve infantry divisions, supply allocations, and the lines between his armies. He was encouraging forward movement, albeit on a relatively modest scale. And this went for Hodges as well as Patton. Bradley includes Eisenhower when he says in *A Soldier's Story* that he told Patton to keep moving ahead.[36] But there's no other proof that Eisenhower was complicit. Surely if Eisenhower himself told the Third Army commander, Patton would have recorded this in his diary. (The entry practically writes itself: *Finally Ike has gotten some real ones and is letting us pull one over that sandbagging phony Montgomery!*)

Bradley was under considerable pressure from SHAEF staff, who clearly wanted the emphasis to come from Montgomery's campaign. At the same time, he saw the opportunity in his sector, as he always had, to shoot into the German heartland. Continuing to probe the defenses, break through those defenses, and move toward the Rhine—Bradley may never have published a map proclaiming that he was aiming to get to and then over the Rhine into the German heartland, but it surely didn't take a genius to see this.

On February 20, Eisenhower gave Bradley instructions that covered his movements for the next phase of Grenade (and Veritable).[37] Working in conjunction with Montgomery's slow-moving offensive, Bradley was to extend coverage along Ninth Army's flank. First Army's VII Corps was assigned to clear a triangular-shaped area between the Erft and Rhine from Cologne to Düsseldorf.[38]

After that, Bradley planned to continue the attack to the Rhine. The plans were worked out following a series of meetings not only with Hodges, Patton, and Simpson, but the corps and divisions commanders. In the First Army area, VII Corps, still under Collins, took Cologne, then began moving south toward Bonn. Huebner's V Corps worked in the direction of the Ahr River. At the same time, Patton had Third Army swing northeastwards.

With the flooding of the Rur subsiding, the Ninth Army leapt across the river and moved toward Wesel, trapping a substantial number of Germans. Hodges and Patton then jumped off, pushing toward the Rhine in a drive whose speed surprised even Bradley. He later said he was prouder of this operation than of any other in the war; within hours of its start, German defenders were falling back in confusion. This was partially because better weather freed the Americans to take advantage of their air power and mobility. It was partially because the depleted German Army couldn't mount a defense-in-depth.

Bradley was so encouraged by the initial progress of Third Army that on March 1 he canceled an appointment with Eisenhower, instead travel-ing to First Army headquarters. He was looking to shuffle forces to improve Patton's drive, undoubtedly encouraged by the possibility of a breakthrough similar to that of the previous summer. With momentum picking up, by the morning of March 6, Bradley found himself managing two strong drives that had broken through the weakened German defenses.

Montgomery continued to believe that Bradley's efforts were secondary to the main thrust by 21ˢᵗ Army Group. It was Montgomery who was going to breach the Rhine and charge into the rest of Germany.

As soon as he had his forces ready.

It's hard to determine whether Eisenhower believed this himself. He says in his memoir *Crusade* that a Rhine crossing was not foreseen until the beginning of May, noting that because of that, he had not seriously planned a crossing campaign.[39] But reaching the river and not crossing it for two or three months would make very little tactical sense, since it would give the Germans an opportunity to build up their defenses. Eisenhower spent considerable time with Bradley during this period. So unless Bradley himself didn't think he would cross the Rhine once he reached it—which doesn't seem possible—Eisenhower surely should have expected something.

This makes it difficult to understand why he then allowed his staff to demand additional divisions that would have blunted Bradley's drives.

Collins VII Corps, back with First Army, was approaching Düsseldorf on March 6 when Bradley journeyed to lunch in Reims with Churchill and Brooke. Unknown to Bradley, the British officials had been accusing him of having too much influence over Eisenhower. But the knives were carefully concealed by all concerned that day. Brooke's aides drew Bradley out about the battle at Avranches, and Churchill himself flattered him, recalling details of the battle.

The discussion over lunch turned to the technology of war and coming developments, including rocket-launched munitions. The discussion was remarkably prescient, touching on airborne combat control centers and remote weapons deployment in the manner of today's missile-carrying UAVs.

"There will come a day when we walk into a cabinet room," predicted Churchill, "break the glass case over a switch, dial to the nation to be bombed and push a button to declare war."[40]

Bradley, thinking back to the conversation he'd had with Roosevelt about the atomic bomb, said nothing.

Soon, the conversation drifted to geo-politics, and Bradley found himself prodding Churchill on the future of Greece, a subject Bradley had not spent much time considering, but one that was dear to Churchill's heart. The prime minister railed against the communists there, and surprised Bradley with his attitude toward Stalin. Bradley had not thought much about the Russians, except in a very vague way as fellow allies. Unlike Patton, who at points saw war with the Soviet Union as inevitable, he thought them mostly benign.

The very next day, Bradley took a phone call in his office from Hodges.[41]

The First Army was at the Rhine.

Better, it was *across* the Rhine—advance units of 9th Armored Combat Command B had shot across the Ludendorff railroad bridge at Remagen, seizing it before it could be destroyed.

"Hot dog, Courtney," Bradley told Hodges. "This will bust him wide open. Are you getting your stuff across?"[42]

"Just as fast as we can push it over."

Bradley talked over the situation, examining the map. He urged Hodges to prepare for a counterattack, though he predicted it would take several days for the Germans to mount it.

A short time later, Harold "Pinky" Bull, Eisenhower's G-3, arrived at Bradley's office. He had come to ask for more troops for Jacob Devers' 6th Army Group. It was a substantial request—one armored division, two infantry divisions, seven battalions of artillery, and assorted support units.

Bradley told him about the bridge. Bull wasn't pleased. Crossing the Rhine wasn't in the plans.

"Sure, you've got a bridge, Brad, but what good is it going to do you? You're not going anywhere down there at Remagen. It just doesn't fit into the plan."

"Plan—hell. A bridge is a bridge and mighty damned good anywhere across the Rhine."

The "plan" was that Montgomery would cross the Rhine first, north of the Ruhr. Maybe later Third Army would cross in the south—but only later.

Of course, Montgomery was still behind the Rhine, and not even close to getting over.

"What in hell do you want us to do?" Bradley asked Bull. "Pull back and blow it up?"

Admittedly, the Remagen Bridge was in the wrong place, even for Bradley, who hoped to swing the Third Army north in the Ruhr pincer. But a bridge over the Rhine was a gift, and Bradley was already thinking of how it could be used.

First, though, he needed permission to keep it. Technically, he had no authority to cross the river.

He called Eisenhower. Ike agreed First Army should get across and hold it.

Before the end of the night, Bradley diagramed a plan for Bull that showed Hodges capturing an autobahn six miles from the bridge. From there, First Army could turn east. Patton, coming from the south, would hook up with them at Giessen. To do this, Patton would need to cross the Rhine near Mainz.

Which gave Bradley even more incentive to hold onto the armies Bull wanted.

"Everything's wrong on the front," Bull argued. "You know what we've selected for a crossing and now you're trying to change it."[43]

No, answered Bradley. It's just that we got a break.

The discussion continued well into the night, with Bull growing more frustrated and tired as Bradley and his staff continued to argue. At one point, Bull admitted that Eisenhower's "heart is in your sector but his mind is made up in the north."[44]

"The 12th Group is harder to get along with than the 21st," concluded Bull when the conference broke up at one in the morning.

How surprised was Bradley that he had taken a bridge over the Rhine?

Perhaps not very. Or at least not as much as he portrayed in *A Soldier's Story*, where the bridge seems to magically appear.

Bradley could not have predicted that any of the bridges across the Rhine would be intact when his troops arrived. But a general who sends an army corps down the banks of a river and doesn't at least *hope* that something will present itself would be a dull thinker indeed.

In the end, Bradley gave up the number of divisions Bull wanted, but managed to take them from First Army and leave Third Army intact. He didn't want to dilute Patton because of what he had in mind next: a variation on the double envelopment of the Ruhr that he had been proposing for months. Now that half of it had fallen into his lap, Bradley was determined to follow through.

The problem was that Montgomery's drive was supposed to take precedence, and it was clear the British would scream if Bradley moved ahead at their expense. Tied to the decision were questions of supply and logistics. More than prestige was at stake; how to proceed was a matter of overall strategy, since the location of the thrust could very well set up the end game of the war.

Eisenhower ordered Bradley to move no more than four divisions into the bridgehead. He was also instructed to keep ten divisions reserved to exploit a breakthrough in the sector reserved for Montgomery.

In other words, Bradley could cross the Rhine, but he had to sit tight. There was to be no encirclement of the Ruhr.

Yet.

Meanwhile, Patton had been moving quickly.

After taking Trier, the Third Army pushed along the Mosel River. This left the Germans in a triangle between Third and Seventh Armies (part of Devers' 6th Army Group), with the Rhine behind them.

Bradley then went to work on Eisenhower to approve a plan for Patton to move south in the Saar-Palatine area, closing off this triangle—and not coincidentally, opening the way for additional attacks across the Rhine. Launched in conjunction with an attack on the Siegfried Line in the south by the Seventh Army, the assault soon turned into a gallop. Patton's army corps swept across the Saar, slicing the German Army Group G to pieces.

Patton's army reached the banks of the Rhine by March 9. Bradley called him each day to congratulate him, and to tell him to keep going—advice Patton hardly needed, though he certainly welcomed the praise.

Bradley's orders remained to hold his line as he waited for Montgomery, but he was barely winking at them. He later confessed to James Gavin that he told his commanders to move ahead about a thousand yards each day, ostensibly to keep the Germans from laying mines in front of them.[45] By this point, neither Hodges nor Patton needed any such directions. The Germans bombed and shelled the bridge at Remagen, succeeding in destroying it on March 17. But by then, Hodges had gotten his four divisions across—and reached the autobahn Bradley had pointed out to Bull.

The way was open for Bradley's envelopment, if Patton could find a way across.

Bradley met with Eisenhower on March 18, their first face-to-face meeting since the lunch with Churchill. The tactical situation had changed considerably—but the political situation with the British had not. Montgomery's offensive remained, in theory at least, SHAEF's priority.

Still behind the Rhine, Montgomery insisted on holding ten divisions to use as a reserve force. Logically, these divisions had to come from the First Army, which was one reason Eisenhower had limited Bradley to using four divisions to establish the bridgehead at Remagen. Apparently at the March 18 meeting, Eisenhower and Bradley worked out a plan that would substitute divisions from the south. This meant either Patton's army or Devers' Army Group.

Bradley was probably thinking they would come from Devers, because he had other plans for Patton. Then again, he may have realized they wouldn't be needed at all.

Later, on March 18, Eisenhower sent a letter to Devers, Bradley, and Montgomery reaffirming that the 21st Army Group had the priority in the attack.[46] But the next day when Bradley visited Patton with Hodges, Bradley detailed the envelopment plan, pointing to a crossing in the Mainz-Worms area as Patton's target. Bradley told Patton that he must move quickly before the 12th Army Group lost any more men to Montgomery.[47]

In other words, even as Eisenhower was reaffirming that 21st Army Group had the top priority in the Allied offensive, Bradley was going ahead with a plan that called for the destruction of a major portion of the German Army. By implication, the offensive would open the a route right through the German heartland. Whatever priority Montgomery might have had officially, if Bradley's forces moved quickly enough, the weight of the push into Germany would belong to him.

★ ★ ★ ★

Bradley traveled to the Cannes area of France March 20, joining Ike for a brief vacation. How much rest they got is debatable, since Bradley seems to have spent considerable time talking with Eisenhower about the eastward push. Bradley didn't want to move ahead only 1,000 or 2,000 yards a night. His goal was to link up with the Soviets.[48]

On March 21, still in Cannes, Eisenhower issued orders to Bull that formalized Bradley's plans and, not coincidentally, authorized Patton to cross the Rhine.[49]

Surprise, surprise, Patton was across the next night.

The sun was just peeking in the windows of Bradley's dining room at the chateau on the morning of March 23 when Patton called to tell him he had gotten across the river.

"I sneaked a division over last night," said Patton. "But there are so few Krauts around there they don't know it yet. So don't make any announcement—we'll keep it a secret until we see how it goes."[50]

That crossing is presented in *A Soldier's Story*—and in many histories of the war—as a surprise, a sudden opportunity offered the Allies that simply had to be capitalized on. Closer examination, however, indicates it was carefully orchestrated by Bradley and possibly Eisenhower to move the American offensive in the south ahead without upsetting the British.

One gets the impression from reading the account in *A Soldier's Story* that Bradley was shocked, just shocked, that this had happened. By an amazing stroke of luck, all of the pieces had fallen in place for the plan he had advocated all along.

The more reasonable conclusion is that Bradley and Eisenhower agreed at least in principle to the plan no later than March 18, worked out the details, then acted in a way calculated to attract the least amount of protest from the British—and from Eisenhower's staff, the majority of whom appeared to back Montgomery. Bradley never minded giving other people credit; one can almost see him winking as he reviewed the passages in his memoir.

True, this is only speculation. But it seems reasonable, especially given the amount of time Bradley and Eisenhower spent together in this period.

During the war, a number of British officials, from Brooke down, contended that Bradley had undue influence on Eisenhower's strategies. A good deal of this criticism stemmed directly from the belief that the British should be the ones leading the ground war, without regard to the actual tactical situation at the time.

A number of writers have agreed with the British contention. Most start from an undeniable premise—Bradley, Eisenhower, Patton, Simpson, and Hodges were all certainly Americans and to varying degrees friends. The debates start when trying to decide whether these friendships unduly influenced Eisenhower's strategy.

There was a basic disagreement between Eisenhower's "broad front" strategy and the strategy favored by Montgomery and Brooke for a single drive into Germany. It's difficult today to argue that Eisenhower's preference was wrong, in so much as it won the war. Nonetheless, there are legitimate arguments for and against the single drive plan as well as the broad front strategy.[51]

Leaving these debates aside, Bradley and the other American generals below him created a situation on the ground that could not be denied. Operating with fewer supplies and lower priority than Montgomery, Bradley presented Eisenhower with the conditions for victory. Even *before* crossing the Rhine, American troops were in a tactical position that simply *had* to be exploited. While some historians insist that Eisenhower made his decisions because he wanted Bradley to get credit for ending the war, all the evidence is to the contrary. If anything, Eisenhower showed remarkable deference and preference to Montgomery despite what, in hindsight at least, appears all logic and common sense.[52]

Once across the Rhine and fully unleashed, Patton's Third Army moved toward Frankfurt, then moved eastward in the direction of Kassel and Eisenach. Part of the First Army headed south to Limburg, and from there turned east, moving parallel to the Third Army. The First eventually linked with Simpson's Ninth Army at Lippstadt. In the pocket between them, 325,000 Germans were taken as prisoners of war.[53]

The drive was not without its reverses. One of the most infamous involved Patton and an ill-advised attempt to rescue prisoners-of-war, including his son-in-law, from a German stalag in Hammelburg.

Patton's 4th Armored Division was marching across the Main River south of Ashaffenburg when Patton received intelligence about the prison camp. While there is some disagreement on the particulars, it seems highly likely that Patton knew that his son-in-law, Lieutenant Colonel John Waters, was among the prisoners.[54] Patton ordered a raid some forty miles behind the lines to rescue them.

The raid was conducted by Task Force Baum, a 300-man, 50-vehicle, armored group led by Captain Abraham Baum and accompanied by Patton aide Major Al Stiller. Setting off March 26, the small group succeeded in liberating the prison, but was overwhelmed by German units responding to the attack. The task force was wiped out, its members either captured or killed. (The 14th Armored Division liberated Hammelburg April 5, freeing the survivors and POWs who had been interned there. In the meantime, some of the prisoners had been moved.)

Task Force Baum actually came close to achieving its goal, but a fair assessment shows the mission was ill advised. Too large to move without being detected, the task force was too small to fend off a sustained attack so far from its own lines. It had no hope of support from other American units. The operation was a diversion from the more important strategic and tactical objectives of the Army. It is generally regarded as one of Patton's worst mistakes of the war, with most critics charging that he let his personal feelings for his son-in-law override sound reasoning.

In his diary, Patton claims that Bradley objected to his sending a full combat command on the mission.[55] It was only because of that objection, Patton writes, that he decided to send such a small force to make the attack. This entry was made a few days after the fact, with the same information repeated in a letter to his wife.

Whether a larger force would have been able to complete the mission or not is an open question. A full combat command still would have been functioning independent of other support far behind enemy lines in a direction away from Patton's thrust. More firepower might have broken through the defenses that the enemy mounted as the Americans left the city, or it might have been spotted earlier, initiating a stiffer defense and an evacuation of prisoners. The size of the force is not a substitute for better intelligence on the enemy or coordinated planning.

The raid was not only a tactical blunder, but a violation of basic leadership; no general should put his men at risk for his own personal reasons. It's on those grounds, not the size of the force, that historians and critics admonished Patton following the war. Depending on one's view, it was at best a grave error in judgment, at worst a gross dereliction of duty.

Was Bradley party to it?

Most historians view Patton's blaming Bradley as either hyperbolic or a lie. Some dismiss it outright; others skip over it. It deserves more attention than that.

It is clearly an instance of Patton making excuses for himself, something he does at several points in his diary and his letters to his wife. It's also somewhat typical in that it doesn't address the real point of his offense. At different points, Patton also blamed the corps and combat commanders for the mission's failure. And finally, in an article published after the war, Patton blamed himself for not sending the larger force.[56]

Yet for all that, there seems to be at least some truth in Patton's statement that Bradley approved the mission, and more than a dollop of dishonesty in Bradley's version.

Bradley says in *A Soldier's Story* that he only learned of the raid "after it had been on the road two days."[57] And further "had George consulted me on the mission, I would have forbidden him to stage it."[58]

Those statements are contradicted by Hansen's diary entry of March 28, the day Bradley claims in *A Soldier's Story* to have heard about the raid:

When Patton ran off on his mission of liberation the other day, Brad told him he would allow it providing Patton did not become involved. He was ordered to withdraw if he did to prevent him from becoming entangled in the wrong direction.[59]

The diary entry, made at the time and recorded even as the Americans were being rounded up, is at least arguably more accurate than what Bradley published in the book. ("Involved" in the entry presumably does not refer to Patton personally, but rather is a military term meaning a battle or firefight. If his forces met resistance and a battle ensued, it would divert Patton's main drive.)

But that still leaves a number of questions. Most prominent among them: Did Bradley veto Patton's request to send a full combat command to the rescue? And did Bradley, contrary to what he claims, know that Patton's son-in-law was among those held prisoner?

Bradley did meet with Patton the day before the raid was launched, and they would have had ample opportunity to discuss the situation. It's certainly possible that Patton would have mentioned sending a relatively large force. At the same time, the comment Hansen makes about not getting "involved" suggests that the raid was presented by Patton as something easily done, perhaps a diversion over uncontested ground only a few miles away from the American lines.

A combat command would have represented a large portion of the corps' firepower, a rather large commitment if the idea was to *avoid* battle. So accepting Hansen's account implies that the situation Patton described to Bradley was less than accurate. Perhaps when Patton told Bradley about the situation, he made it sound as if the target was closer or completely undefended. It's also possible that Bradley said the camp could be liberated if only a small force was needed to do so, or as long as the main drive was not disturbed. While not specifically ruling out the involvement of a combat command, such a directive would strongly mitigate against using one.

The real controversy over the raid stems from the question of whether Patton knew if his son-in-law was there. The evidence from his diary and the letter to his wife make it fairly certain that Patton strongly suspected this was the case, even though he said later on that he did not know. In *A Soldier's Story*, Bradley reports that Patton "assured me he did not learn of his son-in-law's incarceration until nine days after the raid."[60] He implies that he believed him, though he doesn't specifically say so.

Here the truth is hard to discern, and Hansen's diary is no help.

Patton could easily have kept the information about his son-in-law being in the camp to himself. On the other hand, Bradley would have had access to the same intelligence and rumors that Patton had, and had already shown an interest in Waters. The same sort of concern Bradley showed toward John Eisenhower could easily have come into play here; one imagines that knowing Patton's son-in-law was kept at the camp would have made Bradley more rather than less likely to approve of a mission.

Assuming Hansen's diary entry is correct, why did Bradley lie?

That's an even harder question to answer than the others. By gliding past the details, he might have thought he was protecting himself, Patton, or the Army. While arguments can be made for each proposition, none is completely satisfying. Even Bradley's own version doesn't cast him in a particularly good light, as he is admitting (or claiming) he was out of touch with his command.

In any event, the irony is that even historians who are extremely sympathetic to Patton have been more likely to believe Bradley's version of events than his. It's one of the few places where Patton's reputation hurts *him* rather than Bradley.

The clouds were thick as Bradley got out of his staff car and looked across the Rhine River near Ehrenbreitstein. Spread out at his feet was the first American-built two-lane bridge over the river, completed just the night before. Eleven hundred feet of roadway stretched across over twenty barges, all moored against the swift current of the river.[61]

He started across. It was Friday, April 6, 1945.

The United States had been at war with Germany for just under four and a half years. Bradley had spent a little more than two of them either in combat or planning for combat. The evidence of his efforts lay all around him—not just in the flow of trucks and men over the bridge, but in the rubble of houses and the broken defenses on either side of the river.

German civilians, cowed by the sudden collapse of their army, watched from the ruins. Guns thundered in the distance.

Across the river, Bradley climbed into his car and told the driver to take his time, savoring the moment as well as the scenery as they climbed past the broken walls of Ehrenbreitstein, entering the fort built a century before.

The view from the parapet was even more impressive than the one from the bridge.

And shattering. Everywhere he looked, Bradley saw Germany in ruins.

The parade grounds inside the fort had been cleared. A band played at one side. Bradley, early as usual, waited for his army commanders to arrive. The last was Patton, his signature sirens wailing in his procession.

The ceremony began. The color guard raised the flag as the first strains of "Stars and Stripes" filled the air.

There were a host of ribbons to be given out, awards for bravery and courage. Promotions. And a speech by Bradley commending the troops of the United Nations. His staff worried that he would stumble, but he didn't—except in one place, where he said "operations" instead of Nations.

It was a sublime moment for Bradley. Just a few days before, he had received word that congress had approved his promotion to four-star rank.[62]

Bradley passes over his promotion quickly in *A Soldier's Life*; the only mention of it shows him telling one of his orderlies not to jump the gun after rumors of it reached Europe. But it was discussed quite a bit at his headquarters, and it clearly meant a great deal to him. For one thing, it finally put him on par with Montgomery.

Five years before, Omar Nelson Bradley had been a lieutenant colonel. Now he had a reached a rank held by only a handful of men at any one time. It was no exaggeration to say that he had reached higher than he had dared dream as a plebe on the West Point plain.

But there was still fighting to be done.

On April 12, Bradley and Eisenhower went down to visit Patton at his headquarters in an old German barracks at Hersfeld. Once there, Patton shepherded them and some staff people into a pair of L-5s. They flew a short distance to Ohrdoff.

He wanted them to see the Nazi concentration camp there. The scene was wretched. Thousands of starved, emaciated, yellow-skinned corpses littered the ground or were interred in shallow graves. There were scars where desperate survivors had clawed at the corpses, plucking the organs for food.

"I can't understand the bestiality of those German people," Eisenhower told Bradley. "What would compel them to do anything like that?"

Bradley couldn't speak. Patton stood off in a corner, getting sick.[63]

Patton recovered sufficiently to host a dinner later that night in his quarters, inviting four Red Cross girls to join the generals as a diversion. When the girls were gone, the three men sat talking together into the night. The topic was the war, but not all the talk was serious; they traded fantasies on how they would spend the trove of a hundred million in gold Patton's men had confiscated from the Nazis a few days before. The gold, along with American and other currency, had been hidden in a salt mine.

Patton went to bed around midnight. Bradley and Eisenhower turned in not long after.

A short while later, Bradley heard a knock on his bedroom door. He looked up to see Patton standing before him.

"The President has died," Patton told him.[64]

Together they went to tell Eisenhower.

The Allies had divided Germany into zones of occupation at Yalta, and as the end of the war came into sight, Bradley began coordinating his attack plans with those eventual boundaries in mind. His immediate concern was to move a large enough force south to occupy Bavaria and the rest of central and southern Germany to the border of Austria. He wanted to get there before the Soviets did, facilitating the post-war arrangements.

Bradley had also become increasingly concerned about rumors that German diehards were planning to retreat to the mountains in southern Germany. There he envisioned months if not years of difficult warfare to root them out.

American commanders from Marshall on down were extremely worried about a Nazi redoubt, realizing that guerilla warfare against hardened and motivated Nazi survivors would be a daunting task. The rumors had an out-sized influence on the final stages of the war, as Eisenhower shifted forces to cut off any possible retreat. Preventing large numbers of soldiers and equipment from reaching a redoubt area had a much higher priority for the Allies than taking Berlin.[65]

In mid-April, Bradley assigned First and Ninth Armies to move across the central Allied front, holding the northern portion of what would eventually be the American zone of occupation. Patton's Third Army (with some First Army divisions) would drive down the Danube. The Fifteenth Army, which until the middle of March had been used mostly for refreshing units devastated during the Ardennes, would work in behind Bradley's other armies. (Gerow had moved from his corps command to take charge of the army in January.) Seventh Army, part of Devers' Army Group, would push to Munich.

American forces quickly reached the Elbe and Mulde rivers, beyond the boundary between the American and Soviet zones. There they waited, not entirely sure what the Soviet reaction would be. Bradley was once again anxious to avoid a friendly fire incident between the Allies, much less create an international incident. He told Simpson that his Ninth Army was to hold the line, unless the Soviets insisted on advancing to the border of their territory, in which case he was to work out an arrangement for an orderly transfer of territory.

While the Americans concentrated on cutting off a retreat to the redoubt and dividing the remains of the German Army into manageable pockets, the British were taking a much broader view of post-war political geography. The plan Eisenhower had adopted—shaped largely by Bradley—had Montgomery moving north to cut off any German attempt to form a redoubt in Denmark. From the British point of view, their equally important goal was to block Soviet post-war access to the Baltic Sea. At the same time, Churchill was trying to persuade Eisenhower (and other Americans) that Berlin should be taken, and implying that it should be held after the war, a violation of the Yalta agreement.

At the end of March when Churchill began pressing his point, it already looked too late. The Russians were roughly forty miles from Berlin. Montgomery was some two hundred miles away. Eisenhower held to his overall plans, explaining them to Marshall and then Churchill himself. The battle plans did not forbid a push to Berlin, but it had such a low priority that the city was clearly being left to the Soviets to occupy.

But the Russians and the British failed to move quickly in Berlin's direction. By April 11, Simpson's army had crossed into Barby, sixty miles from the city. With a bit of regrouping, Simpson could have walked to the city within a week.

Bradley prepared a plan to take Berlin, though he did not believe it was a good move tactically. A sudden counterattack could have inflicted severe casualties on the Ninth Army; even without that, he thought there would be significant resistance in the capital. He estimated that taking the German capital would cost as many as 100,000 casualties. While the number seems exaggerated, Bradley's unstated goal now was to end the campaign with the minimum of American bloodshed.

At the same time, the Yalta agreement made it clear that the Americans would have to evacuate the eastern sectors of Germany, which were designated for the Soviets; the farther they went now, the more difficult that would be. From a military point of view, Berlin's value was purely symbolic, and Bradley never put much store in symbols.

For a while, it looked as if the Americans would take the city simply by default. Simpson reached the Elbe River April 11 and kept moving east. Finally, on April 15, Bradley got a call from Eisenhower telling him that Simpson must not enter the city. Bradley called Simpson to his headquarters that morning, surprising and disappointing him with the news.[66]

Berlin was left for the Russians.

The decision about Berlin was never Bradley's to make. His thoughts are interesting, however, especially in light of the experiences of post-War Europe, and of Bradley's own tour later as chairman of the Joint Chiefs of Staff during the height of the Cold War. He admitted later that he simply never saw occupying Berlin as being important.

It's not surprising that he would eschew the political symbol for the military reality. For Bradley, military reality trumped all. It wasn't that he disagreed with the vision of post-war Europe espoused by Churchill. Bradley simply didn't have one. He admits to having been somewhat naïve about the Soviets and their intentions following the war. But it seems more accurate to say that he wasn't so much naïve as simply not present—he was focused on the war and military problems. Geopolitics wasn't his thing.

This would prove a severe handicap when he took over as head of the Joint Chiefs of Staff two years after war.

Speculating over Berlin has lost a great deal of its interest now that the Cold War has ended. It does seem obvious, however, that had Bradley

been given the resources that went to Montgomery at the end of the summer, the western Allies would have had a far better chance of punching
into Berlin before the Russians. An earlier capture of Antwerp and its
approaches might have had a similar effect.

Arguments that Montgomery's northern push would have been
quicker had he had more resources are difficult to sustain. Nothing in his
track record suggests that he would have moved any faster, let alone used
the American armies effectively. And the Germans would surely have
been able to divert troops from the static front to the south to further
thwart him.

Bradley worked late into the night of May 6. He'd recently moved to
a new command post in Bad Wildungen, Germany, taking an interior
room at the Fürstenhof Hotel. The building had been recently used as a
hospital, and the place still smelled of antiseptic. Work finally squared
away, Bradley lingered over a letter his wife. Long ago, she'd complained
about how terse his messages were. He had retyped her long letter of
complaint into a short paragraph, showing how easily much could be
said in few words.

He had many things to say to her tonight, but he'd save most of them
for when he saw her.

Going home was very much on his mind. Hitler had killed himself a
few days before, though the body had yet to be found. The German Army
in Italy had surrendered, and there were negotiations between the remnants of the German Army in the homeland to lay down their arms.

Letter finished, Bradley crawled into his bed and fell asleep.

The telephone rang at 4:00 a.m. It was Eisenhower.

"Brad, it's all over. A TWX is on the way."[67]

Germany had surrendered unconditionally.

Bradley spoke with Eisenhower for a few more moments, then called
Patton and told him the news. Then he called Hodges, Simpson, and
Gerow.

He broke the news in his understated, offhand style at his morning press conference a few hours later. No fanfare, no presentation, just "this is off the record."[68]

A few days later, he held a party for some of his officers and staff. Sixty-five women, most of them Red Cross nurses were invited.

Marlene Dietrich came in, ten minutes late, wearing a dress that stunned the others into silence.

Bradley took a dance with her, and each woman in turn.

It was over. The war was over.

CHAPTER 9

At Rest

radley wanted to go to the Pacific once Germany was defeated,
but MacArthur told Marshall that he didn't need another army
group commander for the Japanese invasion. This in effect
ruled Bradley out; going to the Pacific would not only entail a demotion
for Bradley, but would imply that the European theater (and those who
served there) was less important than the Pacific.

Still, Marshall cabled to Eisenhower asking if Bradley wanted to go
as an Army commander. Eisenhower was strongly opposed on prestige
grounds. While Bradley told him, "I will serve anywhere in any position
that General Marshall assigns me,"[1] Eisenhower wrote Marshall that he
recommended against it, effectively ending even the slim possibility.

At one point, rumors were rife that Bradley would succeed Eisen-
hower as head of SHAEF. But he was not to have a role in post-War
Europe. A scandal had been brewing in the Veterans Administration. The
VA's bureaucracy was overwhelmed by the size of the returning Army,

and it was clear the agency would face even greater difficulties as the war wound down. President Harry Truman decided that he needed a prestigious general to clean up the situation and handle its transition to peacetime. He chose Bradley.

The job was not a military position, and Bradley surely perceived it as controversial and thankless—and potentially an end to his Army career. But there was no graceful way to refuse it. Bradley did get an assurance from Eisenhower that he would recommend him in the future as Army Chief of Staff. With Marshall planning to retire, it was obvious that Eisenhower would get the position, and thus be in a position to recommend Bradley at the end of his envisioned two-year term.[2]

Bradley presided over an enormous reorganization of the VA, decentralizing its operations in an effort to make it more responsive to the needs of veterans. The sheer scale of the work was incredible—*A General's Life* says some 300,000 pieces of mail came in every day. The Agency was responsible for some 17 million men by the end of June 1946, more than three times the number when Bradley took over.[3] Bradley worked like a madman, but the task was overwhelming, with reform and improvement needed in nearly every aspect of what the VA did.

Bradley spent roughly two and a half years at the VA. He was most proud of his efforts on behalf of disabled veterans. It was an issue he took a particular interest in, delivering speeches to various business groups urging they be hired and treated like other workers. Recalling their experiences and sacrifices in battle, he argued that they had already proved themselves worthy of any challenge the work world could present.

By the time Bradley became Army Chief of Staff at the end of 1947, the U.S. Army had been reduced and restructured. A new White House National Security Council had taken much of the impetus away from the military chiefs. The Air Force had been elevated to a separate service. Instead of a Navy Secretary and a War Secretary, there was now only a Defense Secretary.

Bradley's stint as Army Chief lasted about a year and a half before he was promoted to chair the Joint Chiefs of Staff. These were difficult years. Bradley found himself leading a military that was far too small and under-funded to adequately deal with the Soviet threat. He presided over the initial phases of the Korean War, where the weakness of the new national security arrangement became shockingly clear. And not even Marshall, who returned as Truman's Secretary of Defense, could properly deal with MacArthur, whose campaign in Korea was marked by confusion, insubordination, and altering bouts of extreme optimism and pessimism bordering on panic.

Bradley was too far removed from MacArthur to play the role Marshall had played with Eisenhower, and in any event the times were very different. MacArthur's relationship with Washington and the policy that resulted were a contentious muddle.

In *A General's Life*, Bradley laments that the Joint Chiefs of Staff did not take a firm hand with MacArthur, agreeing with criticism that the Joint Chiefs—and he himself—were too awed by MacArthur's reputation. Bradley also honored the military tradition of allowing the commander in the field to control tactical decisions, which in Korea amounted to strategic and, potentially, geopolitical decisions as well.

While it's possible, perhaps likely, that nothing Bradley did would have eased the conflicts, it's clear that he didn't try to exert a strong hold over MacArthur. Nor did he attempt to bring coherence to the administration's policy. Bradley's habit of seeking consensus and relying on logic failed in the reality of political disorder and petty jealousies. Much of the ultimate blame for confusion over Korea must go to Truman and his indecision on what to do about the Chinese, but the Joint Chiefs' failure to firmly direct military policy on the peninsula added to the problem.

On the other hand, Bradley did preside over the country's rearmament, a reversal of the nearly disastrous rapid demobilization following the war. As head of the Joint Chiefs, Bradley pushed the development of the hydrogen bomb. He also guided the implementation of the military aspects of what became known as "Containment," the decades-long campaign to keep Communism from spreading until it would collapse under its own weight. Like the other members of the JCS in the early 1950s, Bradley saw Soviet threats to Europe as considerably more dangerous than the invasion in Korea, and directed much of his attention there.

Bradley left as chairman of the Joint Chiefs of Staff in August 1953, not long after Eisenhower began his first term as president. He was sixty years old. In the photos taken at the time he looks considerably older. Promoted by Truman to five-star rank with Congressional approval in September 1949, Bradley was still in the Army, though not on the active list. He retained an office at the Pentagon, but aside from the occasional speech or appearance at the request of the president or the Army, Bradley's military duties were over.

Not ready to retire, he went to work for the Bulova Watch Company, starting as head of its research and development labs and becoming chairman of the board in 1958. He held the position until he was eighty years old, resigning in 1973 for an honorary post.

His wife Mary died in 1965. The following year he married Kitty Buhler, a 43-year-old screenwriter whom he met when she interviewed him for a potential screenplay. (According to his cowriter on *A General's Life*, Clay Blair, Buhler had acquired life rights to Bradley's story. No movie was ever made, but *A Soldier's Story* was eventually used by the producers of the movie *Patton* for background material.)

Among other activities, the Bradleys spent a good deal of time at horse races. Ever the mathematician, Bradley consulted books on horse racing systems before placing his bets.[4]

In 1968, he and Kitty moved to Beverly Hills. A series of health problems struck Bradley in 1975 at age eighty-two. He remained in poor health, often confined to a wheelchair for the next six years. Bradley died of a brain clot at age eighty-eight in 1981.

Bradley's reputation was badly mauled during the political fracas of the late 1940s and early 1950s. As chairman of the Joint Chiefs of Staff, he found himself an easy target for critics of the Truman administration. The attacks peaked during the run-up to the 1952 election, when Republican presidential primary candidate Bob Taft lambasted him and the Joint Chiefs of Staff in general, saying he would replace Bradley and the others if elected.

Taft was quickly criticized by Republicans as well as Democrats for introducing politics into discussions of the military and national security. This was considered out of bounds at the time, and perhaps the fact that Taft thought criticizing the JCS would gain him political points is more a comment on Taft's candidacy and competence than anything he said about Bradley.

Still, the criticism from this period remained in public currency. It was the background against which Bradley's first memoir, *A Soldier's Story,* was reviewed, coloring the reading (when the reviewers actually *read* the book they were commenting on, which was far from always). Some reviewers found his matter-of-fact style to be false modesty. *Time* magazine called him a "boastful winner" with a "persistent if disarming claim to near-infallibility."[5] Bradley was compared unanalytically to Patton, Eisenhower, and Montgomery, and always found wanting, though not on the basis of anything he had said in the book. The yardstick the reviewers were using was in fact their own views of the other leaders, based almost exclusively on the news reports that had run during the war.

The *New York Times* praised *A Soldier's Story* for concentrating on his portraits of other commanders, yet oddly claimed the book did not tell the reader much about who Bradley was.[6] Bradley was criticized for not taking enough blame for the Battle of the Bulge (surprisingly, as he takes more blame than any of the other generals who wrote about it). He was also criticized for not writing enough about the battles of Huertgen Forest. (In fact, Bradley spends about as much time on it as he does the rest of the battles that summer, and he describes it as horrific. But he does so without using the term adopted by historians to describe it. Nor does he separate it from the rest of the First Army campaign— natural, since the forest was not the Army's primary focus.) Bradley's achievements were notably missing from the review, which doubted the book would be of much value to future historians.

Thus, what might have been a moment to analyze Bradley's contributions to the war was lost in the controversies of the moment and the preconceived lines of the past. The Bulge was used as an example of failure. This was in keeping with the already accepted wisdom; initial reporting on the Bulge during the war had indicated it was a terrible setback, and this view remained cemented in popular culture and in the media. Even mention of lesser known struggles, such as those in the Huertgen Forest, complied with accepted wisdom: heavy casualties there must not have been due to the advantages of terrain and defense—to say nothing of the prowess of the German Army—but to failures of command...even if the writer had no idea what those failures actually were.

To a large extent, these sorts of reviews were merely reflections of an American cynicism toward authority. They didn't so much negate Bradley's achievements as imply that they didn't count, or perhaps more accurately, that Bradley didn't count. When D-Day was talked about, Eisenhower was important. It was Patton's army that marched across France.

Bradley was squeezed out, relegated to parenthetical notes, except when the subject of failure needed to be discussed. This was even true in encyclopedia accounts, critical information sources for students and the general public before the Internet.[7]

Other generals—Hodges, Collins, Truscott—can make at least some similar complaints. But none had Bradley's rank, nor were they involved in such a large portion of the war. And none published such a comprehensive and frank account of that participation.

To adapt an old cliché, five-star generals never actually retire; they just go around giving speeches. Bradley continued to make speeches and appearances through the 1950s. These were mostly generic, apolitical, and noncontroversial. They had no appreciable impact on the way he was viewed by the public, the media, or historians.

Bradley in fact had more or less slipped from public view by the mid-1960s when his first wife died, though as a living five-star general he was not exactly unknown within the Army. After he remarried, he journeyed to Vietnam as part of a story for *Look* magazine arranged by his wife. He was seventy-two at the time. He declared America's involvement as "a war in the right place, at the right time and with the right enemy—the Communists." It's difficult to know what sort of influence the story had with *Look's* readers; it seems not to have generated much controversy or notice, lost in the loud debate over the war.

The movie *Patton* came out in 1970. George C. Scott as Patton delivered a classic portrait, searing the image of the "blood and guts" general in the public mind.

Karl Malden starred as Bradley. Unsurprisingly given the film's subject matter, Bradley is a supporting character in the movie. The scenes in which he appears are, naturally, chosen to help portray Patton's character and exploits, not Bradley's. Therefore it's not very surprising that what most people remember from the film is the image of a hard-nosed Patton, not a calm and collected Bradley. The script considers Bradley sympathetically at several points, and even has the Germans praise him. But it doesn't give Bradley the full credit he deserves for guiding the American armies. And in the end, Scott's performance overwhelms Malden's characterization. If the movie didn't actually harm his reputation, it certainly did little to restore it.

Marshall, Eisenhower, Montgomery, and Patton have all had several major biographies, scholarly and popular, devoted to all or part of their lives. Bradley has had none.[8] All are relatively major characters in broad surveys of the war. Bradley is not.

Some of this, certainly in the arena of popular literature, is due simply to luck and timing. Publishers at different times would have been reluctant to compete with Bradley's own memoirs, and certainly during the late 1960s and 1970s, popular biographies of any general would have been, well, unpopular. And there is the changing fashion of histories—

what might be called "top-down" works have become much less popular since the immediate post-War period.

The types of histories of World War II most likely to reach the public now are largely about "regular joes"—the fathers and grandfathers of the present generation. While Bradley may be the closest thing to a "regular joe" among the commanding class of generals during that war, he is still a general.

Bradley's lack of name recognition hurt him as well. While this was due to many factors, it was largely an outgrowth of his personality. Bradley did not actively seek public attention for most of the war, and was very reluctant and late to use the media. While this sprang at least partly from his virtues—he thought publicity was akin to boasting—it also meant that there were far fewer stories about him in the press during the war than there were about other generals. His concern not to rock the boat—whether it belonged to Montgomery or SHAEF—reinforced a low profile in the press.

The cliché that "news stories are the first drafts of history" was never truer than in the case of World War II. While academics may criticize news accounts as unreliable and sensationalistic, there seems little doubt that they greatly influence many historians. *Every* book about Patton traces a character that was known to avid newspaper readers in 1943.

Finally, there is Bradley himself. If ever an undramatic figure walked across history's stage, it was Bradley. He was, by all accounts, a modest, "regular" guy. He liked to shoot, tried not to curse, rarely if ever drank to excess. He broke up fights rather than started them. Bradley's usual method of dealing with subordinates was to listen to their views. He usually agreed with people who made logical arguments. He was often conciliatory to those he didn't particularly like. And as a general rule, the angrier he became, the quieter he tended to be.[9]

These were important assets in the European war, when Bradley essentially had to wheedle his way into being allowed to win the war. But they are clearly not the sort of thing drama is made of, and like it or not, history is written with one eye toward drama.

More poignantly, the elements of Bradley's character that shine so brightly—humility, respect for authority, intelligence—have often been held in deep suspicion in post-War America. Someone who genuinely possessed them, such as Bradley, is deemed a little too good to be true.

But why is it that when Bradley appears in serious historical accounts, the figure bears so little resemblance to the actual man?

It certainly is not for lack of source material—both *A Soldier's Story* and Hansen's diary are fairly well-known to historians, even if the latter is only available in two places. Bradley's account, and to a certain degree Hansen's, underlie a number of historical works, directly or indirectly, credited or not. And while at points it is hard to know who really is talking in *A General's Life* (Bradley or his co-author Clay Blair), the book presents a fairly accurate image of the facts of his life.

Perhaps part of the problem is the fact that he has had no biography or major work devoted to his career, nothing to put his autobiography in context. Indeed, the main place he's found is in biographies focusing on Montgomery and Patton. There he's almost always a foil for the book's main subjects.

Montgomery's memoirs are notoriously revisionist, and most readers take them these days with a good dose of salt. His most anti-Bradley statements, however, generally work by implication. In the section on the Ardennes, for example, Montgomery claims that neither the First nor the Ninth Army commander had "seen"[10] Bradley during the battle—which naturally gives the reader the impression that Bradley was not in touch with them (patently false). It also implies than an army commander needed to have his group commander hold his hand during a crisis—something one imagines Montgomery would not have accepted when he was in that position. Indeed, one might ask how many times he visited Bradley during the Normandy battle, or stopped by for tea in Sicily.

Montgomery's view of Bradley has had enormous influence on British writers, especially as it dovetails with the criticisms of Bradley by other British leaders, such as Alan Brooke, who felt he had too much influence on Eisenhower. By this theory, Bradley prolonged the war by convincing Eisenhower not to let Montgomery run it.

Patton is a more complex and special case. His views on *everyone* are mercurial. He loves someone, he hates him—often at the same time. There are some devastating negative quotes about Bradley in his diary—and some absurdly positive ones as well. Take your pick.

Writers have often focused on the conflict between the men, or else engaged in a high-level version of "compare and contrast." Unfortunately, in many cases both men are caricatured. They *do* stand in contrast in some demonstrable ways. Patton was openly emotional; Bradley was not. Patton was a volatile terror to his subordinates, even those with great skill. If Bradley ever yelled at a subordinate in public, it's not recorded. But too much is made of other differences. It's very romantic to think of Patton as an intuitive dreamer who can look at a battlefield and conjure the future sweep of his army, but that simply didn't happen in real life. Patton's army could never have switched directions so completely during the Battle of the Bulge if it relied entirely on his intuition. By the same token, Bradley's hours staring at a map and his early obsession with walking the terrain to understand what tactics it dictated could just as easily be gilded with romantic overtures.

Occasionally, observers have seized on the differences in the two men's early army training and experiences as evidence that they had a radically different approach to the battlefield. In this view, Patton wanted a speedy, cavalry-like advance; Bradley was a plodding infantryman. Aside from somewhat off-base speculation about how cavalry and infantry were actually used on the battlefield, the contrast misses the point: both men wanted to advance as quickly as possible, knew this called for highly mobilized units, and attempted to use these units to the limits of their capability.

The main differences between Patton and Bradley were in their assessments of danger to their formations—Bradley tended to be somewhat more cautious than Patton, though perhaps it would be impossible for anyone to be otherwise. There are countless examples of times when Bradley was more willing to take risks than other generals, the Ardennes being exhibit A.

Sometimes the contrast can be quite subtle and even inadvertent, with no conscious intent to put Bradley down. In *Bitter Victory*, Carlo D'Este ends one paragraph speaking about the poor performance of landing craft and crews during training for the invasion of Sicily: "Bradley gloomily despaired over the dire consequences of such a performance on D-Day. With time running out, the pragmatic Bradley was entitled to deep concern...." In the very next sentence, Patton and, ironically, Montgomery are praised for a "philosophy of command...rooted in the belief that a commander's personal presence made a difference."[11] Bradley, of course, had the same philosophy. But the casual reader would hardly know that, and could certainly be forgiven for getting the impression from this unlucky juxtaposition that Bradley despaired while Patton marched on the front line.

One has to be careful about misreading developments and lessons learned during the war with actual differences between the two men. Bradley was able to integrate tactical air power with his advancing columns in France in a way that Patton could not in Africa. This was highly successful, and a real achievement. But does this mean that while Bradley was an advocate of air power, Patton was not?

Of course not. But why then call Patton a staunch advocate of tank tactics and Bradley—who used armor as much as Patton did—not?

The point is not that the two men weren't different; certainly they were. The point is that by focusing on the differences, neither man is seen accurately. But since Patton generally emerges as the more romantic figure, ultimately the assessment of Bradley is the one that suffers.

The changing fashions of historical writing in the years after the war multiplied this distortion. Novelistic techniques might have their place in the writing of history, but many writers using narrative techniques formerly used for fiction have found it necessary, or at least convenient, to portray Bradley in broad strokes, often as a foil to other characters.

Battle: The Story of the Bulge, by John Toland, contains no reference notes, but attempts to adhere to the historical record. Bradley comes off as colorless and a bit of a stick figure, especially in contrast to Patton. But the distortions are relatively benign, if somewhat laughable at times. Referring to Montgomery's attempt at reconciling matters with Bradley following the "return" of the First Army to Bradley's command, Toland says:

> Bradley put down the letter. It was obviously an effort to forget the past. As far as Bradley was concerned the past was also forgotten. There was a much bigger problem in hand: the final destruction of the German army.[12]

Whether Bradley really forgot the past is a debatable point, given what he says in his memoir. Still, it's not a distortion that affects Bradley's reputation very much. But in other hands, the use of the narrative technique can be absolutely toxic.

In *11 Days in December: Christmas at the Bulge, 1944,* Stanley Weintraub turns Bradley into the caricature of an out-of-touch general, trotting him out to set up a contrast with the *real* fighters or to establish whatever emotional counterpoint the author is striving for at the moment. The technique is transparent, and made all the worse by source notes that give the work the pretence of scholarship, when it would seem that the original sources were, to be kind, not studied in depth.

Weintraub—I am sorry to pick on him—ends his book with the comment, "Bradley, despite his weak role in the Bulge, became, in 1950, as chairman of the joint chiefs of staff during the Korean War, the last five-star general."[13] At least on the evidence of the book and Bradley's "weak role," one can only conclude that not only Bradley, but the entire American military and political establishment must have been completely out to lunch during both the world war and the Korean conflict.

Which actually is the larger point: Bradley has often been used as a hobbyhorse for a particular point an author is trying to get across. He's more often been a subconscious expression of a viewpoint than the subject of serious study.

So what can we say about Bradley in the end? What were his achievements during the war? His *actual* strengths, his *real* weaknesses?

He was, by all accounts, a modest man, humble in the best sense of the word. His personal values were those of small town, mid-Western America at the dawn of the twentieth century: honesty, charity towards one's neighbors, respect for others.

To these we might add industriousness, a belief in education, and the conviction that reason and intellect were crucial in life. He was neither a puritan nor a libertine; he was not overtly religious, but he refrained from cursing and drank relatively little. He was tolerant of divergent views on his staff, but was not particularly ahead of his time or enlightened in such things as race relations. Athletic in his youth, he liked hunting and gambling. He was good in math, and treated algebra as a hobby on par with doing crossword puzzles.

As a military man, Bradley was above all else an excellent tactician. He was praised on these grounds by men above and below him, at all points in the chain of command: Eisenhower, Collins, Gavin. He had an excellent knowledge of what his troops could achieve. He tended to let his commanders do their jobs, though he could step in when necessary. Above all he was approachable as a commander—he was open to reason and suggestion.

Aggressiveness in battle can be a difficult quality to measure, as it is often a vice as well as a virtue. Bradley was not as aggressive as Patton, but more so than Montgomery or Eisenhower; any assessment finer than that depends on an analysis of actual situations. But it is often the case that the accusations of his being overly cautious are the result of not understanding the conditions he faced, the shortages of supply or the paralyzing effect of his orders. Further, any assessment must take into account the strategic situation the Allied commanders faced as the war continued. At some point, it was clear to them that the only way the Germans could win the war was by an unexpected military stroke.

In other words, Bradley didn't just have to win the war—he had not to lose it. He had to fight in a way that prevented a catastrophic event—or what the Germans would think of as a bold, daring, imaginative, and risky strike that would suddenly reverse the odds. Bradley had to guard against what we would call today a "black swan event" while still being reasonably aggressive. The proof that he was able to do this is his reaction to the Bulge, where he alone correctly assessed the danger and the potential.

Bradley is sometimes criticized as being dull. But was it creative to use carpet bombing to escape the bocage? Was putting radios in tanks creative? Exploiting a bridge over the Rhine? Juggling supplies back and forth between two and then three and finally four armies?

On the other hand, how does one evaluate his failure when it came to projecting German intentions in the Ardennes? The best answer here is that Bradley was as creative as he needed to be under the circumstances; like all of us, his imagination occasionally failed.

Other achievements of Bradley's are rarely mentioned.

He helped shape the training methods and the doctrine used by the Army during World War II. He furthered the coordination of air and ground forces, making this the key to the outcome of the battle in Europe. Bradley did not invent the idea of integrated air power with ground attacks, but greatly helped in its implementation, both theoretically and then practically. This was a lasting achievement, as it influenced not only the war but American military doctrine during the post-war period.

He never went into combat as a division commander, but it must say something about his abilities that the 82nd Airborne, which he commanded stateside, became one of the Army's most elite units. Surely the commanders who succeeded him and the men themselves must get the lion's share of the credit, but Bradley left them a good base to start with, as he did in straightening out the 28th Infantry Division.

Working under Patton, Bradley helped reorganize and energize the Army in northern Africa. This came at a critical juncture in the war. Had a turnaround not been achieved, the rest of the war could easily have been run along the lines of the Sicilian campaign, where the Americans were relegated to a confused supporting role by British ground commanders.

Bradley organized the American invasion forces in Normandy. This was a dramatic logistical achievement. It was also decidedly undramatic—but that in itself might be a sign of his achievement.

Bradley then led the American invasion. There was more drama here, as well as personal danger and a good bit of dash. Bradley's somewhat matter-of-factness about it is a statement of his personality, and a realistic recognition on his part that his men faced considerably more danger than he did.

Bradley engineered the breakout from the Normandy beachhead at a time when both the American and British forces were stymied.

Bradley showed a great deal of flexibility in adding units to standard formations, leveraging American mobility and flexibility to battle. Overall, he established a tone of adaptability to changing combat conditions that was one of the U.S. Army's secret weapons in World War II.

Bradley established the conditions for the Third Army's drive across France in August 1944, adapting a very different Allied plan to the conditions on the battlefield. This involved flexibility and a willingness to accept risk.

Bradley directed the strategy and conditions that established the Allied victory at Falaise.

He worked closely with Patton and Hodges, encouraging both in their advances to the German border.

He recognized the opportunity presented by the German attack into the Ardennes before anyone else, and worked steadfastly to exploit it.

Bradley created the conditions that resulted in the crossing of the American Army over the Rhine. This hastened the end of the war.

Bradley cut off the possibility of a German retreat to a mountain redoubt, lessening the likelihood of a continuing guerrilla war.

Bradley prepared the Army for the immediate post-war occupation of Germany.

Bradley (and his staff) did all of the important though "boring" things required of an Army Group commander to keep his armies in the field, overcoming severe shortages and establishing the conditions necessary for victory. Despite the paucity of supplies reaching his theater at different points, Bradley was effective in helping his armies get those supplies to his units.

Bradley was able to deal effectively with his subordinates, assisting those who needed help, and getting out of the way of those who didn't. The latter is an extremely undervalued skill in a general officer.

His remarkable collaboration with George Patton contributed measurably to the war effort. Patton deserves enormous credit for finding the wherewithal to work under someone he had so recently commanded. But Bradley deserves credit as well. The relationship was not characterized by pettiness or disruptive grudges. On the contrary, Bradley gave Patton a critical role in the campaign, listened to his advice, and made effective use of his abilities as a commander. He was able to modify and occasionally reject Patton's plans without causing him to sulk or lose his aggressiveness. Often the subordinate commander operates in the shadows while his boss gets all the glory; that was reversed here, with no political backstabbing.

It may be true that, as Bradley says, Patton matured between Sicily and France. But this is difficult to perceive from the historical record, especially given Patton's troubles immediately after the war. The most obvious difference, in fact, is Bradley. It would be a mistake to give him too much credit for Patton's successes, or to claim that he was the secret author of Patton's war plans. But he does deserve more credit than he has been given. He worked closely with Patton, reviewing his plans and offering his advice and praise. Even if Patton had rejected everything Bradley said—which, clearly, he didn't do—no other commander had as fruitful a relationship with the brilliant but at times erratic general.

★ ★ ★ ★

Analyzing the campaigns in the European theater, historians have generally criticized American performance in three separate battles that were conducted under Bradley's overall leadership: closing the Falaise Gap, the actions grouped together as the Battle of the Huertgen Forest, and the Battle of the Bulge. Bradley's actions in each can be criticized at least to some extent:

Bradley must (and did) accept blame for the intelligence failure in the Ardennes. Whatever mitigating factors deserve to be mentioned, at the end of the day, he was in command. His orders weakened the line there, and he had a responsibility to remain not only vigilant but imaginatively vigilant about the possibilities of an attack. This is not to take away from his actions following the attack.

In the various battles of the Huertgen Forest, including the campaign for Aachen and the Rur, the case is slightly more complicated. Force changes were made, previous battles were studied, largely to no effect. Bradley's failure here might have sprung from what was often one of his strengths—allowing his commanders enough leeway to accomplish their missions. Just as likely, the situation there was so inherently difficult that problems were inevitable.

Today, the Allies' failure to close the Falaise Gap doesn't seem critical at all. A large part of the German Army was destroyed in the battle, and it is not at all clear that the gap could have closed *and held* in any event, given the units available.

Moreover, Bradley's initial instinct *was* to strike hard at the German force, but he was overruled. He had already put his alternative plan into effect when, belatedly, Montgomery changed his mind about what should be done. At that point, Bradley's moving more of Patton's forces into the pocket would have kept him from deploying Patton to drive farther east.

Beyond these battles, Bradley has been criticized for failing to fully appreciate the complications of the terrain in the bocage. The real problems here were the general location of the invasion area and the related need to secure Cherbourg; these presented obstacles that complicated the job for any commander. Once the problem was recognized, Bradley began addressing it. It's sometimes argued that he should have planned to incorporate British "Hobart's funnies" (specially modified tanks) in his D-Day battle plan, but it's difficult to find real evidence that these would have changed the battle. (Nor is it remembered that he *did* include the waterproofed tanks, with mixed results.) Clearing the bocage of enemy resistance was inevitably going to be a time-consuming, painstaking process, at least until the integration of air and ground power that Bradley introduced with Cobra.

Actually, Bradley's biggest failures were related to his personality and personal beliefs. As such, they are flipsides of his assets, difficult to remove or correct without completely changing the man.

The most obvious has to do with his use, or rather non-use, of the media. Bradley was very slow to understand that his success as a general required him to present a specific kind of image that was easily understood and appreciated: that of a bold, aggressive leader.

Patton continually bragged about the things he did to cement his image as "blood and guts." At one point he gave Bradley advice on the sort of weapon he should carry around. Ever the practical man, Bradley didn't take the advice—but he also didn't understand it.

Image was not just important in rallying his troops. A high profile in the media would have given Bradley's plans considerably more prestige; his armies, rather than Montgomery's, might have gotten the priority in Europe. Had that happened, the war might have been over before Christmas 1944, as many hoped in August of that year.

Bradley was also somewhat naïve and probably ignorant when it came to geopolitics, which hurt him more after the war than during. Nonetheless, a deeper understanding of world dynamics might have helped him make arguments designed to take Berlin more quickly. He might well have lost them, but at least posterity would have a better memory of him.

Omar Bradley was a regular guy who rose through the ranks by hard work and ability. He succeeded, not by cutting a dashing figure or garnering outrageous press, but by persevering. He was personable, intelligent, knowledgeable about war, and certainly brave, but it would be hard to say that he had more of these qualities than anyone else in the Allied command. He simply put his assets to work.

Which is how real wars are fought and won. If an army benefits from having a Patton, it truly succeeds when it has a Bradley to advise him, direct him, and supply him.

Beyond any of these accomplishments, Bradley shows us that a decent man, one whose values are still considered important by a good number of Americans, can and did succeed in one of the most severe crises in American history.

It is an encouraging lesson for us all.

APPENDIX OF MAPS

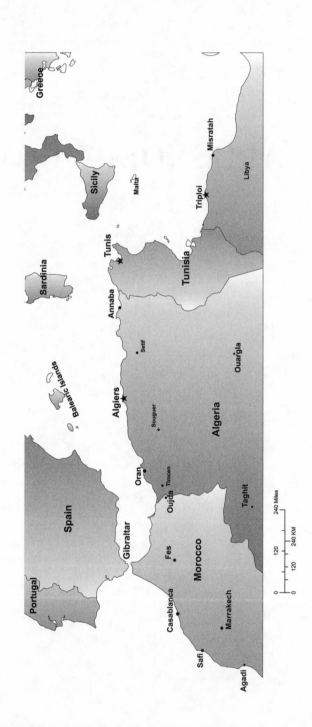

NORTH AFRICA & THE MEDITERRANEAN

TUNISIA: CLOSING IN

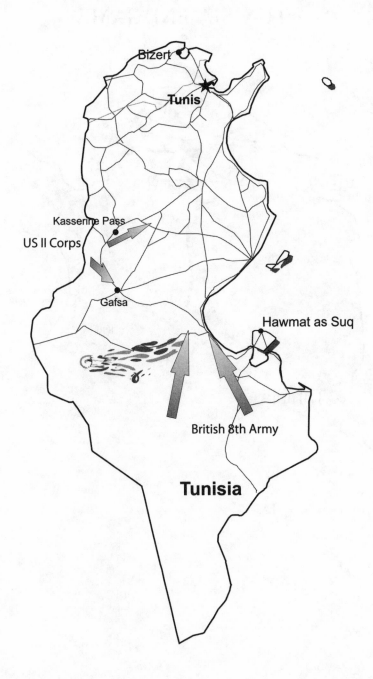

TUNISIA ENDGAME

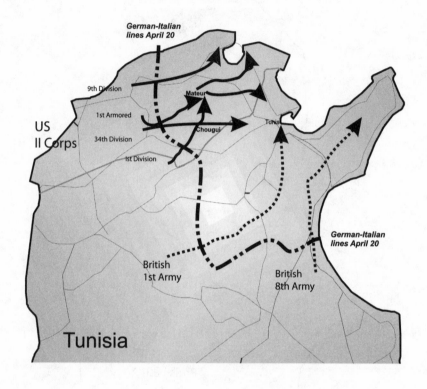

SICILY: OPERATION HUSKY

SICILY: AMERICAN ADVANCE

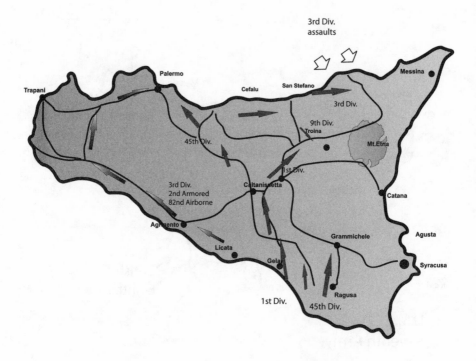

FRANCE: MAJOR CITIES

Dunkerque
Calais
Lille
Valenciennes
Cherbourg
Le Havre
Amiens
Rouen
Caen
Reims
Metz
Brest
Paris
Chalons-sur-Marne
Nancy
Strasbourg
Rennes
Troyes
Le Mans
Orleans
Mulhouse
Lorient
Angers
Tours
Dijon
St-Nazaire
Nantes
Bourges
Besancon
Poitiers
La Rochelle
Limoges
Lyon
Chambery
Clermont-Ferrand
St-Etienne
Grenoble
Bordeaux
Valence
Avignon
Nimes
Nice
Toulouse
Montpellier
Cannes
Bayonne
Pau
Marseille
Toulon
Perpignan

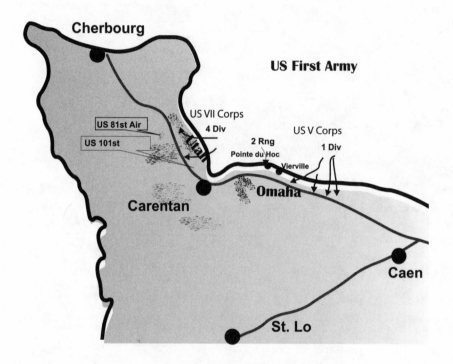

D-DAY INVASION BEACHES

Cherbourg

US First Army

US VII Corps

US 81st Air

4 Div

US 101st

Utah

US V Corps

2 Rng

1 Div

Pointe du Hoc

Vierville

Omaha

Carentan

Caen

St. Lo

FRANCE: AFTER COBRA

GERMANY: MAJOR CITIES

Sources &
Acknowledgments

M y primary sources for this biography have been the collections of General Omar Bradley's papers and the papers of his aide Chester Hansen in the Omar N. Bradley Collection at the United States Military Academy Library, housed in the Special Collections and Archives Division at West Point, New York.

West Point's wide-ranging collections include Bradley's personal and professional papers and documents from the period. (While the bulk are originals, a significant portion of the collection consists of photocopies of documents and other items collected elsewhere.) Of these, by far the most important items are Hansen's typewritten diaries, kept at the time. Hansen served with Bradley throughout World War II (and afterward).

While Hansen's diary is fairly candid, some of the entries toward the end give the impression that it was being kept as the basis for a future book. Hansen notes during September 1944 that the *Chicago Tribune* had asked to bid on Bradley's memoirs, and my supposition is that at some point thereafter (if not earlier), he began keeping the notes with an eye toward eventually writing the book.

As might be expected, Hansen is a strong advocate for his boss, and his entries must occasionally be considered in this light. There are two other limitations: First, for much of the war, Hansen and Bradley's other aide, Lewis Bridges, accompanied the general on alternate days. This somewhat limited Hansen's eye-witness accounts, though he often filled in quite well with details he learned elsewhere. Second, Bradley often conducted his planning conferences without his aide present, or at least instructed Hansen not to include them in his diary. Thus detailed discussions of most of these are missing from the notes. But these are minor caveats; overall, the diary is one of the most thorough accounts of a general officer's day to day conduct in a war ever kept.

Besides the various papers, of special interest at West Point were the collection of maps, including original maps used by General Bradley, those used by Dickson, and some intelligence photographs, including a handful of aerial reconnaissance pictures relating to the Ardennes offensive and the Rur (Roer) dams.

In addition, of considerable use were the papers of Benjamin A. "Monk" Dickson, also collected at West Point. The most valuable part of this modest collection was Dickson's unpublished memoir, *G-2 Journal: Algiers to the Elbe*, collected in typescript.

Though technically not part of these collections, the library's Joseph Fansler Petit Collection of World War II photographs taken by members of the U.S. Army Signal Corps document a portion of Bradley's tour in Europe, and were of considerable value as well.

Bradley published two memoirs, *A Soldier's Story* and *A General's Life*. Collaborators, fully credited, helped with both. They lie somewhere between primary and secondary sources.

A Soldier's Story, devoted to Bradley's experiences in World War II, was published in 1951. Written with Chet Hansen's help, much of the book is based on the contemporaneous diary that Hansen kept during the war, augmented by a series of interviews after the war. That diary still exists, as do notes and drafts of the book manuscript. While the prose clearly belongs to Hansen, there is no question that it accurately reflects not only what happened to Bradley but what he wanted to say about those events.

In a few instances, the descriptions are of things Hansen rather than Bradley saw, and at places it is apparent that Hansen's laudatory views of his boss crept into the book's tone, making Bradley sound slightly more self-satisfied than he probably was.

Bradley is relatively forthright in giving his opinions, with the probable exception of his sections on Eisenhower, whom he only criticizes for siding too often with Montgomery and the British. (Not coincidentally, Eisenhower was still in the Army and was running for president when the book was published.) Bradley went over the manuscript carefully, gave Hansen extensive interviews to supplement what he already had, and at that point was only a few years away from the events.

The book is a well-written model of the genre, somewhat less self-serving and congratulatory than many others. It has been used as a primary source in other works.

From an historical point of view, the real drawback to the book is its omissions. The two that are of interest here:

1) It does not go very deeply into tactical problems, which would be of great interest though admittedly to a very specialized audience.

2) It does not go into any great detail about several of the campaigns, especially when Bradley is army group commander. This is understandable: While the book is some 554 pages in the Modern Library Edition, it is still written for a general reader. More subtly, since the book was born from Hansen's notes, it depends very largely on what Hansen originally saw and recorded.

These drawbacks do not harm the material, nor take away from its value as a first-person account. Besides its own inherent value (and the value of the interviews Hansen conducted with Bradley, and the related material he compiled), the existence of Hansen's diary provides an excellent check on the work. Of course, we must always remember that the *function* of a memoir is to present a one-sided view of things to posterity. Bradley was a straight-shooter in the literal and figurative senses, but even his aim could occasionally get blurry.

Bradley's second memoir, *A General's Life,* was written with Clay Blair. This book is considerably more problematic as a representation of Bradley's thoughts.

Bradley died during the book's preparation; the only section of the book that he read, according to Blair, are the chapters about his years before World War II, which amount to eleven out of sixty-two.

Most if not all of the sources for Bradley's pre-war days are available in the West Point collection. They show that Blair followed them closely. The World War II sections track *A Soldier's Story,* though at times from a broader perspective. There are a few key differences, which seem in answer to controversies that arose following the first book's publication, but in general those sections align with the earlier work.

The post-war section, which among other things deals with Korea and Bradley's time as Chief of Staff, is not directly applicable to this work.

Bradley's death obviously presented Blair with numerous problems, chief among them the fact that the general was not there to add anything beyond what Blair could find from earlier interviews and notes, including *A Soldier's Story.* It is therefore not surprising that much of the book reads as if it is based on third person sources.

Blair notes in the preface to the book that he went to great lengths to assure the accuracy of what is in it. Among other things, he submitted the manuscript to a number of historians, to Hansen, and to Bradley's second wife, having them check it for factual accuracy.

Putting aside the subjectivity of those he consulted—a not insignificant factor—such a process is limited at best to the "known" facts at hand. No "distinguished historian" can say exactly what Bradley felt the moment he first heard a shell flying overhead in Africa. And it is exactly for that piece of information that we turn to an autobiography.

Blair said that he "conscientiously endeavored not to impute any view or opinion to him that I could not verify from at least two sources."

The limits of that approach—a rule taken from daily newspapers, most famously popularized during the Watergate and post-Vietnam era during which he was working—are fairly obvious. Blair recognized the problem and considered publishing a biography instead. He doesn't make clear in the prologue why he decided not to do this, though one imagines that the original book contract had something to do with it. In any event, the book was presented as a memoir, and it is far closer to that than a biography. It can be taken as an accurate account of the events in Bradley's life. As a first-person account of Bradley's opinions on them, however, it can be problematic.

Among other important primary source materials were General Eisenhower's papers, *The Papers of Dwight David Eisenhower*, Volumes I–IV, edited by Alfred D. Chandler Jr., Stephen E. Ambrose, et al, (Baltimore: The John Hopkins Press, 1970–1978). Also important were Patton's diary entries and letters from the period, conveniently collected and edited by Martin Blumenson in *The Patton Papers, 1940-1945* (New York: Da Capo Press, 1996).

The use of other first-person accounts and documents outside of these sources is credited where appropriate below and in the footnotes.

Secondary Sources

I relied on a large number of books and other secondary material as I worked on this book. This does not mean that I necessarily agreed with all their conclusions, of course, but in many cases that made them even more helpful.

The following were the most useful:

Books

Ambrose, Stephen E. *Eisenhower and Berlin, 1945*. New York: W.W. Norton, 1967.

———. *Eisenhower: Soldier & President*. New York: Simon & Schuster, 1990.

———. *The Supreme Commander*. Garden City, N.Y.: Doubleday & Company, 1970.

Astor, Gerald. *Terrible Terry Allen*. New York: Ballantine Books, 2003.

Atkinson, Rick. *An Army at Dawn*. New York: Henry Holt and Company, 2002.

———. *The Day of Battle*. New York: Henry Holt & Company, 2007.

Baron, Richard, Abe Baum, and Richard Goldhurst. *Raid! The Untold Story of Patton's Secret Mission*. New York: G.P. Putnam's Sons, 1981.

Barr, Niall. *Pendulum of War: The Three Battles of El Alamein*. Woodstock, NY: The Overlook Press, 2004.

Beevor, Antony. *D-Day: The Battle of Normandy*. New York: Viking, 2009.

Bigland, Thomas S. *Bigland's War: War Letters of Tom Bigland*. South Wirral, England: T. S. Bigland, 1990. (Self-published)

Blumenson, Martin. *The Patton Papers 1940-1945*. New York: Da Capo Press, 1990.

———. *Kassarine Pass*. Boston: Houghton Mifflin Company, 1967.

Brereton, Lewis H. *The Brereton Diaries*. New York: William Morrow and Company, 1946.

Butcher, Harry C. *My Three Years with Eisenhower*. New York: Simon & Schuster, 1946.

Brendon, Piers. *Ike: His Life and Times*. New York: Harper & Row, 1985.

Burgett, Donald R. *Seven Roads to Hell*. Novato, California: Presidio, 1999.

Carafano, James Jay. *After D-Day*. Boulder, Colorado: Lynne Rienner Publishers, 2000.

Chandler, Alfred D. Jr., Stephen E. Ambrose, et al, editors. *The Papers of Dwight David Eisenhower. The War Years: I-IV.* Baltimore: The John Hopkins Press, 1970.

Cole, Hugh. *The Ardennes: The Battle of the Bulge.* Old Saybrook, CT.: Konecky & Konecky. (No publication date given; text is a reprint of official Army history, with Defense Department maps.)

Cray, Ed. *General of the Army.* New York: W.W. Norton & Company, 1990.

D'Este, Carlo. *Bitter Victory.* New York: E.P. Dutton, 1988.

———. *Decision in Normandy.* New York: Harper Collins, 1994 (anniversary edition).

———. *Patton: A Genius for War.* New York: Harper Collins, 1995.

Doubler, Michael D. *Closing with the Enemy.* Lawrence, Kansas: University Press of Kansas, 1994.

Eisenhower, Dwight D. *Crusade in Europe.* Garden City, NY: Doubleday & Co, 1948.

Eisenhower, John S. D. *The Bitter Woods.* New York: G.P. Putnam's Sons, 1969.

Gavin, James M. *On to Berlin.* New York: The Viking Press, 1978.

Gelb, Norman. *Ike & Monty: Generals at War.* New York: William Morrow & Company, 1994.

Gilbert, Martin. *Churchill: A Life.* New York: Henry Holt & Company, 1991.

Hastings, Max. *Armageddon—The Battle for Germany 1944-1945.* New York: Vintage Books, 2004.

———. *Overlord.* New York: Simon & Schuster, 1984.

Hirshson, Stanley. *General Patton: A Soldier's Life.* New York: Harper Collins, 2002.

Horne, Alistair, and David Montgomery. *Monty: The Lonely Leader, 1944-1945.* New York: Harper Collins, 1994.

Hughes, Thomas Alexander. *Over Lord.* New York: The Free Press, 1995.

Hynes, Samuel, Anne Matthews, et al, editors. *Reporting World War II,* Part One & Part Two. New York: The Library of America, 1995.

Keegan, John. *Six Armies in Normandy.* New York: Penguin, 1994.

Kelly, Orr. *Meeting the Fox.* New York: John Wiley & Sons, 2002.

Kershaw, Alex. *The Longest Winter.* Cambridge, Mass: DaCapo Press, 2004.

MacDonald, Charles B. *The Last Offensive* (U.S. Army in World War II, European Theater of Operations). Washington, D.C.: Office of the Chief of Military History, 1973.

———. *Mighty Endeavor.* New York: William Morrow (Quill Edition), 1986.

———. *The Siegfried Line Campaign* (U.S. Army in World War II, European Theater of Operations). Washington, D.C.: Center of Military History, U.S. Army, 1990.

———. *A Time for Trumpets.* New York: William Morrow, 1985.

Manchester, William. *American Caesar.* New York: Dell, 1978.

Mitcham, Samuel W. Jr. and Friedrich von Stauffenberg. *The Battle of Sicily.* New York: Orion Books, 1991.

Montgomery, Bernard. *The Memoirs of Field-Marshal the Viscount Montgomery of Alamein*, K.G. Cleveland: The World Publishing Co., 1958.

Neill, George W. *Infantry Soldier: Holding the Line at the Battle of Bulge.* Norman, Oklahoma: University of Oklahoma Press, 2000.

Nichols, David, editor. *Ernie's War—The Best of Ernie Pyle's World War II Dispatches.* New York: Random House, 1986.

Nordyke, Phil. *All American All the Way.* Minneapolis, MN: Zenith Press, 2005.

Patton, George S. Jr. *War As I Knew It.* Boston: Houghton Mifflin Company, 1975. (Original edition 1947)

Payne, Robert. *The Marshall Story: A Biography of General George C. Marshall.* New York: Prentice-Hall Inc., 1951.

Perry, Mark. *Partners in Command.* New York: The Penguin Press, 2007.

Pogue, Forest C. *Education of a General.* New York: Viking, 1963. (George C. Marshall, vol. 1)

————. *Ordeal and Hope.* New York: Viking, 1966. (George C. Marshall, vol. 2)

————. *Organizer of Victory.* New York: Viking, 1973. (George C. Marshall, vol. 3)

————. *Statesman.* New York: Viking, 1987. (George C. Marshall, vol. 4)

Price, Frank James. *Troy H. Middleton.* Baton Rouge: Louisiana State University Press, 1974.

Pyle, Ernie. *Brave Men.* New York: Grosset & Dunlap, 1944.

Reeder, Red (Russel Potter). *Born at Reveille,* New York: Duell, Sloan and Pearce, 1966.

Roberts, Andrew. *Masters and Commanders.* New York: Harper Perennial, 2009.

Summersby, Kay. *Eisenhower Was My Boss.* New York: Prentice-Hall, 1948.

Summersby Morgan, Kay. *Past Forgetting: My Love Affair with Dwight D. Eisenhower.* New York: Simon & Schuster, 1976.

Tobin, James. *Ernie Pyle's War.* New York: The Free Press, 1997.

Toland, John. *Battle: The Story of the Bulge.* New York: Random House, 1959.

————. *The Last 100 Days.* New York: Bantam Books, 1985.

Truscott, Lucian. *Command Missions: A Personal Story.* New York: E.P. Dutton and Company, 1954.

Weintraub, Stanley. *11 Days in December.* New York: Free Press, 2006.

Whitaker, W. Denis and Shelagh. *Rhineland.* New York: St. Martin's Press, 1989.

Wiegley, Russell F. *Eisenhower's Lieutenants.* Bloomington, Indiana: Indiana University Press, 1981.

Wijers, Hans. *Battle of the Bulge.* Mechanicsburg, PA.: Stackpole Books, 2009.

Miscellaneous Articles & Websites

A large number of contemporary news and magazines articles are included in the collections listed above. In addition to sources in the Bradley and Dickson collections, a few articles and websites found outside those sources were very useful to me as I prepared this work. Among the most important were:

Berlin, Dr. Robert H. "U.S. Army World War II Corps Commanders: A Composite Biography." U.S. Army Command and General Staff College, 1989.

Billings, Linwood W. "The Tunisian Task Force." U.S. Army War College. Retrieved via http://historicaltextarchive.com/sections.php?action=read&artid=190.

Carr, Vincent M. Jr. "The Battle of Kasserine Pass: An Examination of Allied Operational Failings." Research Report, Air Command and Staff College, Air University, April 2003.

Collier, Thomas. "The Army and the Great Depression." *Parameters.* September 1988.

Johnson, Richard H. "Investigation into the Reliefs of Generals Orlando Ward and Terry Allen." U.S. Army Command and General Staff College (Monograph), 2009.

Muller, Edwin. "How the Rhine Battle Was Planned." *Reader's Digest*, June 1945.

Steadman, Kenneth A. "The Evolution of the Tank in the U.S. Army." Combat Studies Institute. U.S. Army Command and General Staff College, April 21, 1982.

Stubbs, Mary Less and Stanely Russel Connor, "Armor-Cavalry: Part 1, Regular Army and Army Reserve/Armored Force." U.S. Army Center for Military History. Retrieved via http://en.wikisource.org/wiki/ARMOR-CAVALRY:_Part_1;_Regular_Army_and_Army_Reserve/Armored_Force.

Swiercek, Nicholas. "Stoking a White Backlash: Race, Violence, and Yellow Journalism in Omaha, 1919." Paper at James A. Rawley Graduate Conference in the Humanities, University of Nebraska, Lincoln, 2008.

"World Battlefronts, Western Front: Destroy the Enemy." *Time* Magazine, December 4, 1944.

"World: Doughboy's General." *Time* Magazine, May 1, 1944.

Interview with Lt. General Harry W. O. Kinnard. Retrieved via http://www.thedropzone.org/europe/Bulge/kinnard.html

Howitzer Yearbook Collection, USMA Library at West Point.

USMA Library at West Point, collections: Folder of miscellaneous letters belonging to Colonel W. H. Britton (West Point student one year behind Bradley; two letters contain personal views of Bradley as a student.)

Background Sources

In addition to the sources listed above and those listed in the footnotes, I relied on a large number of background sources as I prepared this book. Most especially, the official histories of the war, now available online through the Army history website, provided a critical starting point for my understanding of the battles. (The website is www.history.army.mil. In a few cases I made use of print editions of these works as well, most notably in the case of Cole and MacDonald, and have listed these under books.)

Additional sources for each chapter include the following:

Introduction:

The description of Bradley's arrival is drawn primarily from *A Soldier's Story*, pages 28–31. I should note that here and in scenes where dialogue is italicized, the actual words are based on primary source material, but are not direct quotes.

Chapter One:

Much of my description of Bradley's early life is drawn from *A General's Life*. The portion of the book covering his early life, much of it based on Bradley's self-written but unpublished memoir, was reviewed and approved by Bradley prior to his death. Additional material on his early days, similar to that in the autobiography though with slightly different emphasis and more details, comes from Colonel George Pappas, recorded in Beverly Hills, California, August 14, 1969, and included in the West Point collection. (The interview is also used extensively for the opening chapter of *A General's Life*.)

Background on Patton is drawn from Carlo D'Este, *Patton: A Genius for War,* and Stanley P. Hirshon, *General Patton: A Soldier's Life,* as well as Martin Blumenson, *The Patton Papers 1940-1945.*

Chapter Two:

The scene at the beginning of this chapter, along with the quotes, are from *A Soldier's Story.* Some of the description of the North African battles is drawn from Pyle's accounts and Patton's diary.

My perspective on the African battles was aided by the official history of the United States Army in World War II Mediterranean Theater of Operations, "Northwest Africa: Seizing the Initiative in the West," by George F. Howe (Washington, D.C.: Office of the Chief of Military History, Department of the Army, 1957). Howe's work is the starting point and basis of many accounts of the battle.

Useful analyses as well as archival data relating to the Kasserine battles prior to Bradley's arrival are stored in a variety of places. Of interest and easily accessed are a series of PDF documents gathered at the Army history website, www.history.army.mil/books/Staff-Rides/kasserine/kasserine.htm. The material is, in effect, a seminar course in the battles.

Rick Atkinson's *An Army at Dawn* (New York: Henry Holt, 2002); Martin Blumenson, *Kasserine Pass* (Boston: Houghton Mifflin Company, 1967); and Orr Kelly, *Meeting the Fox* (New York: John Wiley and Sons, 2002) were all useful to my understanding of the campaign.

Among the best descriptions of the battles from the soldier's viewpoint were those written by Ernie Pyle and included in his book, *Brave Men* (1944: New York: Grosset & Dunlap). The book is based on columns written in 1943 and 1944.

Chapter Three:

Among the books that helped me understand and describe the battles on Sicily were Rick Atkinson's *The Day of Battle* (New York: Holt and Company 2007); Carlo D'Este, *Bitter Victory* (E.P. Dutton); and Samuel W. Mitcham Jr. and Friedrich von Stauffenberg, *The Battle of Sicily* (New

York: Orion Books, 1991). The last is subtitled "How the Allies lost their chance for total victory," which gives an indication of its slant.

Pyle's descriptions from *Brave Men* were once again extremely useful, as were news accounts from the period.

Chapters Four, Five & Six:

There is a mountain of literature available on D-Day. Among the most valuable to me while preparing this book were Charles B. Mac-Donald, *The Mighty Endeavor*, updated edition (NY: William Morrow/ Quill Edition, 1986); John Keegan, *Six Armies in Normandy*, updated edition (NY: Penguin, 1994); Max Hastings, *Overlord* (NY: Simon and Schuster, 1984); and Anthony Beevor, *D-Day*(New York: Viking, 2009). James Jay Carafano, *After D-Day*, provided a thorough background on the Cobra breakout, and in my opinion is the best book on the subject.

Eisenhower's Lieutenants by Russel F. Weigley (Bloomington: Indiana University Press, 1981) added substantially to my overview of the battles.

Chapters Seven & Eight:

Charles B. MacDonald, *A Time for Trumpets* (New York: William Morrow and Company, 1985); Hugh Cole, *The Ardennes: The Battle of the Bulge* (with maps and illustrations in the Konecky & Konecky oversized edition, Old Saybrook, Connecticut); and Hans Wijers, *Battle of the Bulge*, Volumes 1 and 2 (Mechanicsburg, PA: Stackpole Books, 2009). Again, *Eisenhower's Lieutenants*, by Russel F. Weigley (Bloomington: Indiana University Press, 1981) provided an important perspective.

Acknowledgements & Thanks:

I was helped by many people, directly and indirectly, as I worked on this book.

My wife Debra Scacciaferro assisted me on this project by doing a great deal of research and offering comments on the manuscript. As always, she was a true partner and coauthor on this work.

Many thanks to the staff at the United States Military Academy Library at West Point. Suzanne M. Christoff, Associate Director for Special Collections and Archives, was generous in arranging extended access to the Omar N. Bradley Collection, where we were given unlimited access to papers, maps, photographs, scrapbooks, and books, along with the other collections and support material cited. Her staff was immensely kind and helpful, especially Susan M. Lintelmann (Mansucripts Curator—English Liaison), Deborah A. McKeon-Pogue (Library Technician), and Alicia M. Mauldin-Ware (Archives Curator), who went out of their way to find obscure documents and items. They offered valuable guidance in tackling such a large collection. Also thanks to Elaine B. McConnell, Acting Associate Director for Access Services—Rare Book Curator—Foreign Languages Liaison, who guided us to rare military memoirs and autobiographies from the general library collection. Reference Librarian Alan C. Aimone generously shared his extensive knowledge of websites, collections, and centennial information about General Bradley, and led us to a rare West Point collection of war photographs that included a number of pictures of General Bradley. Librarian technician Casey Madrick processed the photos.

Current West Point Professor V. Frederick Rickey, a member of the Department of Mathematical Sciences, has compiled data on the history of math classes and teaching at the Point, including information on Omar Bradley. He quite generously shared this information with my wife during her research. He currently maintains a series of web pages regarding mathematical history accessible through the Military Academy web site.

Major Dan Nettling prepared a bibliography of material relating to General Bradley in 1993. His bibliography includes a number of sources that could easily be overlooked by even the most diligent researcher.

The West Point Library's large collection of books on the war and military history were a ready and helpful supplement to the source material. The knowledge and helpful staff made our work not only easier, but very pleasant. In addition, a significant portion of the secondary sources I read and consulted while working on this book were obtained through inter-library loan from the Ramapo-Catskill Library System. Their diligence and efforts, not just in helping me but in building the combined collection, made my work considerably easier. My overdue fines, though considerable, could never begin to repay them.

At Regnery Publishing, my editor Harry Crocker III had faith in the book before many others. Managing editor Mary Beth Baker was not only efficient and effective, but is surely one of the nicest people in publishing. Farahn Morgan in editorial and Amanda Larsen in graphic design also helped make the book better. I appreciate as well the efforts of the marketing department and the salespeople, without whom there would be no readers.

My agent, Jake Elwell at Harold Ober Associates, encouraged me at all stages of the process.

Finally, a large number of friends and acquaintances gave me advice and suggestions as I worked on this book. While I didn't always take their advice, their feedback was important.

And after saying all that, let me add that all of the mistakes are my own.

In a small number of cases, I have recreated dialogue based on source material. While I believe these accurately reflect the conversations, rather than place the material in quotes, I have rendered it in italics.

For more photos, maps, corrections, and updates, visit me at www. jimdefelice.com.

I welcome corrections to the record, and will endeavor to post them when possible.

Notes

CHAPTER 1

1.   Omar Bradley and Clay Blair, *A General's Life* (New York: Simon & Schuster, 1983), 19. The squirrel story appears in Bradley's interviews with Allean G. G. Lottle and Courtney M. Rittgers, collected at West Point. Bradley doesn't give his age in either of the interviews or the autobiography, but it clearly happened well before he was twelve, and more than likely when he was eight or nine.

   One imagines that Bradley told this story about himself throughout his life, perhaps to illustrate various points, altering it slightly. It seems somewhat curious that he would not have sighted the weapon himself before setting out, and one wonders if the real cause of his missing was the difficulty of controlling the weapon's recoil. His shooting quickly improved—a not unexpected consequence of his getting bigger as well as more experienced.

2.   Bradley and Blair, *A General's Life*, 18.

3.   Ibid., 17.

4. The data are from the U.S. Bureau of the Census.

5. Omar Bradley, "Address at the Dedication of Bradley Post Office, Bradley, West Virginia, July 10, 1953," in *The Collected Writings of General Omar Bradley*, speeches 1950-1957, Volume II (West Point archives).

6. Bradley and Blair, *A General's Life*, 20.

7. In a photo supplied by Bradley or his wife to accompany a profile in *Life* magazine (published June 5, 1944), we see John as a solid, well-built man of barely average height, with a moustache and buttoned suit, posing with one hand on his six-year-old son. Omar's mother, in a black dress, is the only one with a hint of a smile.

8. Bradley and Blair, *A General's Life*, 20.

9. Omar Bradley, "Address at the Dedication of Bradley Post Office."

10. The Diary of Chester Hansen (unpublished), 1942–1945. April 23, 1943 (West Point archives). On that day, Bradley told the story to some men who had just been wounded in battle; one wonders whether they found it nearly as amusing as the general did.

11. The cause of John Bradley's pneumonia was not recorded. Comments in the local newspaper and Omar Bradley's own remembrances make it likely that the infection was common in town at the time, though whether it was bacterial or viral is impossible to say.

12. *Higbee Weekly News*, quoted in Bradley and Blair, *A General's Life*, 22.

13. Clay Blair noted that a "casual observer" of the school records could not find evidence that Omar Bradley had been placed back a year and then promoted. But he placed these doubts in a footnote, and there seems no reason to question Bradley's memory.

14. The average pay for all railroad workers in 1910 was $2.23 a day, according to Bulletin 34 of the Bureau of Railway Economics, Washington, D.C., June 1912. Quoted in F. A. Fetter, *Source Book in Economics* (Whitefish, Montana: Kessinger Publishing, LLC, 2008).

15. Bradley and Blair, *A General's Life*, 26. Bradley told the story throughout his life, and it appears in a variety of places.

16. Ibid., 27.

17. Ibid.

18. Ibid., 28.

19. The data on graduates are from the Smithsonian National Museum of American History webpage, West Point in the Making of America, http://americanhistory.si.edu/westpoint/history_6b.html (accessed October 19, 2010).

20. Bradley and Blair, *A General's Life*, 30.

21. Piers Brendon, *Ike, His Life and Times* (New York: Harper & Row, 1986), 38.

22. Quoted from the West Point yearbook 1915, Bradley's page.

23. Bradley and Blair, *A General's Life*, 33–34.

24. Quotes and descriptions, Bradley and Blair, *A General's Life*, 36–37. Perhaps it's only fair to note that *A General's Life* was written very late in Bradley's life and with the help of his second wife. While Omar and Mary are said to have written to each other every week for several years before their marriage, the letters do not appear in Mary's scrapbooks. Clay Blair wrote that they had been destroyed or lost.

25. Bradley and Blair, *A General's Life*, 40.

26. Interview of General of the Army Omar Bradley by Colonel George Pappas, recorded in Beverly Hills, California, August 14, 1969 (West Point collection).

27. The quote is from Bradley and Blair, *A General's Life*, 42–44, which here is based partly on Bradley's unpublished memoir of his early days. For train fares, see the case of *State v. Dickinson*, heard in Kansas in 1917 and recorded in *The Pacific Reporter*, Volume 168 (accessed through Google Books). Interstate fares were regulated at 2.4 cents per mile both in Missouri and Kansas. The actual fare was likely much lower. In any event, he did not go out of his way to bring his mother to his wedding.

    As for a best man, Bradley did have an Army friend whom he considered, but the friend was on duty, and Bradley apparently didn't want to put him to the trouble of standing up for him.

28. Bradley and Blair, *A General's Life*, 43.

29. The Industrial Workers of the World, IWW, was one of the leading forces of the union movement in the early twentieth century, though it was smaller than organizations such as AFL and CIO. Advocating aggressive tactics and not shy about criticizing capitalists and politicians who backed them, the Wobblies recruited blacks, women, and immigrants into their ranks at a time when this was highly unusual. They attempted to organize unions by industry, rather than skill or craft level, a more common approach at the time. Using work slowdowns, sit down strikes, and general strikes aimed at closing an entire community, the Wobblies were considered more aggressive than most other unions, with a more radical and activist outlook. Most of their leaders saw the world divided into two classes—workers and capitalists—and they were decidedly on the side of

the workers. While not necessarily Communist, much of the leadership viewed history through the lens Marx and Engle provided.

The IWW opposed America's entry into World War I, passing a resolution at the union convention in November 1916. While support for the war was hardly universal—President Wilson had just won reelection on a slogan that he had kept the United States out of it—the IWW's strong criticism of the conflict and U.S. involvement helped turn much public opinion against the union. It was in Butte, Montana, in August 1917, just before Bradley's assignment there, that IWW leader Frank Little was lynched while helping organize a strike against the Anaconda Copper Company. At the time, Anaconda was one of the largest and most powerful trusts in the country, controlled by Henry Huttleson Rogers and William Rockefeller. The perpetrators were never caught, and while there are many theories, it is generally believed that the murderers were either hired or encouraged by people in the company. Little's activities in town included speeches against the war and the Army, which a number of local men had recently joined. He called the president a tyrant and troops "scabs in uniform," so there were plenty of emotions besides anti-unionism in the air.

30. Some of the information on Montana's sedition laws and related political strife comes from Clemens P. Work, *Darkest Before Dawn: Sedition and Free Speech in the American West* (Albuquerque: University of New Mexico Press, 1995). Dunn's family spelled their last name with an "e"—Dunne. However, during this period and for a significant portion of his life he left the "e" off, and I have followed that practice here.

31. Omar Bradley personal scrapbook (West Point archives).

32. I was unable to locate documents relating to the trial. The accusations were made during a period of racial unrest, when lurid and often unfounded complaints against blacks were common, as was white on black violence.

33. Photo, *Life* magazine, June 5, 1944. Bradley or his wife apparently supplied the photo which accompanied the story, Christian Wertenbaker, "Omar Nelson Bradley: History and 'the plan' place greatness within the grasp of a quiet man from Missouri."

34. See Press release, February 24, 1975, "The Scottish Rite," Cincinnati, Ohio, in Omar Bradley, *Collected Writings* Vol. VI (unpublished), 107–9 (West Point archives).

35. Bradley and Blair, *A General's Life*, 51.

36. Ibid., 58. Exactly how much he ever drank is open to interpretation. He was not a teetotaler, but certainly in the context of the times he would have seemed something of an abstainer.

37. Ibid., 59.
38. Forrest C. Pogue, *Education of a General* (New York: Viking, 1963), 254. Bradley wrote the foreword to the book.
39. Quoted in Ibid., 258.
40. Pappas interview.
41. Ibid.
42. Marshall, Bradley fitness report.
43. "Mobility" is sometimes misunderstood (and misused) by historians to apply *only* to the combat phase of battle, and epitomized by the marrying of armor and infantry. While that was certainly a central concept during World War II, Bradley understood mobility to be a far more encompassing quality. It included the Army's ability to quickly shift its units from one part of the battlefield to another—an ability essential to the broad front strategy adopted by Eisenhower at Bradley's urging.

    Mobility was *the* critical component in the supply and logistics of armies across battered lands—France 1944, for example. And mobility allowed the army not only to efficiently and effectively combine arms such as artillery and infantry, but to mass those arms for maximum power.
44. See Marshall's comments on machine guns and the communications gear in Pogue, *Education of a General*, 258. The probable result would have been to diminish the use of the weapons in combat.
45. Pappas interview.
46. Omar Bradley, *A Soldier's Story* (New York: Modern Library, 1999), 19.
47. Bradley's personal library at the end of his life included two different volumes on betting; both were annotated. The books are in the West Point collection. The notes appear to include tallies of winnings.
48. Thomas W. Collier points out that more than budget appropriations were to blame for the Army's lack of innovation in weapons development during the years between the wars. The service's top leadership was stagnant intellectually, unable or unwilling to recognize how much warfare had changed. It is not surprising that the people pushing hardest for reform—men like Marshall—were colonels rather than generals. Collier's assessments are found in "The Army and the Great Depression," *Parameters*, September 1988, 102–8.
49. Bradley and Blair, *A General's Life*, 638. Blair does not source the tart expression "right-wing primitives."
50. Ibid., 71.
51. Ibid., 93–94.

52. Officially, Bradley's appointment to general was temporary. The United States was still using a two-track system of permanent and temporary (or war) ranks for the officer corps, though this would soon be disbanded. The temporary ranks were higher as a rule than the permanent ranks.
53. Omar Bradley, "Remarks at a Conference of the Defense Department, Civilian and Military Officials," Quantico, Virginia, July 25, 1953, in *Collected Writings of General Omar N. Bradley, Speeches 1950-1967*, Volume II (West Point collection).
54. In his diary, Hansen uses "Li" to refer to her.
55. Bradley told this to Hansen. See Hansen's diary entry December 27, 1944.

CHAPTER 2

1. Bradley's claim about passing unnoticed on the hike is in *A General's Life* (110). Generals are always dreaming of passing unnoticed among their men, a la Shakespeare's *King Henry V*. But even during World War II, a 49-year-old would have tended to stand out among the younger men, and it would have been a dull private indeed who didn't realize the "old man" marching next to him was someone *very* important.
2. West Point was about forty minutes away by car, close enough for Elizabeth to travel every weekend. Conveniently, she was seeing a West Point cadet, so undoubtedly her visits to her mother's temporary home were doubly motivated.
3. The Army sent messages over a special phone communications system known as TWX. The letters TWX came from Teletypewriter Exchange System, established by AT&T in the 1930s. The system used special typewriters at each end, and would be roughly the equivalent of email today. The term "cable" was often used generically to describe the same type of message.
4. Orr Kelly, *Meeting the Fox* (New York: John Wiley & Sons, 2002), 149.
5. Eisenhower Papers, 951.
6. There is also the question of Mark Clark, who had been appointed to head the Fifth Army, on guard against what proved to be a nonexistent threat from Spain in Morocco and Algiers. Moving Clark over would have in effect demoted him, but Eisenhower had his own misgivings about him as well.
7. In fact, Marshall later made this suggestion. The situation at II Corps deteriorated before Bradley arrived, and Eisenhower ended up offering the corps commander post to Ernie Harmon. Harmon felt he couldn't take the job since he had recommended that Fredendall be sacked.

8. During the Casablanca meetings, Marshall tried to persuade Roosevelt to promote Eisenhower, arguing that he needed a fourth star to keep up with the British he was supposedly commanding. Presidential aide Harry Hopkins related in his diary how he had come in on the end of a discussion with the president about it; Roosevelt made it clear that he wasn't impressed, at least not enough to give Eisenhower a fourth star. "He hasn't knocked the Germans out of Tunisia," Harry Hopkins noted. See for some discussion about Eisenhower, Robert E. Sherwood, *Roosevelt and Hopkins* (New York: Harper & Brothers, 1948). There is no documentary evidence revealing Bradley as a backup for any of the positions.

9. The passage is from Pyle's column dated February 23, 1944. Quoted in *Ernie's War*, ed. David Nichols (New York: Random House, 1986), 88.

10. *A Soldier's Story,* 37.

11. Every description of Tebessa and Djebel Kouif seems to differ on their exact location and relationship to each other. For what it's worth, by Google Earth's reckoning, Djebel Kouif is 13.44 miles to the northeast of Tebessa on a heading of 61.5 degrees. The critical point is that it was far behind the lines, adding to Fredendall's difficulties.

12. *A Soldier's Story,* 39, 46. See also the description, slightly harsher, in *A General's Life*, 135, where the fact that the building had no windows was added.

13. *A Soldier's Story,* 41

14. Alfred Chandler, Stephen E. Ambrose, et al. *The Papers of Dwight David Eisenhower*, I-IV (Baltimore: The John Hopkins Press, 1970), 690. Rick Atkinson also quotes this cable in *An Army at Dawn* (New York: Henry Holt and Company, 2002), 272.

15. A brief summary of Lloyd Fredendall, his shortcomings as a leader, and what might be learned from his example was published in the periodical *Army*, March 2003, by Steven Ossad. It can be found online at http://findarticles.com/p/articles/mi_qa3723/is_200303/ai_n9222724/.

16. *A Soldier's Story* and *A General's Life* have two slightly different versions of how he learned that Eisenhower was visiting II Corps March 5; I've used the version in *A Soldier's Story.*

17. *A Soldier's Story*, p. 42. Dialogue placed in italics is reconstructed based on the sources but is not verbatim.

18. In *A Soldier's Story*, Bradley notes carefully that he had not communicated his opinion about Fredendall earlier, even though he had already formed one. It's possible that he simply hadn't had a chance to speak to Eisenhower. It would also be very much in Bradley's character to withhold a

final verdict on anyone until he had turned over all the stones. But one can't help thinking that, like Harmon, he must have felt it an awkward position. He had, after all, been nearly named a corps commander before getting this assignment. He would have been dull indeed if he hadn't realized that he would be a possible candidate for Fredendall's job. Perhaps his concern was primarily not to look like a backstabber in *A Soldier's Story,* where the reader soon learns that he was in line for the post.

19. *A Soldier's Story,* 47.
20. Ibid., 52.
21. *A General's Life,* 135. Admittedly, this is from the section of the biography that Bradley was unable to review before his death, but his comments throughout his life show that he held Harmon in high regard.
22. Carlo D'Este, *Patton: A Genius for War* (New York: HarperCollins 1995), 466.
23. D'Este insists throughout his book that Bradley hated Patton, no matter what the actual evidence reveals. For example, he claims on p. 485 of *Patton: A Genius for War* that Bradley had "virtually nothing positive to say about Patton in his two postwar memoirs," which is patently untrue. I mention D'Este in particular because he is a well-respected and enormously popular historian, whose works are critical reading for anyone interested in World War II, and from whom I have learned a great deal. But his attitude toward Bradley has and will undoubtedly continue to influence readers and other writers for many years.
24. The incident is reported in many places, including D'Este, *Patton,* 466, where it is cited as an example of "Patton's methods backfiring," rather than a justification of Bradley's misgivings, which are detailed a few sentences earlier. Interestingly enough, Patton gave his driving detail standing orders to get out of their vehicles and run like hell if attacked by airplanes.
25. See Atkinson, *Army at Dawn,* 446, where the incident is used to describe Ward's dysfunctional relationship with Patton. The incident is described in Ward's personal papers, collected at the Military Historical Institute, Carlisle, Pennsylvania.
26. Constantine FitzGibbon tells the story in his Introduction to Charles Whiting, *Bradley* (New York: Ballantine Books, 1971), 7. Whiting is something of an adventure as an historical writer, but FitzGibbon's story was presented by FitzGibbon himself.
27. *A Soldier's Story,* 43. Bradley of course had heard the siren at Bennington.
28. Martin Blumenson makes this case in *The Patton Papers,* (New York.: DaCapo Press, 1995), 195. It seems highly logical, given Patton's general

behavior later on. Additionally it explains why he was so adamant about 1st Armored Division's drive. On the other hand, Bradley doesn't mention it, and Patton's diary contains no direct evidence.

29. Ibid., 52.

30. Kelly, *Meeting the Fox*, 264.

31. *Patton Papers*, 195. Patton wrote in his diary that he was keeping his feelings to himself, though it's likely his emotions were evident to all around him. It was a fairly busy time, however, as he and Bradley were making sure that the infantry advance into the El Guettar region succeeded.

32. Eisenhower's *Crusade in Europe* (Garden City, NY: Doubleday & Co., 1948) appears to misstate what actually happened, a fact that's pointed out in *A General's Life*. Eisenhower's letter to Alexander March 23, 1943—the same date as his meeting with Bradley—contains the suggestion that the II Corps be kept together, which would strongly indicate he was influenced by Bradley. Eisenhower in *Crusade* (p. 152) gives the impression—but doesn't actually *say*—that he decided II Corps should be kept together after speaking with Patton. Patton of course agreed with this idea, but it's clear that Bradley was the one who suggested it, not Patton.

Interestingly, Bradley is completely left out of the picture in Eisenhower's account—in fact, he doesn't make an appearance in *Crusade* until a few pages later (p. 154). It's a small matter, but one more instance of someone else getting credit for what Bradley did.

33. The strength figures are from Kelly, *Meeting the Fox*, 265.

34. This date is derived from Patton's diary. Hansen's diary (March 26, 1943) implies it happened March 25, 1943. Except for the dates, the descriptions agree.

35. Patton's diary, March 24, 1943. (*Patton Papers*, 197–98.) Patton being Patton, he then fretted that he had ordered Ward to his death—but consoled himself by saying he was only doing his duty.

36. Hansen's diary, March 26, 1943

37. Hansen's diary, March 29, 1943. There are several accounts of Bradley firing at enemy airplanes during the war.

38. The planes are erroneously described as twin-engine Ju-87s in *A Soldier's Story*. The Ju-87 was the one engine dive bomber known as the Stuka. The Ju-88 was a two-engine bomber as described here. Both types were common in Africa, but the description of two engines cinches the identification. The Junkers were twin-engined attack planes, formidable weapons in the war.

Originally designed as dive bombers, by this point the planes were considered jacks of all trades. Besides carrying bombs, they were quick and maneuverable enough to be used as nightfighters. They could carry just under 8,000 pounds of bombs (3,600 kilograms), though more often they held roughly 6,500 (3,000 kilograms).

39. In *Army at Dawn*, Atkinson cites statistics showing that Luftwaffe sorties had been reduced to fewer than seventy-five a day from a peak of 370 on February 24 (460). Air coverage and support are notoriously subjective matters, always in the eye of the beholder, and the numbers would have been small consolation to the men being bombed. It would not have helped that the ground troops saw no fighters flying overhead (due to the change in tactics), and felt themselves essentially undefended. Patton is criticized for his complaints, but the circumstances, not the statistics, justify him. At the very least, Conningham should have explained his strategy rather than calling the Americans cowards.

40. Patton described the strafing incident in his April 8, 1943, diary entry. He had met with Conningham himself on April 4, according to the diary, and this meeting would have taken place before then. Bradley, in *A Soldier's Story*, dates it April 3, which seems the most likely date. Slight variations of the story appear in several sources. One curiosity about Bradley's: in his version, the German fighters strafe first and then drop their bombs. That reverses the normal order of things. See, for example, "Dive Bombing," *Intelligence Bulletin*, October 1942, and "Air Force," *Intelligence Bulletin*, June 1942, for a contemporaneous report on tactics used by the Germans.

41. Bradley doesn't give the exact date; the date is the one Ward recorded in his diary.

42. Ward's diary, April 4, 1943, cited in Atkinson, *Army at Dawn*, 452, among others.

43. *A Soldier's Story*, page 65.

44. See Forest C. Pogue, *Organizer of Victory* (New York: Viking, 1973), 189, and Ed Cray, *General of the Army* (New York: W.W. Norton & Company, 1990), 383. Pogue points out that Marshall had read the cables between Eisenhower and Alexander and felt that Eisenhower was not being forceful enough.

45. Lucian Truscott, *Command Missions* (New York: Dutton, 1954), 199. Truscott was disturbed that, while Bradley had said this, none of the division, regiment, and battalion commanders were themselves willing to admit it—itself a sign of the problem.

46. *A Soldier's Story,* 207. It's not surprising that these qualities are cited when contrasting Alexander to Montgomery. Bradley, like most American commanders, was not favorably impressed by Montgomery.

47. The scene is from *A Soldier's Story,* 69.

48. *Life* magazine, June 5, 1944. The story the photo accompanied was published just before D-Day.

49. Summarized from Truscott, *Command Missions,* 189-90.

50. The quote is from Benjamin A. Dickson, *G-2 Journal: Algiers to the Elbe* (unpublished memoir, in Dickson collection at West Point), 63. Dickson's description of the general and his style, which this section is based on, extends from pages 62 to 64.

51. In actual fact, Bradley employed the division's Combat Command somewhat differently than Anderson envisioned. But given how the campaign proceeded, it can be said that the II Corps did clear the road for Anderson; the advance forced the Germans who had been stymieing the British to withdraw.

52. *A Soldier's Story,* 77.

53. Bernard Montgomery, *The Memoirs of Field-Marshal the Viscount Montgomery of Alamein, K.G.* (Cleveland: The World Publishing Co. 1958), 148. The comment has proven too good for just about anyone writing about the battle (including me, obviously) to pass up. See, for example, Atkinson, *Army at Dawn,* 494. Interestingly, Montgomery in his memoirs says he thought the main drive should have come from Anderson's front, which would have implied a bigger role for the Americans. There is no indication that he pushed this idea at the time.

54. Hansen's diary, April 23, 1943.

55. Ibid. The situation in the air had improved greatly in the past month; the harassing attacks by the Luftwaffe that had marked earlier fighting were no longer a factor.

56. Progress wasn't fast enough for Lieutenant General Lesley McNair, who had come to check on II Corps and the fighting. McNair, who oversaw all Army ground troops, had been in World War I, and while he had a reputation back home as a tough fighter, Bradley found him difficult and trying. He'd arrived the day before the battle began, one of a series of senior officers who were more a nuisance than a help to Bradley and his staff. It wasn't just the need to accommodate a VIP with extra food and lodging that bothered them. High-ranking visitors loved to go near the front lines, where their procession of vehicles necessarily attracted enemy attention. VIPs became such a problem that Bradley issued orders that no

one was to visit an artillery observation post without the permission of the senior artillery officer. (The observation posts were particularly vulnerable, since for obvious reasons they had to be on high ground near the front lines, with a clear sight of the enemy—and therefore vice versa. The VIP could leave if the post came under fire, the men there could not.)

Bradley's restrictions didn't stop McNair from going down to the 1st Infantry Division, known colloquially as the Big Red One. Nothing he saw seemed to please him. The soldiers, he said, were too reluctant to face the enemy. Arguing with the division's deputy commander, Ted Roosevelt, McNair proceeded to an artillery observation post.

A hail of German artillery hit the post soon after he arrived. A shell fragment went through McNair's helmet and another landed in his shoulder, knocking him to the ground. Informed that the general was wounded, Bradley dropped everything and headed up to the aid station where he'd been evacuated. McNair had already been taken to the field hospital; Bradley passed through the quiet ward, speaking to the wounded.

"We took the hill, General," said one wounded man. "We took the hill."

Bradley nodded.

"We took the hill, General," repeated the young soldier.

"Good."

"We took the hill."

The soldier kept repeating it until he left.

Bradley caught up with McNair later that day at the 15th Evacuation Hospital; though hurt, he would make a full recovery. A few days later, Bradley visited him again, this time pinning a Purple Heart on him—accidentally upside down, which somehow amused the aides who'd been run ragged by the senior general.

McNair went home, continuing to complain that the troops weren't fighting.

57. Bradley says that he had worked out all the hills in his mind prior to the battle, but most accounts of what happened there indicate that the attacks on the hill were not in the original plans.

58. *A General's Life*, 156.

59. German artillery pounded Hill 523 the day after it was attacked, and the Germans brought up part of the Hermann Goering Division in an attempt to take it back. A thousand Germans stormed the hill from both sides.

Bradley drove to the regimental headquarters to check on the situation as the attack proceeded. The mood was grim. The units on nearby

Hill 523 were greatly outnumbered. There was nothing available to reinforce them. The 34th Division units nearby were still mopping up on 609 and had no one to spare.

What happened to the division reserve? asked Bradley.

Over with the 18th Infantry.

The tanks we ordered up the day before?

All but one destroyed or disabled; the last one's pinned down.

Bradley suggested that the battalion be withdrawn temporarily, but there was no way to do so without putting them in more danger.

All we can do then is wait, he said finally.

A company of tanks were finally scrambled down from the 1st Armored Division, but by then they were launching a counterattack, not reinforcing the battalion. When they reached the hill, they found the entire unit had either been killed or captured. *Meeting the Fox*, 336. The basis of the account is from a rifleman who happened to be at the regimental headquarters.

60.   Hansen's diary, May 1, 1943. Bradley could have been speaking for many in his command; in the same diary entry, Hansen mentions a group of Germans who tried to surrender but were erroneously shot upon.

61.   This is a distillation of the reasoning Bradley gave Hansen and the aide recorded in his May 1, 1943, diary entry.

62.   Bradley doesn't mention this, nor does Truscott go into detail, but it is obvious from the description in *Command Missions*, 189-90.

63.   Armored Divisions during the war were organized around combat commands, which combined tanks, tank destroyers, artillery, and mechanized infantry. While there were some variations in how the units were used, as a general rule there were three combat commands per division, Combat Command A, Combat Command B, and a Reserve. The 1st Armored Combat Command B had been the first in Tunisia and had seen considerable action in the campaign. Robinett had replaced the former commander, Lunsford Oliver, during the winter, after Oliver suffered heavy losses, both to the enemy and the weather.

64.   Bradley writes about the meeting in *A Soldier's Story*, 92.

65.   *A Soldier's Story*, 100.

CHAPTER 3

1.   *A Soldier's Story*, 103.

2.   For all his reputation as a maverick, Patton generally went along with the plans set out by higher authorities in Africa and Sicily. In France and

Germany, he had a commander in Bradley who trusted his abilities in the field, and who generally thought in similar ways; while Bradley always had the final say, both men collaborated, and clearly Patton had no problem objecting to Bradley's initial suggestions.

Regarding Sicily, one theory that students of the campaign sometimes consider is the possibility that Patton—and by extension Bradley—viewed the vagueness of the adopted plan as a way of angling for a bigger role in the battle.

The strategic importance of the Vizzini-Caltagirone Road in II Corps' sector could have opened the way for a role in the final assault, if only to support the larger British force on its flank, and it's possible that Patton had this in mind. The road ran east-west and lay about twenty-five miles from Gela. Securing it would cut off the possibility of an Axis attack against Montgomery's forces from the southwestern portion of the island.

It does seem likely that Patton was assuming that II Corps would be able to move inland quickly, go up from the Vizzini-Caltagirone Road east to Catania, and from there join in Montgomery's northward assault. Patton pushed to have a supply line through Syracuse in the British sector, something that would make sense if the Americans had the road and were working in this area. There is additional evidence that Bradley was eying Caltagirone and Enna, cities further northwards; they would be critical for a push by Patton's Seventh Army to Messina.

Still, it seems remarkable that these goals were not specifically set out. The almost inevitable conclusion is that Montgomery was planning from the start that his army would spearhead the attack, and that the Americans would essentially just watch his flank.

3. Darby was also in charge of the Third Ranger Battalion, but it was not included in Force X.

4. *A Soldier's Story,* 106

5. Admittedly, it is hard to prove a negative. But for what it is worth there is no record of the criticism anywhere, including Hansen's diary. And while Bradley's remarks in his published memoirs must always be put into the perspective of when they were written rather than when the events occurred, there's no overt criticism of the plan there either. Nor is there evidence that Bradley criticized Patton over the plans, as is sometimes said.

6. Bradley's promotion to head II Corps was considered secret, and many war correspondents didn't know about it until Tunisia was won. Some stories about the battles, therefore, credited Patton with the victories, even though Bradley had been responsible.

7. *Newsweek*, May 17, 1943. As colorful as it is, the origins of the snake story are unclear; it's unsourced in the story. It is not repeated in either of Bradley's books.

8. "Second Corps Led By Gen. Bradley," *New York Times*, May 9, 1943 (retrieved online from www.nytimes.com). Patton was listening to the press conference and noted in his diary entry for May 8, 1943 (*Patton Papers,* 245) that "no one bought" the explanation Eisenhower gave and kept asking about it. Eisenhower ended the questioning by saying that Patton was needed for something big that couldn't be discussed.

    The reporters' questions seem to have been directed at discovering whether Patton had been fired. But they also may simply have stemmed from a general ignorance of the battles that had just been fought, and the role of a corps commander.

9. *A General's Life,* 170.

10. *A Soldier's Story,* 118. The semi-amusing way the story is told masks its seriousness, as supplies were a critical problem in the operation.

11. Atkinson, *Army at Dawn,* 442. According to Atkinson, the result was a switch in the code that led to the loss of intelligence for several weeks.

12. *A Soldier's Story*, 121. The USS *Ancon* was known to the military as ACG-4. Launched in 1938, she did duty as a troop transport after being taken by the Army Transport System soon after Pearl Harbor. After taking part in the Torch landings November 8 off of Fedhala, Morocco, she returned to the States and was converted for use as a combined headquarters and communications vessel.

13. LCVPs or "Higgins Boats" were small landing craft; the plans called for them to pick up troops and ferry them to shore. Their draft was three feet.

14. Patton's diary entry May 17 (*Patton Papers,* 252).

15. It's unclear whether Bradley actually watched the landing boats depart, or was simply taking dispatches in his cabin or command center when the assault got underway. The accounts in both *A Soldier's Story* and *A General's Life* are written as if he was on the bridge. However, Hansen indicates in his diary entry for July 10, 1943, that Bradley was angry because he was confined to quarters and missed the start of the campaign due to a "local operation"—a veiled reference to the hemorrhoid operation, which is skipped over in the books.

    Hansen as well as other aides were clearly on the bridge, as detailed in the diary entry. It seems *probable* that Bradley came up for a short while as well. It's also likely that he was planning on going ashore on the first day of the invasion but had to cancel those plans because of the operation, but that is not explicit in the diary entries or the books either.

16. The figure, one out of six, comes from Rick Atkinson, *The Day of Battle* (New York: Henry Holt & Company, 2007), 78. Atkinson made the calculation based on a survey of several sources, as there does not appear to be a definitive tally. All sources agree the jump was fairly catastrophic.

17. Atkinson, *Day of Battle*, 85.

18. Besides the entry in Hansen's diary cited above, my assumption is based on Bradley's activities and expectations on D-Day in Normandy. Bradley says in *A Soldier's Story* that the division commanders had not yet landed and so he had to wait for their communications to be set up. While that's certainly true, Bradley's usual methods would have called for him to personally visit division commanders before the end of the day, as he did the next day.

19. Hansen's diary, July 10, 1943.

20. The account of Hansen's visit is from the July 10, 1943, entry in his diary. Hansen doesn't say how he managed to plunge off the gangplank exactly, but except for his pride, he seems not to have been hurt.

21. *A Soldier's Story*, 128.

22. The description is from Hansen's diary. Some of the entries in this time period are unmarked and the pages appear to be out of order, but these details are consistent with other descriptions.

23. *A Soldier's Story*, 130.

24. See *A General's Life*, 183. There the focus was on Bradley's anger with Patton, not the tactical details. The source cited for the information that Bradley was angry is actually a supplementary interview Bradley did with Hansen, along with a note from Frank Price's book on Troy Middleton that does not bear directly on that battle, though it favorably compares Bradley to Patton. Frank James Price, *Troy H. Middleton* (Baton Rouge: Louisiana State University Press, 1974).

25. *A Soldier's Story*, 131.

26. Ibid., 133; Atkinson, *Day of Battle*, 109.

27. For this exchange, see *A Soldier's Story*, 142; for the overall situation, Dickson memoir, 84-86.

28. Dickson memoir, 86.

29. A diary entry of Patton's (see *Patton Papers*, 283) is cited by several sources, including *A General's Life*, to support this theory. But the entry refers to the friendly fire incident, and the application involves considerable speculation. In actual fact, while Patton expressed outrage with Eisenhower

in his diary and to others, his track record suggests that he rarely protested actual orders, and when he did acquiesced quickly and without much further ado—as would be expected in the chain of command.

30. It's not clear that any protest from Patton would have changed things, at least not with Eisenhower's help. Eisenhower's latest "eyes and ears" near the battlefield, John Lucas, told Eisenhower that Alexander's orders were a terrible idea, but Eisenhower replied, in essence, that if Patton didn't like the orders he would have to stand up to Alexander himself.

31. Darby headed all of the Ranger battalions. Together the units were smaller than an infantry regiment, which would ordinarily be commanded by a colonel. The Rangers were still something of an ad hoc unit. New brigades were being formed even as the proper role for the crack troops was being debated.

32. Patton's diary entry for July 13 implies this, though it does not explicitly state it (*Patton Papers*, 285). Bradley's account, which is longer, mentions the DSC but does not make it explicit that this was when Darby was offered the job.

33. H. Paul Jeffers, *Onward We Charge* (New York: NAL, 2007), 137. The story is repeated in dozens of sources, exactly paralleling Bradley's own account in *A Soldier's Story*, 140, which includes direct quotes of the conversation. Patton's account in his July 13 diary entry (*Patton Papers*, 284–85) is shorter. Curiously, Bradley is generally left out of the story, even though *A Soldier's Story* makes clear he was there.

    Darby eventually did leave the Rangers and accepted a promotion; he was killed in Italy in May 1945.

34. *A Soldier's Story*, 141.

35. Ibid.

36. My account is based on Atkinson, *Day of Battle*, 117–21.

37. *Patton Papers*, 288. The exact timing of Bradley's visit to Patton's head-quarters is not clear.

38. Patton's diary, August 9, 1943 (*Patton Papers*, 316).

39. Atkinson, *Day of Battle*, 120.

40. Hansen's diary, September 3.

41. Ernie Pyle, *Brave Men* (New York: Grosset & Dunlap, 1944), 212.

42. Bradley told Ernie Pyle a story that he had once taken over for a driver who was too cautious at night. See Pyle, *Brave Men*, 212.

43. *A Soldier's Story*, 151. Friendly fire from aircraft was a serious problem on Sicily, as communications between ground units and the aircraft were primitive or nonexistent. The A-36 was a ground attack version of the

P-51 Mustang. Two groups of A-36s were used during the Sicilian campaign. Patton's question was not as far off as it may seem, as the plane superficially looked similar to the Messerschmitt Bf 109. Up close, the markings would leave no doubt.

44. See Carlo D'Este, *Bitter Victory* (New York: E.P. Dutton, 1988), 425. Interestingly, some of the maps from the campaign imply that Seventh Army actually followed these orders; see the official Canadian maps of the campaign, for example. It could also be argued that Bradley's movements, more rapid than anticipated, did divide the island in half about the time Palermo was taken.

45. *A Soldier's Story*, 143.

46. Dickson wrote that looting and rioting among anti-Fascists and the general public were such a problem that the city leaders actually met Truscott's men and begged them to occupy the city quickly. Dickson memoir, 86.

47. Alexander became angry with Montgomery following the latter's meeting with Patton, possibly feeling that his prerogative as commander had been breeched. He nonetheless approved the plan they had discussed.

48. This was Patton's plan. (See *Patton Papers*, 302, and D'Este, *Bitter Victory*, 444, among others.) Today the coastal route would make use of A-20, the Autostrada Messina-Palermo, a much wider road which tunnels through the mountains in roughly the same area.

49. See Hansen's diary for that date.

50. Bradley doesn't actually mention that he was planning the replacement after Troina was taken, but it seems implicit in the planning. See also D'Este, *Bitter Victory*, 463.

51. *A Soldier's Story*, 153.

52. See D'Este, *Bitter Victory*, 460 note. (The source is the interviews Bradley did with Hansen during the preparation for *A Soldier's Story*.)

53. See *Papers of Dwight David Eisenhower*, 1304, where in correspondence dated July 30, 1943, Eisenhower refers to a handwritten note from Bradley and mentions that he has already communicated the decision. (Bradley's note to Eisenhower is dated July 25, 1943, and can be found in the Pre-Presidential Papers Box 3 in the Dwight David Eisenhower Library.) The note was primarily concerned with obtaining a new G-3 for II Corps. Patton made similar notes in his diary around the same time.

54. The dates are based on Patton's diary. Carlo D'Este first laid out the timing in *Bitter Victory*, 468–69.

55. Based on Patton's diary, the date would be August 2, 1943, with Patton seeing Roosevelt and Allen the next day. However, a letter by Allen to his

wife indicates that he saw Patton August 5. See Gerald Astor, *Terrible Terry Allen*, (New York: Ballantine Books. 2003), 219.

56. For a well-written and cogent summary and analysis of what has been the mainstream view until now, see Richard H. Johnson Jr., "Investigation into the Reliefs of Generals Orlando Ward and Terry Allen," monograph published by the School of Advanced Military Studies, U.S. Army Command and General Staff College (Fort Leavenworth: Kansas, 2009). Major Johnson's interpretation largely follows D'Este but adds other material. Like nearly all historians, he leaves out the critical question of alcohol and its relationship to Allen's performance in the Troina battle.

57. D'Este, *Bitter Victory*, 452. Besides documents including Patton's diary, D'Este based his passage on an interview he conducted with General Robert W. Porter Jr., who had been Allen's G-2 colonel at the time. Bradley would have known for sure about the switch for roughly a week, based on Eisenhower's letter to him July 30 indicating the matter had been settled earlier.

58. Ibid., 156.

59. *A Soldier's Story*, 156. Atkinson in *Day of Battle* (160) mistakenly wrote that Roosevelt wrote this to Bradley, which would cinch the theory that the MP story was imposed; his citation to *A Soldier's Story* shows that the text was in error.

60. Astor, *Terrible Terry Allen*, 224–25.

61. Ibid., 223.

62. Astor suggests that Allen's being so sick that he couldn't fight was merely a rumor. *Terrible Terry Allen*, 225.

63. Ibid., 215.

64. Reynolds' story appeared in *Collier's* magazine. Perhaps coincidentally, Reynolds was one of the three reporters who approached Eisenhower about the Patton slapping incidents, promising not to write stories if Patton was removed from command. Bradley's relationship with the press was certainly different than Eisenhower's, but it's not hard to speculate on his reaction if a reporter had told him one of his commanders was drunk immediately before battle. Which, I hasten to add, we don't know was the case.

65. *A General's Life* is much more severe in its criticism of Allen than *A Soldier's Story*, claiming that Bradley took over the tactical planning for the division toward the end of the battle, without giving a date or more detail. (The implication would be that it happened at the very end of the battle, resulting in the final push.) But there the decision to replace Allen is pre-

sented as being made during the battle itself, which is simply not true. (See *A General's Life*, 195.)

66. The idea may have come from Eisenhower, according to Eisenhower aide Harry Butcher. Harold Butcher, *My Three Years with Eisenhower* (New York: Simon & Schuster, 1946), 298. But Pyle received story ideas and suggestions all the time, and there's no reason to give Eisenhower any special credit. The columnist had been with the 1st Division in Africa and would have had ample time to hear about Bradley and make a decision on his own. Given Pyle's personality and stature, the final decision would have been his in any event.

    Some writers have suggested that Pyle saw Bradley as a kind of antidote to Patton's over-the-top style. The contrast in the two men's styles was evident, but there's no evidence that the Bradley piece was done as a kind of answer to Patton. While a friend of Pyle's said he hated Patton's pomposity, that was a reason *not* to write about Patton. Nor was Bradley the only general or "brass hat" Pyle wrote about.

67. Pyle, *Brave Men*, 210.

68. Ibid., 214.

69. "Address by General of the Army Omar Bradley at the dedication of Sigma Delta Chi Bronze Tablet in Memory of Ernie Pyle," Indiana University, Bloomington, Indiana, October 5, 1953, *The Collected Writings of General Omar Bradley, Speeches 1950-1967*, Volume II (West Point collection).

70. Samuel Mitcham Jr. and Friedrich von Stauffenberg, *The Battle of Sicily* (New York: Orion Books, 1991), 288. The landing occurred some fifteen miles behind the American lines. There are several stories of Patton threatening both men with being busted in rank. Given Patton's nature, it's unlikely Bradley or Truscott would have taken it as an actual threat, though the treatment would not have endeared him to either.

71. While it's often written that Patton accompanied the first Americans into the city, technically this is not true. A reinforced platoon from Company L, 7th Infantry, had gone into Messina the night before; other units from the 7th and the 1st Battalion, 157th Infantry, were in the city prior to Patton's arrival. See Garland and Smith, *US Army in WWII: Sicily and the Surrender of Italy*, www.history.army.mil, 415–16.

72. I've used the official U.S. Army statistics, as included in the historical publication, Sicily, downloaded from www.history.army.mil/brochures/72-16/72-16.htm.

    As always, various sources have different numbers on the casualties. Garland and Smith, *Sicily and the Surrender of Italy*, estimated 12,000

Germans killed or captured, with another 8,000 wounded. Many Germans were also victimized by malaria and other diseases.

73. Cable dated August 27, 1943 (#1213), Eisenhower Papers, 1357. The cable is a study in indecision. Eisenhower says there are three possibilities: Clark, Bradley, and Patton. He praises Bradley as the "best rounded in all respects, counting experience, and he has the great characteristic of never giving his commander one moment of worry." He then goes on to say Patton is too much a combat commander for the job, which would require nearly a year of planning. Clark, Eisenhower thinks, is the best planner in amphibious operations, but has not yet been tested. He then says that he's "personally distressed" at losing Bradley, but that he is the obvious choice for the job. But if Marshall wants Clark, then Bradley could take over the Italy campaign. And Patton could be had tomorrow.

The following day, August 28, Eisenhower sent a cable that was a model of decision and brevity, telling Marshall he should take Bradley and he would be available whenever Marshall wanted. (Eisenhower Papers, 1364.)

CHAPTER 4

1. The description of the lunch and ceremony are largely based on *A General's Life*, 205–6.
2. *A Soldier's Story*, 6. Most of the description in this section is based on Hansen's notes for September 3, 1943, and the account in *A Soldier's Story*.
3. Bradley gave his assessment to Clay Blair in an interview for *A General's Life*, 207. He had serious reservations about the plans for the invasion and the follow-up attacks. It's not clear what he thought of the decision to go into Italy in the first place.
4. *A Soldier's Story*, 8.
5. Hansen's diary, September 3, 1943.
6. The 1st Army Group would eventually be renamed the 12th Army Group in France.
7. See Eisenhower Papers, 1357–1358. Eisenhower's hesitation is generally interpreted to have had more to do with concerns about the Italian campaign than Bradley's qualifications. One interesting aspect about Eisenhower's first response is his statement that he had "come to lean on [Bradley] so heavily in absorbing part of the burdens that otherwise fall directly on me." It's not clear what exactly he was referring to, though obviously it's an indication of how close their relationship had become.

8.   *A General's Life*, 208.

9.   Ibid., 209.

10. Omar Bradley, *Speech to Members at the 128th Annual Dinner of the St. George's Society of Toronto*, April 21, 1961. Collected Speeches (West Point collection).

11. *A General's Life*, 210. The characterization in the text apparently comes from the Hansen-Bradley interview. The text says that Bradley formed this opinion over the next few days. It's odd that he makes no reference here to his opinions of Devers from the West Point baseball team or his days as an instructor, for he surely would have had ample opportunity to form an opinion there. Whether his later opinion was an amendment or an emphatic confirmation is not clear.

12. The First Army existed as a skeleton structure at the time. Its commander was General Hugh Drum, who retired due to his age. General George Grunert took over briefly, serving mostly in name only, before Bradley took the post. Marshall appointed Grunert, Bradley says, as a way of honoring his long service before he retired.

13. Interview with General Omar Bradley by West Point cadet Ross Wollen, The Pointer Fiftieth Anniversary Issue, 1973-1974. (West Point Collection. This is a reprint of an article originally published in the 1964–65 issue.) Bradley in *A Soldier's Story* says that neither Eisenhower nor Marshall mentioned the American A-Bomb to him. *A Soldier's Story*, 179.

14. Eisenhower letter to George Marshall, December 17, 1943, Eisenhower Papers, 1605.

15. Eisenhower letter to George Marshall, August 27, 19443, Eisenhower Papers, 1357.

16. Bradley also tried to get Truscott to command his third corps, XIX. The post eventually went going to Charles H. Corlett. Bradley and Corlett did not get along on a personal level. Bradley found his personality difficult to deal with; Corlett believed his experiences in the Pacific were too easily and often dismissed. Corlett was succeeded by Major General Raymond McLain in October, 1944.

17. *A General's Life*, 232.

18. Kay Summersby Morgan, *Past Forgetting* (New York: Simon & Schuster, 1975), 52. Summersby had remarried by the time this memoir, her second, was published.

19. Kay Summersby, *Eisenhower Was My Boss* (New York: Prentice-Hall, 1948), 172. She made this statement in relation to a visit by Bradley to Eisenhower's Normandy headquarters, a little later than London.

20. Summersby Morgan, *Past Forgetting*, 124.

21. Ibid., 232.

22. Ibid., 211.

23. The quotes and most of the description are drawn from *A Soldier's Story*, 234. The quotes were from memory and are unlikely to be verbatim, but appear in quotation marks in Bradley's book.

24. Utah was VII Corps' area, under Collins' command. The beach landings were to be handled by the 4th Infantry Division, which would strike in the area between La Madeleine and Pourperville and move in the direction of the 82nd and 101st Airborne troops.

25. The scene is described by Anthony Bevor in *D-Day* (New York: Viking, 2009), 9. Bevor's description is based on the captain's personal recollections, collected at the Second World War Experience Centre Archive, Horsforth, Leeds, England.

26. To lessen some of the casualties, the commander of V Corps, Major General Leonard Gerow, suggested that the assault begin in darkness. He hoped that would allow engineers to clear away at least some of the German obstructions before the men came ashore. Bradley also favored an early assault in darkness. But once the overall assault time was set for high tide, at 0630, Bradley had to insist on simultaneous landings. If one beach was hit before the others, it would become the focus of a German counterattack, making the landing even more dangerous.

27. The two battalions equipped with DD tanks on Omaha were the 741st and 743rd. On Utah, the 70th battalion was equipped with DDs. All told, there were over one hundred DDs included in the battle plan on American beaches.

28. *A Soldier's Story*, 238.

29. See, for example, his letter to Beatrice, February 26, 1944, *Patton Papers*, 419.

30. Gaffney was actually not happy about leaving the division, but felt he owed it to Patton. See Patton's diary, March 6, 1944, *Patton Papers*, 422.

31. *A Soldier's Story*, 230.

An earlier incident, not recorded by Bradley, gives a sense of how things went even when Patton was on his best behavior. One evening, Bradley went to dinner with Eisenhower. Patton was there, along with Assistant Secretary of War John McCloy and Marshall's deputy chief of staff, Joe McNarney. At some point, the subject turned to the incident where American troops on Sicily had murdered prisoners of war. At the court martial, the men had claimed that Patton had directly encouraged them, claiming that his speeches about the enemy's brutality amounted to orders to show them no mercy. The Inspector General had followed up the claims with an investigation which eventually resulted in no charges. Patton had heard about the investigation, and had been concerned enough to talk to Middleton (the division commander) about it a few days before, asking if he remembered the speeches the men had claimed had incited them.

Now he began speaking about the incident a little too freely. Eisenhower reacted angrily. He told him he spoke too much. Patton refused to back down, saying he would shut up if ordered to.

Eisenhower told him he had better watch what he had to say.

Bradley, as usual, was utterly silent. The court martial had been instigated at his direction, and while he thought the defense ploy of misconstruing Patton's speeches was preposterous, it was not an issue to be raising to the assistant secretary of war or Marshall's secretary.

32. The account is in *A General's Life*, 222–23. Unfortunately, the usual caveats about this section having to be completed after Bradley's death apply.

33. Patton diary entry, January 18, 1944, *Patton Papers*, 398. The announcement actually did *not* specify that Bradley was to be army group commander, though Patton interpreted it that way.

34. Included in Bradley collection at West Point, miscellaneous papers. The assessment is not generally included in appraisals of either man, but then again it is not as readily available as Patton's well edited and published diary.

35. Phil Nordyke, *All American All the Way* (Minneapolis: Zenith Press, 2005), 186, and Bradley, *A General's Life*, 227.

36. Much of this description is drawn from *Time* magazine's cover story dated May 1, 1944 (retrieved online). The reporter had accompanied Bradley in April. According to his aides, Bradley often stopped to hunt during the war, but it's not clear that he did so in England.

37. Gene Ford, Letter to the Editor, *Life* magazine, 1950, page 367. The letter is included in the Omar Bradley collection at West Point.

38. *A Soldier's Story*, 242.

39. Ibid., 242. Brigadier General Manton Eddy was the division commander.

40. The incident was reported by General J. Lawton Collins in *Lightning Joe* (Baton Rouge: Louisiana State University Press, 1979), 192. Carlo D'Este followed up on the account by interviewing the general about it, *Decision in Normandy* (New York: Harper Collins, 1994), 97, note.

41. Hansen's diary, May 4, 1944. Hansen writes that one or both of the women were in the WAF. The unit identification is in doubt, since the WAF or

Women's Air Force was not officially begun until after the war. I've extrapolated his direction from his normal schedule, though it's possible he could have been heading toward Bristol.

According to an undated news item included in the personal scrapbooks in the West Point collection, Bradley's car was involved in a minor traffic accident near Slough near London at some point during his time before D-Day. According to the article, he was in the hospital for five days following the accident, which left a minor scar under his left eye. It's not recorded anywhere else.

42. Keegan, *Six Armies in Normandy,* 62.

43. Dickson memoir, 114.

44. See Hansen's diary entry for February 12, 1944, where Hansen connects rumors of a German long-range "rocket gun" with Bradley's mention of high explosives. The Germans were experimenting with a number of long-range weapons capable of hitting London (at least theoretically). These included a high-pressure gun whose site preparation work was detected and bombed by the Allies in late 1943. The long-range artillery never became a serious threat.

   The V-1 and V-2 missiles were a different story. Both were being actively developed at this point, though it's not clear that Hansen was referring to them. The first V-1 was not used until June 13, 1944.

45. *The Pointer,* 1973–1974, Interview with General Omar Bradley. West Point collection. Unmanned missiles would be a more suitable delivery system for radiological weapons than conventional aircraft, as contact with the poison could be minimized. The possibility of the bombs was top secret.

46. *Time,* May 1, 1944 cover story. It was in this story that Bradley's comment about the likelihood of casualties was reported. He called it "tommyrot."

47. *A General's Life,* 241–42. The section is based on *A Soldier's Story,* where Hansen argued that Bradley should allow Pyle to travel with him.

48. Hansen's diary, June 2, 1944. The staff was still smarting from their treatment by Seventh Army in Sicily, and had become completely disillusioned. Hansen's attitude toward Patton softened as the war went on, very likely a reflection of Bradley's own opinions. Bradley's feelings toward Patton were always more nuanced than Hansen's or the rest of his staff. He could have easily found an excuse not to go to Montgomery's with Patton—he was just about to board his command ship and the meeting was primarily a social one.

49. Patton's diary June 1, 1944 (*Patton Papers,* 461).

50. *A Soldier's Story,* 251. He received word June 1, 1944.

51. The description of the events from June 1 to 3 is based on Hansen's diary entries for those days.

CHAPTER 5

1. This section is based on *A Soldier's Story* and Hansen's diary. Some small details in the accounts are at variance, but do not contradict the overall story.

2. One of the villains of the novel is a general whom Hershey modeled on Patton. Bradley had also planned on bringing a book by Pyle, presumably *Here Is Your War,* but couldn't fit it in his gear. See Hansen's diary, June 4, 1944.

3. This section is based on Hansen's diary for June 3, 1944, and on *A Soldier's Story,* 251–65. Bradley later calculated that had Eisenhower not decided to go ahead with invasion that day, D-Day would have had to wait until July; the winter campaign would have taken place in France, with massive damage to French cities, including Paris. (Bradley liked to share this calculation with businessmen during his speeches, perhaps because it gave him a chance to talk about logistical matters he felt would appeal to them.)

4. The quote is from Hansen's diary, June 6, 1944. The description of Bradley in this section is primarily based on that entry, as well as *A Soldier's Story,* 266–70.

5. The difficulties on Omaha Beach have led to mountains of literature about it, debating about what might have been done, and what went wrong. Allied intelligence underestimated the strength of the defenses, though in truth the mistake was not massive. It's sometimes argued that a larger force should have been used to take the beachhead; besides the fact that landing craft were short, that argument ignores the obvious—the craft that were there had trouble reaching the right beaches and then jammed up before they could get their men on land.

    Two things are often forgotten in the accounts of the landing:

    1) Forces opposing a landing from properly prepared defenses *always* have a tactical advantage, even more so than similar forces in defensive positions anywhere else on the battlefield. Or to put it another way—it's damn hard to run through even ten yards of water with a full kit and bullets firing all around you.

    2) The planners, Bradley included, always realized this was going to be the most difficult task of the invasion. They felt they had no choice but to make the landing there.

There's one other thing that the debate at times skips over: for all its difficulty and loss, Omaha was a victory for the Americans. It just wasn't an easy one.

Not that it was a cakewalk anywhere else.

6.   Bradley's memoir, *A Soldier's Story*, introduces some confusion on when he learned the identity of the troops they were facing on Omaha. On page 272, Bradley writes that he was disheartened at noon on June 6 to hear that the troops the Americans on Omaha were facing were members of the German 352nd Division rather than the coastal infantry they had anticipated. This meant not only were they fighting experienced troops, but there were more of them. Added to the natural advantages the Germans enjoyed on the beach, this made Omaha even more deadly.

Bradley says the information came from Gerow, the corps commander. But he then immediately writes that Dickson had obtained information about the 352nd moving into the area of the assault beaches for an exercise on the day Bradley and his staff headed for the *Augusta*. The information, Bradley notes, had been passed to V Corps and First Division, but because of security precautions apparently was not forwarded to the units "sealed" on their ships.

Huh?

Here's what most likely happened:

Almost certainly Bradley had the information, given the amount of time Dickson was spending with him. Certainly Gerow would have been given the information shortly thereafter, whereupon the division commander would receive it. How much lower it got from there, however, is an open question; certainly most of the lieutenants and captains who hit the beach would not have had it.

At that point, however, the identity of the units facing them would have been irrelevant.

The actual identification of the unit in this case would have depended on identification from enemy dead, the capture of enemy POWs, or some other local intelligence. Thus the intelligence speculation about the better unit would not have been confirmed until the actual fighting began, and reports of that confirmation didn't reach Bradley until noon.

What truly disheartened Bradley were the reports that the Americans were still pinned down.

7.   Hansen's diary, June 6, 1944.

8.   The division deputy commanders were ashore and were having an impact. Brigadier General Norman D. Cota, the deputy commander of the 29th

Division, waded in around 0730 on Dog White beach on the far right of the American line at Omaha. Though wounded, Cota personally led a small band of men through mortar fire, managing to get past the bluff. He put together a temporary force of Rangers and regular infantrymen, sending them inland to a key village. He roamed the beach, kicking men into action, and personally made the hookup with the deputy commander of the 1st Division, who had landed to the left. He later received a Distinguished Service Medal for his bravery.

9. *A Soldier's Story*, 274. Bradley adds that Gerow grinned as he changed the plans, implying he was eager to go.

10. Hansen's diary, June 9, 1944. Bradley made the remark to Collins. In the Navy's defense, their ships cost considerably more than an Army truck.

11. The scene is based on Hansen's diary for June 6, 1944, and *A Soldier's Story*, 277–78. Hansen may have polished the ending for the book, though the general flow and description follow the diary closely.

12. For a brief discussion of fears in Bradley's army about secret weapons at the time, see Dickson, unpublished memoir, 158.

13. Hansen's diary, June 8, 1944.

14. Dickson, unpublished memoir, 123.

15. Hansen's diary, June 10, 1944.

16. The quotes are from Hansen's diary, June 10, 1944, morning entry. The description is based primarily on that entry.

17. Hansen's diary, June 14, 1944.

18. In his diary, Hansen mentioned D-Day plus 15 as the actual target for its capture.

19. Dickson, unpublished memoir, 134.

20. Ibid., 135.

21. Hansen's diary, July 3, 1944.

22. Ibid.

23. An example cited by Beevor, *D-Day*, 235.

24. Hansen's diary, June 30, 1944. The conversation was carried out in front of Hansen. Needless to say, Hansen was not among Montgomery's admirers.

25. Brest, on the northwestern tip of Brittany, is usually written of as the main objective. Eisenhower and Bradley both said after the war that Quiberon Bay, further south between Lorient and St. Nazaire, was considered a higher priority, though Brest received all the headlines at the time.

26. Bradley's quotes are from Hansen's diary, July 3, 1944.

27. An excellent discussion of the tactical limitations of fighting in the bocage, and some of the doctrinal deficiencies the Americans had there, is found in James Jay Carafano's excellent but too little known book, *After D-Day* (Boulder: Lynne Rienner Publisher, 2000). Carafano debunks many of the myths regarding the battles here. Another little known but excellent discussion is found in Michael D. Doubler's *Closing with the Enemy* (Lawrence, Kansas: University Press of Kansas, 1994). Doubler gives somewhat more importance to the mechanical inventions than Carafano, but both authors detail the importance of ground tactics and the infantry's learning curve.

28. Dickson, unpublished memoir, 126.

29. Beevor, *D-Day*, 113.

CHAPTER 6

1. Obviously, his selection of the target area also depended equally on his own abilities to create and then exploit it, as well as the difficulty the Germans would then have in filling it. Had the gap been created in a place where the multi-layered German defenses could have quickly rushed troops to plug the space behind the hole, it would have been worthless. But the defenses here were hardly soft.

2. Dickson actually seems to have slightly overstated German strength before the battle. In this case, that proved better than the alternative.

3. Collins is sometimes credited as the author of the plan, but clearly none of the changes he suggested were radical alterations, and in fact it can be argued that they made the plan weaker. Bradley made two major changes at Collins' suggestion. The first had to do with the corps organization. Bradley's original plan would have put the 83rd Infantry Division (from XIX Corps) under Collins for the attack, but Collins felt this would have given him too many divisions to supervise. Instead, a regiment from the division was temporarily attached for the assault and assigned to protect the flank of one of the assaulting divisions. Collins also suggested a rearrangement of the envelopment forces, putting more infantry and making the turn shallower. The latter had the effect of speeding up the initial phase of the drive, though in theory it would bag fewer prisoners.

   Collins also suggested a change in the plan following the breakthrough. Bradley had originally wanted to block all of the Germans to the west by holding and cutting off the roads there. But Collins was afraid that VIII Corps, advancing following the initial phase of the attack, might get tangled with elements of VII Corps. So he suggested leaving a major road open for VIII Corps, even though this would give the Germans a way to escape as well. Bradley agreed.

Bradley probably agreed to make the envelopment shallower to keep the timetable brisk. Agreeing to leave open an avenue of escape may have reflected the fear that Collins' force might be disorganized or perhaps overpowered by the retreating Germans; this would impact on the next stage of the battle.

In looking at Bradley's overall strategic and tactical mindset during the war, it's significant that Collins was the one who wanted less emphasis on the armored force in this battle.

4.   My description comes nearly verbatim from *A Soldier's Story*, 332. Collins' gesture may or may not be a literary addition, as it does not appear in the Hansen diary entry on which the memoir is mostly based.

5.   An excellent discussion of the ground-level tactics and their evolution can be found in Michael D. Doubler, *Closing with the Enemy* (Lawrence, Kansas: University Press of Kansas, 1994), 31-62.

6.   Hansen's diary, July 15, 1944. The shell blew holes in one of Bradley's uniforms.

7.   *A Soldier's Story*, 334.

8.   Originally designed as a trainer, the five-seat C-78 was ungainly looking, its two engines appearing oversized for the relatively small plane. It could cruise at about 175 knots, which was faster than the C-47 but far slower than a fighter or bomber. It even *felt* slow; in his memoir, Bradley would later recite the old joke about it as a "double-breasted [Piper] Cub with a built-in head wind." (*A Soldier's Story*, 339.) The only easier target for the Luftwaffe to shoot down would have been a balloon.

9.   *A Soldier's Story*, 337.

10. While the outlines of Quesada's contributions to Cobra and the European battle are given in several places, as far as I know, the only book to give a full view of the airman's career is the biography by Thomas Alexander Hughes, *Over Lord* (New York: The Free Press, 1995).

11. While Culin is usually singled out, several other soldiers seem to have come up with the idea around the same time. The fact that the "rhinos" were invented so late in the campaign is one more indication that the hedgerows were not taken as seriously as they should have been. The invention is sometimes given credit for winning the breakout; while they were certainly an important weapon, that would be giving them more credit than they actually deserve.

12. The account of Culin's invention is found on page 342 of *A Soldier's Story*; it parallels but adds to the account in Hansen's diary. Notably, examples of the invention's actual contribution to the campaign are missing in the pages that follow.

13. In his letter to Montgomery the next day, Eisenhower highlights these as one of the reasons that Montgomery must push his own advance. Eisenhower to Montgomery, July 21, 1944, Eisenhower Papers, 2018.

14. Hansen's diary, July 20, 1944.

15. Hansen's diary, February 11 and 12, 1945 (combined entry). One suspects that Hansen was among the subordinates cited.

16. Hansen's diary, July 21, 1944.

17. The toll here is from First Army records and the official report following the incident, Headquarters, First U.S. Army, Air Support Report, Investigation of Bombing of Ground Troops by Friendly Planes on 24 and 25 July 1944. McNair was the most prominent casualty. It was a substantial toll, generally considered the highest single friendly fire incident of the ground war. It probably should be stated that a frontal assault without a large-scale bombardment would have cost considerably more.

18. Bradley attended McNair's funeral on July 26. It was a small affair: Patton was there; so were Hodges, Major General Ralph Royce, Major General Elwood Quesada, and McNair's aides. The funeral was secret as was McNair's death. He was an important part of the deception plan aimed at convincing the Germans that the real attack was still coming at Pas de Calais, and announcing where he had died would have given much away. Even at this late date, it was thought the deception was valuable, holding the Germans back from committing more troops against the Allies.

19. Historian James Jay Carafano makes a strong argument that this objective was unachievable, given the division's strength at the time. See *After D-Day*, chapter 8.

20. Carafano (*After D-Day*) points out that Collins did not change the orders for 3rd Armor, and it thus remained on a track toward the original envelopment. It's not clear why, given the changes in Bradley's overall plan. Bradley didn't discuss this in *A Soldier's Story*, where in fact he gave little attention to the nuts and bolts of the drive. *A General's Life* is equally silent on the matter.

21. Hansen's diary, July 28, 1944.

22. Collins would come to blame the slowness of the 3rd Armor Division's advance for this failure, but a good argument can be made that his revision

of the original Cobra plan had failed to take into account the tactical situation: the smaller penetration in the envelopment doomed the trap to failure. Regardless of whether the flaw lay in the plan or the execution, Collins did not alter his original plan July 28 when it became clear that the envelopment could not be completed in time.

23. Montgomery, *Memoirs*, 200, and 227–33. Montgomery's exaggerations have been fairly well pulled apart by any number of historians on both sides of the Atlantic.
24. Ernie Pyle, *Brave Men*, 295.
25. See Carafano, *After D-Day*, 263–64. Carafano's book is an antidote to those earlier studies.
26. Montgomery, *Memoirs*, 231.
27. Bradley seems actually to have been told it would have been at least three times as long as his plan called for; the shorter time period is from the report.
28. Author Thomas Alexander Hughes, in *Over Lord*, contends that the reason had more to do with the technical limitations of the early radar guidance system used by the Americans, which induced larger deflection errors in a parallel attack than in a perpendicular one. (*Over Lord*, 209.) That begs the question of why that wasn't explained to Bradley, or Quesada for that matter. The mission sorties for the day—special weather reconnaissance flights were conducted to make sure the targets were visible—suggest that visual identification of the targets remained the primary targeting method.
29. Hansen's diary, June 9, 1944.
30. *A Soldier's Story*, 350.
31. There are countless examples. See, for example, Hansen diary entry August 7, 1944, where Bradley presents his plan, listens to Patton's suggestions, then "sells his own." It was Bradley's plan that was followed.
32. *A Soldier's Story*, 357.
33. Hansen's diary, July 5, 1944.
34. *A Soldier's Story*, 394.
35. This section, including the quotes, is based on Hansen's diary entry of August 2, 1944.
36. Hansen's diary, August 2, 1944.
37. Perhaps it was just a coincidence, but Middleton had given Patton a similar excuse a few days before when asked why he hadn't gone across the Selune River.

38. Patton Papers, 498. Interestingly, Hansen's record of the meeting does not mention Patton's objections—somewhat odd, given Hansen's attitude toward both men. In his diary, Patton says that it had been almost a year since he had to order Bradley to make an attack in Sicily—a reference no doubt to the dubious amphibious attacks, which in Patton's mind remained brilliant tactical thrusts.

39. Bradley's unusual session with Hansen July 28 (cited above) shows at least some of what he was thinking. Patton noted in his diary entry for July 30 that "they are getting more ambitious," adding characteristically, "they are just what I wanted to do."

40. Some critics have cited Bradley's "delay"–depending on the perspective, from July 28 to August 1 or 2 – in ordering the turn as a failure not only on Bradley's part but on Patton's. According to them, Bradley should have recognized the changing nature of the battle sooner—or Patton should have pressed him to do so—if not simply disregarded orders. Most arguments imagine that both commanders possessed the sort of data about the enemy that's not even clear in the historical record, to say nothing of unlimited supplies of ammunition, fuel, and men. They also assume that an Army Group commander could change orders promulgated two levels above him without much thought. (Bradley did actually change those orders on his own authority, though he seems not have been upbraided for it.)

   The keystone of this criticism is the request to turn eastward by General John Wood, the 4th Armored Division commander, who in fact disobeyed Patton's orders and moved toward Rennes, necessary for an eastward turn. Unfortunately, especially for the historians who make this argument, Wood didn't have enough infantry with him to take Rennes, which was barely defended when he arrived. (Tanks operating without infantry would have been easy targets, no matter where they advanced, but especially in an urban environment.) He had also stretched his fuel stocks and supply line to the limit. Patton recognized both problems and kept him pointed toward Vannes and Lorient, angered that Wood wasted a day by turning his unit eastward without orders to do so or the force necessary to make such a decision work. Thus the entire reasoning for the criticism is based on false premises.

   It seems to me that Patton understood the situation far more clearly than any historian.

41. The operation was canceled as unnecessary by Eisenhower August 15, just as the Falaise pocket operation was closing up.

42. See Hansen's diary entry for August 12, 1944. Had the Germans been able to retreat on the timeline Bradley envisioned, the failure of the Canadians to close the gap would have been much more critical than it was.

43. The estimate is from Blumenson, *General Bradley's Decision at Argentan*, collected in *Command Decisions* (Washington, D.C.: Center of Military History, Department of the Army, 1960), page 417. (The book is available online at http://www.history.army.mil/books/70-7_17.htm). By Blumenson's estimate, as few as 20,000 and as many as 40,000 escaped. As wide a range as these numbers are, all have been subject to great debate.

     Some number of support people had already been pulled from the pocket, and would continue to be evacuated over the next few days. There may have been some initial disagreement on Montgomery's part about the turn north, or at least the timing; Hansen noted in his entry for August 12, 1944, that he had heard of some "alleged disagreement" between Bradley and Montgomery, but though he gives the reasoning for the turn, never really gets to the bottom of the rumors.

44. *A Soldier's Story*, 376. After Cobra, such fears were magnified.

45. Ibid., 378.

46. Ibid.

47. Hansen's diary, August 12, 1944. As a general rule, Hansen rarely discussed strategy in the diary, even at key moments in the campaign. Fortunately, he did so here.

     Naturally, the decision on objectives affected the disposition of the units involved.

     The alternative theory that makes the most sense is that when he made the decision, Bradley thought the Germans had far less men in the pocket, and that he had already missed his opportunity to catch them. By that theory, his second-guessing the next day would be because of fresh intelligence or analysis indicating there were more Germans trapped than originally thought.

     Strong arguments can be made either way. My vote goes to the dispute over strategy because of how often it shows up in the diary.

48. The account in *A General's Life*—as in many American accounts stemming largely from Blumenson's early analysis of the battle—leaves the Poles out completely. It also neglects to discuss the terrain the Americans held (and, conversely, that which the Germans "escaped" through), and takes the highest of all estimates of the number of German units that forced the gap. The tone of the section is extremely reactive and defensive – without, in fact, mentioning the strength of the arguments in favor of Bradley's actual

decisions. Without delving too deeply into textual analysis and the questions of authorship, one may say that this is not the most persuasive section of the book.

49. See, for example, the transcript of the press conference between Patton and journalists conducted September 7, 1944, conveniently collected in the *Patton Papers* 539–45; the Falaise questions are on page 542 and, while very brief, are the sort that would only have been raised if there had been criticism.

50. Blumenson, General Bradley's Decision at Argentan, collected in *Command Decisions*, 416.

51. Eisenhower, *Crusade in Europe*, 279.

52. In his memoirs, Montgomery doesn't explain the decisions surrounding the Falaise Pocket; in fact, he does little other than to basically take credit for the destruction there. To take the most charitable view of his arguments with Bradley, one can see the drive toward the Seine as a drive toward Paris, the political capital of France. Not coincidentally, this parallels Montgomery's later plans for a northern campaign against Berlin. If his focus was as much on political as military goals, then it might make sense to forgo the destruction of the army Falaise offered.

It's a tenuous argument, but it could be made.

CHAPTER 7

1. Montgomery seems to have argued that he needed the entire Allied force just to face the Germans in front of him. Eisenhower apparently did not buy this argument, but still agreed that he would receive top priority in supplies and a substantial portion of First Army. Eisenhower summarized his feelings in an office memorandum dated September 15, 1944 (Eisenhower Papers, 2121).

2. The plan is characterized in *A General's Life* as "conservative and conventional" (312). That is, frankly, ridiculous. And implying that it followed exactly the course laid out before Normandy (same page) is, at best, misleading. Bradley was calling for a blitzkrieg below the main German defenses, supported by air and artillery, spearheaded by armor, and supplied largely by air. His thrust ignored the main body of the German army and stuck at that army's breadbasket and supply line, as well as the army's political base. This wasn't a Leavenworth maneuver. He may, as the text claims, have envisioned a "pause" at the Siegfried Line and/or Rhine River—but clearly events would have dictated when or even if such a "pause" would take place.

3.   The quote is from notes made by Patton aide Alexander Stiller on the conversation; the notes are included in the *Patton Papers*; this quote comes from page 522. Stiller said later that Bradley's arguments centered around the weakening of the shoulder of the Falaise pocket, and he interpreted Bradley's concern along those lines. But while Bradley must have been worried about a German counterattack to some degree, he had already taken steps to deal with that. His real concern, reflected even in Stiller's notes, was that Patton not do anything that would jeopardize his plan to strike eastward. And an examination of Hansen's diary shows that Bradley was in fact *pushing* Eisenhower and Montgomery to approve his moves in exactly that area. Placed into that context, the meeting takes on significance different than what a few historians have supposed.

The unanswered question is whether Patton knew what Bradley's plans were. It seems likely, though it's difficult to tell. He says in an August 22, 1944, diary entry that Bradley wanted to do what he (Patton) wanted to do, only with *two* armies not one – and of course at this point Patton wanted to go east as fast as possible.

Whether they would have agreed on every specific or not, the two men clearly had the same general idea. That being the case, it's not surprising that Patton quickly calmed Bradley down.

4.   *A General's Life,* 314. Montgomery claims in his memoirs that Bradley had originally agreed to his plan but changed his mind by the 23rd. That clearly is mistaken. To be charitable.

5.   Eisenhower told Marshall on August 24 that he no longer felt it possible to push east as well as north, and that he was directing Bradley to put the bulk of his forces on Montgomery's right. (Eisenhower to Marshall, August 24, 1944, Eisenhower Papers, 2091.)Though the plan that Eisenhower adopted was not exactly what Montgomery wanted—in effect, Montgomery wanted *everything*—Bradley correctly saw that it would essentially take control of First Army from him, allowing Montgomery to "coordinate" the 12th Army Group's left wing with the push.

6.   Patton's diary, August 23, 1944. *Patton Papers*, 526.

7.   Hansen's diary, August 25, 1944.

8.   Eisenhower to Montgomery, Eisenhower Papers, page 2100.

9.   Bradley said in *A Soldier's Story* that he felt in retrospect Eisenhower had made the proper decision – something he clearly did not believe at the time, as Hansen and Patton's diaries make clear. In the memoir, he is critical only of Montgomery's decision to command what he says was a disproportionate share of his resources. He also gives the impression that he welcomed

the compromise of giving a single corps to Montgomery, which does not appear to have been the case. Reading that section, it's difficult to escape the impression that Bradley is being far too polite toward Eisenhower, if not Montgomery.

In *A Soldier's Story*, Bradley limits his speculation to what might have happened had Third Army been given two extra corps; he says that he doubts the force could have crossed the Rhine on its own. This was meant as an answer to critics who believed that Patton, if let loose, could have proceeded to Berlin that fall and early winter. Bradley notes that there was still a substantial army in Germany, and it also reflects the fact that the force would have had less of a priority in its supplies than if it was the main force. But that statement begs the question of what might have happened if the plan had been given top priority from the start, and what would have happened if early success had led to the introduction of more forces behind the spearhead.

A General's Life (pages 316–17) has Bradley disagreeing but ultimately supporting Eisenhower's decision in retrospect. The book also declares:

"Alternatively, what if we had backed Patton in an all-out pursuit without pause? Could he, as he claimed, have brought the war to an early end?

"I am not aware that anyone other than Patton has taken this idea seriously" (page 317).

The statement was probably supposed to echo Bradley's thoughts in *A Soldier's Story*, but it seems to go beyond it by implying that Bradley believed his plan was not as good as Montgomery's: if it would not have ended the war earlier, what then was the point?

The phrasing is very unfortunate. If Bradley did not think his plan— it was *not* Patton's, as described here—was better, why would he have argued so vehemently and so long for it? The statement inadvertently puts Bradley in a very passive role in commanding the battle, one that doesn't fit with the actual facts. Here as elsewhere, Bradley—or his coauthor—is being far too circumspect.

Candidly, all the evidence is in favor that the quicker thrust which he originally helped design and fought for would have ended the war sooner. Saying that only Patton thought this is nonsensical and distorts the record.

10. *Patton Papers*, 532.
11. Bradley gives conflicting dates for the order in his biography; it was either August 22 or August 23.
12. *A Soldier's Story*, 395.

13. Admittedly, Bradley never took the allocations from SHAEFE about which armies should get the supplies too seriously, but he was always, in the words of the old saying, robbing Peter to pay Paul – or in this case, Courtney and George.

14. Eisenhower outlined the objectives in a letter September 4, 1944. The inclusion of Frankfurt is key; this was a deep, strategic penetration in Germany.

15. The direct quote comes from Hansen's diary, September 15. The paraphrases are from the diary, *A Soldier's Story,* and Patton's diary, September 15, 1944, which have slightly different though parallel accounts. Bradley had called his Army commanders in to help make the argument.

16. Hansen's diary, September 14, 1944. This was actually an improvement over the earlier situation.

17. Hansen's diary, September 15, 1944.

18. This comes from Patton's diary, September 15; it is not mentioned in Hansen's diary or in *A Soldier's Story.*

    An ultimatum like this seems somewhat out of character, and it's possible that Patton was exaggerating. However, Bradley had clearly reached the end of his considerable patience. Giving Montgomery First Army would have meant handing him total control over the offensive. At this point, Bradley thought he could win the war quickly if allowed to proceed. Not only did he feel that the Third Army alone was not large enough to run through Germany, but Montgomery's plans would hold it in position. Holding Patton back under any circumstances was a thankless task, but surely it would have driven even Bradley to drink.

19. Hansen's diary, September 22, 1944.

20. This scene and what follows is based on Hansen's diary, September 24, 1944.

21. Hansen's diary, September 28, 1944.

22. According to *A General's Life*, the dams "while they were not specifically set forth in Hodges' or my directives as a key objective...were a constant source of worry and discussion. This, in turn, led directly to the decision to order General Norman (Dutch) Cota's 28th Division, heavily reinforced with artillery and engineers, to attack the town of Schmidt on November 2. While the Roer [Rur] dams were not an assigned objective, the whole point was to gain control of the dams and spillways." (341)

    According to the co-author's footnote, the claim is based partly on an interview with Hansen in preparation for *A Soldier's Story.*

In *The Siegfried Line Campaign* (Washington, D.C.: Center of Military History, U.S. Army, 1990), page 325. Army historian Charles B. MacDonald provides a cogent and concise rebuttal—actually written before *A General's Life*—complete with notes referring to various intelligence reports and other data.

One point that MacDonald doesn't make: The following February, when the dams' significance *was* understood, when the Americans had every advantage, and when the dams were clearly a threat to the plans to cross the river, American troops weren't even able to get close to the dam to begin an attack before it was blown. The Germans were able to destroy enough of Schwammenauel to flood the valley for nearly two weeks. One can speculate about the possibilities of more imaginative plans, but the location of the dams, the fact that they could be wrecked by relatively simple and small precautions, and the terrain and proper training and planning by the Germans combined to present long odds against capturing them intact.

23. Total casualty numbers are, as always, elusive. The toll was horrific, certainly, but perhaps not as high as some accounts suggest. MacDonald's official history (*The Siegfried Line Campaign*) lists a total of 6,184 casualties for the second attack on Schmidt. But First Army statistics show the *total* of wounded in the entire army from October 27 to November 15, the period of that attack, was "only" 4,270 wounded, with 884 QM burials—known deaths from all causes. The addition of non-battle injuries still brings the casualty list for the entire First Army to a little under 6,000. (The numbers are from the medical annex to the First United States Army Report of Operations 23 February-8 May 1945, 136; they are included in a table at: http://history.amedd.army.mil/booksdocs/wwii/HuertgenForrest/BattleforGermany.htm)[accessed November 30, 2010].

One sign of the severity of the fighting is the fact that a significant portion of soldiers who became casualties suffered from psychological ailments, predominantly battle fatigue.

24. James M. Gavin, *On to Berlin* (New York: The Viking Press, 1978), 259-66. Gavin was of the opinion the battles shouldn't have been fought. The problem in that case would have been how to deal with any German counterattack through the sector—a problem with obvious parallels in the Ardennes battle that followed.

25. Gavin, *On to Berlin*, 268, note 1.

26. Russell F. Weigly, *Eisenhower's Lieutenants* (Bloomington, Indiana: Indiana University Press), 432.

27. In *Eisenhower's Lieutenants*, Weigley makes an odd argument that Bradley (and other American generals) was *not* offensive minded *because* he aimed to take the dams. Even if the attacks *had* been aimed at taking the dams, it's difficult to see the logic there, especially given that destruction of the dams would have stopped an offensive (and did). Weigley proposes that a southern attack against the dams would have been effective—a proposal that seems even further out of touch with the actual terrain and defenses than the plans actually followed. (Weigley, *Eisenhower's Lieutenants*, 432-444.)

    Weigley draws parallels to Grant's Wilderness Campaign – an inventive and provocative parallel unfortunately not supported by facts. He ends his chapter by claiming that the German army was staggering before Patton, an equally tenuous claim.

28. The 28th Division was later involved in a scandal that nearly cost Cota his command: in February, Cota's signal company lost top secret encryption gear when their truck was stolen. An investigation castigated Cota and several of his officers. Cota was recommended for removal. Devers, who by that point had the 28th Division in his army group, recommended that Cota's punishment be reduced to a reprimand; Marshall accepted the recommendation.

29. Some historians have made a case that Cota was handcuffed by the Corps and Army planning; see for example Doubler, *Closing with the Enemy*, 172.

30. Hansen's diary, December 1, 1944. There the reference is to a dam whose water threatened part of the Ninth Army's advance; an entry December 9 indicates his concern was much broader.

31. Eisenhower to Devers, October 23, 1944, Eisenhower Papers, 2249.

32. Kay Summersby, *Eisenhower Was My Boss*, 193.

33. Choosing a building for a command post, especially that one had relatively reliable heat, may be an indication that Bradley felt he was going to be staying for a while, that the rapid advances of the summer would no longer be possible.

34. *A Soldier's Story*, 438. Bradley didn't go into detail on his reasoning. Aside from the fact that he had (parts of) two armies involved in the northern thrust (which made sense in any event because of the conditions and the units he was facing), it's difficult to see this priority in the actual orders. Interpreting from his later actions, he seems to have felt that he would get a breakthrough in one of these spots, which he would then exploit.

35. See Hansen's diary, January 2, 1945. This was a significant deadline, but Bradley apparently did not share this fact with Hansen at the time.

36. Eisenhower letter to Marshall, November 11, 1944, Eisenhower Papers, 2297.

37. *A General's Life* describes the three-week campaign in the Huertgen area as the Huertgen Forest battle, essentially blaming it for the failure of the entire northern offensive (page 343, 352). That is an exaggeration, and frankly it's not clear to me that Bradley ever believed that.

38. Bradley made a remark to Bedell Smith around this time, saying that he wanted a counterattack. (There are several accounts; see *A Soldier's Story*, 450, for example.) When the counterattack did come, it was clearly more than he had expected, let alone wished for.

39. Hansen's diary, November 22, 1944. Dietrich remained a friend throughout the war, and Bradley later tried to help her locate her sister in Germany. There are no indications that the relationship was anything but platonic.

40. Dickson, unpublished memoir, 171. He is quoting from Estimate No. 37.

41. See Bradley's interpretation – admittedly after the fact—of Dickson's report in *A Soldier's Story*, 463. While disagreeing that Dickson predicted the offensive, he does go to great lengths to praise his former G-2 elsewhere. Admittedly now it's very easy to reinterpret the reports the 12th Army was receiving at the time, but at least in retrospect it's clear that the Germans were marshalling forces for an offensive; the only question was where.

42. Dickson, unpublished memoir, 172. Dickson describes his changing opinion in his manuscript, 170–72. The contrary opinion of 12th Army Group's G-2 was almost universally shared.

43. *A Soldier's Story*, 453.

44. Bradley, *A Soldier's Story*, 465. In his biography of Bedell Smith, *Chief of Staff* (New York: Greenwood Press, 1991) D. K. R. Crosswell says that Eisenhower committed the divisions himself over Bradley's objections (page 283). But Crosswell's apparent source for this, Eisenhower's December 23, 1944 memo (Eisenhower Papers, 2373) gives no indication that Bradley had to be argued into accepting this move. On the contrary, every evidence is that Bradley himself was behind the division shifts.

45. Smith's biographer D.K.R. Crosswell, citing General Everett Hughes, says Eisenhower and Bradley relieved some of the tension that night by playing five rubbers of bridge. Crosswell also says that an entire bottle of Scotch was consumed at Eisenhower's table. If so, it's unlikely Bradley drank

much if any of it at all. Not only was he not much of a drinker, but he disliked Scotch. Crosswell, *Chief of Staff*, 282.

46. The city of Liege, Belgium, was behind First Army's drive in the Aachen area. Bradley's analysis was much more tactically sound than the actual goal, and in fact was the target in von Rundstedt's original plan for the offensive, the so-called "Small Solution," which was over-ruled by Hitler. It's not surprising that the two military professionals, though enemies, viewed the battlefield similarly.

47. Hansen's diary, December 17, 1944. The account is similar but slightly rearranged in *A Soldier's Story*. The portion of Hansen's diary covering the Bulge contains several indications that it was either added to or perhaps rewritten following the actual events. This wasn't a wholesale revision, however; Hansen's entries reveal the confusion and misinformation typical in a day by day recording of battle. Most likely the specific entries were retyped from earlier notes or dictation a few days after they were made.

48. Hansen's diary, December 17, 1944.

49. Ibid.

50. Summersby, *Eisenhower Was My Boss*, 200.

51. *Patton Papers*, 596 (from a letter to Major General Fox Conner).

52. This is based on Hansen's interpretations of Bradley's remarks to him following the meeting; see Hansen's diary, December 18, 1944. See also *A Soldier's Story*, 469.

53. Bradley tells this story in *A Soldier's Story* (467–69) in conjunction with the visit to First Army on December 18, but it's not in Hansen's diary entry for that day.

54. Hansen's diary, December 18, 1944. According to Alex Kershaw in *The Longest Winter* (Cambridge, Massachusetts: DaCapo Press, 2004), 83, members of the 394th Platoon captured and passed on a copy of von Rundstedt's order of the day during the early hours of the campaign; a veteran told Kershaw that Bradley confirmed he had seen it "in a timely manner." The order would have made clear the goal of the offensive, though by now Bradley saw it.

55. Bradley had put Middleton's VIII corps under Patton to make it easier to coordinate the defenses and counterstrike.

56. *Crusade in Europe*, 350.

57. Ibid. The description of the start of the meeting—which is used in many of the histories of the battle—is clearly meant to portray Eisenhower as calm and confident in the battle. Eisenhower's subsequent actions belie the optimism it suggests.

58. The original plan sketched at Verdun included Middleton's divisions, which were in no shape to mount an offensive. The revised plan, arranged by Bradley and Patton the next day, brought XII Corps and a good portion of XX Corps into the southern offensive.

59. *Patton Papers*, 599–600. Bradley in *A Soldier's Story* says that he asked the question, but it's not clear in that account where he asked. Most likely they would have discussed a possible timeframe the night before.

60. *A Soldier's Story*, 472.

61. Ibid.

62. Hansen's diary, December 19, 1944.

63. *A Soldier's Story*, 476. Interestingly, Hansen's diary entry for December 19, 1945, indicates that the changeover was decided at the Verdun. This seems to have been a mistake by Hansen, who was apparently writing after Smith had talked to Bradley.

CHAPTER 8

1. Bradley's army group actually had three different headquarters; Luxembourg City was "forward." The main part of his headquarters was actually located back in Verdun, where the meeting with Eisenhower took place. It would have been easy to relocate there, but doing so would have meant long commutes to his army commands.

    It's sometimes suggested that his stubborn refusal to leave Luxembourg contributed to the decision to remove his armies. It's impossible to know what was going on in Eisenhower's mind, but Bradley displayed a relatively balanced estimate of dangers throughout the war, and while he did take personal risks, they were never foolhardy ones. In this case, it seems reasonable to assume that his assessment was prudent and in line with his earlier ones. Since he was *already* in communication with his commands, moving back would not have improved them. And had he moved back, he could just as easily have been criticized for running from the fight.

2. Patton's diary, December 20, 1944. *Patton Papers*, 601.

3. *A Soldier's Story*, 477. *A General's Life* follows the same line. Hansen's diary does not contain an account of the conversation. Hansen, undoubtedly recording what Bradley told him, says the move "probably" makes sense given the state of communications. There is some talk there about the possible need for British help and the possibility of German advance into Luxembourg, but the overwhelming sense one gets is that Bradley was looking at the situation as an opportunity to attack.

4.   Eisenhower, *Crusade*, 355.
5.   *A General's Life*, 367. The message quoted is from Arthur Bryant, *Triumph in the West*, (Garden City, N.Y.: Doubleday, 1959). 272.
6.   Eisenhower letter to Bernard Law Montgomery, December 22, 1944, Eisenhower Papers, 2369. Hodges does appear to have been either sick or exhausted at the start of the battle; Hansen implies this in a diary entry for February 11 & 12, 1945. He was older than Bradley and had been commanding the troops for many months without a break. If he was exhausted, he recovered sufficiently to lead his army through the rest of the war.
7.   See, for example, Hansen's diary entry of February 7, 1945, for Ridgeway's sentiments about the withdrawal, or the entry for January 8, 1945, where Dan Faith speaks of the withdrawal. On the other hand, James McGavin, commanding general of the 82nd Airborne Division and acting commander of the XVIII Corps at the time, is relatively positive about Montgomery's command, and noted that the withdrawal was "very much in order." (Gavin, *On To Berlin*, 238.)
8.   See, for example, John Eisenhower's description of the orders for 82nd Airborne to retreat to straighten his line, or his straightening of the St. Vith line in *Bitter Woods* (New York: G.P. Putnam's Sons, 1969), 358. Whatever one thinks of the moves themselves, it's clear they would have been presented and discussed differently by Bradley.
9.   Hansen's diary, December 25, 1944. The description in this scene is largely based on the diary entry, augmented by *A Soldier's Story*, 480–81, where Bradley made some corrections to Hansen's original account.
10.   In *A General's Life*, the presence of the car is a coincidence, and this is taken as a deliberate slap against Bradley. It's not clear from Hansen's diary entry that this was so, however. Montgomery may have sent someone from his own headquarters who arrived late, or seeing that Bradley was late and the weather bad, may have concluded he wasn't coming. It's also possible that the American escort might have seemed preferable to Montgomery, or that the orders to pick up Bradley were simply confused.
11.   *Triumph in the West*, 278. Montgomery's account of the meeting is contained in a letter to Alan Brooke. While it may have some bits of exaggeration, on the whole it seems pretty typical for Montgomery.
12.   *A Soldier's Story*, 482.
13.   Ibid., 480. According to historian John Eisenhower in *The Bitter Woods*, Montgomery's main objection was the fact that Collins would have had to support his thrust via a single road. Collins was confident it could be done.

14. Hansen's diary, December 27, 1944.

15. Eisenhower to Montgomery, December 29, 1944, Eisenhower Papers, 2384.

16. Eisenhower to Montgomery, December 31, 1944. Eisenhower Papers, 2386–2387.

17. Historians generally credit de Guingand with talking Eisenhower out of asking the Combined Chiefs for a showdown, arguing that Montgomery was only being his usual insensitive self. It was a plausible excuse. Montgomery continued to believe against all evidence that he had done a remarkable job saving the American army in the bulge.

18. Bradley apparently tried to push Eisenhower into giving him the Ninth Army back by announcing at the press conference that all American forces were being returned to his control. (See Hansen's diary, January 9.) This seems like an uncharacteristic ploy, and from the diary entry wording one is tempted to conclude that it was something done by the staff rather than Bradley, who would have a fairly realistic view of what the result was likely to be—Eisenhower was not influenced in the least.

19. Hansen's diary, January 6, 1945.

20. Or Roer River.

21. Hugh Cole, in the Epilogue to his *The Ardennes: Battle of the Bulge* (part of the *U.S. Army in World War II* official histories) estimates that the Germans had a three to one overall advantage in infantry, ranging to a six to one ratio during the breakthrough and initial assault. The advantage in tanks was closer: two to one if only medium tanks are counted; four to one if self-propelled guns used as tanks are added in. In no other battle did the Germans have such an advantage [Hugh Cole, *The Ardennes: The Battle of the Bulge* (Old Saybrook, CT: Konecky & Konecky, no publication date given), 650.]

    The tank totals can be a little deceptive, given the landscape and the wide area of the battle. The Germans were able to concentrate their armor at the start of the offensive; the large American concentrations occurred mostly in the middle and end.

22. Charles MacDonald, *A Time for Trumpets*, (New York: William Morrow, 1985), 618.

23. MacDonald, *Time for Trumpets*, 614.

24. Ibid., 618.

25. The numbers, again only representative, are rounded off from *Armageddon* by Max Hastings (New York: Vintage Books, 2005), 235.

26. *A Soldier's Story*, 495. Bradley uses the passage to mention proximity fuses, which were used for the first time in the battle.

   One wonders what would have happened if Bradley trusted Dickson's estimates in late November, or if there had been some other intelligence coup that alerted Bradley fully to the German plans. Surely he would have had Patton and Hodges waiting on the shoulders, noose in hand. But how far would he have let the German forces advance—would he have had the courage, to use Patton's word, to let them get far enough to run out fuel? The irony is that if the German assault had been quickly repulsed, substantial forces might have gone back to the West Wall, once again reinforcing the defenses and making it that much more difficult for the Americans. The sacrifices of the men lost in the early hours and days of the Ardennes battle saved countless Allied lives later on.

27. The numbers are from Alexander M. Bielakowski and Raffaele Ruggeri, *African American Troops in World War II* (New York: DaCapo Press 1996), 21. Weigley, *Eisenhower's Lieutenants* (Bloomington, Indiana: Indiana University Press, 1981), 570, gives similar numbers.

28. See, for example, Hansen's diary, April 15, 1945.

29. A news story covering his early military career talks of his good sportsmanship in a special football game with black players. Undated news clipping, Mary Quayle scrapbook in West Point collection. Bradley was a major at the time.

30. See, for example, Hansen's diary November 15. Hansen doesn't spell out what Bradley's concerns were, though his later actions would seem to make that clear.

31. Bielakowski and Ruggeri, *African American Troops,* 22.

32. Restored and renovated, the building is today a small four-star hotel.

33. Patton's diary January 24, 1945. *Patton Papers,* 628. It wasn't actually the only time, not even in Patton's presence, but it was relatively rare.

34. *A Soldier's Story* has Gerow as commander of V Corps. He was assigned to lead 15th Army January 15, 1945, and while there could have been some overlap, Huebner was in charge of the corps at this point.

   The task of taking dams intact is extremely difficult, especially under the conditions surrounding the Rur dams. Even so, the operation seems to have proceeded without a full appreciation of the tactical situation, and the main dam was dynamited by the Germans before being seriously threatened with capture. *A General's Life* (396) criticizes the staff planning for the operation in one of the few times either Bradley book is directly critical of First Army. From start to finish, through a succession of commanders, there seems to have been a real lack of understanding about the task.

35. Patton's diary, February 27, 1945. *Patton Papers,* 648.
36. *A Soldier's Story,* 501.
37. Eisenhower to Bradley, February 20, 1945, Eisenhower Papers, page 2489.
38. Charles B. MacDonald, *The Last Offensive* (Washington, D.C.: Office of the Chief of Military History, 1973), 185.
39. Eisenhower, *Crusade,* 372.
40. Hansen's diary, March 6, 1945.
41. The exact description of the incident differs between Hansen's diary and *A Soldier's Story.* I have chosen details from both, giving more weight to the diary, where there appears to have been less "literary license."
42. All quotes in this scene except where noted below are from *A Soldier's Story,* 510–12. The account there is based on and parallels Hansen's diary entry Wednesday March 7, 1945, (Hansen has another March 7, 1945 entry marked Tuesday; presumably he got the date wrong.) Internal evidence in the Wednesday entry suggests that it was written after March 10, as there is a reference to something said on that day.)
43. Hansen's diary, Wednesday, March 7, 1945.
44. Ibid.
45. Gavin, *On To Berlin,* 276.
46. The letter was a revision of one that Bull had prepared but not sent two days earlier. Eisenhower to Devers, March 18, 1945, Eisenhower Papers, 2536.
47. Patton's diary, March 19, *Patton Papers,* 658. The significance of this meeting has often been overlooked. The concern about losing the troops to Montgomery is mentioned here. While Patton doesn't attribute it, it's exactly the concern that Bradley has elsewhere. Bradley in *A Soldier's Story* claims that both he and Eisenhower had urged Patton to continue.
48. In his book, *On to Berlin,* James Gavin says he spoke to General Bull about Eisenhower and Bradley's "vacation" on the Riviera. "They didn't get much rest," Bull told him (277). Gavin believes that Bradley planned the eastern push from the time the Remagen bridge was seized, implying that he used the vacation to elaborate the plan with Eisenhower. Kay Summersby, who was also along for the stay, says that Eisenhower spent most of the time while Bradley was there in bed sleeping (Kay Summersby Morgan, *Past Forgetting,* 217), in which case Bradley would have argued his plan on the trip down, or even beforehand.

49. Cable to Jacob Loucks Devers, et al, March 21, 1945, Eisenhower Papers, 2536.

50. Bradley, *A Soldier's Story*, 521.

51. Most discussions assume that the best place for a single-thrust attack was where Montgomery's forces made it. That clearly wasn't the case. As Patton and Bradley both pointed out before Market Garden, the canals and river crossings in the Low Countries and the mountains of northeastern Germany were barriers to the rapid mobility that characterized the successful campaigns on both sides of the war. A single front strategy to the south—say, where Third Army operated—would have made considerably more sense.

    There is also the question of what Montgomery would have done with First Army if he had it.

    Truly, a Montgomery single front strategy might have won the war, but it's hard to demonstrate that it would have been better or faster than what was actually done.

52. See, for example, W. Denis Whitaker & Shelagh Whitaker's *Rhineland: The Battle to End the War* (New York: St. Martin's Press, 1989). The book gives the Canadian Army long overdue credit for its part in the final months of the war, which makes it a valuable read. But besides exposing a prejudice against Eisenhower for his alleged grand living, the early chapters reveal an uncritical acceptance not just of Montgomery's superiority as a general but of the single front strategy as well. This slant directly influences the rest of the account. According to the Whitakers, Ninth Army was slow to join Montgomery's offensive not because Montgomery was slow to employ it or even because of the flooding of Rur Valley (the actual reasons), but because it was (supposedly) engaged elsewhere in Bradley's ill-conceived plot to win the war on his own. It's an unfortunate distortion of the record.

53. Estimates of the POWs taken vary; the figure is the one Bradley uses in *A Soldier's Story*, 525 map.

54. See for example the eye-witness account of Donald B. Prell, one of the prisoners, posted at http://www.indianamilitary.org/German%20PW%20Camps/Prisoner%20of%20War/PW%20Camps/Oflag%20XIII-B/Prell/Prell-Donald.pdf

55. Patton's diary, March 31, 1945, Patton Papers, 668.

56. Richard Baron, Major Abe Baum, and Richard Goldhurst point this out in their book, *Raid! The Untold Story of Patton's Secret Mission* (New York: G.P. Putnam's Sons, 1981), 271. (The assertion was made first in an article published in the Saturday Evening Post, August 1948.) The book is

the definitive account of the raid. The contents of Chet Hansen's diary entry cited on the page are correctly described, but erroneously attributed to "Joe Hansen" and at another point General Hansen's Third Army diary.

57. *A Soldier's Story*, 542.
58. Ibid., 542–43.
59. Hansen's diary, March 28, 1945. There is a second reference in the entry for April 13, 1945, but it doesn't shed more light on the matter.
60. *A Soldier's Story*, 542.
61. The description of this scene is based on Hansen's diary, April 6, 1945.
62. *A Soldier's Story*, 528.
63. The scene is described, slightly differently, in *A Soldier's Story*, 539–540, and Hansen's Diary, April 12, 1945.
64. The scene is based on Hansen's diary, and *A Soldier's Story*, 541, where it is repeated almost word for word.
65. They had similar fears that a redoubt might be formed in the north as well.
66. John Toland, in *The Last 100 Days*, (New York: Bantam Books, 1966), 385. Toland sources the information to an interview with Simpson. Stephen E. Ambrose, *Eisenhower and Berlin, 1945* (New York: W.W. Norton & Company, 1967), 92, provides a similar scene, based on Toland. (The dates in the accounts differ. Ambrose gives April 14, Toland April 15. Hansen's diary indicates a meeting took place April 15; he doesn't record what happened there.)
67. *A Soldier's Story*, 554.
68. Hansen's diary, May 7, 1945. Bradley and his staff discussed the advisability of telling the correspondents before SHAEF made the formal announcement; Bradley decided to go ahead. The party is from Hansen's diary, May 12, 1945.

CHAPTER 9

1. Eisenhower to Marshall, April 26, 1945, Eisenhower Papers, 2647.
2. Bradley lays out their thinking in *A General's Life*, 440.
3. The statistics are from *A General's Life*, 450.
4. The books, with neat notes in Bradley's handwriting, are in the West Point collection.
5. *Time* magazine, *A Soldier's Story* (review), Monday, June 18, 1951.
6. Hanson W. Baldwin, "General Bradley Calls the Roll," *New York Times*, June 17, 1951.

7. See, for example, the *Universal Standard Encyclopedia* entry on World War II, which follows the entry from an earlier *Funk & Wagnalls Encyclopedia* (1953), or the various *Encyclopedia Britannica* entries published in the post-war period. But at least Bradley got his own, albeit brief, entry in the works.

8. There is a brief Palgrave biography (2008) written by Alan Axelrod, based very largely on *A General's Life.* Charles Whiting also wrote a brief overview of Bradley for Ballantine's Illustrated History of the Violent Century series (1971) which, frankly, is not reliable.

9. While this is obvious from others' descriptions, especially Patton's, Bradley himself confessed as much to several people. See, for example, the Pappas interview (West Point collection), where he recounts an incident as chairman of Bulova.

10. Montgomery, *Memoirs,* 276.

11. D'Este, *Bitter Victory,* 155. D'Este's portrayal of Bradley is considerably more negative in his biography of Patton, *Patton: A Genius for Victory,* where he seems to go out of his way to criticize him at different points, even taking some gratuitous shots at Bradley for being a teetotaler. On the other hand, D'Este is an eloquent defender of Bradley's actions at Falaise in *Decision in Normandy.*

12. John Toland, *Battle: The Story of the Bulge* (New York: Random House, 1959), 330.

13. Stanley Weintrab, *11 Days in December: Christmas at the Bulge,* 1944 (New York: Free Press, 2006) 179–80.

Index